Magic Words, M

CRITICAL EXPLORATIONS IN SCIENCE FICTION AND FANTASY

A series edited by Donald E. Palumbo and C.W. Sullivan III

Earlier Works: www.mcfarlandpub.com

Magic Words, Magic Worlds

Form and Style in Epic Fantasy

MATTHEW OLIVER

CRITICAL EXPLORATIONS
IN SCIENCE FICTION AND FANTASY, 80
Series Editors Donald E. Palumbo *and* C.W. Sullivan III

McFarland & Company, Inc., Publishers
Jefferson, North Carolina

This book has undergone peer review.

Library of Congress Cataloguing-in-Publication Data

Names: Oliver, Matthew, 1978– author.
Title: Magic words, magic worlds : form and style in epic fantasy / Matthew Oliver.
Description: Jefferson, North Carolina : McFarland & Company, Inc., Publishers, 2022 |
Series: Critical explorations in science fiction and fantasy ; 80 |
Includes bibliographical references and index.
Identifiers: LCCN 2022021531 | ISBN 9781476687131 (paperback : acid free paper) ∞
ISBN 9781476645889 (ebook)
Subjects: LCSH: Fantasy fiction—History and criticism. | Narration (Rhetoric) |
BISAC: LITERARY CRITICISM / Science Fiction & Fantasy | LCGFT: Literary criticism.
Classification: LCC PN3435 .O426 2022 | DDC 823/.0876609—dc23/eng/20220525
LC record available at https://lccn.loc.gov/2022021531

British Library cataloguing data are available

ISBN (print) 978-1-4766-8713-1
ISBN (ebook) 978-1-4766-4588-9

Front cover images © 2022 Tithi Luadthong / Dima Zel / New Africa / Shutterstock

Printed in the United States of America

*McFarland & Company, Inc., Publishers
Box 611, Jefferson, North Carolina 28640
www.mcfarlandpub.com*

To Lucy and Maggie,
whom I have joined in many imagined worlds

Contents

Contents

Section IV: Narrative Frames

Acknowledgments

Any acknowledgment of my intellectual debts in creating this book has to begin with the International Conference on the Fantastic in the Arts. As I teach at a small, teaching-focused university, the community of scholarly inquiry at the conference has been crucial to generating and maintaining my energy for this project, to say nothing of the personal and social connections it has made for me. While I would love to list here every friend that I have made while attending annually for the better part of the last decade, I will confine myself to thanking two whose conversation, debate, and academic work have particularly sharpened my own: A.P. Canavan (whom I can always count on to challenge my certainties) and Daniel Creed. I also thank the established scholars in the field who have taken the time to offer words of encouragement after hearing earlier versions of the material in this book: I particularly recall such moments with Brian Attebery, W.A. Senior, and Kathryn Hume. Furthermore, ICFA creates an opportunity for academics to interact with writers, and I have been delighted to find that the same people who create the worlds I enjoy reading also create a warm, accepting, and entertaining social environment. I am particularly grateful for the friendship and generous encouragement of my academic reading of their work offered by Steve Donaldson, Steve Erikson, and Cam Esslemont. Finally, I may not have found the conference had it not been for my teaching colleague, Judy Collins, whose knowledge of those involved in the field has deepened my own. Judy, I am fairly confident that without you, this book would not exist.

I am also grateful to my other colleagues at Campbellsville University who have supported me in writing this book. Much of the text of this book was drafted during a sabbatical provided by the university in spring 2020 (which corresponded to the start of a global pandemic, but I was grateful not to have to deal with that complicated teaching environment while also working on a book). Particular thanks go to my department head Sarah Sims and the rest of the department for covering for my absence that semester. I also want to extend recognition to the library staff for assisting my research. As we work at a teaching-focused school, our library sometimes has limited resources for research, but Kay Alston always seemed willing to order a book if I needed it, and I have relied heavily on Interlibrary Loan librarian Regina Thompson.

I also want to thank those who have helped to publish this research: Brian Attebery, Christine Mains, and the editorial staff of the *Journal of the Fantastic in the Arts* who published an earlier version of Chapter 1 (vol. 29, no. 3, 2018, pp. 355–379) and C.W. Sullivan (whom I also met through ICFA) and Susan Kilby from McFarland.

Finally, I want to thank my family. Reading with my daughters, Lucy and Maggie, has allowed me to share my work in some degree (and provided an epigraph for Chapter 5). Although they are still a bit young for most of the texts covered here, re-experiencing Oz and Narnia and Middle-earth through their eyes has been energizing. I am also grateful to my wife, Natalie, who (among too many other virtues to list here) has served as a second set of eyes to search out good sources for analysis. I am not a rapid reader, and epic fantasy is very long, so both due to reading books aloud together or getting her recommendations (I read Jemisin largely on her suggestion), my reading experience (like my life experience) would be poorer without her.

Preface

As I prepared to submit the final draft of the manuscript for this book, I received an e-mail from a scholarly journal asking me to review a recent submission about the use of epigraphs for world building in epic fantasy novels. The article's abstract particularly referred to the striking fact that such epigraphs are often part of the fictional world itself, an unusual feature for the epigraph form.[1] As I have devoted an entire chapter of this study to a similar argument, this might have seemed like a fantastic coincidence … if it was the first time this had happened. Several years ago, shortly after writing the original version of what is now Chapter 4 in this book, a chapter discussing how Glen Cook uses subjective first-person narration that seems not to fit conventional expectations for epic fantasy—a paper that was foundational to my research defining the *epic* component of epic fantasy—I was asked to review an essay about Glen Cook and his unconventional treatment of epic fantasy. This occurrence may have been less coincidental, as the journal's editorial assistant had heard me present the Glen Cook paper at a conference and knew I was familiar with his work. However, there was an astonishing amount of overlap (and some key differences) between the arguments I was making and those being made in the paper I was reviewing. That essay, "History and Precarity" by Dennis Wilson Wise, has subsequently been published, and I have now included it in my arguments below. What is exciting to me about these stories is that in each case, academics working independently have come to similar conclusions, guided by the language of the texts they are reading.

This focus on the effects of language has been the motive force behind this study. As I will discuss at more length in my introduction, I have long been disappointed with the academic work (including my own) on writing style and affective reading experience in the fantasy genre. While style is frequently mentioned, rarely is there systematic or extensive analysis to back up broad generalizations about it, nor has much consideration been given to how the fantasy context itself interacts with stylistic choices to

1

create the unique fantasy reading experience. A number of earlier critics gesture towards this, but more often their methods point them in other directions. As I decided to embark on a longer research project, I wanted to apply the type of close reading analysis of style that I find most satisfying to a set of popular texts (epic fantasy) that generally does not get such attention, in a sustained fashion, to see what I turn up. At the time I started, only a couple book-length studies focused on form in fantasy, one by Farah Mendlesohn from a structuralist perspective, another by Susan Mandala with a linguistics approach, neither precisely doing the type of close reading I wanted to do. Yet both of these studies were comparatively recent when I started (Mendlesohn's published in 2008, Mandala's in 2010), so it seemed that the time was right for the study of fantasy style and form that I had in mind.

My experience writing this book suggests to me that the time for studying epic fantasy style has indeed arrived.

As I have been working on this book, it has been difficult to keep up with all of the good new scholarship focusing on issues of style in fantasy. In the same issue of the *Journal of the Fantastic in the Arts* as Wise's article appears, Kim Wickham analyzes N.K. Jemisin's use of second-person narration in the Broken Earth trilogy. Similarly, at around the time I was completing the draft of my book in 2020, C. Palmer-Patel published a book called *The Shape of Fantasy* that focuses on the form and structure of epic fantasy novels, which I have retroactively incorporated with my own frequently similar observations. This pattern has continued throughout the process of writing this book, and as I have already suggested, I find it exciting because it seems to confirm one of my theses in this book. I argue that fantasy is particularly adept at creating connections between people, using language that generates empathy by shaping similar patterns of thought. As I observe these recent literary analysts focusing on the language of epic fantasy, it is striking to find such parallel thinking from readers who (to this point, at least) have had little to no interaction with each other. Naturally, we are all approaching these texts within the context of a similar critical and scholarly discourse, so it would be best to be cautious about rhapsodizing here about the power of fantasy to bind together a community, yet I cannot help but feeling that in some way the texts we are reading are shaping our perceptions in similar ways.

My work differs from these others primarily through my focus on close reading passages of text in detail—a method I have seen little used in relation to epic fantasy. I am aware that close reading has long been a somewhat embattled approach, often questioned by ideologically focused criticism for cutting out historical or social context and questioned more recently by cognitive reader-response or something like Franco Moretti's "distant reading" which focus more on broad patterns of how readers process texts. Certainly, close reading, by entangling itself in specific, localized details, has more difficulty generalizing about the effects of language use, but this is part of the appeal to me. Critics like Isobel Armstrong and Caroline Levine have done much to rehabilitate the perception of close reading, demonstrating that it need not be divorced from social context or apolitical, that form is, in fact, tied to the very fabric of our social reality. Often, close reading (especially when attentive to that wider context) touches on something those other approaches leave out—the affective experience of reading a particular text, the possibilities created by specific forms. I am more interested in that affective experience, which is often compromised and contradictory, as different forms collide in fascinating ways. Perhaps this is nowhere truer than in epic fantasy, a genre full of collisions between various formal possibilities. Thus, while I will only touch on the historical or social context behind these texts lightly, and while I will draw some general conclusions about what epic fantasy is *capable of*, what the language of epic fantasy *can* do, the meat of this book will be found in the case studies that examine how specific writers of epic fantasy manage the affordances of the genre in ways that reveal the *capabilities* of language in a fantasy context.

And what I find is that epic fantasy speaks to core questions about literature. It raises questions of history and the novel's relation to history, of how literary invention works and why fictions about the world matter. Crucially, it engages readers in patterns of similar mental operations that are distinct from, if clearly derived from, the mental patterns necessary for everyday life. All readers who have visited Tolkien's Middle-earth, Le Guin's Earthsea, or Erikson's Malazan world have a particular communal bond through the mental processes these texts impress on their minds. While differing circumstances of different readers will often lead to different conclusions, those shared mental patterns create a social world much like the texts themselves aim to create imaginary worlds. That relationship between textual world and social world is, I believe, at the core of the study of literature and is nowhere more transparent than in epic fantasy.

Introduction
Building Worlds with Words in Epic Fantasy

"Wizards operate in the subjunctive mode."—Ursula Le Guin,
"From Elfland to Poughkeepsie" (footnote to 1989 revision)

Magic is closely linked to language. When we think of magic, we often think of spells, those magic words that re-shape the world according to the will of the spell caster. From "bippity-boppity-boo" to "avada kedavra," stories about magic suggest that the form of language aligns with the form of the world. Epic fantasy stories frequently connect magic to discourse. In a study of spells in fantasy fiction, Jes Battis characterizes magic use as follows: "we describe in coherent, elegant detail what we want to occur, and if our will is in the spell, then what we desire comes to pass" (37). Indeed, such a "descriptive and grammatical" magic system can be found in nearly all "quest" fantasy novels (Battis 37).

At the same time, language has long been closely linked to magic. From the ancient world through the Middle Ages, language was often thought to shape the essence of things in the world. Many traditions in naming children, for instance, establish a connection between a child's name and identity. While the Enlightenment attempted to disentangle such magical thinking from the abstract, representational function of language, the insistence that language *does things* persists. Speech act theory, for instance, argues that discourse does not simply represent actions that take place in a material world, but that it should be viewed as an action itself with tangible consequences. J.L. Austin created categories like "performative utterance" to describe language that changes reality (such as in the simple example of an employer saying, "You're fired"). Similarly, scholarly authors metaphorically gesture toward the linkage between language and magic with article titles like "The Magic Spell of Language: Linguistic Categories and Their Perceptual Consequences" and "The Magic of Words: Teaching Vocabulary in the Early Childhood Classroom."

More importantly, in the latter part of the twentieth century, postmodernism and linguistic philosophy began to question the Enlightenment separation of rational language from the irrational "spiritual" world. Older models of language ascribed spiritual properties to language, as Ryan Stark traces in his account of the Enlightenment struggle between "plain style" and "enchanted rhetoric": "In most forms of Renaissance mysticism and magic, tropes have a spiritual dimension, ontologically speaking. Rhetoric invokes. But this idea is obscured by modernity's materialization of language, where words and tropes become only cold instruments, mere ornaments, trapping the human voice in the bric-a-brac of the material world" (5). Clark identifies a return of the earlier numinous approach to language in Martin Heidegger's hermeneutics, Stephen Toulmin's "return to cosmology," or even his own "return of enchanted rhetoric" (6). Indeed, the postmodern turn, with its questioning of Enlightenment binaries like "rational/irrational," has enabled a whole range of ways of thinking about language acting on the world, from Jacques Derrida's philosophy that the world exists only as a web of signifiers to the more empirical explorations of cognitive linguistics, which link language to the materiality of the brain. In this intellectual climate, the popularity of fantasy stories, particularly fantasy novels, may seem less like the archaic, pre-modern throwback that it is sometimes characterized as, for nowhere is the world more obviously constructed of language than in a fantasy novel, where the words on the page literally create the world, without even the illusion of referentiality found in various forms of realism (even the speculative referentiality of science fiction). As the magic words of fantasy construct the magic worlds its characters inhabit, the form those words take—the style a given fantasy novel uses—clearly has significant implications for how that novel constructs our understanding of the world and positions us as actors in a political and social world.

However, epic fantasy in general, and its style in particular, have not necessarily received extensive attention from literary critics. This project emerged out of my realization that when I wrote about epic fantasy, even I ignored my own preferred practice of focusing on style and wrote differently than when I wrote about more canonical literature. My strongest formative influences as a scholar involve close reading, which I still believe to be the cornerstone of literary analysis. My work has always grappled with the New Critics, reader-response theory, and the more recent return to form found in the New Aestheticism and New Formalism. When I read, I want to know how the structure of the language shapes the reader that is reading that language. Yet I realized that when I approached fantasy, I looked at broad motifs, archetypes, and plot structures, not the language being used. One of my earliest forays into academic writing about the genre was a conference paper about "parasitic magic," a motif in fantasy fiction of magic objects (particularly magic swords) that gain power for their users by stealing it from others (such as Elric's vampiric sword Stormbreaker).[1] I discussed this use of magic as a metaphor with political implications about ambiguous uses of power, especially connected to the criticism of imperialism (as empires are also a common plot feature of epic fantasy fiction). While that essay certainly contained quoted passages to illustrate how the magic worked in the text, the form of those passages—the style of the language used to describe the magic—was largely irrelevant to my argument. When I survey the criticism about epic fantasy, I find much the same thing dominating the literature. Naturally, issues of style and form are discussed, but typically not in a systematic or central fashion.[2] What, I asked, might I find if I read Stephen R. Donaldson or Robert Jordan with the same critical eye that I apply to Joseph Conrad and Henry James? What if I withhold my assumptions about what the style will look like in a fantasy novel and instead attempt to *analyze* what I find there, and then draw conclusions about its effects? The answer to those questions (at least in part) is this book.

I aim here to identify the affordances of epic fantasy as a genre and the forms and styles most frequently used in it. In my use of the word "affordance," I am following Caroline Levine in her recent study of form, where Levine suggests using the word "affordance" to understand how forms work: "To capture the complex operations of social and literary forms, I borrow the concept of *affordance* from design theory. *Affordance* is a term used to describe the potential uses or actions latent in materials and designs" (6). Just as physical forms have particular affordances (glass is fragile but transparent, steel is durable), Levine suggests that all other forms (including literary ones) have specific, describable potentialities. The goal of a formal analysis, then, is to identify these affordances: "Rather than asking what artists intend or even what forms *do*, we can ask instead what potentialities lie latent—though not always obvious—in aesthetic and social arrangements" (Levine 6–7). An important consequence of this type of analysis is that forms do not simply reflect pre-existing political and social realities (14); instead, many social structures *are* forms, and aesthetic forms interact with those other forms in complex ways. This reinvests literary form with political purpose, as when forms "collide," they result in "minor forms sometimes disrupting or rerouting major ones" (18).

The image of "collision" is especially important. Literary theory frequently analyzes various tensions and conflicts within texts, but often these conflicts are seen as paradoxes or ironies that resolve, or dialectics that achieve a synthesis, or, when they do not resolve, it is interpreted as an aesthetic failure. The image of collision calls attention to an experiential aspect of form, how different forms, with separate affordances, struggle and combine in unique ways that may reshape or redirect each other. Rather than the metaphor of conflict-followed-by-mastery inherent in the resolution of irony or synthesis, collision returns to the dynamic experience of asking questions without necessarily finding satisfactory answers. Levine explains at length how the notion of collision reinvests form with political purpose, as introducing new forms into an existing system can push that system in new directions. If all social behavior is viewed as different types of forms, then any form that causes us to re-think the shape of social experience has tremendous potential. And this is where the concepts of affordance and collision are particularly useful for studying epic fantasy. As I will argue, the epic fantasy novel is built on formal and ideological collisions that make it a productive location for reshaping other forms. While epic fantasy itself is more commonly classified as a "genre" rather than a "form,"[3] it nonetheless tends to use particular formal structures, which are themselves shaped by the types of stories epic fantasies tell. Thus, when I discuss the affordances of epic fantasy throughout this book, this could more accurately be taken as shorthand for "the affordances of the forms which epic fantasy often gravitates towards." Those forms are not exclusive to epic fantasy, nor will all epic fantasy take advantage of those formal opportunities to the same degree. Certainly, I am not arguing for some "essence of epic fantasy style" (although my rhetoric may at times, for concision, imply such a thing). Instead, fantasy writers (especially since the genre was more formally defined in the 1960s) tend to ask similar questions and aim for similar effects, and they tend toward similar solutions to their representational problems. I want to investigate how the shared conventional forms of epic fantasy intersect and collide with the specific individual forms and contexts of different writers in the genre. In doing this, I will not be creating a systematic index of "epic fantasy style features" so much as I will be exploring a set of shared social conventions and thinking about the typical ideological impact of introducing those repeated forms in a variety of contexts. (My own reading of these stylistic features should be understood as yet another of these ideological contexts, and any seeming essentialism in my analysis as the result of a collision between the texts I am reading and the conventions of literary analysis which require bold claims and confident assertions.)

Thus, by examining the affordances of epic fantasy, we may trace the ways in which its forms *can be used* to intervene and shape other political and social forms surrounding it, including the conventional epic form it frequently draws upon. In this book, I will attempt to sketch out an approach to analyzing the style used in epic fantasy novels, specifically identifying what forms are used in fantasy writing and how they enable epic fantasy's aesthetic and ideological potential. However, before I can describe these affordances, I will have to identify the materials being used. Thus, before diving into the details of epic fantasy style, I will have to establish what I mean when I say "epic," "fantasy," and "style."

The Quest for a Definition of Fantasy

For a number of years, at the International Conference on the Fantastic in the Arts, the Fantasy Literature division held a "state of the genre" panel. Unfortunately, these panels gained a checkered reputation with their regular attendees due to a tendency to get bogged down in the problem of defining "fantasy." Regardless of the intriguing issues raised by the panel's organizers—such as the role of violence in fantasy—at some point the conversation always turned to questions of what fantasy is and defensive discussions of why it does not receive sufficient academic attention. Inevitably, some frustrated conference-goer pointed out that questions of definition are at the lowest levels of Bloom's taxonomy, expressing a wish that we would proceed to more sophisticated analyses.

As I open this study of fantasy fiction, I want to heed the lesson of these panels and not get mired in the issue of definitions. Yet any academic project must define its parameters, and in a genre as infamously amorphous as fantasy, these parameters can be especially tricky: too many academic papers sidestep the issue by using Brian Attebery's useful term "fuzzy set" as an intellectual short cut,[4] or simply resorting to the "I know it when I see it" approach. Many of the standard theoretical texts on fantasy—such as Tzevtan Todorov's *The Fantastic* (1970) or Rosemary Jackson's *Fantasy: The Literature of Subversion* (1981)—focus largely on the subtle invasion of non-mimetic elements into everyday settings in novels such as Henry James's *Turn of the Screw*. Jackson even includes Pynchon's *The Crying of Lot 49*, a postmodern mystery story with no apparent non-mimetic plot elements but with an atmosphere of the fantastic. Gothic fiction and magical realism are fantastic subgenres that have been well-represented in critical analyses, but "fantasy" also extends to the very different narratives of heroic battles and perilous quests in the recently popular worlds of J.R.R. Tolkien's Middle-earth and George R.R. Martin's Westeros. Clearly, despite their non-mimetic elements, the reading experiences of *Lord of the Rings* and Angela Carter's *Nights at the Circus* are radically different, so the broad category "fantasy" presents too much variety for a detailed analysis.

At the same time, those studies which attempt to distinguish too narrowly often have difficulty teasing apart similarities. Farah Mendlesohn's

Rhetorics of Fantasy (2008), for instance, while it has much to recommend it, tries to separate secondary world fantasies into two categories based on a rhetorical difference in how the world is introduced to the reader: "portal-quest" where a guide introduces the world to a novice, and "immersive" where the reader is "immersed" in the world without explanation. Yet, as its name suggests, the category of "portal-quest" fantasy (which Mendlesohn associates most with the epic due to the narrative structure of the quest [3]) confusingly melds two different narrative categories in its name—the plot element of a "portal" and the narrative structure of the "quest." In an attempt to alleviate this confusion, Mendlesohn treats the "portal" more symbolically than literally, including secondary world novels that do not have travel via "portal" between worlds on the basis that "the portal is about entry, transition, and negotiation" (xix). Thus, any novel that contains initiation or coming-of-age fits in this category, and yet, one cannot help but feel that this murky distinction between "immersive" and "portal-quest" fantasy largely boils down to fantasy Mendlesohn likes and dislikes, as she categorizes as "immersive" novels such as Michael Swanwick's *The Iron Dragon's Daughter* (76) which contains both a literal portal and a coming-of-age structure and China Miéville's *Perdido Street Station* (xx, 16–17) which contains a classic quest structure complete with party building and tracing the monster to its lair (albeit in a heavily disguised form). To some extent, Mendlesohn recognizes this instability and discusses *The Iron Dragon's Daughter* and Miéville's *The Scar* in a lengthy section about "subversion of the portal-quest fantasy" (the longest section of specific analysis in the chapter on portal-quest fantasy), where she talks about "the refusal of portal," says Swanwick's novel "barely belongs in this category" (48), and calls *The Scar* an "anti-quest novel" (58). Clearly, it is difficult maintaining such rigidly defined category boundaries. This is not to say that Mendlesohn's classifications are not useful analytical tools, but instead to point out the difficulty of creating too precise a system of classification.

For these reasons, I have chosen to classify my subject for this book broadly as "epic fantasy." By "epic fantasy," I am referring to **non-mimetic novels that take place predominantly in a secondary fantasy world and that in some way run contemporary social and psychological concerns through a filter derived from past models of history** (ancient epics, medieval folk tales, etc.). To be clear, the narrative structures are derived from past models, but the content need not be knights, kings, and pseudo-medieval technological development. In such novels, there is typically an emphasis on world building, which often involves magic or other elements that are not considered possible in the rational, empirical universe, thus resulting in a breakdown of the reader's usual cognitive framework for categorizing the world. This definition contains two key elements: (1) a sense of "past-ness"—the "epic" part of the term indicates the work's connection to ongoing themes, a sense of continuing history and past tradition, a chronotope of enduring time; and (2) the secondary world setting that is manifestly artificial, and which the reader knows from the outset has been entirely constructed, which distances and defamiliarizes every element such that the reader must start from ground zero in building an understanding of the world (or at most start with an analogy to the real world) rather than by extending from our consensus reality by way of additional elements (as in magical realism or gothic horror) or speculative elements (as in science fiction). These two features make epic fantasy a particularly useful term for this book because they encapsulate the twin affordances of this genre that, I argue, can be found in the most characteristic forms and structures associated with epic fantasy: **mental flexibility** (often manifesting through empathy) and **continuity** (a sense of ongoing connection from past to present). The removal from reality to a secondary world requires a more strenuous exercise of imagination on the part of the reader, a greater act of projecting the self into the other, which results in fantasy often generating an invitation to flexible mental states, curiosity, and heightened empathy. At the same time, the epic scale creates links between the individual perspective and the communal or historical perspective. Epic fantasy is particularly adept at creating systems to manage the relation between individuals and larger group identities, leading to large-scale social mapping and the construction of community.

I should pause here briefly to discuss how this definition relates to other definitions of the fantasy genre. With some small variations, this definition largely follows a common pattern extending back at least to Lin Carter and L. Sprague de Camp. As Jamie Williamson summarizes, for them fantasy meant "narratives set in worlds in which the supernatural or magical are part of the fabric of reality and that center on the themes of quest, war, and adventure" (12). It may be objected, then, that my definition does not sufficiently distinguish between different subgenres of secondary-world fantasy (such terms as "epic fantasy," "heroic fantasy," or "sword and sorcery"). However, it is not my intention to make fine distinctions between these. I use epic fantasy as a term to distinguish between secondary-world fantasy and non-secondary world fantasy (such as magic realism or intrusion fantasy), and I believe "epic" is a useful term for describing what such fantasy *does*, as I hope to make clear in the next section of this introduction. For now, I simply want to note that my definition of epic focuses on temporality more than scale. By way of contrast, consider C. Palmer-Patel who discusses "epic" as part of setting and contrasts epic fantasy to "localized" fantasy, making statements such as "Epic

Fantasy must culminate in the hero transforming and remaking the world or land as a whole, and not just a city or village" (8). I would contend that the epic is less "world-altering" than "world-revealing." Some ancient epics such as *Gilgamesh* or Homer's *Odyssey* do not tell world-altering stories but instead reveal the world by serializing a group of individually localized incidents set in an artificial past time that constructs a relation between the past and present cultural identity. One consequence of this emphasis on my part is that I do not find the distinction between epic fantasy and sword and sorcery to be analytically significant in many cases. Despite being more "localized," sword and sorcery still engages in a chronotope of enduring time, I would argue. However, this issue of scale is not entirely irrelevant, and I explore its impact at more length in Chapter 6.

While the significance of the "past-ness" of epic fantasy will be the subject of my next section, this definition will not be complete without a bit more background for the second key element: what I mean by calling epic fantasy "non-mimetic" and an explanation of why the artificial secondary world setting is so crucial. In fact, this portion of the definition touches on why I believe *epic* fantasy has been largely undertheorized even among critics concerned with fantastic literature. Most major studies of fantasy at some point engage with Tzvetan Todorov and Rosemary Jackson in defining the genre, and while these two sources have much to offer, they have shaped the definition of the fantastic in ways that exclude epic fantasy from the conversation. Todorov begins by defining the fantastic not as a genre but as a moment of "hesitation" in a narrative when a reader (or a character) attempts to determine whether the seemingly impossible events of a narrative (e.g., the appearance of ghosts) are the product of a disturbed imagination or an actual violation of the laws of reality as we understand them. If a narrative prolongs that uncertainty, it belongs to the fantastic, but if it resolves it, the story becomes either "uncanny" (if the supernatural is imagined by the character) or "marvelous" (if the supernatural is actually happening) (Todorov 25). Jackson takes this definition and extends it by arguing that the fantastic "enters a dialogue with the 'real'" (in the Bakhtinian sense), "interrogating single or unitary ways of seeing" (36). In contrast, epic fantasy (which Jackson typically calls "high fantasy") more properly belongs to the marvelous, as it does not contain that hesitation. Readers and writers approach epic fantasy with an awareness of its unreality *from the beginning*; thus, there can be no moment of "hesitation." When Tolkien describes an orc, the reader does not ask whether the orc exists but instead assumes it exists *in that story world* (because it is not our world).

Thus, while Todorov and Jackson describe an area that borders on epic fantasy, and they have much to say about shared concepts such as defamiliarization (which I will discuss in Chapter 1), they are not precisely talking about epic fantasy. Yet the consequences of lumping "the fantastic" and "fantasy" together are evident in a number of largely unwarranted conclusions Jackson draws about the marvelous and "high fantasy" without any extensive textual analysis. Setting up the marvelous as a straw man in binary opposition to the fantastic, she argues that "its version of history is not questioned and the tale seems to deny the process of its own telling," that it "discourages reader participation [...] carrying the implication that their *effects* have long since ceased to disturb," and that the effect is "one of a *passive* relation to history" (33). Thus, when she does briefly discuss Tolkien and mentions other "high" fantasy (including writers like Ursula Le Guin and Stephen R. Donaldson), she dismisses them "as conservative vehicles for social and instinctual repression" (155). While a number of critics have dismantled this position,[5] the definitional confusion she creates is evident in the shift in titles from Todorov's *The Fantastic* to Jackson's *Fantasy: The Literature of Subversion*. By taking the specific effect of "interrogating the real" (Todorov's "fantastic"), valorizing it, and naming it "fantasy," Jackson effectively ghettoized an entire portion of fantasy literature. If fantasy is "the literature of subversion," and "high" fantasy does not subvert anything, then it is not even really fantasy.[6] By trying to accrue critical capital for the term "fantasy," Jackson effectively denies access to the category for texts with less cultural capital. Fantasy, for Jackson, is Franz Kafka, or certain works by Henry James and Thomas Pynchon, not Tolkien, Le Guin, and Donaldson. Nonetheless, critics writing about those fantasists continue to return to Todorov and Jackson's categories. (For instance, Farah Mendlesohn's argument about "portal-quest fantasy" is largely a more nuanced and detailed re-skinning of Jackson's argument.)

However, there are two things to learn from Jackson's influence. First, while epic fantasy may overlap with the fantastic in many ways, it needs to be defined on its own terms, rather than simply in relation to the broader "fantastic." I will argue that epic fantasy actually does quite a bit of what Jackson wants fantasy to do—it questions the constructed category of the "real," it encourages an *active* relation to the text and to history, it supports a dialogic understanding of the world—but I am not doing so in order to claim for it a spot in "the fantastic" as defined by Jackson. These similarities are, I believe, simply the result of overlapping considerations between various types of fiction that deal in the unreal. This leads to the second thing we learn from Jackson's definition—"the fantastic" and "epic fantasy" do *not* line up due to differing reader (and authorial) expectations. One of the key elements of genre is that it pre-structures reader expectations. When a reader approaches an epic fantasy novel, everything from the setting to the cover art and marketing blurbs condition the reader to expect "unreal" events. The world is predefined as *constructed*. For this reason, my definition of fantasy is shaped less by Todorov and Jackson than by Stefan Ekman's thoughtful definition: "Fantasy, in short, is fiction *acknowledged by reader and writer* to contain 'impossible' elements that are accepted as possible in the story and treated in an internally consistent manner" (6, emphasis added).[7] Unlike Todorov's fantastic, which requires hesitation and uncertainty, this definition more accurately describes the rhetorical situation in epic fantasy, where the emphasis is on *building* worlds that are *manifestly unreal*. As I will argue below, the radical possibility for subversion here simply manifests itself differently. The world is artificially constructed and *only* exists in language (in contrast to, say, Dickens's London, which is certainly a linguistically constructed world but is not expected to exist *only* in language by a reader—in fact, the expectation of a link to reality is crucial both to the sentimental effect of Dickens and the social action he wants to spur in his readers). The fact that the reader is aware of this world as a construction enables a range of possibilities in the text for raising the reader's awareness of the role language plays in constructing that reality. These possibilities may be activated to a greater or lesser degree by the style of the text—the words it uses to construct that reality. That the "epic" part of epic fantasy also links the text to time, history, and a communal imaginary only increases the subversive potential of these constructivist inclinations, but to understand this will require further explanation of what makes such fantasy "epic."

What Is "Epic" About Epic Fantasy?

The designation "epic fantasy" itself requires a bit of explanation, as the average reader (or publisher) does not typically use the term in a precise fashion. "Epic fantasy" is frequently disdained as a marketing category and not a productive theoretical term. Marek Oziewicz dismisses it as "impressionistic" (79) and Gary K. Wolfe's glossary of critical terms for science fiction and fantasy notes that "publishers have come to use the term somewhat more loosely to describe almost any multivolume fantasy work" (31). It does not help matters that much fiction that codified "epic fantasy" was consciously created not out of the epic tradition but out of the attempt to market to Tolkien fans. Lester del Rey, according to David Hartwell's account, "mapped out a strategy [...] using mass-marketing techniques" to "satisfy the hunger in the marketplace for more Tolkien" ("Making" 375). Such self-conscious marketing certainly seems far removed from the aestheticized ideal of the ancient epic. Nonetheless, even though "epic" is often not being applied in an analytical way, much epic fantasy *does* include the superficial features of the epic—elevated language, vast scale (and length), the relationship between gods and humans, and idealized, larger-than-life heroes. Matthew Fike identifies a similar list of traits in a discussion of Robert Jordan's Wheel of Time series: "the series' martial activity is Iliadic. [...] The series also includes an Odyssean emphasis on romantic relationships among the main characters. [...] As well, epic tells the story of one action—in this case, the (one hopes successful) fight with the Dark One" (145). While certainly not all features of the epic will be present in any given fantasy work, it would be a mistake to overlook the importance of conventional expectations and authors exploiting and developing those conventions. Epic fantasy may *also* be a marketing category; however, I am not sure that it should be dismissed out of hand for that reason. To argue that audience demand for "more Tolkien" helped create genre fantasy simply sidesteps the question of what features, shared by Tolkien, his imitators, and others influenced by the same sources as him, appealed to those readers and how those textual features function. Whether a publisher's marketing creates audience demand or responds to it, marketing categories often refer to a set of specific audience expectations, and form itself interacts significantly with audience expectations, whether it follows those expectations or works against them.

Nonetheless, whether a given work has an epic invocation, begins *in medias res*, or involves "Iliadic martial activity" are to some extent superficial characteristics. As I suggested in my definition above, I am not even interested specifically in whether the epic served as an influence to the writer of the text. More importantly, epic fantasy shares several structural affordances with the epic that are crucial to this study: depth of time, communal identity building, and a "double narrative" of its own genre development. Each of these affordances is linked to an affordance of epic fantasy that I will trace through a variety of texts: depth of time spurs an awareness of "continuity" or "ongoingness" that is linked to a group understanding of history; communal identity building connects to empathy and mental flexibility; and the reflexive focus on genre creates a metanarrative awareness of the narrative construction of reality. I will here define each of these three in some detail.

Depth of Time

Definitions of epic most frequently return to length as the central feature, but it would seem to be trivial to define epic fantasy solely in terms of being "long," as Wolfe suggests publishers do, or as one less-than-helpful Internet definition (out of many) puts it: "[Epic fantasy] has to be more than one book in length. To qualify as an Epic Fantasy there needs to be at least a trilogy to resolve the problems in the books" (Ganiere). Considering length itself as a defining feature may lead to such impractical assertions, but it may be more productive to consider length a symptom of a deeper affordance of the epic, namely its attitude toward time and history, what Bakhtin named a novel's chronotope. According to Bakhtin, the chronotope is the "intrinsic connectedness of temporal and spatial relationships that are artistically expressed in literature" ("Forms" 84). Attitudes towards time take on physical representation in literature. Thus, as Bakhtin argues in his essay "Epic and Novel," the narrative world of the epic exists at a distance from the contemporary reality of the narrator or writer. Epic time is complete and therefore unchangeable, its possibilities exhausted. The distance between the epic narrator and the reader, the "singer and his audience," is fundamental: "To destroy this boundary is to destroy the form of the epic as a genre. But precisely because it is walled off from the all subsequent times, the epic past is absolute and complete. It is as closed as a circle" (16). This may remind us of Jackson's definition of the marvelous, which is similarly marked by "complete knowledge of *completed* events" (33). While not all readings of epic time see it as closed off and unchanging in the way Bakhtin does, most agree that there is some sense of stability, enduring values, ongoing connections from a past time that reflect on the reader's present changeable state. This epic temporality typically contrasts that of the novel, the subject of which is the changing, inconclusive contemporary world (even when it is written about events in the past).

Georg Lukács illustrates this tendency to assign the epic a stable, fixed time in contrast to the novel, calling the novel "the epic of an age in which the extensive totality of life is no longer directly given, in which the immanence of meaning in life has become a problem, yet which still thinks in terms of totality" (56). In other words, while epic and novel seek to achieve the same thing (totality, a unity of all elements of life), they approach it with from quite different temporal coordinates. Epic envisions an unchanging static totality, an essentialist world where everything is defined and nothing changes. Conversely, the novel must attempt to *create* a totality that no longer exists out of the changing, subjective perspectives of everyday life. While it is not my intention here to engage fully with the critical concept of totality as it extends from Marx to Lukács to Lyotard, Lukács illustrates the same fundamental split as Bakhtin does between the epic (completed past time, immanent totality) and the novel (incomplete present, absent totality). Thus, the novel as a form is founded on a fundamental collision between different ways of viewing time and history. To be sure, this contrast between epic and novel is highly questionable. E.M.W. Tillyard, for instance, sees the epic not as replacing the ancient epic but instead as a mode or "kind" that could appear in the novel as well as in poetry. Frederick Griffiths and Stanley Rabinowitz similarly argue that a defining feature of the epic is that it adapts to the mores of its current age, that Wordsworth's *Prelude* or the nineteenth-century Russian novel could contain these features of the epic, that the epic only has "a tendency to become fixed and monolithic when viewed over the shoulder" (32), that is, retrospectively to appear to have this fixed quality.

Nonetheless, this debate serves to illustrate that one of the primary stakes of the epic is the temporality of narrative, the relationship between past and present. The epic never just tells a story about a single time period. It always concerns some form of continuity across time. This may be why the epic elements have seemed attractive to politically conservative writers such as J.R.R. Tolkien, a Catholic medievalist, who would have had no problem with the essentializing tendencies of a closed world view in a distant past time sadly lost to us in the changeable, technological spiritual wasteland of the present. However, such a narrative structure is also ripe for critiquing the ideological narrativization of history: to the extent that epic fantasy novels are both epic (in their concern with deep temporality) and novels (in their concern with individual subjectivity and agency), they embody an inherent and productive collision of paradigms. This collision between epic and novel may be inherent in the structure of the novel itself, but the structure "epic fantasy novel" puts pressure on the split between a totalizing view of history and culture (epic) and a changing inconclusive one (novel), sometimes to the breaking point, allowing thoughtful writers to slip into the fissures and illuminate the relationship between narrative, history, and totalizing understandings of the world.[8]

Epic fantasy is, therefore, a productive place to interrogate the very concept of stable historical narratives. While structurally relying on a continuity of past with present for its effect, epic fantasy frequently raises questions about the stability of that past as an unchanging, static basis for making meaning. Such a compromised and contradictory position does not lack value. In fact, stable forms of social organization are often necessary for political action, even if they are problematic.[9] Levine argues that literary theory has been so concerned with "breaking forms apart" in order to "rid ourselves of particular unjust totalities or binaries" that we lose sight of the fact that "it is impossible to imagine a society altogether free of organizing principles. And too strong an emphasis on forms' dissolution has prevented us from attending to the complex ways that power operates in a world dense with functioning forms" (9). With the core collision in epic fantasy between stable historical narrative and contingent narrative, the genre has much to offer in showing both how group understandings of history can be structured and how these artificial understandings can be taken apart. I see in epic fantasy a contradictory movement both toward construction and deconstruction. With its connection to the epic, a form with an affordance for totalizing views of history, the genre reflects on stable historical narratives—even creating its own artificial totalities to reflect how power circulates—yet it does so in a way that nonetheless maintains an awareness of the artifice of those systems (through its manifestly artificial world creation), encouraging a flexibility in how we construct these structuring forms rather than a rigid sense of the world. In this study, I will examine a number of writers who overtly leverage the temporal elements of epic in order to reveal the ideological or hegemonic order of stable historical narratives, writers such as Glen Cook, Steven Erikson, and N.K. Jemisin. This is why I choose to label this affordance of epic "continuity" or "ongoingness"—in order to strip it of essentializing associations with reactionary politics that words like "tradition" would invoke. The epic creates an opportunity to explore temporality and the relationship of history and value in narrative.

Communal Values

In fact, values are a key element of the epic, and not merely the values of any single individual. The epic expresses the values of an entire social group. Odysseus is not only an individual character but in many ways the "ideal Greek." While certainly some epics generalize these values as universal or timeless, the key factor here is that the epic involves shared values. This is what E.M.W. Tillyard refers to as the "communal or choral quality" of epics (15). The characters in an epic are not simply defined by their individual feelings but by "feelings [...] shared by a great body. [...] That sharing [...] forms the psychological ground and the justification of the epic" (15). This communal sharing is similar to what Marek Oziewicz's sees as definitive in "mythopoeic fantasy," a category which overlaps with my chosen texts quite a bit (despite his dislike of the term epic fantasy), which he characterizes as "fulfilling vital human needs, as concerned with human values and spiritual yearnings" and as "assert[ing] that humans are moral beings who want to understand right action and live it" (67). While Oziewicz is primarily concerned with a narrower subset of fantasy that deals with predominantly Christian values, this focus on the individual as more than an individual but as an expression of the community is a feature found throughout the epic tradition. As a result of this tradition, characters in the epic often feel less like individuals and more like types. Tolkien, for instance, can be easily criticized for the lack of dimension in his idealized heroes such as Aragorn or even Frodo.[10] More recent writers show increasing reticence about idealizing characters and essentializing particular communal values, yet they will often resort to indirect means to portray these values, such as frame narratives, bathos, or the use of average humans as point-of-view characters to present idealized figures without fully embracing them.

Furthermore, this epic structure of communal values manifests in fantasy novels in an emphasis on empathy.[11] Empathy, as defined by Suzanne Keen, is "a vicarious, spontaneous sharing of affect" (4) and has been one of the principal benefits ascribed to novel reading. Due to fantasy novels' complete removal from consensus reality, they must work particularly diligently to aid readers in identifying with characters and cultures that are, in some cases, quite alien from "real world" experience. Ironically, the alien otherness of the world almost contradicts the communal values being established by the epic context. Once again, this collision at the heart of the epic fantasy novel forms a productive point of conflict. Epic fantasy novels are both a good place for producing the pro-social response known as empathy and also for interrogating the value of empathy as a potentially hegemonic response that absorbs the other into the self, erasing cultural difference. Keen's study of empathy and the novel has pointed out both sides of this debate as well: the benefits of a compassionate and fair society generated by empathy and the contrary possibility of "the empathetic individual's erasure of suffering others in a self-regarding emotional response that affronts others' separate personhood" (xxiv). Epic fantasy—through its consideration of communal values, its representation of otherness, and its defamiliarizing language—examines both sides of this relationship between individual and community.

Due to the ambiguity surrounding the value of empathy, it may be more accurate to describe the affordance here as mental flexibility. The imaginary nature of fantasy requires the reader to be open to more connections, more possibilities, other experiences. This requirement of flexibility is present even in the language. Robert Reid-Pharr illustrates the "liberating" quality of SF language through the sample sentence, "Her world exploded." In realist fiction, this sentence could only be understood metaphorically, as the end of her past way of life, but in the SF context, it could also have a literal meaning that is "outside of human experience" (Reid-Pharr 925): the planet she lived on exploded. Even the syntax of fantastic literature is destabilized "in a manner that might be described as 'liberating'" (925). This illustrates how fantastic fiction in general demands a certain amount of mental flexibility that is not necessary in more realistic fiction, a feature that simply becomes more likely the further a text drifts from representing consensus reality. I argue that this flexibility manifests in a variety of ways, including how fantasy encourages readers to imagine others: the other becomes a construct in the reader's mind (as they must be in such a manifestly fictional form), but the reader is also made aware of the problem of absorbing the other into the self. Regardless of whether this awareness of community is ironic or not, the "epic" component of epic fantasy fundamentally enables a conversation about communal values and definition in a way that is not always readily available elsewhere in a postmodern era.

The Epic Double Narrative

Perhaps most intriguing, given that epic fantasy is often maligned for formulaic use of tropes or conventions, the self-referential interest in itself as a genre is a feature of the epic. Frederick Griffiths and Stanley Rabinowitz refer to this as the "double plot" of the epic: epics are both stories about heroes and about the epic itself as a genre. Griffiths and Rabinowitz describe all epics as quests leading to the same destination (16). Virgil, in writing the *Aeneid*, is consciously attempting to re-write Homer, while Dante builds on Virgil in *The Divine Comedy*, and Joyce builds on all of them in *Ulysses*. In fact, Griffiths and Rabinowitz argue that this interest in its own tradition defines "epic" more than any list of formal features: "The term is closer in use to classic, a perspective or sense of literary topography describing a corpus with a center, than it is to lyric or drama as they refer to original modes of performance [...] the term is applied with no sense of such election and is constantly being redefined by what is produced" (21). This may be a feature that epic fantasy shares with epic more than other novels do—an interaction with its own tradition (not just "tradition" generally), and a conscious extension of that tradition in each text, particularly since fantasy was defined as a separate genre in the 1960s.[12] This may be taken to an extreme in overtly imitative texts like Terry Brooks's *Sword of Shannara* (1977), which has been describes as a "slavish imitation" and an "unauthorized sequel" to *The Lord of the Rings* (Hartwell 375), but nearly every text in this study bears the marks of some type of conscious interaction with the fantasy tradition, an attempt to extend or in some cases distance itself from what comes before—to an extent that goes beyond what we see more generally in literature. This goes beyond an "anxiety of influence" to a larger sense of contributing to a tradition of cultural storytelling, both extending and altering that tradition.

For the past fifty years, authors and critics frequently connect fantasy (and particularly epic fantasy) to this self-conscious awareness of its place in the tradition of mythmaking and storytelling. Speaking of literary history more generally, Tolkien refers to the "Cauldron of Story" ("Fairy Stories" 52–55), the collection of myths and legends that writers draw varying elements from in fashioning their own stories. Ekman extends

Tolkien's argument more explicitly to fantasy, saying, "fantasy writers in particular rely on material from the Cauldron. As a rule, they are also quite frank about using such material" (6–7). In this sense, epic fantasy is a genre about storytelling and its value, a genre of "old tales … brought to life again" (Ekman 7). Similarly, John Clute, in his essay "Beyond the Pale," frequently talks about fantasy in relation to "the Ocean of Story," to which popular storytelling forms have more "uncensored" access (421). While discussing specific examples of fantasy stories that are "a conversation with the Ocean of Story," Clute suggests the purpose of the fantastic: "in a world of convulsive instability, […] it is the task of the fantastic to make [the world] storyable" (431). While Clute is not specifically writing about epic fantasy here (although some of his examples, like an early excerpt from Gene Wolfe's *The Wizard Knight* clearly are), it is nonetheless possible to see the constant concern with convention and even formula in epic fantasy as a heightened example of this project. Epic fantasy is often a self-aware narrative about narrative, about the importance of story for constructing our world. By seeing itself, like the epic, as extending the story of a *genre* rather than masquerading as a transparent representation of the world, epic fantasy has a surprising affordance for metanarrative, constructivism, and other perspectives associated with postmodernism (much to the contrary of its reputation for focusing on the pre-modern).[13] Ironically, the interest in origins, traditions, and continuity manifests in a self-conscious development of "the genre" as a whole, which enables a powerfully subversive potential. As with the previous two affordances, this is another affordance that involves making connections between subjects and constructing forms for imagining the world. As Clute sums up, "The final lesson of any examination of the fantastic is connection. Touch one story and we touch them all" (432). From connections across society, between individuals, and across genre, epic fantasy is a genre of constructing connections, building forms. The style, then, the building blocks of language that create these worlds, plays a crucial role in enabling these affordances.

Style, Politics, and Fantasy

Despite its importance for this study, "style" proves to be as resistant to clear definition as "fantasy." Even when consulting the classic style guides for writing instruction, books like William Strunk and E.B. White's *Elements of Style* (1959) or Joseph M. Williams's *Style: Ten Lessons in Clarity and Grace* (1981), one finds a surprising reluctance to give a direct definition. While it seems particularly odd that textbooks intended to teach style never tell the reader what style is, we can at least derive some idea from the subjects they cover. Strunk and White divide style into two categories: "what is correct, or acceptable, in the use of English" (64) (that is, rules of grammar and syntax) and the "broader category" of "what is distinguished and distinguishing" (64). This latter category makes up the final chapter of their book, and they insist there upon the mysterious nature of style, even going so far as to re-write famous sentences (such as Thomas Paine's "These are the times that try men's souls") to demonstrate that what makes the style is something undefinable. This, of course, does not prevent them from writing the rest of the chapter in the form of rules, even though they acknowledge that these are "cautionary remarks" and "mere gentle reminders" (64). Thus, even the most rule-bound of stylists acknowledge some difficulty in definition. Style is some combination of the words being used and the ineffable "voice" of the author.

Literary critics also acknowledge this latter component of style, although often with less mystification and more conceptual rigor. Rebecca Walkowitz, in *Cosmopolitan Style* (2006), often treats "the concept of style more broadly conceived—as attitude, stance, posture, and consciousness" (2). By connecting style to posing, Walkowitz treats style as the *construction* of identity, not the revelation of identity. (In contrast, note how Strunk and White say writers use style to "*reveal* something of their spirits" [64, emphasis added].) The core feature of the writers Walkowitz discusses is that they "seemed to invent identities rather than inhabit them and [...] dramatized this process of invention" (22). This will be a fundamental assumption behind my analysis of style in epic fantasy as well: the arrangement of words on the page is not a neutral formulation of grammatical rules, and it is not simply a mysterious revelation of the author's essence. Style constructs reality by shaping perceptions of it. Style creates identity positions for authors, readers, and characters to inhabit. Thus, whenever I use the term style throughout this book, I mean the following: **the specific arrangement of words in a text (syntax, patterns of grammar, use of perspective, etc.) that shapes a reader's experience of the textual world.** The style is the textual "magic" that invokes these invented worlds, and by constituting those worlds it also constitutes a relation to the world for the reader. In fact, this should be nowhere more obvious than in epic fantasy, where the words on the page must by necessity create the reality we read. This means that rather than being a derivative and intellectually impoverished genre, epic fantasy can actually play a role in crucial debates about language, politics, style, and aesthetics both in the discipline of literary studies and in society at large.

Debates about the role of style in literary analysis take place in the larger discussion about the role of aesthetics, and by considering the aesthetic to be an inherently political category (rather than a disinterested "objective" domain), I am particularly following the aesthetic philosophy of Jacques Rancière. Rancière's theory of the politics of aesthetics is built on a definition of politics in terms of perception. Rancière frequently describes politics as a "distribution of the sensible," or as he explains in *The Politics of Aesthetics* (2004), "Politics revolves around what is seen and what can be said about it, around who has the ability to see and the talent to speak" (8). Politics determines who gets to speak, who can be seen, what categories can be used to organize and structure interactions between people. Consequently, art, as a shaper of perceptions, is inherently political. However, significantly, the politics lie not in how the aesthetic motivates action or even changes how people think; instead, it changes how they perceive. The politics of aesthetics is "about creating forms of perception, forms of interpretation" ("Interview" 80). For Rancière, this perspective on art returns agency to aesthetics as a category for change: "Political statements and literary locutions produce effects in reality. […] They draft maps of the visible, trajectories between the visible and the sayable, relationships between modes of being, modes of saying, and modes of doing and making" (*Politics* 35). Rancière provides a compelling explanation for how style does not just shape politics but is inherently political, an argument that touches on common arguments about defamiliarization in literary criticism (which I will expand in more detail in Chapter 1). Furthermore, his map-making metaphor allows us to circle back to how epic fantasy offers a particularly interesting test case of this theory. As I have defined it, epic fantasy is a genre about world creation, so it may be possible that a genre that focuses so much on building its own maps (even to the extent of often including literal maps in the text) might also have something to show us about how the aesthetic "drafts maps of the visible." In fact, Rancière specifically sees the role of the critic as explicating the world created by the text: "The role of the critic […] is to draw the outlines of the kind of common world that the work is producing […] to explain the forms—as well as the possible shifts in the forms—of perception" ("Interview" 80). While Rancière surely does not intend this literally as an analysis of world building in fantasy, it describes reasonably accurately what I intend to do in this study: analyzing the synergy between the fantasy world and the textual world built by the writer's style to describe what kind of worlds are proposed by epic fantasy.

Thus, I will approach style in this book by starting with textual details—the formulation of words on the page—and extrapolating from those how the style shapes the perception of the reader and thus their political world. Style creates cognitive forms in the mind of readers, or as Isobel Armstrong puts it, the "subject of representation" is "not a self, or an object, or a thematics, but the structuring movement of thought and feeling" (17). Isobel Armstrong's close reading methodology, and her rationale for it as explained in *The Radical Aesthetic* (2000), underlie much of my method in this book as well. Armstrong's book attempts to rehabilitate the category of the aesthetic after it was largely dismissed by the "hermeneutics of suspicion" practiced by Marxism, deconstruction, and similar theoretical approaches. Armstrong attempts to rehabilitate the aesthetic by uniting cognition and affect in a detailed "closer than close" reading of the text. She sees cognitive attempts to master the text (ranging from the New Critics to the Marxists) as fundamental to the problem of aesthetics, as such readings tend to distance themselves from texts, creating artificial closure by imposing their theoretical paradigms rather than embracing the messy, often exploratory and non-finalized affective experience of reading the text. Thus, redefining emotion as part of the cognitive experience of a text is crucial to her definition of aesthetics, as she attempts to find a close reading method that accepts the text's difficult wrangling with reality and avoids imposing a masterful theoretical interpretation on the reading experience. She seeks an "analytical poetics of emotion" (13)—she wants emotion to be part of cognition in our analyses. This split between cognition and affect in aesthetics is the same as the split I identified in the definition of style: the rules of usage are the cognitive analytical component, while the mysterious "voice" that gives a text its personality is the "affect." As I observed, the Strunk and White definition tends to mystify affect, making it a numinous, experiential quality of the text that cannot be analyzed. Armstrong, however, suggests a method for unifying cognition and affect within a single definition through extremely close reading. She practices a form of close reading that embraces the experience of the text as it is embodied in the language in order "to rethink the power of affect, feeling and emotion in a *cognitive* space" (87). Close reading, she says, "has never been close enough" (95) because it has always been engaged in attempting to master the text. When one does not read for mastery, one instead "necessarily gets caught up with, imbricated in, the structure of the text's processes" (94). When Armstrong gives a sample reading of Wordsworth's "Tintern Abbey," she focuses on small details of style, such as syntax or the use of prepositions like "of." Doing so allows her to account for how the language of the text involves the reader in its processes.

In the following chapters, I will carry out a number of similarly close readings of epic fantasy texts, with frequent attention to how small details of style structure the reader's *experience* of the text and thus the world the text creates. I am influenced in this also by the phenomenological critics like Wolfgang Iser, but New Formalist approaches like Armstrong's and Levine's allow a clearer account of the political consequences of these readings: texts shape reader experience and therefore re-structure how the mind functions in relation to the world. Like Armstrong, I am attempting to analyze the text's affect rather than make masterful interpretive pronouncements about meaning. This means that conclusions about texts will sometimes appear as tensions or contradictions rather than statements, as this method embraces the questions raised by the reading experience. For instance, my reading of certain linguistic structures (such as syntactic complexity) leading to empathy should not be understood as the creation of mechanistic, essentialist rules ("complex sentences lead to empathy") but a situated reading of how various forms (epic temporality and scale, secondary-world fantasy structure, and syntactic complexity) intersect to form an experience that unveils possibilities within the language. These possibilities are realized in varying degrees depending on the writer, the specific text, and the context of the reader (whose widely variable expectations and goals while reading will certainly influence the effect in unpredictable ways). My own position as reader will often be invisible due to my following the conventional forms of literary criticism, but the reader of this book should not forget that the enabling possibilities I describe are processed through my own ideological position as I make my claim to "the ability to see and the talent to speak." Nonetheless, the ultimate effect will be, I hope, a better understanding of how style interacts with genre.

Currently, such close analysis of style is largely missing from literary criticism of epic fantasy. This is not to say that considerations of style are utterly absent, nor that close reading is never done, but few studies offer sustained analysis of style, certainly not in the "closer than close" mode of attention to syntax, form words, grammatical patterns, and the like. The strongest and most influential studies are often organized around considerations other than form and style, and even those that focus on form often do not emphasize close readings of style. Most major studies either focus on broad modes of fantasy (Ann Swinfen, for instance, organizes her chapters around subjects like talking animal fantasy, time fantasy, secondary world fantasy, or philosophical ideals behind fantasy) or content issues relating the text to real-world social or psychological models, under which heading I include more recent efforts to link the development of the fantasy genre to its historical context in various Marxist-inflected theoretical works (as in James Gifford's excellent survey of the genre's roots in anarchism and late modernism). Even those who write about form more extensively, such as Brian Attebery or C. Palmer-Patel, focus broadly on narrative structures like plot and characterization rather than style. While the lack of sustained attention to style is not necessarily a flaw in these works (they are attempting quite different projects), either critics who practice close reading are not applying it to epic fantasy, or critics are choosing different types of projects when faced with fantasy.

Two relatively recent studies do give sustained attention to matters of style in epic fantasy; however, both approach it somewhat differently than I will. Susan Mandala's *Language in Science Fiction and Fantasy: The Question of Style* (2010) examines how patterns of syntactic and grammatical choices enable writers to construct convincing alternate worlds. Her study provides much concrete evidence to support years of critical generalizations about world building in fantastic fiction, but her methodology comes primarily from linguistics and is therefore more descriptive. The conclusions typically confine themselves to observational comments about how style creates plausibility rather than any theoretical consideration about, say, why "plausibility" might be ideologically important to a text. On the other hand, Farah Mendlesohn's *Rhetorics of Fantasy* is one of the most ambitious studies of form and structure in the fantasy genre and has provided a new critical vocabulary for describing various rhetorical forms of fantasy, in addition to numerous analytical examples of how each of these broad categories uses specific stylistic forms. Her study is certainly a landmark in studying fantasy, as she is one of the few to consider form in fantasy at length. Her structuralist methodology still tends to lend itself better to broad sampling rather than the more extensive analysis I will be attempting, but there are still many insightful observations about style to be found in her book. However, despite (or perhaps because of) this overlap of interest in style, and because I find many of her conclusions about epic fantasy (largely found in the mode she describes as "portal-quest fantasy") to be inaccurate, she frequently encapsulates the attitudes toward epic fantasy that I will argue against—namely, its association with conservative, essentialist, static modes of thinking. Thus, I will most often discuss her work as a point of contrast to my arguments.

In summary, then, I am arguing that specific patterns of language usage shape reader experience in a way that we can describe as political. When I call style "political" throughout this study, I am referring to this experiential, relational component of the text—the relationship of self to other, and the form we imagine communal relations taking, is the foundation of politics (in the sense Rancière means) and also the foundation of the epic (as I defined it above). While I may talk much more about "perspective" and "empathy" in this book than conventional "political" issues, that underpinning is always present, and it is fundamental to my definition of style. In technical terms, this definition of style includes many of the categories found in those style guides or in foundational theoretical works like Wayne Booth's *Rhetoric of Fiction*: sentence length and rhythm; use of metaphor and figurative language (or lack thereof); syntax (how character and action relate to subject and verb of sentence, coordination and subordination, active vs. passive); narrative voice; diction and tone; structural issues of cohesion, coherence, and emphasis (such as telling vs. showing); and patterns of grammar and punctuation. Some of these will organize sections of this study, while others will be recurring points of discussion.

The Elements of Epic Fantasy Style

In order to test the affordances of the forms epic fantasy gravitates towards, this study will pull in two directions. First, and perhaps most obviously, I want to examine many of the common formal features ascribed (fairly or not) to epic fantasy, ranging from florid writing style to paratextual apparatus. How will taking seriously these features that support and reinforce the themes and purposes of fantasy narrative inform our understanding of fantasy as a genre? To be sure, to understand the affordances of fantasy, we will need to look to seemingly typical examples. At the same time, however, to see how fantasy as a field of possibilities shapes the narratives that are run through its filter, we must also examine the exceptional cases: how are features less often used by epic fantasy writers (first-person perspective, minimalist style) also indicative of the enabling possibilities fantasy affords? Thus, this book will alternate between examinations of common formal features of fantasy style and less common cases in order to find the through-lines—the opportunities epic fantasy offers to literary narrative. Each section of this book has a pair of chapters. The first chapter will explicate the affordances of a common feature of epic fantasy style and structure, in some cases arguing that certain effects of style persist despite apparent evidence that they run contrary to the author's "intentions" (although intentionality will largely be discussed as a rhetorical perspective of texts, not a property of some transcendental authorial subject). The second chapter in the pair, by focusing on less typical cases, will examine exploitation of the generic expectations seen in the first chapter, either making a negative argument through the absence of a feature (as in Chapter 2, where moments of editorial simplicity contrast the stylistic excess I discuss in Chapter 1) or by self-reflexively commenting on a feature of fantasy (as in Chapter 8, where I discuss writers who use frame narratives to comment ironically on the framed nature of fantasy narrative). These alternating chapters are based on what is often *perceived* as common or uncommon in epic fantasy narrative. Genre expectations shape reception, so while it may be empirically true that first-person perspective is far less common in epic fantasy than in mainstream fiction (and I provide some evidence of this in Chapter 4), it is more important that readers expect first-person narration less, and thus canny writers can use it to shape reader experience in revelatory ways.

Finally, I should note that this study focuses on similarities and connections in style. Many of these works were produced in substantially different contexts: Fritz Leiber begins his career before the fantasy genre is formally defined and writes much of his fantasy during a crucial period of definition; Glen Cook responds as much to Vietnam war fiction as to the fantasy genre; and N.K. Jemisin interacts with a fantasy canon that has been established for decades suffering from baked-in exclusions. While I will attempt to gesture towards how these varying contexts influence these writers' styles in particular ways, it is not in the scope of this study to examine this historical context in great detail. Instead, I will focus on how the choice to write about magical fantasy worlds influences the use of language in these writers and leave the historical differences to be developed in future studies.

The first chapter, in some ways, continues this introduction as I interrogate the theoretical consequences of one of the core evaluative assumptions about fantasy style: namely, that epic fantasy is written in a florid style, prone to excessive details and archaisms; that it suffers perhaps from purple prose.[14] I argue that this elaborate "excess" of style has an important consequence: it generates the mental flexibility that leads to empathy in the reader. I re-examine the now familiar critical truisms about fantasy excelling in defamiliarization and argue that by exercising the reader's imagination so intensely, epic fantasy is particularly capable of enabling readers to imagine others' lives. Chapter 2 will then examine the reverse of this argument: rather than empathy being simply a constructive, pro-social behavior, it can also turn into a voyeuristic appropriation of the other. Epic fantasy, in its attempts to emotively link readers to characters, runs the risk of crossing this line and reducing depictions of violence to occasions for readers to experience a vicarious emotional charge. Writers who resist the expectations of an emotive style often do so by strategically deploying moments of editorial simplicity. The notable elision of descriptions of emotion or scenes of violence illustrates how working contrary to stylistic norms generates a powerful critique of the reader's expectations for what it means to imagine the other.

These questions of how fantasy shapes the social imaginary—the relation of the subject to the other—continues into the second section of the book, where I will explore the broader questions of perspective and point of view. Epic style is often associated with a distant perspective and a hierarchical, totalizing world view, and unsurprisingly, then, epic fantasy tends by far to prefer third-person narrative to first-person. Most epic fantasy deploys some form of narrative distance, ranging from omniscience to what is often referred to as "third-person limited," frequently with generous helpings of free indirect discourse, with an omniscient narrator dipping in out of the consciousness of various characters, often in sections of the book named for those characters. In Chapter 3, I will consider the implications of the various forms of narrative "omniscience" in third-person narration, arguing that the "head-hopping" omniscience so common in epic fantasy has the surprising potential to break down hierarchies and level distinctions between characters, quite the opposite of the hierarchical effects usually ascribed to it.

In Chapter 4, I will examine the more exceptional case of first-person narration in epic fantasy. First-person epic fantasy even more directly deconstructs the ideology of epic essentialism, breaking down the fundamental tension I have already noted in the form "epic fantasy novel" between the epic (with its static, totalizing impulses) and the novel (with its attempt to create communal identities out of a contingent present). While this tension is to some extent present in all novels, epic fantasy is surprisingly well-suited to deconstructing the totalizing impulses at the heart of the novel, particularly when it uses first-person narration, a highly subjective, immanent form of narration that seems conventionally ill-suited to the distant form of the epic.

In the second half of this study, I shift to examining form and style on a larger scale within the text, while still mapping those onto sentence-level style choices. In Chapter 5, I look at the "sense of wonder" frequently cited as foundational to the fantastic. As a "sense," the concept of wonder is often treated as a form of mystification, too experiential for concrete, cognitive analysis. Yet this experiential quality of wonder is precisely why an extremely close reading of style is valuable here, as it allows us, in Armstrong's terms, to see the cognitive and the affective united in the aesthetic. I explain the "sense of wonder" in concrete stylistic terms by examining the use of what might on the surface appear to be gimmicks—plot twists and withheld information. Carefully structured moments of narrative surprise create a feeling of transcendence, first establishing a system of rules before breaking those rules to suggest the existence of a wider system, spurring curiosity and a desire for discovery, a questioning attitude toward the world that is not fixed but open to revision. However, some fantasy steadfastly refuses the sense of wonder, either outright rejecting it through a focus on the mundane or parodically pulling away from its own magical elements. In Chapter 6, I analyze these writers who resist "fantasy" as a category even as they deploy its tropes. Such fantasy often operates at the fringes of the "epic fantasy" category, resisting epic idealization through various strategies of ironic deflation while simultaneously employing some epic features. By operating on the edge of subgeneric distinctions, such writers clearly display the collisions at the heart of the fantasy genre, deploying one set of conventions (cynical war fiction or sword and sorcery action-adventure) to comment on another (epic idealization). Such writing creates a language for fantasy out of a fundamental tension, unveiling the artifice at the heart of all social formations yet simultaneously arguing for the necessary illusion of such order to create communal identity.

All of these arguments indicate how the style of epic fantasy assists it in framing our understanding of networks of social relations. In the final section, then, I turn my attention to how epic fantasy uses elaborate framing mechanisms to create maps of social form. Chapter 7 focuses on the framework of maps, appendices, epigraphs, and glossaries meant to present the fantasy text as an artifact in a larger fantasy history. I principally examine epigraphs and appendices, showing how such paratexts intersect with the main body of the narrative. Paratexts often function to construct the relationship of the text to the larger social world, yet in epic fantasy, the paratexts are frequently *part of* the fictional world. By fictionalizing these margins of the text, epic fantasy has a tremendous capability for generating metatextual awareness of the constructed nature of our assumptions about historical truth. While Chapter 7 analyzes the *implicit* framing of epic fantasy, Chapter 8 shows how the overall frame of fantasy often translates into a literal frame narrative. Using frame narratives allows writers of epic fantasy to maintain an ironic distance while nonetheless creating the visceral narrative immersion on which the genre's popularity often depends. A function of the frame is to render all content within it suspect, as it is run through the subjective filter of the frame narrator. While the assumption is most often that epic fantasy requires "suspension of disbelief" and therefore avoids such perspectival ironies, these writers create frames that exert pressure on the main text of the story, a pressure that ironically warps the style of that text to reflect the subjectivity of the frame narrators. As a result, such stories have the radical potential to subvert stable hegemonic views of history by revealing stories as ideological constructs that attempt to shape the world, a fitting overview of how fantasy style creates worlds that shape the reader's political and social perceptions.

A Note on the Selection of Texts

This study focuses largely on writers working after fantasy is established as a genre with its own conventions and expectations, which happens primarily from 1960 to 1975. As Jamie Williamson argues in *The Evolution of Modern Fantasy*, prior to this period no unified concept of a fantasy genre existed; thus, any attempt to analyze the style of the genre prior to that period would be complicated by the fact that its writers had different ideas of what they were attempting to accomplish. My selection of texts, on other hand, predominantly includes writers who are working with an established set of conventions. Only three of my focus texts even come from this definitional period (Leiber's Fafhrd and Gray Mouser stories, parts of Moorcock's Elric series, and Le Guin's *Tombs of Atuan*), and these texts illuminate the genre in intriguing ways. Furthermore, because part of the motive for this study is an attempt to redress significant gaps in scholarship about epic fantasy, I have tried to discuss writers who have typically not received critical attention. Thus, I have largely avoided J.R.R. Tolkien, not because there is not much to say about style in Tolkien, but because much has already been said (more than about any other writer in this book). If I could make the same argument with a less familiar text that also rewarded close attention, I chose to do so, and the result is that Tolkien is mostly absent from this book. Several writers proved too useful to this study to exclude, though, so I included them despite a relative abundance of critical material, a group that includes Ursula Le Guin, Stephen R. Donaldson, and Samuel Delany, but as with much of epic fantasy, style has often not been a central focus of the criticism on these writers. On the other hand, I have included many writers for whom little to no scholarly work currently exists, including Glen Cook, Steven Erikson, R.F. Kuang, N.K. Jemisin, Brandon Sanderson, and David Gemmell. Some of these are recent writers and some have been overlooked for years, but all make important contributions to the conversation about epic fantasy.

A Note on the Style of This Book

Perceptive readers may note that various elements of the structure of this book reflect the structures I am analyzing. For instance, you may find that the syntactic structures I am analyzing can also be found more frequently in chapters or passages analyzing those structures. Some of this was intentional as I drafted these chapters, some was discovered (and refined) upon revision, and no doubt some can still be found that I have not noticed. To be sure, this is playful and somewhat gratuitous, and readers who take pleasure in detecting such ironies may enjoy guessing which were placed intentionally and which were not, but retrospectively there is a serious point: the style of this book demonstrates how immersing yourself in particular forms of language changes the way you think. Structures of language influence structures of thought, and as I spent so much time absorbing particular linguistic structures, to some extent they tended to imprint on my own use of language. That some of these echoes are unintentional simply reinforces that embracing the language you read shapes how you see the world.

Syntactic Complexity

CHAPTER 1

"The Riotous Conflagration of Beauteous Language"

Flowery Style, Defamiliarization, and Empathic Imagination

> One can listen to words, and see them as the unfolding of a petal or, indeed, the very opposite: each word bent and pushed tighter, smaller, until the very packet of meaning vanishes with a flip of deft fingers. Poets and tellers of tales can be tugged by either current, into the riotous conflagration of beauteous language or the pithy reduction of the tersely colourless.—Steven Erikson, *Toll the Hounds*

In the middle of Steven Erikson's massive novel *Toll the Hounds* (2008), itself the eighth volume in a gargantuan ten-volume epic fantasy series, the whimsical narrator Kruppe takes a moment—in the epigraph to this chapter quoted above—to consider the difference between two extremes of writing style, wordiness and terse simplicity. The metaphor of flowers is appropriate as such linguistic excess is often saddled with the term "florid," yet here Erikson (via Kruppe) reverses the implications of "flowery" prose; his metaphor suggests that such language is open and embracing, "unfolding" to encompass more people and experiences than a language so ruthlessly simple that even the "meaning vanishes." Certainly, Kruppe illustrates the florid style, as his language is erupting with convoluted syntax, Latinate diction, and perhaps too many images. Critics of such excessive style could easily point to the mixed metaphor of the final line, where writers are first "tugged by" a "current," and then they are apparently in flames (a "conflagration") before finally returning to the flower metaphor with the word "colourless." Naturally, this is the point, and Kruppe immediately contrasts himself to another character, Gaz, a brutal murderer and wife beater, who is "terse" and "views his paucity of words [...] as a virtue, sigil of rigid manhood. [...] in his endless paring down he strips away all hope of emotion and with it empathy" (279–80).

The gender coding of language is noteworthy here, as the flowery imag-ery of the term "florid" suggests decoration and femininity, while terse simplicity signals "rigid manhood." Yet, again, Erikson reverses the tradi-tional valuing of such terms by associating terse simplicity with ruthless-ness and violence: the "manic editing" of his perspective enables Gaz to commit great violence, whereas Kruppe's more emotive language leads us to empathy. Erikson here seems to be engaging in an almost metafictional moment touching on one of the great debates surrounding literary analy-sis of writing style. For over a century, the dominant canons of "good writ-ing style" have favored what I will call (via Erikson) "ruthless simplicity" and have devalued flowery excess. However, I will argue alongside Kruppe (and perhaps Erikson) that such an ideological evaluation of style is "ruth-less" in that it reinforces stereotypically masculine, clinically cognitive attitudes that "manically edit" out parts of life, leaving only what they deem worthy, whereas a flowering style has potential uses beyond being sloppy or pretentious: it can be open and embracing, leading the reader to a more empathic and accepting view of the world.

From this standpoint, it is particularly ironic that one of the com-mon charges leveled against epic fantasy—a genre known for masculine heroics, bloody battles, and sexualized sorceresses—is that it too often descends into excessive, florid style. In an early attempt at a scholarly defi-nition of fantasy fiction, Jane Mobley credited the genre with an "essen-tial extravagance": "The language of fantasy is itself extravagant, creating oftentimes by the mere unpronounceability of names the wonder and great-ness of it all" (124). Mobley seems to concede that this is a fault, suggesting that "craft is secondary to material" (126) in the mythic functions of fan-tasy, that myth has a "sturdy ability" to "survive even mediocre retelling" (126–7), and that "our aesthetic standards must be altered somewhat to allow the inclusion of 'function'" (127). While we might assume that criti-cal attitudes have shifted in the last forty years, Susan Mandala cites ample evidence of a consistent pattern in critics accepting assumptions that fan-tasy style is "downright poor: clumsy, intrusive, and unconcerned with lit-erary quality" (15). Mandala gives examples from the 1970s up through the first decade of the twentieth century, noting "great strides" (18) in accept-ing genre writing (both science fiction and fantasy) on the level of theme, but not on the level of style. While many of Mandala's examples accuse fantasy of being too simple, plain, or non-experimental, she also notes the influence of pulp fiction style, with its overwritten traits that reviewers of fantasy novels still cite as problems in contemporary fiction, such as "intrusive and over-long passages of exposition; [...] needless repetition of adjectives and adverbs that serve as little more than fillers; a depen-dence on third person omniscient narration; dialogue that is too complex

syntactically to convincingly represent talk; and a tendency to use unnatural synonyms for the speech reporting verb 'said,' and to modify those
synonyms with equally unnatural adverbs (e.g., 'No!,' he blustered roar-
ily)" (16–17). Mandala even includes an entire chapter on the use of archaic
forms in fantasy fiction, and while she argues that such forms are often
used artfully and thoughtfully, she cites further examples of criticism that
archaisms are a clumsy affectation (77).

Even fantasy writers perpetuate this stereotype about the genre. Samuel Delany contrasted the prose he attempted to construct in his Nevèrÿon
series with the traditional style of sword and sorcery: "an adjective-heavy
exclamatory diction that mingles myriad archaisms with other syntactical distortions meant to signal the antique" (214). Ursula Le Guin even
more ruthlessly mocks the use of florid writing by "novice" fantasists.
While Le Guin overall argues that fantasy requires elevated distance
from everyday life, she believes that such style requires a careful balancing act that can be achieved through "[c]larity and simplicity" (89). The
"novices" (among whom she seems to imply are many published writers) arrive at mistaken ideas about elaborate prose through imitation of
more skilled "master fantasists" (85) like Dunsany: "I have never seen any
imitation Dunsany that consisted of anything beyond a lot of elaborate
made-up names, some vague descriptions of gorgeous cities and unmen-
tionable dooms, and a great many sentences beginning with 'And'" (84).
She further cites traits such as "the archaic manner," "the use of the subjunctive," the "She-To-Whom Trap" ("I shall give it to she to whom my love
is given!"), and "fancy words": "Eldritch. Tenebrous. Smaragds and chal-
cedony. Mayhap. It can't be maybe, it can't be perhaps; it has to be mayhap,
unless it's perchance. And then comes the final test, the infallible touch-
stone of the seventh-rate: Ichor. You know ichor. It oozes out of severed
tentacles, and beslimes tessellated pavements, and bespatters bejeweled
couriers, and bores the bejesus out of everybody" (85). At the same time as
she mocks this excess, Le Guin recognizes the impulse lying behind this
style, the same impulse that Mobley identified: "what is wanted in fantasy
is a *distancing from the ordinary*" (Le Guin 85). These stylistic excesses
are part of a removal from the everyday, which is part of what defines epic
fantasy.

In this chapter, I will attempt to identify how this tendency toward
flowery style intersects with other conventions of epic fantasy to enable
its aesthetic and ideological potential. We may view florid style not as a
"weakness" of epic fantasy (an evaluative term) but an affordance of epic
fantasy (a descriptive term) and examine what the consequences are for
fantasy's collisions with other social forms. Specifically, elaborate syntax
and colorful diction, which I will call "flowering" style in contrast to the

evaluative connotations of "flowery" or "florid," are particularly suited to epic fantasy as they support two important functions: (1) they defamiliarize the world, enabling readers to perceive the world through the eyes of people who do not exist and in ways that are not actually possible in the real world; and (2) they reveal in fine detail the interior subjectivity of characters, the ways in which a character's perspective is projected onto the world around them. To illustrate how an analysis of flowering style may function in fantasy literature, I will focus on two writers—Stephen R. Donaldson and Steven Erikson—each of whom has been criticized for perceived stylistic excesses for not following the conventions of ruthless simplicity, but who both thereby illustrate the link between epic fantasy style, defamiliarization, and empathic imagination.

The "Ruthless Simplicity" of the Writing Classroom

Before launching into samples from Donaldson and Erikson, we should consider briefly what the conventions of "ruthless simplicity" are. We could go back to the American New Critics of the 1930s–1950s and discuss the likes of John Crowe Ransom and Cleanth Brooks, whose practice of close reading is foundational to literary criticism and who gave us such terms as "organic unity" to describe how not a single word should be "wasted" in a "great" piece of literature.[1] (They also exhibited the masculine ethos of this ruthless simplicity in their vicious opposition to sentimentality.) However, perhaps even more influential on the practice of *writing* is William Strunk and E.B. White's guide *The Elements of Style*, which first appeared in 1918 (written by Strunk alone, with White updating in 1959) and has been standard reading in writing courses from the 1950s up to the present day. While Strunk and White acknowledge that style should fit the occasion, that sentence rhythm and rhetorical purpose may dictate the use of more elaborate language, they repeatedly hammer home the point that good style is short, brief, efficiently edited. For instance, they say, "A sentence should contain no unnecessary words, a paragraph no unnecessary sentences. [...] This requires not that the writer make all his sentences short [...] but that every word tell" (23). To be fair, this passage partly refers to expressions like "the reason is because," but they continually repeat this refrain about style. For instance, they urge the reader "to reread your writing later and ruthlessly delete the excess" (72), interestingly echoing Erikson's exact diction when describing Gaz. Elsewhere, they state, "The approach to style is by way of plainness, simplicity, orderliness, sincerity" (69). In fact, anything that potentially disturbs clear writing is not only stylistically but morally suspect: they admit "there are occasions when obscurity serves a literary yearning, if not a literary purpose" (which is some heavy hedging), but they go on to say, "Clarity, clarity, clarity. [...] Muddiness is not merely a disturber of prose, it is also a destroyer of life, of hope: death on the highway caused by a badly worded road sign" (79), following with several similarly melodramatic examples.

Strunk and White's harping on clarity returns us to the debate about the relationship between aesthetics and politics. Too often, according to its opponents, the rhetoric of "clarity" veils a mechanistic and unchallenging approach to hegemonic authority. Such is the gist of Theodor Adorno's argument in a frequently quoted passage from *Minima Moralia*, "Morality and Style": "[A]nything specific, not taken from pre-existent patterns, appears inconsiderate, a symptom of eccentricity, almost of confusion. [...] Only what they do not need first to understand, they consider understandable; only the word coined by commerce, and really alienated, touches them as familiar" (101). "Clear" language, according to Adorno, is "clear" only because it does not challenge conventional ways of thinking; if we de-couple language from commerce and commodification, it will become less "clear" (even if, presumably, it is still structurally, grammatically correct). To be fair, Adorno is partly objecting to the same sort of conventional vagueness as Strunk and White. The difference, however, as Adorno points out, is that "clarity" too often means repeating the familiar rather than challenging the reader with new or unfamiliar forms. Walkowitz sums up Adorno's argument neatly: "literature that repeats familiar generalizations [...] helps to maintain fixed conceptions by living up to them, and it generates in its readers habits of inattention and intellectual automatism" (56). While Adorno is partly arguing against a generic homogenization of literature of which (some would argue) genre literature is particularly guilty, he also suggests a contradiction in those claims. If difficult or unconventional language challenges the reader's conventional perceptions (and challenging conventional perceptions could be seen as a staple of fantasy in general), then it seems odd to criticize an entire genre for using such language, even if that language may exist in tension with other more formulaic genre elements. Too often critics do not pay enough attention to how style "generates habits in its readers" or how the words on the page construct an understanding of the world that will affect how readers interact with it. Instead, "clear" style is used to establish a separation between a cultural elite who know the proper use of the tools of language and those who lack such knowledge.

Strunk and White especially seem to use "clear writing" to separate social order from disorder, particularly through their recurring metaphor linking writing style and eating: "Young writers often suppose that style is a garnish for the meat of prose, a sauce by which a dull dish is made palatable" (69) and "Rich, ornate prose is hard to digest, generally unwholesome, and sometimes nauseating" (72). While this latter passage seems intended to ironically illustrate the rule they are expounding, nonetheless Strunk and White link simple prose to order, social hierarchy, and general good culture just as the rules of good eating are a part of the social discipline by which subjects show they are able to regulate the body. As such, writing style is a limiting factor that determines who belongs, who counts, based on who knows the rules. They make this abundantly clear when they ask, "What is wrong, you ask, with [using the word] *beauteous*? No one knows, for sure. There is nothing wrong, really, with any word—all are good, but some are better than others. A matter of ear, a matter of reading the books that sharpen the ear" (77). Good style, therefore, is a matter of taste, which comes from developing your ear, or, in other words, being educated in the proper way. All of these examples illustrate how the ideology of "good plain style" functions to fragment social groups by testing who has received the proper education and who has not. In contrast, epic fantasy moves towards unity (specifically, uniting the reader with alternate perspectives), and consequently tends toward more elaborate, flowering styles to attempt to create a more embracing, empathic language.

This classroom experience—involving the use of language to fragment social groups into a hierarchy based on style—certainly influenced Steven Erikson's creation of Kruppe's narrative style. Erikson has specifically noted his experience in the Iowa Writers' Workshop, where the imitation of minimalist writers such as Raymond Carver dominated. Erikson has argued that imitating another author's voice without having lived the same life is ineffective writing (personal interview).[2] Yet Erikson's style here goes beyond simple satire: it exposes some potentially problematic affordances of minimalist style. Specifically, Erikson (via Kruppe) suggests terse style more readily represents fragmentation and alienation, pushing away from empathy. Many critics acknowledge some such fragmenting effect of minimalist style. For instance, Ihab Hassan writes of Ernest Hemingway (an important influence on Carver) that his "distrust of language" (88) results in an "anti-style" (89) that entails "a deliberate restriction of feelings" (109). We should particularly note the social dimension here, as the characters themselves are isolated: "the ethic of Hemingway's characters is not only reductive but solitary. What they endure, they can never share with others" (91). Interestingly, the same tends to be true of Carver's characters, as Robert Clark points out in his study of American minimalism: "Many of the figures that populate Carver's stories seem to lack the capacity to comprehend the perspectives of others or empathize with those they have hurt" (65).

Both of these characterizations are visible in Erikson's character Gaz, who, in his "endless paring down [...] strips away all hope of emotion and with it empathy" (280). Gaz views himself as an "artist" of violence, and his creed is to "keep things simple" as the "secret to staying sane" (280). We should also note again how this terseness of language supports a toxic masculinity: Gaz "views his paucity of words [...] as a virtue, sigil of rigid manhood" (279–280), and his idea that his abused wife belongs to him is "artfully whittled from his world view" (280). Such "whittling" metaphorically connects violent action (cutting an object), art (whittling is an art that involves reducing an object's size, cutting parts out) and "manic editing" (minimalist style, like whittling, involves "cutting" words out). It may also remind us of the heavily masculine ethic of Hemingway or Carver, or their own "manic" tendency to cut out words. Kruppe (and perhaps Erikson) suggests that this overly editorial eye aligns with a distrust of language and emotion that can ultimately result in justifying violence or other anti-social behavior (as Gaz uses it to justify beating his wife).

This "tighter, smaller" logic (as Kruppe might call it)—which values a simple, laconic, emotionally-restrained style over a verbose, emotional one—may in part account for the attitudes toward fantasy I cited at the start of this chapter.[3] In fact, I have chosen one of my principal examples, Stephen R. Donaldson, because his style has often been subjected to this sort of criticism. David Pringle's response to Donaldson's Thomas Covenant novels is a good example. Pringle, once the editor of the academic journal *Foundation* and the editor and publisher of *Interzone* until 2004, has written a number of guides to science fiction and fantasy, including in the 1980s a pair of volumes on the 100 best novels in each genre. While Pringle is certainly not the only critic writing about fantasy at this time, he is a characteristic example of the attitude towards fantasy style when Donaldson was first publishing (and when Erikson was studying).[4] Pringle's preference for simplicity and objections to perceived overwriting are nowhere more evident than in his entry in his list of "hundred best" fantasy novels for Stephen R. Donaldson's Chronicles of Thomas Covenant, which Pringle seems to include grudgingly. In particular, he dislikes the style on grounds that Strunk and White would approve, calling it "long-winded," "hamfistedly Latinate," and "difficult," criticizing the use of metaphor and the dependency on "a sheer *piling on* effect" (180). This has been a common complaint about Donaldson's Thomas Covenant novels, and Donaldson has acknowledged in an interview with W.A. Senior that the style of the novels is "occasionally misjudged" (Senior 26) but points out that the style was also a deliberate choice: "I believed that the Covenant books required an operatic prose in order to generate the colors and feelings that I wanted, and that it was better to err on the side of excess than it was to make the mistake of not providing that particular rhetorical richness" (26).

In order to analyze epic fantasy style, we should take Donaldson's claim at face value and analyze the style for what it affords—how the tools it offers intersect with an author's other structures—rather than simply evaluating our preference for a given set of features. From that standpoint, Donaldson's work, and particularly the Thomas Covenant novels, are an excellent case study. In fact, Senior's study of the series is one of the few critical works to discuss epic fantasy writing style at length, although Senior does point out a number of problematic elements, such as "difficult vocabulary," "arcane usages," and "contorted, overwrought images" (25), all of which might remind us of how Strunk and White tell us to "avoid fancy words" and use Anglo-Saxon rather than Latin words. By way of illustration, Senior cites a passage in which Covenant "chewed the gristle of such thoughts for leagues" (*Lord Foul's Bane* 118). However, Senior puts this in context by connecting this stylistic tendency to the larger goals of epic fantasy to defamiliarize the world: "Part of the problem is that fantasy authors must try to define in words what does not exist, and so the language of fantasy is always pushing against the barrier of meaning and significance" (25). This defamiliarizing power of fantasy language is crucial to its flowering style and the primary means by which it creates the potential for mental flexibility, empathy, and social connection.

Linguistic Defamiliarization

It should not be surprising to claim that defamiliarization is one of the affordances of the fantastic. Many critics who discuss science fiction or fantasy focus on defamiliarization as a key component. Rosemary Jackson's influential study of the fantastic primarily argues that fantasy subverts categories for understanding meaning: it is "an art of estrangement, resisting closure, opening structures which categorize experience. [...] By drawing attention to the relative nature of these categories the fantastic moves towards a dismantling of the 'real'" (175). Jackson, though, favors the study of fantasy that begins nominally in the real world and then introduces fantastic elements (what she calls "paraxial" fantasy), seeing this uncertainty as the locus of fantasy's estranging effects. In contrast, Jackson sees epic or secondary-world fantasy as refusing the desire to break down categories and "frequently displacing [that desire] into religious longing and nostalgia" (9). Her blanket assumption that epic fantasy will "defuse potentially disturbing, anti-social drives and retreat from any profound confrontation with existential dis-ease" (9) is one claim that I hope to counter here. By locating defamiliarization in style, and not content or structure, I hope to point to elements *in the language itself* which generate this effect of estrangement.

In addition to Jackson's arguments about fantasy, it is difficult to discuss "estrangement" in relation to any fantastic literature without addressing Darko Suvin's classification of science fiction as "literature of cognitive estrangement" (4). While acknowledging that "estrangement" can be found not only in science fiction but also in fantasy, myth, and folk tales, Suvin sees science fiction distinguishing itself through the addition of the cognitive framework, which sees the world as "changeable" in contrast to the "fixed and supernaturally determined" view of myth and fantasy (7). For this reason, Suvin sees science fiction as a good form for materialist critique while fantasy is largely reactionary wish-fulfillment. Typical counterarguments to Suvin focus on refuting his claim that fantasy is fundamentally non-cognitive. China Miéville, for instance, points out that science fiction is as likely to use incoherent and irrational speculation as fantasy, and that by creating internally consistent and internally plausible systems fantasy can also be rational and use the same type of cognitive estrangement to comment on material reality. He concludes that even though fantasy does not give a "clear view of political possibilities," "the fantastic, particularly because 'reality' is a grotesque 'fantastic form,' is *good to think with*" (46). While I agree with Miéville's argument, I want to take the argument in a slightly different direction by suggesting that an element usually taken as a weakness of fantasy, its potential for the irrational and non-cognitive, actually enables its transformative potential, rather than consigning it to nostalgia and reaction. Essentially, I am reversing the polarity of Suvin's argument to suggest that revolution also appears in the breakdown of cognition, and that this breakdown happens not only at the level of content but at the level of language. That is, defamiliarized language breaks down habitual forms of thought—in many ways the very same type of habitual forms that create the rules of style that fragment the audience into an elite who have been educated in proper taste and an outsider class who lack the proper training. Thus, fantasy language is capable being used to generate unified communities—not the naïve unity conceived as based on some preexisting essence, but a unity based on empathy within difference.

Julia Kristeva offers a theoretical foundation that shows how this might work on the level of writing style, and how the specific features most frequently found in epic fantasy particularly afford such opportunities. While the psychoanalytical theoretical model has been influential on scholars of fantasy (Rosemary Jackson, for instance), Kristeva adds a dimension that is not as often explored, a focus that moves beyond broad identity structures to look at style, diction, and syntax. Defamiliarizing language crucially breaks that linkage between objects and categories, allowing for new, more embracing ways of seeing the world. Thus, one of the affordances that fantasy literature brings as a form is a particular affinity for the role of fantasy (in broader psychological terms) to disrupt rigid, habitual forms of language.[5] Kristeva separates language into two parts, the symbolic (the part of language with determinate meanings) and the semiotic (the part of language based purely on the physicality of language, the experience of feeling the sounds one makes). She then analyzes how the semiotic, experiential elements of language break down its meaning-making functions and are therefore a "means of overriding" the "constraints of civilization" (140). These "constraints" are, of course, the rules that create categories separating people into different groups, the same rules that Strunk and White gesture toward through their metaphors of style as eating. The semiotic provides a crucial disruptive undercurrent to all attempts at fixing a stable or absolute symbolic meaning in language. The semiotic not only exists outside the realm of meaning but can even produce in a text "nonsense effects that destroy [...] accepted beliefs and significations" (133). Kristeva goes even further to posit an almost revolutionary force for the semiotic. Against the repressive position of "transcendental mastery over discourse" which is possible within the symbolic, Kristeva sets up the semiotic as a resource which challenges this repression and creates "a means of overriding this constraint" through "a *discordance* in the symbolic function" (140). Thus, a text with the resources to break down a reader's meaning-making (symbolic) functions would be well-positioned to disrupt any form of ideology claiming a rigid, transcendental essentialism. Epic fantasy, with its resorting frequently to invented words and unfamiliar, archaic diction, would seem to be in a particularly strong position here.

Kristeva's methodology for analyzing literature in general suggests a direction for the analysis of fantasy literature as well. Kristeva's analysis of language looks for features of the text ("semiotic functions") that disrupt the ability of a "judging consciousness." In "From One Identity to Another" (1980), she examines sentence rhythms and obscene words in Louis-Ferdinand Celine's novels to demonstrate how they emphasize experiential pleasure over meaning. Kristeva's discussion of obscene words is particularly comparable to the use of language in fantasy. According to Kristeva, obscene words serve a "desemanticization function": obscene language does not refer "to an object exterior to discourse and identifiable as such by consciousness. [...] The obscene word, lacking an objective referent [...] mobilizes the signifying resources of the subject, permitting it to cross through the membrane of meaning where consciousness holds it"

(142–3). In other words, obscene words refer to language itself, not to an outside thing, and therefore provide a "cathartic" (143) escape from meaning, which by extension leads to an escape from restrictive identity categories. The word "escape" is mine, not Kristeva's, and I have chosen it because of its loaded connotations when discussing fantasy. While fantasy has been derided for "escapism,"[6] I am suggesting here a further twist on the notion of escape, one based less on content—the escape from technological modernism—and more on language and style—the escape from repressive, rigid systems of meaning-making. As I have suggested above, these rigid systems fragment social groups into hierarchies and classifications. By breaking down these hierarchies, fantasy is well-positioned to create unity and community by generating the mental flexibility leading to empathy.

Consequently, much of Kristeva's description of the semiotic and profanity applies to fantasy, particularly epic fantasy, which is full of invented vocabulary with no objective referents in the real world. Consider the case of Donaldson's Thomas Covenant books, where magical phrases like the words of power—*Melenkurion abatha duroc minas mill khabaal*—are frequently used even though they mean nothing to the reader and even within the world of the Land their meaning has been lost (at least in the first six books of the series). At times, characters will use words in ancient languages that are not translated, as when one of the Ramen, a tribe who cares for the powerful magic horses called the Ranyhn, calls them by shouting, "*Kelenbhrabanal marushyn! Rushyn hynyn kelenkoor rillynarunal! Ranyhyn Kelenbhrabanal!*" (*Lord Foul's Bane* 371–2). Even when words are given a denotative meaning, though, their alien form "desemanticizes" them much like Kristeva's obscene language as the physicality of pronouncing the words (or imagining their sound while reading silently) often dominates the denotative meaning (just as obscene language often has a denotative meaning that is de-emphasized when used). Examples abound, such as the abovementioned Ranyhn, the treasure-berries called *aliantha*, or the adhesive fabric called *clingor*. Similarly, the text is filled with names for places and people that the reader will not habitually recognize as names, therefore again having that distancing effect, place names such as Andelain or Mithil Stonedown, or character names such as Mhoram, Baradakas, Tamarantha, or Jehannum. Barely a page passes without such coinages to take the reader beyond the signifying function of language.

Erikson's novels are similarly filled with such semiotic terms. The Malazan Book of the Fallen overflows with invented terms, and although many of those terms have denotative meanings, Erikson frequently introduces those terms without explanation, allowing readers to figure them out as they read. This means that expositional passages are often initially confusing to readers, divorcing the sounds and rhythms of the words from their denotative meanings. Consider this passage from relatively early in the first book, *Gardens of the Moon* (1999), from before many of these terms are likely to be familiar to the reader (or have even been defined in the text):

> The Moon's reappearance here on Genabackis had been a surprise. And this time, there was no last-minute reprieve. A half-dozen legions of the sorcerous Tiste Andii descended from Moon's Spawn, and under the command of a warlord named Caladan Brood they joined forces with the Crimson Guard mercenaries. Together, the two armies proceeded to drive back the Malaz 5th Army, which had been pushing eastward along the northern edge of Rhivi Plain. For the past four years the battered 5th had been bogged down in Blackdog Forest, forcing them to make a stand against Brood and the Crimson Guard [57].

While Erikson makes some concessions to the reader's lack of familiarity (Caladan Brood is given the explanatory tag "a warlord named"), some of these do very little to help the reader create mental pictures—calling the Tiste Andii "sorcerous" does little to allow the reader to picture them. Thus, while the passage is an excellent example of subtle exposition (for instance, we can intuit that Blackdog Forest is swampy because of the verb choice "bogged down"), such passages are first experienced as an overwhelming wash of sound and rhythm. The sound and shape of these words is foregrounded much more than if they were replaced with familiar words, in which case the meaning would likely dominate. (If we rewrite the passage with familiar, real-world analogues, the effect is quite different: "The airplane's reappearance here in Europe had been a surprise. A half-dozen squads of British paratroopers descended from the plane.")

This fantasy tactic of overloading the reader's signifying functions often combines with an emphasis on sound and rhythm. Erikson's second book, *Deadhouse Gates* (2000), opens with a similar sentence:

> He came shambling into Judgment's Round from the Avenue of Souls, a misshapen mass of flies. Seething lumps crawled on his body in mindless migration, black and glittering and occasionally falling away in frenzied clumps that exploded into fragmented flight as they struck the cobbles. The Thirsting Hour was coming to a close and the priest staggered in its wake, blind, deaf and silent. [...] The brothers had then moved in procession out onto the streets of Unta to greet the god's spirits, enjoining the mortal dance that marked the Season of Rot's last day [1].

Here, in addition to the unfamiliar terms (e.g., Judgment's Round, Thirsting Hour, Season of Rot), the desemanticizing function is supported by the passage's emphasis on sound, particularly alliteration: "misshapen mass," "mindless migration," "fragmented flight," "greet the god's." Further, the sentences have a rhythmic cadence with a main clause followed by an adjectival verbal phrase (or in one case, simply a list of adjectives). These elements work together to pull the passage away from semantic meaning and push it toward a feeling of rhythmic incantation (in this case, also appropriate to the religious ritual being described). This rhythmic quality also characterizes fantasy's invention of names. Many of these names could be rhythmically scanned like lines of poetry. Two of the examples I cited from Donaldson—Baradakas and Tamarantha—are made up of two trochees. Erikson[7] infuses a similar sort of rhythm in the names of the Tiste Andii, with names like Anomander Rake and Sandalath Drukorlat. Often, characters are introduced as much through the sounds of their names as through more conventional characterization, and even when the characters are familiar, their names can have a similar effect. In Erikson's *The Crippled God* (2011), when many of the characters are known to the reader, a list of names interrupts a climactic scene: "When Fiddler turned, he saw the soldiers. And, feeling grief grip his heart, he forced himself to look from one face to the next. In his mind, he spoke their names. *Tarr. Koryk. Bottle. Smiles. Balm. Throatslitter. Deadsmell. Widdershins. Hellian. Urb. Limp. Crump. Sinter. Kisswhere. Maybe. Flashwit. Mayfly. Clasp. Nep Furrow. Reliko. Vastly Blank. Masan Gilani*" (885). While some of these names belong to characters with significant narrative arcs, for many readers, most of these names are simply shapes on the page, collections of sounds, and a narrative moment that is thematically about soldiers making empathic connections to each other becomes, for the reader, entangled with a semiotic wash of sound.

On top of the desemanticizing function of invented terms, even real words can have a semiotic effect in a fantasy context. Donaldson in particular further defamiliarizes his fantasy world through his unusual figurative language and vocabulary. Senior's list of rarely used words in *Covenant* include "anodyne," "roborant," "attar," "carious," "bedizened," and "verdigris" (25), to which we could add words like "visage," "mien," "expostulation," "incarnadine," and even the conventional fantasy word that Le Guin mocks, "ichor." Many other more familiar words are used in unfamiliar ways; throughout the series, the word "despite" frequently appears in its archaic sense as a noun form of "despise" to refer to contempt, disdain, or hatred. This word is particularly important as it often refers to the primary antagonist, Lord Foul, and the attitude of his followers. Such diction might traditionally be criticized as overwriting, but it nonetheless contributes to the semiotic element of style. Furthermore, the seemingly odd metaphors can be seen as an attempt to render a sensory experience that is impossible in our world: in the Land, people can literally *see* abstract things like health. Donaldson enables the reader to experience the world through the eyes of such people by making singular metaphors to represent abstract feelings. The first description of the Soulsease River contains a characteristic example: "its water was as clean, clear and fresh as an offer of baptism" (*Lord Foul's Bane* 173). Metaphors often function to assist the reader in creating a mental picture and thus work by comparing something abstract or unfamiliar to something familiar and embodied (such as "his happiness felt like a warm hug"). Donaldson's metaphor here reverses that typical structure: rather than comparing something abstract to something concrete, the example compares something concrete (a river) to something abstract (an offer). This pattern is common throughout the Covenant books and serves both as a means of allowing the reader some access to the characters' altered perceptions and as a "desemanticization"—the language has the form of a metaphor but not the expected function, so it emphasizes the rhythm of the sentence rather than the content or meaning. In both ways, such metaphors serve as a means to defamiliarize the text and distance the reader from habitual forms of thought.

Critics of Donaldson often overlook this crucial defamiliarizing function of the style. For example, the metaphor that Pringle singles out as "risible"—"she raised her head, showing Covenant and Foamfollower the crushed landscape behind her eyes"—is both fitting in its attempt to render a perception the reader literally cannot have and appropriate by pointing us to her eyes, trying to help us to see the world as she sees it. Farah Mendlesohn also overlooks this facet of Donaldson's style in her analysis of other passages in *Lord Foul's Bane* (1977). Mendlesohn actually argues that portal-quest fantasy is characterized not by defamiliarization but by familiarization, as it works to make the unfamiliar "comprehensible" (9). This, to Mendlesohn, accounts for the layering of details, the "diegetic overkill" (9) she finds, and a host of other stylistic defects that lead away from polysemy and toward a more rigid, essentialist view of the world. She offers Donaldson as an illustration of this, as she asserts that the limited-omniscient point of view leads to passages where "descriptions must tell us more than we can possibly know" about characters "because we do not have time to learn about people, nor do we believe that minor characters can change, because they are as much scenery as is a tree" (42). Mendlesohn particularly singles out the following passage: "But where Lena was fresh and slim of line, full of unbroken newness, Atiaran appeared complex, almost contradictory" (*Lord Foul's Bane* 67). This leads Mendlesohn to the conclusion that one of the affordances of the portal-quest fantasy is a form of character stereotyping, as characters are described as objects and exist primarily to fulfill plot functions: as she puts it, the portal-quest fantasy is "the last resting place of physiognomy" (11). However, she does not seem to be accounting for how the magic of the world is infusing the style of the novel. The characters are not being described like objects; rather, Covenant, as the point of view character, has the ability to see inside people. In other words, rather than being evidence that such fantasy fundamentally flattens its characters, Donaldson's style illustrates how fantasy can create images of empathy-in-process (Covenant seeing inside other people) and can infuse empathy into its own language (the reader sees as Covenant sees due to the style of the passage) by using an affordance unique to fantasy, the magical world it takes place in.[8] This process of creating empathy, therefore, is a product of fantasy's structure of defamiliarization intersecting with the form of complex, elaborate language, as the irrational, magical elements of the world are rendered in the style itself. While semiotic, defamiliarizing language is certainly a feature in other genres, the imaginative resources of fantasy writing are especially well-suited to it and perhaps account for why so many fantasy writers (like Donaldson and Erikson) are drawn to the more elaborate, "flowering" epic fantasy style to achieve their aesthetic goals.

Donaldson's Semiotic Parallelism

I will illustrate how this dense style works in practice with a few detailed analyses, taking passages from each of these writers. A close reading of Donaldson will demonstrate how dense epic fantasy style works through doubles and parallels that thicken the texture of the prose, while Erikson will illustrate a style that acquires density more laterally, by stringing together multiple syntactic units. I would visualize this difference by saying Donaldson's style acquires density vertically, while Erikson's does so horizontally. Additionally, Donaldson exemplifies epic fantasy operating within a traditionally humanist paradigm, while Erikson exhibits many of the same affordances within a postmodern, constructivist approach, showing that this affordance can operate independently of other thematic variables. From Donaldson, we will examine a pattern that achieves its most characteristic form in the climactic passage from the final Covenant novel, *The Last Dark* (2013).[9] In this passage, Covenant defeats his foe, Lord Foul the Despiser, not by killing him in combat but by absorbing him into himself. This is thematically significant because, as Donaldson writes elsewhere, Foul has always been an externalization of Covenant's internal struggle with self-hatred. As Donaldson argues, in epic fantasy "internal crises or conflicts or processes of the characters are dramatized as if they were external individuals or events" (*Epic Fantasy* 7). In an interview with Senior from before the publication of *The Last Dark*, Donaldson explains the logic that leads to this climactic passage:

"Following the psychological paradigm through, what happens at the point that you become your own other self is that you become whole, and the universe is made new" (236). Perhaps just as important is that this conflict is resolved not through violence but through *embracing* the other, literally accepting the enemy as part of the self rather than continuing to exacerbate the conflict. This psychological movement toward unity opposes separation, and on a linguistic level, Donaldson uses unifying language rather than language that separates into rigid categories. Separation is a feature of stereotyping, one of the most common types of rigid language use, as Homi Bhabha explains. According to Bhabha, the stereotype is "a form of splitting and multiple belief" (77) and "dramatize[s] [...] a separation—*between* races, cultures, histories" (82). Stereotyping requires the erasure of difference by paradoxically insisting obsessively on the mechanistic character of that difference. The self does not have to feel threatened by the other because the other's nature is integrated into a coherent, consistent narrative (that has been projected by the self, of course). At times, epic fantasy echoes this mental process of stereotyping by presenting any number of orcs, ogres, and monsters whose unchanging nature makes them an appropriate target for the hero's expulsive violence.[10] However, Donaldson reverses that trope and shows that fantasy can also lead the reader to recognize the stereotyping mental processes and instead reintegrate the self by embracing the other. Significantly, he does so not only on the level of thematic content but also on the level of language.

A particularly salient feature of Donaldson's dense style is an insistent syntactic parallelism, which can be found at key points throughout the Thomas Covenant series. Before examining its appearance in *The Last Dark*, we should examine how this parallelism develops throughout the series, often proliferating at narrative climaxes, as descriptions pile up multiple noun phrases, verb phrases, or parallel sentences that describe similar objects, actions, or emotions using slightly different words but the same syntactic form. While certainly, this parallelism is a part of Donaldson's linguistic imagination (probably what Pringle criticized as a "piling on effect"), it is heightened in important passages regarding Covenant's empathy (often with antagonists but nearly always with characters with whom Covenant has had conflicts). This parallel style can be found even in the first book, *Lord Foul's Bane* (1977). Throughout this novel, Covenant refuses to believe in the existence of the Land, the fantasy world he finds himself in, which leads him to dehumanizing behavior towards its inhabitants, behavior manifested most notably in his rape of the young woman Lena. As Covenant refuses to acknowledge Lena as a real person, he denies that the action is a rape until a key moment late in the novel. In a passage that parallels his internal reverie with descriptions of external action, Covenant struggles with a growing empathy that contradicts his refusal of belief: "Lena! Swinging his staff like an ax, he chopped at the blaze [campfire]. But he could not fight off the memory, could not throw it back" (369). The passage parallels Covenant's internal and external states as he is matching his perspective to Lena's, and the last sentence characteristically matches this parallelism syntactically by doubling the verb. While "could not fight off" and "could not throw it back" are not precisely redundant, they are not both needed strictly for semantic meaning. Thus, the sentence emphasizes rhythm in a way that brings together parallel forms.

This effect also engages Kristeva's semiotic function of language. In addition to obscene words, she identifies "sentential rhythms" as a source of the semiotic: "the aim of this practice [...] is, through the signification of the nevertheless transmitted message, not only to impose a music, a rhythm [...] but to wipe out sense through nonsense [...] that obliges the reader not so much to combine significations as to shatter his [*sic*] own judging consciousness in order to grant passage through it to this rhythmic drive" (142). The unnecessary doubling of verb phrases emphasizes the emotive rhythm of the passage rather than the sense of the passage, bringing the reader into the "feeling" of being Thomas Covenant just as Covenant experiences the feeling of what he did to Lena. Similarly, in the climactic battle of the book, Donaldson consigns the struggle with the villainous Drool Rockworm to the narrative periphery while Covenant feels remorse for a dying Bloodguard: "He could not refuse a Bloodguard, could not deny the appeal of such expensive fidelity" (448). Throughout the book, Covenant has often found himself at odds with the Bloodguard, the defenders of the Land's Lords, yet Covenant's empathy for this man at his death is expressed through another redundant multiplication of verbs. As Covenant matches his mind to others, the syntax also multiplies, doubles, and mirrors itself.

However, these examples only show Covenant empathizing with allies (albeit allies he has treated poorly). Significantly, Donaldson allows Covenant a similar humanizing of his enemies, demonstrating how the language specifically combats the stereotyping function in fantasy. In *The One Tree* (1982), Covenant tames a monstrous Sand Gorgon named Nom, forging an alliance that lasts throughout the remainder of the series. Nom, a literally faceless creature, could be taken as a representative of the faceless other that society usually constructs as a monster. Covenant's entire fight with Nom is filled with parallel structures and doubled verb phrases: "Its head had no face, no features, betrayed nothing of its feral passion" (329) and "With wild magic, he gripped the beast, bound it in fetters of flame and will" (331). Their conflict is ultimately resolved not through the violence but through negotiation for mutual benefit (if Nom stops fighting

Covenant, he can go free, as the spell summoning him from imprisonment only ends when Covenant dies). This connection between self and other is emphasized by the doubling of the syntax. In the description of this combat, their connection is demonstrated through an image of enemies embracing: "He and Nom wrapped arms around each other and embraced like brothers of the same doom" (330).

This image of embracing the other rather than expelling it is crucial to the entire series, and central to the series' climax. The ultimate enemy of the series, Lord Foul, is subject to the same sort of empathic embrace. The climactic passage in *The Last Dark* provides perhaps the most complete example of Donaldson's style in the series, as it reflects this theme of embracing and finding similarity through the insistent structural parallelism of the sentences. During the preceding action scene, Donaldson frequently doubles up on the metaphors and verbs: "Unnatural heat and cold gusted at Covenant's face like gasping, like strained exhalations of time. [...] Wild magic ripped through [Lord Foul's] fleshless form, sent fiery harm careering everywhere along his disembodied nerves" (520). "Strained exhalations" could serve as a solid definition of "gasping," making the first phrase redundant, and while "ripped through" and "sent fiery harm careering" are not precisely equivalent, they are close enough in meaning that an insistently minimalist editor would cringe. This second example illustrates a crucial feature of the scene, though, as the fragmenting violence of the fight ironically contrasts with the conjoining effect of parallel structure. The structural parallelism works against the presumptive effect of violence, and instead the reader is preoccupied with conjoining linked phrases. As in the examples above, the sentence rhythms have the effect of Kristeva's semiotic: the rhythm overtakes the meaning-making function of the passage, requiring the reader to give up on judgment (the category-separating functions of the mind), which, in Donaldson's case, prepares the reader for the unification with the other in Covenant's climactic exchange with Lord Foul.[11]

In that climactic moment, Donaldson again uses insistent repetition to achieve the effect: "The Despiser was smaller now, beaten down or reduced by the bane's retribution. He was almost Covenant's size" (520). Note here that the parallel syntactical structure is supported by the parallel between the characters' physical bodies—which links to the parallels the reader is meant to recognize in Covenant's and Foul's identities: "He hunched into himself as though he sought to hide. As though he wanted to be smaller still. With wild magic and leprosy, Covenant reached out to him. With pity and terror, Covenant lifted Lord Foul upright. This was his last crisis. There could be no more" (520). Again, the grammatical parallelism is striking (the repeated "as though" clauses and "with" prepositional phrases at the beginnings of sentences), while the last phrase is clearly redundant—if it is the "last," of course there can be "no more." However, that seeming redundancy (which Strunk and White might hate) continues to invite the idea of doubling (by using two functionally identical phrases), and thereby of inclusion rather than division. Covenant sums up the moment by saying,

> "If I'm yours, you're mine. We're part of each other. We're too much alike. [...] If we want to live, we have to do it together." [...] [Lord Foul's] eyes were not fangs. They were wounds, gnashed and raw [...] [Covenant] was blinded now, not by fires and fury, but by tears as he closed his arms around his foe. Opening his heart, he accepted Lord Foul the Despiser into himself [522].

There is almost too much parallelism here to mention it all: the balanced chiasmus of "If I'm yours, you're mine," the near redundancy of the next two sentences, the repeated structure of "they were not ... they were" (repeated in "blinded now, *not* by fires and fury, *but by* tears"). Again, there are nearly redundant pairs of items ("gnashed and raw," "fires and fury") that primarily contribute to the semiotic rhythm of the sentence. Even the alliteration of the letter "f" (fangs, fires, fury, foe, Foul) emphasizes sound over sense, contributing to making semiotic connections across the passage. The final balance of "closed" and "opening" as Covenant literally *embraces* his foe, linguistically and mentally underscores for the reader the act of bringing together. This may have the appearance of the "flowery" epic fantasy prose so often censured in genre writers, but here it clearly serves a purpose by leading the reader through a cognitive process that reinforces the thrust of the passage. Readers are invited into the process of juxtaposing and combining sounds and language via a passage that itself talks about doing the same thing, combating the social fragmentation inherent in stereotyping and habitual representation.

Erikson's Empathic Parataxis

Erikson's *Toll the Hounds* similarly invites the reader to imaginative empathy through style, but in his case, it does so not as much through redundant layering and doubling but instead by stringing together syntactic units paratactically. An especially clear illustration of this horizontal density emerges late in *Toll the Hounds*. Gaz, the character discussed at the beginning of this chapter, is sacrificed by his abused wife in order to enable Hood, the God of Death, to physically enter the world. As Hood walks through a crowded city to a climactic confrontation, his presence causes countless deaths in the city. In a virtuostic passage of nearly six pages, Erikson recounts six micro-short stories about the deaths Hood has caused, in each case encouraging the reader to empathize. The ironic juxtaposition of the compressed short story method and the overabundance of detail highlights the power of flowering excess language to enable the reader to imagine another person's point of view. Kruppe presents this theme directly in the prologue to this section: "Plunge then, courage collected, into this welter of lives. Open the mind to consider [...] if all was met with but a callous shrug, then, this round man invites, shift round such cruel, cold regard, and cast one last judgement. Upon thyself" (714). By encouraging us to feel, not just think, Kruppe once again argues for the importance of flowering language as more than mere sentimentality.

A sample of one of the stories illustrates how this works. Ironically, this is the shortest of the stories, but it starts with a 99-word sentence, structurally re-emphasizing the contrast within the whole passage:

> Kanz was nine years old and he loved teasing his sister who had a real temper, as Ma always said as she picked up pieces of broken crockery and bits of hated vegetable scattered all over the floor, and the best thing was prodding his sister in the ribs when she wasn't looking, and she'd spin round, eyes flashing with fury and hate—and off he'd run, with her right on his heels, out into the corridor, pell-mell straight to the stairs and then down and round and down fast as he could go with her screeching behind him.
>
> Down and round and down and—
>
> —and he was flying through the air. He'd tripped, missed his grip on the rail, and the ground floor far below rushed up to meet him [715].

This sentence is full of extraneous detail and flowering with extra clauses, such as the interruption beginning with "as Ma always said." Strictly speaking, the details about the mother's reaction to his sister's temper are not essential to the story about Kanz accidentally falling to his death (does the reader really care that his sister hates vegetables?). Certainly, to insert this clause in the middle of an already lengthy sentence could just add to the verbal clutter. In addition, the repetition of "down and round and down" is similarly unnecessary, and in some ways oxymoronic. While it serves to mark the repetitive action of running down the stairwell, it simultaneously lengthens the passage, working against the effect of speed which the passage is describing. A primary point here is how suddenly and abruptly death comes for Kanz, and by not providing any stopping points in the form of periods, the lengthy sentence imitates the breathless rush of a child's thoughts and also the too rapid rush of his running that leads to his accidental death. At the same time, each of these lengthening devices serves instead to delay death's arrival (an arrival the reader anticipates at this point, as the pattern of these stories has already been established). Thus, the run-on form of this sentence unifies the effect of the passage by speeding it up while the length works against the overall effect by delaying the climax.

This simultaneous uniting and fragmenting effect also manifests in the paratactic style of the sentence. Parataxis is the use of coordination rather than subordination to link together clauses in sentences. Stringing together multiple clauses with "and" is not usually considered good style,[12] and this sentence has eight "ands" and five separate main clauses. The paratactic use of "and" at the beginnings of sentences and between clauses is a frequently noted feature of epic fantasy style. In an interview, Michael Moorcock describes epic fantasy's "slightly elevated prose style, with a certain amount of purple in it" (Greenland, *Michael Moorcock* 9). This style features rhythms reminiscent of the King James Bible, particularly through "using a lot of *ands* to begin sentences ... to keep the whole thing shifting forward all the time" (Greenland, *Michael Moorcock* 10). Mendlesohn similarly notes that the "narrative use of 'and,' as in Old Testament language and the narratives of the Anglo-Saxon Chronicle, provides the story with extra authenticity" (33), suggesting that such style functions to create an authoritative, monologic voice.

However, I would suggest another possible affordance that Erikson particularly reveals, an affordance springing from how parataxis organizes information. Parataxis is often faulted for not providing logical links between actions,[13] as Erikson's sentence clearly shows, for instance, in the following clauses: "and the best thing was prodding his sister in the ribs when she wasn't looking, and she'd spin round." The "and" between these two clauses could be said to weaken the sentence, as it does not clearly indicate the cause and effect relationship between Kanz's "prodding" and her spinning. However, rather than viewing this focus on coordination as a weakness, I want to view it as one of the principle stylistic strategies of the passage. In one of the most influential theoretical essays on paratactic style, Theodor Adorno describes parataxis as "artificial disturbances that evade the logical hierarchy of a subordinating syntax" (131). This may remind us of Kristeva's argument about the semiotic more generally. Adorno links parataxis to a musical quality in language: language itself is "chained to the form of judgment and proposition and thereby to the synthetic form of the concept" (130), while paratactic constructions are "straining away from what fetters them" (132). By avoiding the imposed logic of subordination, parataxis breaks away from habitual forms of perception, allowing for "aconceptual synthesis" (130). As I noted above about the oxymoronic character of this passage, Adorno finds a similar contradiction in paratactic structures in that they simultaneously unite and divide: on the one hand, language unites by creating coherent subjectivity ("Without externalizing itself in language, subjective intention would not exist at all" [136–7]); on the other hand, by resisting hierarchy and subordination, parataxis "disintegrates" subjectivity (137) by calling attention to its artificial construction.

Thus, by resisting the logical cause-and-effect links of subordination, the passage avoids constructing Kanz as a subject and instead plunges into the *experience* of being him. The passage reflects the thoughtless rush of the child's mental state, and the abrupt break-off of his thoughts at the end of the passage, with the dashes and the short sentence, indicates the abruptness of his death. The description of his death lacks some of the expository markers of causation. After the break caused by the dashes, the text simply says "and he was flying through the air." Again, the "and" is insufficient by itself to indicate causation, just as Kanz himself is unaware of exactly what happens as he is in the middle of experiencing it (he has not "externalized" the experience "in language"). Even the sentence that does explain what happened is a coordinated list: "He'd tripped, missed his grip on the rail, and the ground floor far below rushed up to meet him." While this final phrase, the subjective description of falling as the ground "rush[ing] up to meet him," is so familiar as to be a cliché, here it is fitting as it again emphasizes the experiential nature of the passage. By violating the tenets of "good, simple style," the passage thrusts the reader into the experience of another consciousness.

In the context of these observations about style, particularly Adorno's argument about parataxis resisting the linguistic construction of the subject, we should return to the interrupting phrase from the beginning of the passage: "he loved teasing his sister who had a real temper, as Ma always said as she picked up pieces of broken crockery and bits of hated vegetable scattered all over the floor." The mother throughout the passage illustrates the attempt to use language to "externalize" experience and create subjectivity in her children. In the earlier interrupting phrase, we see her explicitly interpellating the sister. The phrase "real temper" could almost appear in quotation marks, as it represents a linguistic label that Kanz has learned from his mother to apply to his sister. The mother has translated the concrete experience of broken crockery and scattered vegetables into the abstract signifier "temper." The story ends by picking up on the thread of the mother's signifying activities: "'You two will be the death of each other!' Ma always said. Zasperating! She said that too—He struck the floor. Game over" (715). Again, this passage describes the scene experientially rather than rationally—it delays the moment of death, stretching it out unnaturally long (does he really have time to remember this while flying through the air?). This delay particularly calls attention to how the mother uses language to classify her children. It suggests an almost magical construction of their futures through language, as her empty cliché ("you two will be the death of each other") becomes the literal truth. However, this ability to construct identity through language is taken from her by Kanz's death, suggesting the failure of language to fully encapsulate the subject. At the same time, in the final paragraph the story's style changes markedly. We are told that the mother stops saying "zasperating" because it was "the last word he'd thought. He'd taken it, as would a toddler a doll, or a blanket. For comfort in his dark new world" (715). Note here how suddenly we have elision in the metaphor rather than wordiness ("as a toddler would [take] a doll"), and a sentence fragment in contrast to the endless coordination of the first sentence. Thus, the style of the passage echoes the fragmentation, the separation, of death, creating a gut punch of a sentimental moment that encourages us to *feel* what the mother feels. The signifying function of language is taken away from her, just as the excess language drains from the passage, in the wash of experiential emotion.

Erikson, like Donaldson, consistently associates his dense style with empathy for the other. Erikson uses this horizontal, paratactic density throughout the series, and—as with Donaldson—prominently in the climactic portions of the final book, *The Crippled God* (2011). The finale has a lengthy battle sequence in which a group of Malazan deserters, the Bonehunters, fight against a variety of forces seeking to usurp a source of tremendous magical power. In a surprising twist, that source of power the Bonehunters defend is the Crippled God, who has served as a significant antagonist for the series, and who readers might assume is the story's Dark Lord/Sauron figure. In this context of empathy for the "enemy" (also reminiscent of the climax of *The Last Dark*), the style frequently uses non--hierarchical additive parataxis, often revealing a feature not seen in the previous example. Sequences of actions are described in parallel without the hierarchizing effect of subordination, usually through lists of participle phrases (these lists differ from the parallel redundancy in the Covenant books in that each one typically adds new information). This style is particularly useful for allowing readers to experience the chaos of battle: "The collision lifted soldiers from their feet, shoved them into the air" (852). In a sense, these function as a paratactic list of verbs with "and" omitted. For instance, "His horse lagging beneath him, beginning to weave, Paran cursed and slowed the beast. He fumbled in the saddlebag on his left, drew out a lacquered card. Glared at the lone rider painted on it" (865). In this case, the final item is even punctuated as a separate sentence fragment yet still joined to the previous list by the elided "and."

The Crippled God himself stands at the center of both the battle and the thematic movement toward empathy. He is actually a being from another universe who has been exploited for centuries by the gods of this world to fuel their own power, and consequently he has frequently struck back throughout the series in revenge for his pain. However, in being defended by the Bonehunters, who selflessly sacrifice their lives for him, he starts to feel empathy for them. This narrative arc that has spanned the series reaches its crescendo in a passage where the Crippled God has an empathic breakthrough, a passage filled with rolling rhythms and paratactic connections:

> Lying beneath the weight of the chains, the Crippled God, who had been listening, now heard. Long-forgotten, half-disbelieved emotions rose up through him, ferocious and bright. He drew a sharp breath, feeling his throat tighten. *I will remember this. I will set out scrolls and burn upon them the names of these Fallen. I will make of this work a holy tome, and no other shall be needed.*
>
> *Hear them! They are humanity unfurled, laid out for all to see—if one would dare look!*
>
> *There shall be a Book **and** it shall be written by my hand. Wheel and seek the faces of a thousand gods! None can do what I can do! Not one can give voice to this holy creation!*
>
> *But this is not bravado. For this, my Book of the Fallen, the only god worthy of its telling is the crippled one. The broken one. **And** has it not always been thus?*
>
> *I never hid my hurts.*
>
> *I never disguised my dreams.*
>
> ***And** I never lost my way.*
>
> ***And** only the fallen can rise again.*
>
> He listened to the laughter, **and** suddenly the weight of those chains was as nothing. *Nothing* [873–4, bold-text emphasis added].

I quote the entire passage with the original paragraph breaks in order to emphasize the parallelism. Particularly the last section—"I never…. I never…. And I never…. And only"—benefits from the paragraph breaks, which heighten the visual parallelism on the page (a unifying effect) at the same time as they ironically call attention to the separation of distinct clauses. The simultaneous unifying and dividing of the paratactic list is dramatically staged in this heightened narrative moment. The passage also features other semiotic, rhythmic elements I have been examining throughout this chapter, such as its use of alliteration ("hid my hurts … disguised my dreams"). This emphasis on the sound and rhythm, breaking down the sense of the text, is supported also by the Crippled God's thoughts: "*Not one can give voice to this holy creation!*" The experience of sacrifice and unity of identity exists beyond language, beyond signification; it is literally unspeakable, and yet ironically it will also be communicated, in language, through a book (metatextually, the book the reader is currently holding while reading the passage). Ironically, one can only tell the story by being broken, crippled, impure and imperfect (outside the hierarchy of representation). Only by losing one's position in the symbolic order can one make these empathic, communal connections. Through its semiotic, defamiliarizing, non-hierarchical density of style, the text manifests this collision between the orderliness of community and the disorderly erasure of subjectivity beneath experiential drives.

Conclusion

These passages from Erikson illustrate some possibly surprising features of the affordances of epic fantasy language. It may not be surprising to claim that empathy is a feature of fantasy language, as fantasy is often linked to the humanist tradition and emphasizes wholeness and unity over social fragmentation (as Donaldson demonstrates directly). However, Erikson's Malazan Book of the Fallen shows how fantasy can deconstruct the linguistic formation of subjectivity. This suggests that epic fantasy, through its lengthy, often paratactic style and structure ("and then another thing happened, and then another thing happened, and then…"), can accomplish the same goals of social unity and empathy *side-by-side with anti-subjectivity and constructivism.* Even one of the often-cited affordances of epic fantasy, its great length, works against the habitual linguistic constructions of subordination and favors something like what Kristeva describes with her category of the semiotic, the breakdown of social hierarchies that would fragment social unity. Paradoxically, fantasy's humanistic unity can proceed from postmodern fragmentation that breaks down conventions just as much as it can from a more traditional, conventional approach, suggesting that this potential within epic fantasy style operates independently of other thematic or philosophical variables.

Thus, as these examples demonstrate, while epic fantasy is frequently drawn to an often-maligned, seemingly old-fashioned style—"flowery writing"—that style has revolutionary potential. The imaginative resources epic fantasy offers can be a strong tool for revolutionizing a reader's perspective. By breaking down the semantic, hierarchizing functionality of language and restructuring habitual perceptions of reality, epic fantasy is capable on both a plot level and a *linguistic* level of making connections between self and other. Therefore, studying the style of epic fantasy can perhaps alter our academic perceptions of the use of language, revealing how seemingly opposed approaches (such as humanistic empathy and ironic postmodern constructivism) can collide within the same linguistic form. Careful attention to the language of epic fantasy might uncover more such surprising affordances and allow us to practice the same kind of flowering embrace for which Kruppe's style of epic fantasy strives.

CHAPTER 2

"A Necessary Subtraction"

Simplicity, the Violent Emotion of Editing, and the Editing of Violence

The death of one soldier was a tragedy. [...] But she could not possibly multiply that by thousands. That kind of thinking did not compute. The scale was unimaginable. So she didn't bother to try. [...] Those weren't lives. They were numbers. They were a necessary subtraction.
—R. F. Kuang, *The Poppy War*

In the last chapter, I presented empathy in an entirely positive light, as a largely pro-social emotion, but this is only part of the story, if not a simplification. Suzanne Keen's in-depth analysis of the subject in *Empathy and the Novel* (2007) not only introduces some skepticism about the extent to which empathy gained from novel reading actually affects behavior, but she also gives a useful overview of arguments that empathy has an overtly negative effect. She classifies one group of critics of empathy as "false empathy" critics, those who "emphasize the self-congratulatory delusions of those who incorrectly believe they have caught the feeling of suffering others from a different culture, gender, race, or class" (159). Such arguments often come from a post-colonial perspective, where there is great suspicion that erasing otherness in order to emphasize fellow feeling is a hegemonic power play, and at the very least, taking someone else's emotions—their suffering—and incorporating it into your self is a narcissistic move motivated by the ego. At their most extreme, such critics "construe empathy as antipathy under the guise of compassion" and argue that "a sense of shared feeling does violence to the object of one's regard and hurts the object through aggressive identification or projection" (159). Marcus Wood goes so far as to characterize empathy as "a pornographic indulgence of sensation acquired at the expense of suffering others" (Keen 147). While many of these criticisms focus on appeals to empathy that seek to motivate altruistic action for perceived others (based on difference in race, ethnicity, gender, orientation, etc.), and not for the more general cognitive structure of mental flexibility I focused on in Chapter 1, it nonetheless raises serious questions about the limits of any literature, much less epic fantasy, to generate a form of pro-social empathy in readers.

Some fantasy writers, such as R.F. Kuang, express similar concerns about attempts at empathy turning into cultural appropriation. Kuang's first novel *The Poppy War* (2018) includes a fictional account in a fantasy world of the Rape of Nanking, the massacre of a Chinese city by Japanese forces in the Second Sino-Japanese War, and she has spoken in interviews and written in essays about both the need to remember such historical violence and the dangers in its representation. She writes in her essay "How to Talk to Ghosts" (2018) about telling the stories of family trauma. Towards the end of the essay in a section titled "The Intruder," after discussing the difficulty of talking to her grandparents about their experiences during World War II, or her parents' experiences as immigrants from China to the United States, Kuang responds to those who would try to tell her family's stories for them, arguing that "you have not faithfully recorded their testimony, you have turned them into kitsch. You have done something worse than silence them—you have transformed them into an image of you" ("Ghosts"). Asking "why are you drawn to profit off of our pain?" she concludes that "the duty of the outsider should simply be to listen." While she does not give a specific referent here, Kuang suggests that an attempt to empathize with cultural others might be (to use Wood's words) an intrusive "indulgence of sensation," an attempt to "profit" in some way (materially or emotionally) from personal suffering. Kuang contrasts the appropriation of emotional stories as distanced objects of empathy by describing the emotional difficulty of writing the chapter of *The Poppy War* based on the Rape of Nanking, a writing process that became intensely personal. Kuang singles out a story about two young girls, one of whom watched from hiding while her older sister was raped and murdered. After a direct recitation of the facts of the story, Kuang simply follows up in a brief paragraph by saying, "I have a younger sister. I wrote only a single paragraph that week" ("Ghosts").

This final sentence demonstrates the style I will discuss in this chapter: this clipped, seemingly emotionless, efficient, summary statement style for discussing emotional—even violent—content. In Chapter 1, I raised the possibility that minimalistic style, through its "endless paring down [...] strips away all hope of emotion and with it empathy" (Erikson, *Toll* 279–80). However, we should keep in mind that this is an argument given to a character, and not an overall theoretically-driven damning of minimalism, nor do those potential affordances tell the whole story. Furthermore, I will not be discussing minimalism as an overall style in this chapter; instead, I will examine a tendency, particularly in emotionally charged moments of a narrative, to pull back as Kuang does above, to play against the stylistic conventions of the genre by using doses of minimalism and simplicity in places where a reader might expect emotive or expressive writing. This clipped, editorial style, I will argue, is both an alternative to the more common fantasy technique of elaborate syntax discussed in Chapter 1—a paradoxically emotionally-charged way of inviting the reader to participate in feeling the characters' emotions—and at the same time, a critique of the potential indulgences of empathy (or at least a hesitation when confronted with that potential), the egoistic sensationalism and erasing of otherness that may result, particularly in cases involving racial or sexual violence. From this standpoint, it is perhaps not surprising that my two primary examples are from women writers—R. F. Kuang and Ursula Le Guin—writers who have a strong commitment to writing about issues related to the representation of women in fiction (something else epic fantasy is not stereotypically known for).[1] In fact, given the history of women writers being critically dismissed due to perceived sentimentality or excess emotion,[2] it is perhaps especially useful for these writers to choose a strategy more often coded as masculine: one that generates emotion by downplaying it, by editing out excess. Furthermore, these writers are perhaps particularly attuned to the potential problems raised by a voyeuristic excess of emotion. While Erikson's Kruppe points out the sociopathic masculine gender roles involved in the violent cutting out of emotion, the flip side of that is how the pleasure of reading epic fantasy is often built on depictions of violence and violent emotion, and Kuang's *The Poppy War* and Le Guin's Earthsea books (particularly *Tehanu*) are written in a style that employs moments of editorial simplicity in order to interrogate that pleasure by pulling back from it. At the same time, they also show us that the pulling back is *part of the problem*, that empathy is still necessary. In the simultaneous generating of empathy and critique of the voyeurism of empathy, there are no easy answers in these texts.

Counterexample: George R.R. Martin and the Red Wedding

As this simple, editorial style I am discussing in this chapter is a style characterized by absence, it will be helpful to start with a contrasting example, one that demonstrates the kind of emotive writing readers might expect so that it is easier to perceive what Kuang and Le Guin are excising from their texts. George R.R. Martin provides a particularly useful example, as Martin tends to write about many of the same types of material—most notably violence toward women—and his prose has been praised by critics. Furthermore, his epic fantasy series A Song of Ice and Fire is massively popular, so clearly it connects to readers on some level, but both the books and the TV series based on them (HBO's *Game of Thrones*) have been criticized for their use of violence, particularly violence against women, as a plot device, as character motivation, and in ways that often suggest the type of "pornographic indulgence of sensation" with which Wood is concerned. However, I mention this debate primarily as context, as it is not my intention here to discuss the merits of Martin's presentation of women or the historical "realism" of his violent fantasy world.[3] Instead, I will examine the style he uses to present violence to readers in order to build a list of features of an emotive style to contrast to Le Guin and Kuang.

To do so, I want to consider perhaps the most (in)famous and powerful scene from the series, the Red Wedding from A Storm of Swords (2000). The Red Wedding is a scene that famously shocked audiences (both of the TV series and the books) for its sudden violence and the deaths of two key characters, Catelyn Stark, matriarch of the Stark family (who at least conventionally appear to be the protagonists of the series), and her son Robb Stark. The Frey family, seeking revenge for an earlier slight by the Starks, use a wedding as a trap to brutally massacre the unsuspecting Starks. The horrifying scene is presented from the perspective of Catelyn, a mother who (incorrectly) believes all of her other children have been killed in this war. She watches her oldest son get murdered in front of her and then loses her mind, attempting to claw out her own eyes, before she is finally killed herself. In looking at how Martin presents this passage, we should first note how much detail he uses to describe the violent actions themselves, as in this passage when the violence first starts:

> Robb gave Edwyn [Frey] an angry look and moved to block his way ... and staggered suddenly as a quarrel sprouted from his side, just beneath the shoulder. If he screamed then, the sound was swallowed by the pipes and horns and fiddles. Catelyn saw a second bolt pierce his leg, saw him fall. [...] She ran toward her son, until something punched in the small of the back and the hard stone floor came up to slap her. "*Robb!*" she screamed. [...] Ser Wendel Manderly rose ponderously to his feet, holding his leg of lamb. A quarrel went in his open mouth and came out the back of his neck. Ser Wendel crashed forward, knocking the table off its trestles and sending cups, flagons, trenchers, platters, turnips, beets, and wine bouncing, spilling, and sliding across the floor [701–2].

While this passage is largely factual, using a minimum of modifiers and value-laden words, the amount of detail here is notable. Martin slows down the action of a few seconds' time to describe the scene at length:

we are told where each quarrel hits Robb, Catelyn, and Manderly—with Manderly in particular the detail seems almost extraneous, as Martin emphasizes that the quarrel not only goes in his mouth but "out the back of his neck," and when Manderly falls on the table, Martin gives a catalogue of items that fall to the floor (perhaps a convention drawn from the epic), but they do not simply "fall"—there are also three action words to describe their movement, "bouncing, spilling, and sliding." Rather than simply saying that a hail of crossbow fire came down from the balcony and began killing the Stark soldiers in the room, Martin makes the reader experience this violence on a moment-by-moment basis. Furthermore, point-of-view is important here as well: this passage is so deeply embedded in Catelyn's perspective that it is nearly free indirect discourse at times. Quarrels "sprouted" from Robb's side—this is clearly not a factual description but intended to place the reader within Catelyn's perspective. Similarly, the overused trope of "the hard stone floor came up to slap her" warps the description of her falling to correspond to the character's perspective, while the interjection of her calling out her son's name, while not overstated (she does not, for instance, "call out in horror"; she simply "screamed") does nonetheless overtly indicate her emotional response to the reader.

As the scene continues, Martin at times interjects sentences that seem designed to communicate emotion, as when soldiers enter and Catelyn briefly thinks they are rescuers before they start killing more Stark allies. At this point, Martin departs from factual description to give a sentence describing her emotions: "Hope blew out like a candle in a storm" (702). The figurative language here is another feature that seems intended to heighten the emotional response. While Martin is a canny enough writer not to overextend himself, he is still clearly here pushing for an emotional effect. This is also visible in the climactic moment: Robb is killed with the same emphasis on detail as above, as the soldier "thrust his longsword through her son's heart, and twisted" (704) (note the subtle reminder of their emotional tie here—it is "her son's heart," not "his" or "Robb's" heart), and then Catelyn, in her excess of grief, kills Frey's adult grandson whom she has been threatening in order to force an exchange of his life for Robb's: "She tugged hard on Aegon's hair and sawed at his neck until the blade grated on bone. Blood ran hot over her fingers. His little bells were ringing, ringing, ringing, and the drum went *boom doom boom*" (704). In both passages, the repetition, the excess of words, indicates her heightened emotional state, while Martin gives us painful details of the violent actions ("the blade grated on bone"). Finally, just before Catelyn is killed herself, the style is again distorted by her perspective, thrusting the reader deeply into her traumatized psyche: "Ten fierce ravens were raking her face with sharp talons and tearing off strips of flesh, leaving deep furrows that ran red with blood. She could taste it on her lips. *It hurts so much,* she thought" (704–5). This scene is certainly horrifying, and Martin ensures that you see its horror by having Catelyn directly tell the reader that it hurts, yet at the same he (and Catelyn) shy away from the pain through figurative language: rather than directly telling us that she tears at her own face, her fingernails are metaphorically "ten fierce ravens."

In summary, Martin demonstrates several features of emotive writing: (1) painfully detailed description of violent action, (2) intimately close perspective that distorts the style through the character's emotion, (3) figurative language to express emotion, and (4) even *telling* the reader how the characters feel (and by extension, then, how the reader should feel). This scene is certainly effective, even horrifying, and Martin clearly intends for the reader to empathize with Catelyn.[4] While I would not go so far as to argue that this scene is a "pornography of sensation," the controversy surrounding the series suggests that some readers might even read moments like this as catering to a self-centered desire for sensationalism. However, more importantly for my purposes, Martin's approach to generating empathy in his depiction of violence is markedly conventional. Le Guin and, even more so, Kuang, resist this conventional style, suggesting a concern that reading pleasure can overwhelm empathy and transform it into something prurient or self-absorbed.

Martial Style in Kuang's *The Poppy War*

While R.F. Kuang's style in *The Poppy War* is not, on the whole, minimalist, she often uses sparseness of detail at key moments, editing out extraneous content to achieve various effects. At times, the effect can be humorous, as in this anecdote from a combat training sequence early in the book: "Kureel knelt down next to Kitay and Han, who were rolling around the ground in mutual headlocks. 'Biting is an excellent technique if you're in a tight spot.' A moment later, Han shrieked in pain" (64). This is the entire anecdote, one of several similar moments strung together in a montage form, and while this is not a particularly important narrative moment, it shows how the book often handles violence: the key action here (Kitay biting Han) is only implied, not directly stated, and details are few. In this case there is also little access to the characters' interiority, which is sometimes the case, but not always. In fact, Kuang will often give lengthy descriptive passages full of character introspection, only to end them abruptly with a few simple, oblique climactic sentences.

Later in the novel, after the protagonist Rin has completed her military training and is now fighting in a war, one such incident involves a man dangling from the wreckage of an upper floor of a building in the aftermath of a battle. A lengthy passage, largely of interior monologue, describes Rin's feelings of helplessness in the situation (agency is a key theme in the book): "Rin felt like a spectator, like this was a show, like the man was the only thing in the world that mattered, yet she couldn't think of anything to do. [...] Because all the Cike [her magic-wielding military unit] knew how to do was destroy. For all their powers, for all their gods, they couldn't protect their people. Couldn't reverse time. Couldn't bring back the dead" (333–4). The shorter syntactic units (short sentences and fragments, or longer sentences made up of strings of short phrases) are generally characteristic of Kuang's simpler style, but the passage itself is nonetheless fairly detailed in its description both of Rin's emotions and the scene itself. Yet when it reaches the crucial climactic moment, as the man falls to his death, the text reverts to three terse sentences, each written as a separate paragraph: "He seemed to hang in the air for a moment before he fell. The crowd scrambled backward. Rin turned away, grateful that she could not hear his body break on the ground" (334). The additional white space on the page due to the paragraphing (and a section break follows the last sentence, adding even more white space) highlights the absence of detail here, editing out such potentially dramatic details as shouts, flailing limbs, or splatters of blood (the type of details that Martin's style might condition a reader to expect). The violence happens out of sight as the text tells us that Rin literally "turned away" from it. In fact, the question of whether or not to "turn away" from violence is very much central to *The Poppy War*.

This latter example also illustrates a rhythmic form Kuang uses throughout the novel that I will call a "summary style." Frequently, she will follow up longer passages of description or exposition with a brief, efficient summation, usually in one or two single-sentence paragraphs. A characteristic example appears in the first chapter, which tells about Rin's background: she is a war orphan, raised by drug-dealing adopted parents who want her only as a cheap source of labor, and to escape them, she bribes a tutor into helping her study for the entrance exams for the elite military academy of Sinegard. One such passage sums up the plans of her adoptive parents, the Fangs, at the end of a lengthier passage explaining their intentions to marry her to a rich merchant with political connections: "It was a much better deal than a war orphan like Rin, with no family or connections, could otherwise hope to secure. A husband for Rin, money for the matchmaker, and drugs for the Fangs" (7). Such pauses for summation happen throughout the novel, meaning that a reader will frequently see a full account of events followed by an edited version that simply hits the high points. On the one hand, this very efficiently draws together a large amount of material, making a reader aware of just how far the narrative has traveled. On the other hand, it means the reader is constantly comparing these edited accounts to the fuller, more complete, more nuanced accounts that have just been given. The summary of the Fangs' marriage plans is typical: the brief version actually reads as an ironic comment, because the more complete version tells us how Rin *feels* about the marriage, that she does not want it, and in that context, this summary clearly takes on a sardonic tone, a sneer at the Fangs and the matchmaker for exploiting her. Thus, the novel's style is constantly making the reader aware of the editing of events and raising questions about why certain details are included or excluded, and what effects those exclusions may have. At times, the novel overtly calls on the reader to consider these issues. Later in the book, Rin reacts to a propagandistic puppet show that she attends, noting that the show presents the story of the previous war without including a key event that ended that war, the genocide of the Speerly people: "I notice the puppeteer glossed over how we actually won the Second Poppy War. [...] You know. Speer. Butchery. Thousands dead in a single night" (174). In this instance, we see the editing out of violence having a political purpose, yet Rin's presentation also takes on an efficient, summary style—the implication of which is that what has been edited out is something that everyone knows. She does not need to explain it again, but this war crime is an absent presence in this culture, shaping it in ways people refuse to acknowledge.

This shaping power of the violence we refuse to acknowledge is a central thematic concern for Kuang and influences the simple, edited style of the novel. Kuang has gestured at this in interviews, sometimes citing a version of Hemingway's famous iceberg theory: "You need to know the entire iceberg but the reader only needs to see the tip" ("R. F. Kuang on Writing"). In other places, as in "How to Talk with Ghosts," she approaches the issue with more theoretical sophistication. In the essay, she interweaves her personal reflections on the influence of her family's largely repressed traumatic past (the "ghosts" of her family) with references to "hauntology" in the work of Jacques Derrida, Frederic Jameson, and Nicolas Abraham & Maria Torok. She identifies the distinguishing mark of these past hauntings in absences: "The clearest indication of a ghost is in what is not. Look for the blank spots" ("Ghosts"). In the case of her family, she links this editing of history to immigration: "historical suppression is a kind of self-induced amnesia, a psychic protective shield of immigrants. [...] The mental burden of trauma is too great." Yet, even as she acknowledges the psychological need to look away from past trauma, she more strenuously argues for the need to recognize and narrate that trauma; the ghosts, after all, haunt you because they want their stories told. Yet to tell these stories directly would be too damaging, as it would exhume that past trauma and force the survivors to experience it again. As Kuang explains in another interview, "sometimes [due to] painful, intergenerational trauma and memories … autobiographies are really difficult to produce because it requires talking to people who are dead or asking people who are alive to relive their trauma for hours and hours" (Sondheimer). Furthermore, the difficulty of discussing trauma, the mental editing it entails, leads to fiction that cannot possibly generate the "radical empathy" (Sondheimer) that it should: "To transcribe literally their experiences would not only feel cold and clinical, it would ring sparse. There are too many details we don't have access to. But if I spin their lives into stories then I can give voice to the frustration, despair, terror, relief, and pain" (Kuang, "Ghosts"). Thus, it is necessary to "fabulate their testimony." This explains, to some extent, the need to write a fantasy novel about the Rape of Nanking rather than historical fiction or non-fiction. While witnessing is necessary, looking too directly at the trauma is psychologically damaging (and, as I discussed earlier, also presents the danger of sensationalistic voyeurism). Yet at the same time, failing to look at it, editing it out completely, is both damaging and unjust. The solution is an oblique account, partially edited, that tells the story and lets the reader experience the weight of emotion without being too direct.

Of all of her theoretical backgrounds in this essay, Abraham and Torok are perhaps the most important. Their central concepts of "the phantom" and "the crypt" are developments of Freud's psychoanalytic theory of mourning and melancholy. For Freud, the healthy process of mourning involves ultimately detaching the self from the lost object of desire, while melancholy entails the refusal to detach. Instead, melancholy is characterized by continuing to incorporate the lost object into the self ("Mourning *or* Melancholia" 127). Thus, because the self cannot recognize the loss, the result is "a radical denial of the loss […]. The words cannot be uttered […] everything will be swallowed along with the trauma that led to the loss. […] Inexpressible mourning erects a secret tomb inside the subject" ("Mourning *or* Melancholia" 130). This burying the loss deep inside is what Abraham and Torok refer to as the "crypt." Because of the "radical denial," the crypt cannot be discussed directly. Evidence of it can only be found in the form of absences and failures of language (Rand lix). Thus, the edited moments and absences that characterize Kuang's style gesture toward the absent or repressed traumas that her characters face, their refusal, via the free indirect discourse of the novel's point of view, to acknowledge their losses, but I would like to suggest a further, more radical effect.

Abraham and Torok's revolutionary addition to Freud's account of melancholy was the idea that the "crypt" can be passed on from one generation to another through what they call the "phantom." The concept here is that parents pass on their own repressions to their children through their behaviors, by the way they use language, through what they are willing to confront and what they avoid. Thus, the "presence of the phantom indicates the effects, on the descendants, of something that had inflicted narcissistic injury or even catastrophe on the parents" ("Notes on the Phantom" 174). Abraham and Torok even suggest that symptoms of the phantom can be found in things like choice of hobbies, leisure activities, and professional pursuits. In other words, our repressions are never entirely our own but are a legacy of the history of repressions that shaped our identities. This clearly has a powerful significance for Kuang and her account of the immigrant experience and her family's traumatic past, and the silences in her fiction index refusals to experience trauma, but I want to go a step further. The phantom is an "alien" subjectivity that has been placed in the self, and Abraham and Torok define the phantom as the result of *"a direct empathy with the unconscious or the rejected psychic matter of a parental object"* ("Story of Fear" 181). For this reason, I would suggest that "phantoms" can be communicated through reading as well, although certainly not in as powerful a form, as a reader is not likely to experience quite the "direct" empathy, nor is the writer likely to have the full authority or emotional connection of a "parental object." Yet as novels can be "tool[s] of radical empathy" (Sondheimer) according to Kuang, and they imprint an alien subjectivity onto the reader's mind, *they can potentially also imprint its repressions, its traumas, its phantoms.* If that is the case (and Kuang's writing style suggests a sense that it may be), then a writer must take great care with how they handle presenting or editing the material they write about.

To apply this theory about gaps and absences to the way literary form imprints on the reader's consciousness brings us close to Wolfgang Iser's phenomenological reader-response theory. Iser's theory of reading configures texts as blueprints or road maps that shape the reader's experience by offering varying perspectives that the reader can step into, standpoints from which to view the material in the text. For Iser, meaning is created through the interaction of the reader's experience with these prestructured experiences. One of the most important elements of that theory is his idea that texts leave "gaps" which readers must fill in, which forces the reader to become active in formulating the text, but also limits the extent to which they can freely think anything they wish about the text (as the nature of these gaps is defined by the surrounding text). Throughout his explanation of this theory in his key text, *The Act of Reading* (1978), Iser repeatedly describes the effect of these gaps as "stimulating" reader interest: "in literature, [...] the text does not reproduce facts but at best uses such facts to *stimulate* the imagination of the reader" (87, emphasis added). In fact, Iser sees the attempt to fill gaps, to understand others' minds, as the driving force motivating all communication. For instance, Jane Austen, he says, "*stimulates* us to supply what is not there" in order to create a deeper emotion than what is on the page: the reader "is *drawn into events* and *made to supply what is meant* from what is not said" (168, emphasis added). Significantly, the gaps and omissions make the reader an *active* part of imagining the world. It may be understandable that fantasy novels would hesitate to embrace too many such gaps, as building imaginative new worlds would seem to require the invention of new details, and writers might be reluctant to allow for the variations that too many gaps would result in.[5] Yet Iser suggests that literature plays an important role in involving the reader's imaginative efforts in creating the world of the text, thus implicating the reader in some sense in both the positive and negative aspects of that world. The language of "stimulation" is important here, as well, because even though it avoids the overtly sexual connotations of words like "seduction" or "titillation" (and certainly "pornography of sensation"), there is still a suggestion here that texts trade on desire, the voyeurism of wanting to know what is in someone else's head leading to the imaginative efforts of communication. The more a text (like Kuang's or Le Guin's) presents the reader with excised gaps that the reader must fill, the more the reader becomes drawn into and implicated in the imaginative production of the violence or trauma that the text is leaving out. (*All* texts involve the reader's imagination to some extent, but the difference here is the degree of involvement.) Then, if the text turns around and questions that violence, it questions the very grounds of our narrative pleasure, the possibility that we were drawn into this narrative by the pleasure of imaginatively creating that violence. Thus, through the style, the reader is made to experience the repressions of the text and at least to question the extent to which looking at or turning away from the man falling from the wreckage is an ethical activity. The reader becomes the site (the "crypt," in Abraham and Torok's terms) in which this conflict plays out.

Kuang questions this voyeuristic-but-still-necessary empathy by employing this simple edited style frequently in places that link violence with aesthetic response. As the conflict between Mugen (the novel's Japan analogue) and Nikan (the China analogue where Rin lives) builds in the background of Rin's training at Sinegard, Kuang employs a summary style to announce that the war is about to come to Rin's door when the following message arrives: "It read simply: *Horse Province has fallen. Mugen comes for Sinegard*" (229). This whole sequence is noteworthy for two reasons: first, it is a narrative turning point between the first half of the novel (structured largely as a boarding school coming-of-age tale, rather like a dark, adult Harry Potter) and the second (structured largely as a military fantasy), but while the threat of Mugen has lingered in the background throughout the novel, the transition here is abrupt and efficient, editing out extraneous details about the sources of the violence to come. Second, this passage calls attention to the fact that this efficient, almost telegraphic, style is a military style.[6] This final message requires no rhetorical frills, no emotion or interiority of the sender; it simply reports the necessary factual information. From this standpoint, we might consider how all of the edited moments in the novel might be by-products of a militaristic mentality that focuses on pragmatics at the expense of ethics and treats people as automata serving functions—again I would suggest Rin's turning away from the falling man as paradigmatic here.

Yet even though this simple, edited style can be linked to dehumanizing violence in the novel, violence is also linked to beauty, to aesthetic pleasure. Combat style and martial arts form a central part of Rin's training in the early part of the book, leading to a number of discussions that possibly reflect back on the style of the book itself. Early on, Rin reacts negatively to the elaborate, dance-like display of martial arts put on by her rival Nezha. As they watch him show off for other students, her expository friend Kitay explains, "A lot of old arts are like that—cool to watch, practically useless. The lineages were adapted for stage opera, not combat, and then adapted back" (65). Thus, Nezha's early fighting style while beautiful is not particularly practical or violent. In contrast, the school's star tournament fighter (and eventually Rin's leader and mentor in the army) Altan has a very different style, still aestheticized but more efficient, without Nezha's elaborate flourishes: "His movements were dancelike, hypnotic. Every action bespoke sheer power [...] as if at every moment Altan were a tightly coiled spring about to go off" (72). Here Kuang links economy of movement in a violent context to an economy of style, something we might associate with the arts, something that we see in the style of the novel we are reading. Unlike useless conventions adapted from a different era (which could be a description of the common conventions of epic fantasy style), Kuang's writing is tight and efficient. Later, almost as if to cement the analogy, Rin finds her study of martial arts history "almost more entertaining than novels" (102).

Thus, we can perhaps add another descriptor to the edited, efficient style of this novel: it is a martial style, simple, hard-hitting, and efficient, and these qualities are linked to its reading pleasure, just as the fighters in Sinegard's tournaments build a base of fans that enjoy watching them fight. The linkage between this style and violence, however, is problematic, as aesthetic pleasure seems to be derived from the voyeuristic pleasure of watching violence inflicted in this most concise, efficient manner. I should also note that while a martial style is efficient and concise, it is not necessarily direct: Altan, for instance, "always attacked from angles, never from the front" (104). Just as Kuang's edited moments narrate indirectly and draw the reader in to fill in the gaps, Altan attacks indirectly and draws in his opponents for punishment. Ultimately it is a style of omission, and too often, what Altan leaves out is emotion: early in the book, he fights with a flat affect, "impassive, detached" (72), the type of sociopathic hero that Kruppe criticizes in *Toll the Hounds*; later, after Altan and Rin's military unit discovers the aftermath of the Golyn Niis massacre (the novel's analogue for the Rape of Nanking), Rin finds Altan escaping from the emotional trauma by smoking opium, a vision of numbness that she calls "the most terrible thing she'd ever seen" (426). The novel sets up Altan's martial aesthetic as an analogue for its own moments of martial style but consistently criticizes that style for what it cuts out.

The best examples of *The Poppy War*'s deployment of martial style for such ambiguous effects can be found in its battle scenes, particularly the battle of Sinegard in the middle of the book. Kuang describes Rin's fighting like this: "Metal met sinew. She was blinded by the blood streaming into her eyes; she couldn't see what she was cutting, only felt a great tension and then release, and then the Federation soldier was at her knees howling in pain. She stabbed downward without thinking. The howling stopped" (244). This passage starkly contrasts the violence of the Red Wedding: the action is described briefly, without the tremendous detail; even though we are limited by Rin's perspective (or lack thereof as she is blinded in this passage), the style remains largely factual, the narration not distorted by her emotions; and there is no description of interiority here. The central moment of violence, as in so many other instances in this book, is edited out: she "stabbed downward" and the "howling stopped" but there is no description of the violence of the sword penetrating the body or the soldier's death—the reader only infers it imaginatively from the absence of howling. The description is largely stripped of emotion, rather like Altan's fighting, but inversely it gains an emotional impact by calling upon the reader's imagination to step in and supply the details (or not, if we choose to "look away"). In fact, the style of the entire passage could be explained by two words in it: "without thinking." The repetitive violence of combat reduces Rin to an automaton, acting on instinct without thinking or emotion. Consequently, the passage itself is stripped of many of those details.

However, while this seeming lack of emotion dramatizes problems of violence Kuang critiques elsewhere in the novel, she also presents this martial violence as a surprising opportunity for empathy. While Nezha has been Rin's primary rival at Sinegard, in the heat of battle, they become allies, in a moment of martial simplicity that immediately follows Rin's execution of the soldier in the passage above. An enemy soldier

> pulled his sword back to deliver the finishing blow while [Rin] was down.
> His sword arm faltered, then dropped. The soldier made a startled gurgling noise as he stared in disbelief at the blade protruding from his stomach.
> He fell forward and lay still.
> Nezha met Rin's eyes, and then wrenched his sword out of the soldier's back. With his other hand he flung a spare weapon at her.
> She pulled it from the air. Her fingers closed with familiarity around the hilt. A wave of relief shot through her. She had a weapon.
> "Thanks," she said [244–5].

While this passage is fairly detailed, the details it leaves out are more noteworthy. This suspenseful moment is described with factual simple sentences and little underlining of emotions: the killed soldier looks at the blade "in disbelief" and Rin feels "relief" at getting a weapon, but otherwise this passage omits many opportunities for describing emotions, such as Rin's fear that she will be killed, her surprise that she has been saved, her surprise that *Nezha* saved her, possibly embarrassment at being in a subordinate position to Nezha, or gratitude for being saved. The passage is almost entirely simple sentences describing the facts. It employs frequent paragraph breaks, using white space to emphasize the short, punchy paragraphs. Key facts are not explained but left for the reader to infer: we are not told that the enemy soldier is stabbed; we only see the effects. Note that the passage never states directly that Nezha saved Rin—the reader must infer it. Her gratitude can also be inferred by her actions, but we are not told how she feels about Nezha saving her. By forcing the reader to fill in the gaps, making these inferences, Kuang makes us imaginatively produce the interiority of these characters.

This empathic move is then paralleled by Rin and Nezha's ability to fight together in the following passage: "Without thinking they sank into a formation. [...] They made a startlingly good team. [...] It wasn't as if she could read his mind. She had simply spent so much time observing him that she knew exactly how he was going to attack. [...] They were a spontaneously coordinated dance" (245). Kuang repeats the phrase from a few paragraphs above, "without thinking," again emphasizing the automatism of combat, but here that automatic behavior leads to coordination, thinking as someone else, acting "as if she could read his mind" because she has so closely observed him. While this moment of joining with an antagonist to fight a common enemy could be a cliché, by choosing not to underline it and let the reader supply that connection, Kuang makes it effective and suggests the powerful empathic possibilities. However, there is an important caveat: this is in-group empathy against a largely faceless out-group, a flaw that Kuang addresses when it leads to Rin perpetrating genocide against Mugen at the end of the book. Finally, this passage also aestheticizes their violence through the figure of the dance. Once again, the novel links martial style, martial violence, and aesthetic pleasure. Here, the presentation seems largely positive, and the reader is drawn in via the gaps to imaginatively produce both the violence and the characters' emotions, but this may to some extent lead the reader into a narrative trap, as there are still hints that the editorial turning away from violence and the empathic voyeurism here are not wholly positive features.

Perhaps to describe this as a narrative trap may be an overstatement; however, as the novel presents the aftereffects of violence in the massacre of Golyn Niis and Rin's ambiguous but certainly empathic response to that violence, it fully reveals that the violent editing and empathic imagination the reader has been invited to engage in throughout the novel are ultimately troubling. Chapter 21 narrates the Cike's discovery of Golyn Niis and constitutes the central moment of the novel. The emotional structure of the chapter moves from the edited, martial style that constitutes much of the novel—a largely factual recitation of what has happened—to an increasingly emotive account, until finally peaking with an explosion of emotion. This structure first lulls readers into dulling their responses to traumatic material that many readers will want to turn away from before overwhelming them with a horrifying reality that, uncharacteristically, the text refuses to turn away from. This pattern starts with the first approach to the city via boat. The Cike begin to realize that the river is filled with corpses in a series of brief, factual, single-sentence paragraphs: "They were riding through a river of blood. [...] Then the bodies began to float toward them. [...] Their boat stopped moving completely. They were surrounded by corpses" (411). This flat affect continues when Rin enters the city: "an appalling stink assaulted them like a slap to the face. Rin knew the smell. She had experienced it at Sinegard and Khurdalain. She knew what to expect now" (413). Here, the absence of conjunctions communicates Rin's fragmented, disconnected state. It would be natural to join these shorter sentences together in ways that indicated their logical relationships through subordination or coordination—for instance, "She had experienced it, **so** she knew what to expect now." By leaving these out, Kuang makes the text feel more like a succession of disconnected images entering a mind that is not processing how those images are connected.

However, as they proceed further into the city and see more of the effects of violence, value-laden language begins to creep in despite the still largely factual, simple descriptions: "Close to the city square, the Federation had arrayed the corpses in states of *incredible* desecration, grotesque positions that *defied human imagination*. Corpses nailed to boards. Corpses hung by their tongues from hooks. Corpses dismembered in every possible way" (413, emphasis added). The short sentences and parallelism keep the description tight and efficient, and much of it simply describes what is present in factual terms, yet value-laden words and phrases start to crop up—it is "incredible desecration," it "defied human imagination." This is also the novel's most extreme example of "artful" violence: "the destruction possessed a strange artfulness, a sadistic symmetry. Corpses were piled in neat, even rows, forming pyramids of ten, then nine, then eight. Corpses were stacked against the wall. Corpses were placed across the street in tidy lines. Corpses were arranged as far as the eye could see" (413). This passage suggests again the violence underlying art, that efficiency and rules of beauty are separate from ethics and morality and may actually be an evasion of human emotion. The style here parallels that orderliness with its own symmetrical parallels and "tidy lines" (in the sense of lacking extra words and showing careful arrangement), perhaps once again an ironic reflection on the edited, martial style used throughout the entire novel, which implicates the reader as this passage reflects back on the "artful" violence the reader was invited to enjoy in earlier passages.

The martial style is increasingly set aside as the chapter continues, suggesting its insufficiency for handling trauma—looking away from and aestheticizing violence fails to do justice to the ghosts of past trauma. The turning point happens when Rin attacks a bloated dog that she finds scavenging the corpses. The text overtly tells us that "something inside [Rin] snapped" (416), which is followed by an unusually detailed (for this novel) description of her fight with the dog:

> Her sword found its way through the dog's ribs. The dog's jaws went slack. She stabbed again. The dog fell off her. She jumped to her feet and jammed her sword down, piercing the dog's side. It was in its death throes now. She stabbed it again, this time in the neck. A spray of blood exploded outward, coating her face with its warm wetness. She was using her sword like a dagger now, bringing her arm down again and again just to feel bones and muscle give way to metal, just to hurt and *break* something [416].

The scene gradually builds up from factual description that is nonetheless highly detailed (in the same way that the violence in the Red Wedding is detailed and less inferential than is characteristic in this novel), through longer sentences as Rin's emotion increases, to direct descriptions of interiority as the end of this passage explains *why* she is acting this way ("just to feel bones and muscle give way"). This type of overt description of emotion is particularly jarring as it more closely resembles the more conventional style of emotive writing than what has been typical in this novel.

This more overt emotion continues after they find her friend Kitay, one of the few surviving soldiers in the city, and he asks about Nezha (who died in a previous engagement): "Rin opened her mouth to respond, *but* a horrible prickling feeling spread from the bridge of her nose to under her eyes, *and* then she was choking under wild, heaving sobs, *and* she couldn't form any words at all" (418, emphasis added). In the only moment in the chapter where Rin directly expresses grief, the conjunctions so carefully excised from the text earlier appear, and the entire passage is strung together into one long, connected sentence, an entire emotional reaction and not a list of fragmented facts.

However, these passages still describe emotions in an external fashion, telling the reader how the character feels, and while the style invites the reader to feel it, this still allows the pleasure of aesthetic distance—I can admire the parallelism of the description of corpses or the syntax in the description of grief and not think about it as a description of corpses, not feel the grief. Yet *this* is the narrative trap, for it is precisely this disinterested distance that enabled the violence of Golyn Niis in the first place. Thus, Kuang has to push this description to the limit, to explode our comfort level and force us to either confront or turn away from the horror here. To do so, as the climax of the chapter, she uses the eyewitness testimony of Venka, another of Rin's rivals from Sinegard. Venka's testimony is presented in contrast to Kitay's, who precedes her, but as he is "numb," the suffering "normalized" (419), his narration resembles the opening of the chapter: largely flat and factual, only occasional hints of emotion in the cracking of his voice. Venka's story, however, contains all of the marks of emotive narration as she tells of her horrific experiences in a "relaxation house" where she was repeatedly raped and dehumanized, her and the other women being described as "public toilets" (423) by the soldiers. The peak of this chapter-long crescendo is Venka's account of watching a general rape a pregnant woman and then tear open her belly and kill her child in front of her. This overwhelmingly sensational story is told with all of the marks of emotive description: painfully detailed description (I will break the academic tone here to point out that I will attempt to spare readers of my book by "turning away" from all but a single passage to illustrate this focus on precise, direct details: "The general howled and grabbed at her stomach. Not with his knife. With his fingers. His nails"), figurative language ("the general ripped her baby in half the way you'd split an orange" and "Her [Venka's] eyes were like shattered glass" [425]), and even telling the reader directly how the characters feel, as Rin stands in for the reader as audience for this story: "Rin didn't want to hear any more. She wanted to bury her head under her arms and block everything out. But Venka continued, as if now that she had started her testimony she couldn't stop" (425).

This sudden outpouring of sensationalistic, emotional writing, particularly in the context of the prevailing style the reader has come to expect throughout the entire novel, seems like a calculated attempt to overwhelm the reader. Like Rin, we likely want to turn away from this passage. In fact, a number of Internet message boards provide resources for readers who want to read the book without reading Chapter 21 (often because their own personal trauma would make the experience difficult),[7] and Kuang herself has spoken of the difficulty not only of writing the chapter but of going back to revise or re-read it (in a podcast, she says, "[it was] difficult to edit and revise […] I don't even want to go back and read it […] I will not go back and read that chapter" ["R. F. Kuang on Writing"]). On one hand, the testimony of victims of violence is important—Kuang discusses the silencing of women's voices in particular and the "ongoing erasure of sexual violence against women who aren't white across military history" (Sondheimer). In that sense, this passage is showing us something that is too often edited out by the "efficiency" and "aesthetics" of historians, society, and "good" style. On the other hand, she clearly recognizes not only the impulse but the need to look away—continually confronting such trauma directly, refusing to let it go (as the melancholic internalizes the lost object) is emotionally destructive.

But is making the reader experience this tension "empathy"? Do we "empathize" with Venka, or do we feel horror on her behalf? Worse, do we take voyeuristic pleasure in the sensation of horror, and talking (half boastfully) afterwards to others about having survived the horrifying experience of reading this story? These are difficult questions that Kuang poses here without giving answers. She does, however, show us the ambiguity of Rin's responses. Venka specifically calls upon Rin not to *feel* for her but to *act* on her behalf: "I don't need your pity," she says. "I need you to kill them for me" (425). However, Rin's subsequent actions are clearly motivated by her empathic, emotional response to the suffering she witnesses in Golyn Niis. In revenge for horrors she has witnessed, Rin uses her shamanistic connection to the phoenix god to destroy Mugen, killing everyone on the home island in a vast magical conflagration. In the aftermath, she reflects on what she has done in terms that describe her actions as editing reality: "She had not just altered the fabric of the universe, had not simply rewritten the script. She had *torn* it, ripped a great gaping hole in the cloth of reality" (503). Furthermore, she thinks of the people she has killed in terms that suggests she feels sympathy or even empathy, yet she still justifies her actions: "Once, the fabric had contained the stories of millions of lives—the lives of every man, woman, and child on the longbow island—civilians who had gone to bed easy. […] In an instant, the script had written their stories to the end. At one point in time those people existed. And then they didn't" (503). The end of the passage uses the same editorial style that the passage itself discusses, a summary ending that omits and ignores the suffering she has just described in so much more detail. Finally, she justifies her actions by generalizing them, cutting out specific individuals because the scale is too large to comprehend:

> she could not possibly multiply that by thousands. That kind of thinking did not compute. The scale was unimaginable. So she didn't bother to try. [...] Those weren't lives.
> They were numbers.
> They were a necessary subtraction [504].

Again, the summary style here parallels the mental process she is going through—she is thinking of her actions in "summary" terms so that she does not have to confront the human details (the very same mental activity that ironically reflected Rin's erasure from the Fang's plans when it appeared early in the novel). The simple, edited style in this novel is a style of subtraction, of leaving things out, and in this case, by leaving out moral context and empathy she is able to justify her actions by abstracting them, an abstraction that seems pale in comparison to the very specific emotion of Venka's narration.

Yet, to be accurate, I should point out that she is not cutting out empathy—she is just being selectively empathic. Keen describes how studies of empathy show that *"empathy for group members emerging from categorical identity with a group does not, on its own, lead to an ethics of compassion"* (164), and Kuang dramatically illustrates this through Rin, whom she compares to the historical trajectory of Mao Zedong, asking, "how does somebody go from being an irrelevant, backwater, peasant nobody to being a megalomaniac dictator capable of killing millions of people? [...] suppose this person is actually deeply empathetic and cares deeply about her friends and the people close to her, genuinely wants to do the right thing and save people, what do you do with a character like that?" (Sondheimer). Empathy, it seems, is a double-edged sword, capable of forming compassion but also capable of motivating genocide. Furthermore, if novels are indeed capable of generating empathy, then this may not be the pro-social effect that we would expect. *The Poppy War*, I would therefore argue, uses its simple, martial style as a trap for readers, stimulating their imaginations to empathy before pulling back the curtain and revealing that they are being made to empathize with genocide, being forced to question whether their engagement with trauma is a "pornographic indulgence in sensation" that is ultimately self-serving and destructive. The reader is compelled here to confront the fact that the book's pleasure is built on violence (as is much epic fantasy), but its style interrogates that pleasure by pulling back from it and then showing us that the pulling back—the refusal to see—is also part of the problem. After all, the book also shows that empathy is necessary, as the victims need a voice, and it is up to the readers to hear.

The Violence of Editing in Le Guin

While Kuang uses a simple, edited style to express a tortured ambivalence about the value of empathy, Le Guin raises similar issues with a more positive focus. Like Kuang, Le Guin's Earthsea novels are not wholly characterized by minimalism (in fact, their prevailing style tends to be more elaborate), but she uses similarly edited moments in key places. Just as in Kuang, for Le Guin these moments often indicate the importance of confronting trauma, but they do so by inversely and ironically using a style that edits out details. Le Guin also at times deals with the trauma of violence, particularly violence towards women, and questions the blindness toward women that is structured into our culture. However, Le Guin's ultimate focus tends to be on undoing these repressions, revealing the beauty of life and undoing conventional, stereotypical ways of seeing (particularly as it relates to seeing gender). Thus, I will end this chapter by looking at examples from two of Le Guin's novels: *The Tombs of Atuan* (1970) for an early example of Le Guin's focusing more generally on individual freedom, and *Tehanu* (1990) for its more concrete work on freedom from stereotypes about fantasy and gender.

In Le Guin's books, there is often a significant interplay between stylistic simplicity and complexity. Le Guin has written about the need for fantasy to straddle this line in her essay "From Elfland to Poughkeepsie" (1973), where she argues that *simplicity* is a feature of epic style: "Most epics are straightforward in language, whether prose or verse. They retain the directness of their oral forebears. Homer's metaphors may be extended, but they are neither static nor ornate. [...] Clarity and simplicity are permanent virtues in a narrative. Nothing highfalutin is needed. A plain language is the noblest of all" (89). This simplicity does not exclude stylized, elevated language, though, as much of this essay criticizes not overly ornate fantasy language but the flat, plain "Poughkeepsie" style that Le Guin was seeing too often in fantasy: "The tone as a whole is profoundly inappropriate to the subject. To what then is it appropriate? To journalism. It is journalistic prose. [...] A language intended to express the immediate and the trivial is applied to the remote and elemental. The result, of course, is a mess" (89). The writing of fantasy, then, is a balancing act for Le Guin between simple style and elevated tone. This tension can be illustrated by a description of the sea from relatively late in *The Tombs of Atuan*: "It never rested. On all the shores of all the lands in all the world, it heaved itself in these unresting waves, and never ceased, and never was still. The desert, the mountains: they stood still. They did not cry out forever in a great, dull voice. The sea spoke forever, but its language was foreign to her. She did not understand" (169). The second sentence of this passage clearly illustrates that simplicity is not a function of sentence length, as even though many of the sentences here are simple and direct, the longest sentence gains its length not from subordination but from the listing of prepositional phrases and multiple verbs in a grammatically simple sentence—essentially it is a list of short phrases ("On all the shores / of all the lands / in all the world,/ it heaved itself / in these unresting waves/, and never ceased, / and never was still"). Yet the rolling rhythm of these parallel phrases (reflecting the rolling waves of the sea) is certainly a stylization, as it includes features like left dislocation ("The desert, the mountains: they still") and figurative language ("the sea spoke"). The language imparts beauty and nobility to the world, according to an aesthetic that simplicity is beauty. The passage does not necessarily attempt to edit our perception of the world.

However, in *Tombs*, Le Guin seems keenly aware of the ties between this editorial descriptive style and an edited perspective of the world. The novel's protagonist, Tenar, was selected in childhood to serve the ancient Nameless Ones, the gods of the Tombs, a process which entails the loss of her identity (her name is taken from her and she is called Arha, the Eaten One). The Tombs give her a singular, narrow focus to her experience of the world. Le Guin calls our attention to the editing of her memory and identity in several early passages: "As she grew older she lost all remembrance of her mother, without knowing she had lost it. She belonged here, at the Place of the Tombs; she had always belonged here" (8), and "she could not remember. What was the good in remembering? It was gone, all gone. She had come where she must come. In all the world she knew only one place: the Place of the Tombs of Atuan" (12). Even her name is almost literally edited out, as it is given to the Nameless Ones to be "eaten." After this ceremony of rebirth, a moment of simple, edited style reflects the editing out of emotion from her life. The eunuch Manan, who has served as a parental figure for the young Tenar, approaches her as she goes to bed and attempts to sympathize with her. However, "The child said nothing. Manan slowly turned around and went away. The glimmer died from the high cell walls. The little girl, who had no name any more but *Arha*, the Eaten One, lay on her back looking steadily at the dark" (7). This passage is strikingly similar to the emotionally numb moments in *The Poppy War*: the point of view is external, and her emotions or reasons for rejecting Manan's comfort are not spelled out but implied in a series of short, simple sentences. The style of the scene reflects the way that Tenar is being taught to restrict her responses to other people, cutting out her emotions to become the perfect servant of the Nameless Ones.

This editing of social ties may be linked to Le Guin's politics, specifically her anarchism. In one sense, we may think here of anarchy as a politics of subtraction, one which seeks to remove the restrictions on behavior, and it would be tempting to draw an analogy here to her style as well, which seeks to restrict the number of grammatical rules in play by being as simple and direct as possible. Yet this tempting analogy is also not entirely accurate: instead, Le Guin seems to see anarchy as a perception of wholeness, of seeing the self as integrated with the world, in contrast to the alienation[8] caused by fragmentation of the world by social codes and rules. James Gifford, who argues that Le Guin's anarchism finds a more congenial form in fantasy than in the science fiction it is more usually associated with, sums up this conflict in relation to Tenar's transformation over the course of the novel: the "rescue of Tenar works through her same struggle toward an antiauthoritarian *being* rather than an authority-crippled *doing*" (208). Defining the self through actions places one under the authority of social codes that shape those actions, whereas simply be*ing* frees one from those expectations and allows a focus on self-definition. Gifford argues that the magic of Earthsea, based around finding the proper names of objects, dramatizes this conflict as it is a magic of subjectivity and self-possession. However, I would point out that this theme of self-possession is also embodied in the style, which reframes the reader's perceptions.

This contrast of *being* and *action* in the style (and the novel's magic) is best illustrated when Ged demonstrates magic to Tenar by calling a rabbit to their campfire. Ged is the foreign wizard who catalyzes Tenar's escape from the restrictions she has been raised with, and he serves as a mentor and teacher throughout the final portion of the novel. As he uses the rabbit's true name to call it to them, there is a shift over the course of the passage in how the rabbit is described:

> Silence. No sound. No motion. Only presently, at the very edge of the flickering firelight, a round eye like a pebble of jet, very near the ground. A curve of furry back; an ear, long, alert, upraised.
>
> Ged spoke again. The ear flicked, gained a sudden partner-ear out of the shadow; then as the little beast turned Tenar saw it entire for an instant, the small, soft, lithe hop of it returning unconcerned to its business in the night [157-8].

The paragraph break marks the transition: while both halves of the passage use the same simple style of short phrases that I have remarked on elsewhere in *Tombs*, the first passage is full of sentence fragments that break the rabbit up into a sequence of separate parts—an ear, a back, an eye. The sentence fragments reflect the fragmented description, as the edited style of the passage chops up the rabbit into a sequence of separate perceptions. The second passage (after "Ged spoke again") is one long sentence that sees the rabbit "entire." Even its actions are not seen as separate from the rabbit as a subject, as indicated by the nominalized verb "hop"—the only specific detail that she "sees" in the second passage. This transition from the fragmented, simple (edited) first half to the more complex holistic second half is a transition from seeing the rabbit as an object that is separate from its actions to seeing it as an entire being that cannot be separated into component parts.

While this may be the most dramatic and extended example in the novel, Le Guin's syntax is filled with this movement from part to whole, as many sentences invert our expectations (and sometimes the syntax) by first listing descriptive details before completing the picture by naming the object being described. For instance, in a description of the Tombs early in the novel, Le Guin does this in two consecutive sentences: "*Behind the Hall and encircling the whole crest of the hill* ran a massive wall of rock, laid without mortar and half fallen down in many places. *Inside the loop of the wall* several black stones eighteen or twenty feet high stuck up like huge fingers out of the earth" (16, emphasis added). In each of these sentences, the reader must wait for the main clause of the sentence and then go back to details given before it to reconstruct the entire picture (it may seem less stylized to say, for instance, "a massive wall of rock encircled the hill"). In one of the key moments of the novel, when Tenar discovers Ged in the Tombs, using light to illuminate the Tomb (which by rule is required to be kept in darkness), a lengthy passage of description ends with another inversion: "the great vaulted cavern […] was jeweled with crystals […] immense, with glittering roof and walls, sparkling, delicate, intricate, a place of diamonds, a house of amethyst and crystal, from which the ancient darkness had been driven out by glory. *Not bright, but dazzling to the dark-accustomed eye, was the light that worked this wonder*" (70, emphasis added). Again, this follows the pattern of complex and detailed description followed by simplicity, which in this case reflects the return of that which has been edited from perceptions. The final sentence also adds the pattern of lists of details preceding the unifying, holistic descriptor ("the light that worked this wonder") that pulls the entire description together after the fact. This may be mildly reminiscent of what I called "summary style" in Kuang's writing, but whereas summary style often called attention to what was missing, this inverted style brings everything together, replacing the partial fragments back into the whole.

A final instance of this interplay between simple and complex in

Tombs occurs in the novel's climactic character moment, when Tenar is tempted to return to serving her masters by killing Ged. The scene begins with silence, as Ged's failure to talk to her as they rest serves as the impetus for her questioning of whether he is manipulating her: "He made no answer. [...] His silence became not absence of speech, but a thing in itself, like the silence of the desert" (170). Here we have silence as editing, the absence as a palpable thing. The lack of language in Ged's silence leads to an excess of interiority to fill the silence. This building of complexity throughout the description of Ged's silence leads into several paragraphs of reflection in Tenar's mind, as she questions her newfound "freedom" and considers returning to the service she grew up in. Intriguingly, the excess here is associated with returning to rules rather than exploring her new freedom, as though more syntax means more rules and less freedom. Thus, appropriately, the moment of doubt ends, stylistically, with a clipped, simple moment, as Ged says her name: "At the sound of his voice the fury left her. She was afraid" (172). The moment of crisis dissipates without further explanation in these brief, simple sentences. This sort of clean efficiency seems at odds with what we have seen elsewhere in this novel, where the edited and fragmentary moments point to parts of experience being left out, but we should note that emotion is not being suppressed, as it was, for instance, when Manan spoke to her after the unnaming ceremony. Her feelings are named here, and shortly after this moment, as they take the final steps to sail away from the island and she feels truly free, her feelings are described at length in perhaps the most expository passage in the novel as "She cried for the waste of her years in bondage to a useless evil. She wept in pain, because she was free" (173), and Le Guin speaks in volubly metaphorical terms of "the weight of liberty" and the road "upward towards the light" that the "laden traveler" may never reach the end of (173). Thus, while the climactic moment itself is edited and simple, it is not the editing of something being left out. Rather the absence suggests a fullness of emotion, spurring reader involvement by leaving out overt description. The reader is expected to provide the emotion as the context is already present, inviting participation in the wholeness of life that we have presumably learned alongside Tenar.

However, this final scene—Tenar being taught "freedom" by a male authority figure—might give us pause. By treating the issue of human freedom so abstractly, does *Tombs* fall into the trap of confirming regressive gender stereotypes about male power and agency that are all too common in epic fantasy? Women are too often "edited" out of epic fantasy. Charlotte Spivack's study of women fantasy writers (written just a few years before Le Guin's *Tehanu*) offers a number of ways in which fantasy has often been written from a male perspective, ranging from primarily male protagonists (8), traditionally masculine subject matter like "battles and politics" taking priority over "human relationships and reactions" (9), "the power principle in politics" (10), and the favoring of "transcendence" over "immanence" (a feature particularly of writers from "the Christian school, including the Inklings") (14). Thus, in the conclusion of *Tombs*, Tenar is perhaps displaced by Ged—as the hero of the first and third books in the series, he may still appear to many readers as the primary perspective rather than Tenar. Le Guin herself seems to have come to similar conclusions, for when she returned to the character of Tenar nearly two decades later in *Tehanu*, the simple style she uses much more overtly thwarts anticipated patterns of language involving masculinity, a simplicity much more about exclusion (as Kuang used it) than about wholeness. (Or perhaps, the simplicity here is only indirectly about wholeness, as Le Guin is introducing an alternative, egalitarian perspective.) Namely, by excluding what might be thought of as the usual (traditionally masculine-coded) content of epic fantasy—action and violence, power politics, transcendence—and instead focusing on the simple and everyday, the domestic, the immanent, *Tehanu* leaves out the salient elements of epic fantasy in order to suggest an alternative view.

I will be making this argument specifically in relation to Le Guin's use of simple, edited style, but I should note that this argument about the novel, more broadly, is not particularly unusual. Melanie Rawls explains it most directly and perhaps most forcefully in her claim that the last three books of Earthsea (*Tehanu*, *The Other Wind*, and *Tales from Earthsea*) are "revisionist history" that rewrites the original trilogy (141). Rawls makes a particular distinction between the nature of male and female power: women's power entails "joining what needs to be joined and dividing what needs to be divided, in the name of healing and wholeness. This is the practice of women—their art and their power. From the beginnings of the written histories of Earthsea, the men of power have separated themselves from women and from ordinary life. They have existed in epic—including in their selfconstructed would-be epics" (140). Clearly, this concern is present even in *Tombs*, with its emphasis on wholeness over separation, and it is therefore already a component of Le Guin's simple, edited style, a style that is about "joining and dividing" where needed in order to bring wholeness. Furthermore, Rawls suggests that the epic is often coded as masculine, therefore suggesting that novels like *Tehanu* are deliberately anti-epic (or at least transformed epic, as Le Guin is clearly not opposed to the epic as such).

In respect to how she presents the content, though, Le Guin must walk a tightrope: how does one introduce the domestic and everyday into fantasy without falling prey to other gender stereotypes, such as the "over-emotional woman"? And further, would this not lead to the potential problem of empathy as a superficial emotional voyeurism? Scenes drenched in blood and violence can be emotive without seeming "effeminate" because they activate traditional masculine scripts. Simply to edit these elements out of the content of the text risks reinforcing the gender binary by writing "feminine" fantasy. Thus, Le Guin counters the stereotype by marrying emotion and empathy to a sparse, non-emotive, non-voyeuristic style—a clipped style that hints at emotions and brings it out of readers without insisting on it. The misogynistic antagonist in *Tehanu*, Aspen, sums up the position Le Guin is countering: "She has so much to say. Women always do" (247). Aspen associates women with excess language and excess emotion. A good example of Le Guin's rebuttal to Aspen's assumptions about women and emotive language comes on the first page of the book, as Le Guin tells the reader that Tenar (now called Goha) is widowed: "It was dusk, but she did not light the lamp, thinking of her own husband lighting the lamp: the hands, the spark, the intent, dark face in the catching glow. The house was silent. 'I used to live in a silent house, alone,' she thought. 'I will do so again.' She lighted the lamp" (2). Le Guin uses no directly emotive language. Instead, she *suggests* emotion by giving a list of detail associated with Tenar's dead husband, which invest emotion into the actions that follow. But those actions are described through a series of simple, direct statements, and Le Guin leaves it to the reader to infer the emotion.

While she edits out direct description of emotion, she leaves in an array of minor, domestic details. For instance, the plot begins when a woman named Lark comes to ask for Tenar's help caring for a child named Therru who has been beaten and burned. As they leave Tenar's house together, we are told that "Goha went to shut the farmhouse door, and they set off along the lane" (3). Rather than being editorial and simple, this added detail seems extraneous—how often in fiction, when a character leaves their house, does the author tell us that the door was shut? The narrative is filled with such small, everyday details, reminders of the simple immanence of the world they live in, certainly a contrast to the high level of violent detail in scenes like the Red Wedding. This scene also continues the pattern of implying emotion rather than directly stating it: as Lark tells Therru's story, emotion occasionally overwhelms her, but Le Guin does not overtly says so. Instead, she pauses the narration and says, "Lark stopped talking for several steps. She looked straight ahead, not at Goha" (3) and "She stopped again, went on again" (4). This may remind us of the Golyn Niis incident in *The Poppy War*, as again we have a restrained retrospective narration of a horrifying act of violence against a girl, although certainly it contrasts the extreme emotion of Venka's narration.

The emotion is left for the reader to infer from a simple description of the facts.

Le Guin's editorial restraint is also particularly in evidence at the end of the novel. Throughout the narrative, the absence of traditional adventure elements is noteworthy: the story focuses predominantly on life on Tenar's farm, as even Ged loses his magical powers (a consequence of the ending of the original trilogy) and comes to herd goats with her, struggling with his change in status. However, the story seems to set up an adventure climax as Ged and Tenar are led into a magical trap by Aspen, a follower of Ged's old antagonist the wizard Cob. Aspen intends to execute them by pushing them off a cliff, but they are saved by the arrival of the dragon Kalessin, who has been summoned by Therru who, it turns out, is a dragon child in human form. Kalessin kills Aspen and his gang and reveals Therru's true identity. However, to even give this summary requires filling gaps that are not explicitly stated in the book. The entire incident takes up roughly twelve pages of a 250-page novel (and the scene with Kalessin, a mere four pages), so, proportionally, this is only a minor part of the narrative. Furthermore, the highest concentrations of physical action are largely edited out of the narrative. Tenar is beaten by Aspen's men the night they are captured, but as was the case in Kuang, this violence toward women is handled in a brief, factual fashion: "Then she was kicked and made to crawl down halls. She could not crawl fast enough, and was kicked in the breasts and in the mouth. Then there was a door that crashed, and silence, and the dark. She heard somebody crying and thought it was the child, her child. She wanted the child not to cry. At last it stopped" (243). The sentences are simple and largely stripped of modifiers and emotive language. The effect is a narrative distance that does not allow the reader a perspective from which to voyeuristically relish the horror of violence. The final detail, the description of the crying, is perhaps puzzling, but it appears to be an oblique description of Tenar herself crying. Again, the emotion of the scene is implied and indirect. The reader must supply the connection, which potentially gives the scene more emotional power even as it refuses to dwell on the emotion.

This editing out of the most active portions of the narrative reaches its apex when Kalessin arrives in the next chapter. While generically, the reader might expect this to be a central focus of the book, Le Guin shows no interest in the dragon's actions, which are completely omitted from the story. Even the dragon's introduction into the story is fragmentary and implicit: "[Tenar] could not speak, but she pointed to the sky above the sea. 'Albatross,' [Aspen] said. She laughed out loud. In the gulfs of light, from the doorway of the sky, the dragon flew" (247). What Tenar points at is not initially described. At first, we have only Aspen's guess that he is seeing a bird, so we know it is something flying toward them. From this and some very general hints earlier, the reader may guess that it is a dragon, but it is likely still not clear until the narrator names him "the dragon"—note however that "the" implies that this is not new information, as though the reader should already know based on the scanty evidence above. This final sentence is also another "inverted" sentence, as a list of descriptors ("in the gulfs of light, from the doorway of the sky") precedes the object described. After this passage, the entrance of the dragon brings with it a comparative wealth of descriptive language, filled with adjectives, imagery, and figurative language: "In the gulfs of light, from the doorway of the sky, the dragon flew, fire trailing behind the coiling, mailed body. Tenar spoke then. 'Kalessin!' she cried, and then turned, seizing Ged's arm, pulling him down to the rock, as the roar of fire went over them, the rattle of mail and the hiss of wind in upraised wings, the clash of the talons like scythe-blades on the rock" (247). However, after this brief moment of voluble description (which is still a bit impressionistic) activates the reader's expectations that "now we will finally get the action climax," there is a break on the page, and the next section begins: "The wind blew from the sea. A tiny thistle growing in the cleft in the rock near her hand nodded and nodded in the wind from the sea. Ged was beside her. They were crouched side by side, the sea behind them and the dragon before them" (248). The action—what the dragon did to Aspen and his men—is completely omitted. Instead, the action is replaced by small, domestic, peaceful details (the wind, the thistle). This displacement may have been subtle in the first chapter, but it glaringly calls attention to itself here, and the style returns to its core simplicity, simple sentences either short or gaining length by accumulating a list of prepositional phrases. Rather than allowing the reader to take pleasure in retributive violence toward the othered enemy, this passage focuses entirely on the peaceful healing aftermath of violence, with the only concession to described violence being a brief, vague mention of the dead bodies when Kalessin leaves: "Where it [the dragon] had been lay scorched rags of cloth and leather, and other things" (250). What these "other things" are (body parts?) is entirely left to the reader's imagination.

To fully recognize how subversive this is, it may be useful to return briefly to Iser's theory, particularly his concept of "negation." Texts often shape the meanings that readers arrive at by "negating" expected genre norms. Iser applies this concept mostly to modernist fiction (like Joyce's *Ulysses*), but what he says clearly has relevance here as well: "It is typical of modern texts that they invoke expected functions in order to transform them into blanks. This is mostly brought about by a deliberate omission of generic features that have been firmly established by the tradition of the genre" (208). Le Guin's structuring of the end of *Tehanu* can certainly be described as a "deliberate omission of generic features," and the effect, according to Iser, is an increase in the "disorderliness" of the text (209). In other words, the reader is confused and must then supply the connections themselves: "the blanks created by the nonfulfilled, though expected, functions demand increased productivity on the part of the reader, for with every connection he [*sic*] establishes he must also supply the code that will enable him to grasp it" (209–210). In this case, the reader must imaginatively supply the violence that is lacking, but doing so creates the awareness that this violence has been *edited* out of the narrative and that it was something *the reader expected in the first place*. Faced with the (potential) disappointment, the reader must recognize the extent to which reading pleasure is derived (voyeuristically?) from the violent meting out of punishment on the other and not the pleasure of reconciliation. As Iser explains, "the reader's own position cannot remain unaffected by the process: if the norms of his society are exposed in this way, he has the chance to perceive consciously a system in which he had hitherto been unconsciously caught up, and his awareness will be all the greater if the validity of these norms is negated" (212). This is, of course, just a "chance": some readers (perhaps many readers) will respond to the climax of *Tehanu* simply by saying the book was disappointing or boring. However, through her oblique and edited style, stripping out the details, Le Guin subverts masculine-coded genre expectations and provides readers an opportunity to face the extent to which their narrative pleasure is fueled not by a prosocial empathy but by a violent, authoritarian desire for violence and coercion of the other.

Thus, both Kuang and Le Guin ironically use an edited style to reveal absences too often at the heart of our fantasy narratives. By omitting details and context, they allow readers space to create those emotions for themselves, paradoxically leading to a greater emotional empathy, and at the same time by way of contrast to the edited text, enabling a confrontation with the assumptions that lead us to want to imagine those emotions. Those assumptions, we may find, can be bound up in flattering self-regard, in pornographic voyeurism, in authoritarian discipline, in the silencing of gender or racial others, just as much as they may involve more positive emotive connections to imagined others. While Kuang and particularly Le Guin ultimately tell a positive story of moving forward through self-critique, they add a shade of complexity to any utopian considerations about empathy, and a significant indication of how, by playing against conventional expectations, fantasy affords useful opportunities for politically subversive writing.

Narrative Perspective

Chapter 3

Third-Person Heroism

Authority, Omnipotent Narration, and the Distribution of Visibility

> For an instant, Cnaiür thought, it seemed the God watched
> him through a man's skull. [...] But then his lover fell away,
> burning as he must, such was the force of what had pos-
> sessed them.—R. Scott Bakker, *The Thousandfold Thought*

Picking up any epic fantasy novel, a reader is likely to find some form of narration similar to this passage from Patricia McKillip's *The Riddle-Master of Hed* (1976):

> They stood unmoving, their faces flushed, while Morgon's farmers looked on
> in unabashed amusement. They were not alike, the three children of Athol of
> Hed and Spring Oakland. [...] Morgon, with his hair and eyes the color of light
> beer, bore the stamp of their grandmother, whom the old men remembered as
> a slender, proud woman from south Hed [2–3].

Superficially, there is nothing striking about this passage: it provides a serviceable third-person description of the protagonist (Morgon) and his family. The point of view is ostensibly focalized through Morgon through-out the novel, but much of the narration, particularly in this chapter, verges more on what we would likely call "omniscient." There is little in this description that suggests thought processes specific to Morgon, and in fact, this passage is actually focalized more generally through the farmers watching them, as the passage repeatedly emphasizes how the characters look from the outside and how "the old men remembered" them in rela-tion to their ancestors. Many of the following descriptions continue in the same vein. Some passages use Morgon to focalize the narration but suggest a degree of knowledge beyond his (or at least heightened perceptiveness on his part), such as when his sister faces him with "a hint of uncertainty in her eyes" (3). Here, rather than jumping into her head to tell us she is uncertain, the narrator stays with Morgon but has him "read" her emo-tional state through her expressions. The narrative follows Morgon, largely

91

reports what happens to him and makes him the subject of most sentences, yet it would be fair to describe the narration as an omniscient narrator that largely limits itself to Morgon.

In contrast, consider another passage of narration characteristic of what a random reader is likely to come across, drawn from early in Joe Abercrombie's *The Blade Itself* (2006). Logen, the point-of-view character in the first chapter, hangs from a ledge after being attacked by an enemy the reader knows very little about:

> It was quite a scrape he was in. He'd been in some bad ones all right, and lived to sing the songs, but it was hard to see how this could get much worse. That got him thinking about his life. It seemed a bitter, pointless sort of a life now. No one was any better off because of it. Full of violence and pain, with not much but disappointment and hardship in between. His hands were starting to tire now, his forearms were burning [9].

Again, there is little noteworthy here. As with McKillip, the point of view is third-person but focalized through a single character. However, this is more clearly an instance of what is usually called "third person limited"— all of the information in the passage is limited to what Logen thinks or knows ("that got him thinking" is a specific signal that we are in his head). The passage emphasizes his interiority, how *he* sees events rather than giving an abstract external view. In fact, the passage even slips into free indirect discourse—a form of third-person narration that uses the character's own words, as though written in first person with "I" changed to "he." Logen's words describe the situation but substitute "he" for "I" ("It was quite the scrape he was in. He'd been in some bad ones"—the informality of the word "scrape" and the contraction even sounds more like dialogue or oral narration rather than formal narration). The narration here calls attention to itself (perhaps playfully), as it seems artificial to slip this reverie of character self-analysis into a moment fraught with the stress of self-preservation. In a pattern typical of much contemporary epic fantasy (and unlike McKillip), Abercrombie's book does not follow a single character but cycles through numerous point-of-view characters, typically shifting perspective between chapters. A small list of similar examples includes some of the most popular fantasy of the past thirty years, including George R.R. Martin's A Song of Ice and Fire, Robert Jordan's Wheel of Time, and Brandon Sanderson's Mistborn Trilogy and Stormlight Archive.

My argument in Chapters 3 and 4 will discuss narrative perspective in epic fantasy, particularly taking up the relationship between "focalization" and "voice," which often shifts and blurs in interesting ways. Gérard Genette defines this distinction between "mood" or "focalization" (answering the question "who sees?" in a narrative) and "voice" (answering the question "who speaks?"), both of which make up "perspective" (Genette 186). Furthermore, Genette takes issue with the conventional terminology that equates grammatical voice with narrative voice: informally, if the story uses "I," we call it "first person"; if "he" or "she," "third person." Typically, when we speak of first-person narrative, we mean a narrative with an "I" narrator *who is also a character in the plot*, but it is possible for a narrator to refer to himself or herself in the first person but not also be a character *in* the story. (Genette's example is Virgil's *Aeneid*, which begins "*I* sing of arms and a man" [244].) For this reason, Genette uses the term "homodiegetic" to refer to stories narrated by characters in the story and "heterodiegetic" to refer to what we would typically call "third-person" narration, stories narrated by a voice from outside the story (244). While these terms are generally used now in narratology, I will largely avoid them as the terms themselves are unintuitive and examples of heterodiegetic first-person or homodiegetic third-person narratives are quite rare (and largely absent from the texts I am considering). Thus, "first person" will refer to narratives predominantly narrated by a character in the storyworld (and also using "I") and "third person" will refer to narratives where (the reader assumes) the narration is *not* provided directly by those characters (and which therefore uses third-person pronouns to describe them). I will also at times refer to "focalization" or "focal narrators" in relation to third-person narratives to refer to instances where the point-of-view of a specific character limits the information provided by the text (although this "limited" narration only becomes "free indirect discourse" when the language of the narration also seems to come from the character, and not just the perspective).

What is striking about the two examples with which I started, then, is that both fit broadly into the same category of narration, "third person" or "third person limited," despite being so markedly different—the language is shaped by the narrator's distance from the character, the privileged access given to the reader into the character's mind. At the same time, they are unremarkable, almost invisible to analysis, because they are so typical. The vast majority of epic fantasy novels are narrated in a way similar to these examples, to one extent or another. In fact, epic fantasy relies more heavily on third-person narration than is typically the case in fiction. While this may seem intuitively obvious to fantasy readers, an informal statistical survey provides hard evidence. As a point of comparison, consider a list of the "Best Books of the Twentieth Century" from goodreads.com ("Best Books"). (While such a list does not exactly constitute a random sample, it does provide a range of genres, largely focused on literary or mainstream fiction, and suggests popular attitudes, as the list is ordered by over 9,000 voters.) Of the top 100 books, 59 use third person, 35 use first person, three use a mix that included substantial uses of first person (*The Sound and the Fury*, *Ulysses*, and *Franny and Zooey*), and four did not fit these parameters in a reasonable way (*Green Eggs and Ham* is told entirely in dialogue, as is the play *Waiting for Godot*, and *Mere Christianity* is the only non-narrative book on the list). This means that 38 percent of these books make some substantial use of first person rather than third person. As a basis for my contrasting list of epic fantasy, I used a similar list of "The Best Epic Fantasy," again from Good Reads (largely to prevent this sample from being limited to novels I am aware of), keeping in mind that the list maker's definition of "epic fantasy" is not as precise as mine ("Best Epic Fantasy"). Because much epic fantasy is published in serial form, this list attempts to give each series one entry rather than listing each book separately; however, after removing duplicates, I added further entries from the list in order to get a top 100 series, then added some additional items from the list, my personal library, and other popular fantasy series. The resulting list had 129 fantasy series, and the numbers were striking: 108 primarily use third person, only 17 use first person, and four use a mix that includes first person (L. E. Modesitt's Recluce novels, for instance, include some books written in first and some in third). From these numbers alone, we find just 16 percent of epic fantasy series making substantial use of first person rather than third, although I suspect a more in-depth study might find the numbers even more skewed toward third person.[1]

The numbers themselves also do not entirely account for reader expectations. First person appears rarely enough in epic fantasy that it is often a marked feature when it does appear. It might seem odd for a reviewer or a reader in informal conversation to say something like, "I liked Kazuo Ishiguro's latest novel even though I don't normally like first-person narrators," but this sort of comment appears commonly when applied to, say, Glen Cook's Black Company series. Readers expect third-person narration so much in epic fantasy that it is largely invisible and noticeable mostly by its absence. This raises a significant question for this study: why is epic fantasy so drawn to the third-person perspective? I will suggest some possible answers to that question in Chapter 4 when I analyze the use of first-person perspective in epic fantasy novels. In this chapter, however, I re-direct the question slightly: what affordances of third-person narrative perspective does epic fantasy's use of the technique reveal? In other words, what uses do writers of epic fantasy find in third-person narration, and what do those uses help us to understand about it? I will analyze why perspective matters in fantasy, what effect it has, and what fantasy can reveal about how it works.

To begin to answer these questions, I will consider why perspective matters in fiction. Perspective is typically a matter of agency, authority, and subjectivity: Who knows what? What can they do with that knowledge? Who gets to speak, and why should the reader believe them? These are always key questions in fiction, but epic fantasy is particularly positioned to deal with them, as the magic of fantasy worlds is often about uses of power and subjectivity, and questions of narrative authority become particularly important when describing worlds outside of the consensus reality, worlds the reader accepts almost entirely based on the words of the text. As a result, epic fantasy puts particular pressure on the narration, and what happens under these pressures can be quite revealing. I will start by looking at this issue of narrative authority and agency in third person from a theoretical perspective before examining two test cases from epic fantasy. In choosing these test cases, even though third person is the conventional form of narration in epic fantasy, I select more exceptional cases, as these reflect more consciously on the overall use of perspective in fantasy fiction. Thus, I will analyze the unusual omniscient narration in Stephen R. Donaldson's novella "The King's Justice" (2015) and the rapidly shifting third-person limited perspective of R. Scott Bakker's Prince of Nothing trilogy. These two texts have some substantial differences: Donaldson holds classic humanist values while Bakker has a markedly post-human philosophy of subjectivity and agency; Donaldson is experimenting with a traditional style of narration while Bakker uses an extreme form of the more common contemporary style. Nonetheless, these two approaches reveal a striking similarity: in both cases, the third-person narration erases distinctions between narrating voices (while still respecting their difference), creating an egalitarian, non-hierarchical distribution of voice that corresponds very closely with what I have been calling "empathy" throughout this study, or which could be considered a way of "mapping" society without the hierarchical structures more commonly associated with traditional forms like epic fantasy.

Who Tells the Story?: Authority, Knowledge Agency

In talking about perspective in terms of an equal "distribution of voice," I am following Jacques Rancière in his definition of both politics and aesthetics as areas of human activity concerned with the "distribution of the sensible" (a phrase Rancière frequently uses). In *The Politics of Aesthetics* (2003), Rancière argues that "Politics revolves around what is seen and what can be said about it, around who has the ability to see and the talent to speak" (8). He contrasts aesthetics to the "police order" (which is not just the police as an institution): the social roles that create a communal distribution of the sensible, a "system of self-evident facts of sense perception that [...] establishes at one and the same time something common that is shared" (7). The police order is characterized by exclusion, by saying "these people belong in these roles and have access to these activities and perceptions." In contrast, aesthetics is fundamentally political (for Rancière, the term political always involves dissenting from the consensual order of perception), as aesthetics inherently intervenes in perceptions—it changes the distribution of the sensible. Aesthetic practices are "forms of visibility," "'ways of doing and making' that intervene in the general distribution of ways of doing and making as well as in the relationships they maintain to modes of being and forms of visibility" (8). Rancière, therefore, sees the relationship between aesthetics and politics specifically in terms of perspective: literature is aesthetic (and political) in terms of how it handles perspective, the degree to which it intervenes in consensual distributions of the sensible and replaces them with an alternative regime of perception. This shifts the grounds of the conversation about the politics of literature from the question of representation (whose works do we read? How do we give access to literature to marginalized subjects?) to questions of literary form, how those perspectives are embodied in the language of the text itself.[2] Rancière's argument significantly alters prevailing Foucauldian assumptions about power in narration, particularly those such as D.A. Miller makes in *The Novel and the Police* (1988). Miller argues that omniscient narration and free indirect discourse form a disciplinary regime of narration that accustoms the reader to the intrusive gaze of a hegemonic power structure. The omniscient narrator, "never identified with a *person*, [...] a faceless and multilateral regard" (24), is the panopticon, accustoming the reader to the all-seeing disciplinary gaze of social authority. However, in this chapter I am troubling the hierarchical distinction between author, narrator, and character that this argument relies on, and Rancière's alignment of aesthetics with a disruption of the police order similarly questions Foucauldian assumptions about narration.

At issue in the form of narrative perspective, then, is narrative authority: who shapes the reader's perceptions and how does the text model that shaping of perspective? Perhaps Rancière's most frequently used example of non-hierarchical perspective is Gustave Flaubert, who introduced many of the stylistic traits now associated with third-person narration, from free indirect discourse to the removal of authorial commentary, allowing characters to "speak for themselves," so to speak. Rancière sees this as a "democratization" of style, as older canons of good writing insisted on a hierarchy of different styles for different subjects (a system classically referred to as "decorum"). According to Rancière, "The system of decorum that governed representative fiction [...] rested on a determinate set of ideas about how a given situation should produce a given feeling" (*Mute Speech* 116) and Flaubert's style frees things from that "regime of signification" (*Mute Speech* 117). The old system of decorum created a hierarchy of the sensible (which in turn translates into hierarchical social forms), but by insisting on a non-hierarchical perspective in his fiction, where the markers of social importance are removed and instead any character may be given voice with any style, Flaubert begins to move us toward a non-hierarchical style (and a non-hierarchical way of perceiving the world). Timothy Bewes, who also extensively uses Rancière as the basis of his argument about free indirect style, sees the goal here as "producing an utterance that is devoid of hierarchy, any privileging of one sense or perspective over another; an utterance in which all normative values or orienting ideologies are merely latent or ineffective" ("Free Indirect"). It is not enough to simply have a protagonist from an underrepresented group; instead writers must find a means of representation that frees up the ability to perceive subjects without placing them in a sensible hierarchy. Bewes and Rancière both seem to argue that free indirect discourse (and more broadly a third-person perspective closely limited by what a character sees) are ways of moving toward this ideal of a narrative voice "devoid of hierarchy" "when visibility will be distributed equitably" (Bewes).

However, does epic fantasy actually creates this narrative voice "devoid of hierarchy"? Even Ursula Le Guin, an anarchist who values individual identity over consensus perceptual regimes, in her concerns about style in "From Elfland to Poughkeepsie," seems to suggest a return to the classical system of decorum. Her essay objects to what she calls the "Poughkeepsie style," dialogue that seems like it could come from our everyday world if we simply changed a few superficial plot markers. The gist of this objection sounds much like a system of decorum: the "tone as a whole is profoundly inappropriate to the subject. [...] A language intended to express the immediate and the trivial is applied to the remote and elemental. The result, of course, is a mess" (89). Le Guin does not object to this mundane style on its own terms but on the basis of its being "inappropriate" in context. Farah Mendlesohn takes this even further, suggesting that the fundamental narrative style of the portal-quest fantasy is built on what we might call, via Rancière, a hierarchical consensual perceptual regime. Drawing on John Clute's arguments, she sees the foundation of the narrative style of portal-quest fantasy as the "Club Story," which she defines as "a tale or tales recounted orally to a group of listeners foregathered in a venue safe from interruption" (4). The Club Story has as its roots the exclusive men's clubs particularly common in the Victorian era, and as a result she sees this narration as picking up the same exclusion as that social milieu, as the narrative voice is "an assertion of a particular type of Victorian masculinity, a private place uninterrupted by the needs of domesticity or even self-care (there are always servants in the club), combined with a stature signaled by the single-voiced and impervious authority" (6). According to Mendlesohn, the narrator's authority is unquestioned and unquestionable, which is necessary for establishing the believability of the imaginary world, and it gives a sense of completion (as it recounts a tale that has happened in the past), and thus it is universal, pure, and reliable, not allowing for discourse or polysemy. For Mendlesohn, this sense of authority (via Rancière, we might call this a police regime) is fundamental to portal-quest fantasy: "the modern portal-quest narratives are hierarchical: some characters are presented with greater authority than others […] and this hierarchy is frequently encoded in speech patterns and the choice of direct or indirect speech" (6). In other words, Mendlesohn gives voice to a common argument about epic fantasy—that it is conservative, reactionary, perhaps even racist, sexist, and/or classist—but she does so using the *form*, specifically the narrative perspective that she links to a classical system of decorum.

Mendlesohn properly identifies the key issue in narrative voice being one of authority, but I believe she incorrectly generalizes how narration works in epic fantasy because she perpetuates a theoretical hierarchy, that of author-narrator-character. Too often, narrative theory personifies characters and narrators as subjects in a hierarchical relationship with authors, with diminishing levels of agency and authority, an assumption that has significant consequences for our theoretical assumptions about a text's ability to construct social forms and disrupt hierarchy. Susan Lanser, whose book on narrative voice extensively considers the issue of authority, places the point-of-view character (or focalized narration) at the bottom of the hierarchy of narrative authority, as everything that a character thinks is limited to a single perspective. However, at the same time, she acknowledges that "Even when the narrator adopts some of the character's vocabulary or register, dual perspective discourse is the narrator's rather than the character's text" (Lanser 142). In other words, in third-person narration, the roles blend rather than maintaining a rigid separation. This becomes even more evident when considering the common critical description of certain third-person narration as "omniscient." Contemporary narrative theory has begun to question whether the anthropomorphized figure of an "omniscient narrator" is even a useful concept. Richard Walsh, for instance, has questioned the need to posit the narrator as a character with omniscient access to everything in the story world: "there is nothing about the internal logic of fictional representation that demands a qualitative distinction between narrators and characters" (72). In fact, in narratives that are "impersonally narrated" (such as *Mrs. Dalloway*) or "authorially narrated" (including much eighteenth- and nineteenth-century fiction, such as *Middlemarch*), Walsh suggests that we need make no distinction between author and narrator: "'Omniscience,' I would suggest, is not a faculty possessed by a certain class of narrators but, precisely, a quality of authorial imagination. [...] the reader is not obliged to hypothesize a narrator who really is omniscient in order to naturalize the authorial imaginative act" (73). Thus, unless the narrator is a character within the story (i.e., a homodiegetic narrator, which is typically only the case in first-person narration), this distinction between focalized character and authorial narrator is potentially misleading. The narrator *is* the author. Jonathan Culler has effectively spelled out the consequences of our insistence on referring to narrative omniscience, namely that it misleads us from perhaps more crucial issues: by imagining a narrator relating a story, we overlook the artistic choices made in creating that story: "Rather than translate novels into stories that are reported by someone, we should, I suggest, try to work with other alternatives (whether telepathic transmission, a reporting instance, etc.) that allow us to focus on the art with which these details have been imagined" (Culler 30). To place this in the context of Rancière's theories, if we can erase the distinction between authors and narrators, we may have a more "democratic" narration that shows language as an intervention in perception (the creation of a world through artistic choices) rather than a description of a fixed hierarchy (a god-like, omniscient overlord).

Thus, I disagree with Mendlesohn's conclusions about narrative hierarchy in epic fantasy because I disagree with her insistence on personifying a narrator that relates the story, as in the following passage:

> There are almost always two clearly identifiable narrators in the portal-quest fantasy: the narrator of the microcosm (the world within a world) that we call the point of view character; and the narrator of the macrocosm, she who "stories" the world for us, making sense of it through the downloaded histories so common to this form of fantasy, or in the fragments of prophecy she leaks to us throughout the course of the text. Usually, but not always, this person is the implied narrator [8].

It is misleading to think of the character as separate or independent from the one who "stories the world for us." Narrative authority always still belongs to the third-person narrator, whose responsibility it is to indicate whether or not a particular point of view is trustworthy.[3] Seeing this as a hierarchical relationship leads Mendlesohn to conclude that the point-of-view character (and therefore the reader who rides along with her) has no agency in a world that is presented as already fixed and finished: "we ride with the point of view character [...] as if we are both with her and yet external to the fantasy world" (8), and by giving us this travelogue of the world, "the hero *moves through* the action and the world stage, embedding an assumption of unchangingness on the part of the indigenes" (9). Thus, if we see the author-narrator-character hierarchy as discreet and unchallenged, we forget the contingent, constructed nature of the fantasy world, the authorial agency in creating that world.

Certainly, some writers of epic fantasy may prioritize the formation of a convincing fantasy world to the extent that they present a static, finished structure that denies its crafted nature and the authorial agency that implies. However, I would suggest that such texts work counter to the affordances of a genre that so strongly emphasizes created worlds. The question should not be whether or not the author establishes narrative authority (indeed, all third-person narration does to one extent or another), but what creative choices in the use of that narration shape the storyworld, and those choices are likely to vary by author. Epic fantasy potentially offers much to narrative theory by assisting it in breaking out of the hierarchical regime of storytelling. This is similar to what Culler is seeking in his critique of the term "omniscience." Rather than thinking of narration purely in terms of knowledge (as the term "omniscience" implies), Culler playfully suggests we use the word "omnipotence": "the power to decide what will be the case in this world is a product of a conventional performative power of language, or, at best, omnipotence, not omniscience" (24). Shifting the grounds from omniscience to omnipotence means shifting from questions of knowledge to questions of agency and power (albeit this does not mean abandoning knowledge, as any good Foucauldian knows that knowledge and classification are linked to power and agency). The question "who is telling this story?" is a question about subject identity, agency, power, and authority. Who has the right to tell the story? How do we classify them? How controlled are characters by authors? How much of a power hierarchy does the story exhibit? Rather than simply leveling the entire narrative structure under one particular ideology, as Mendlesohn does, we should look at how specific authorial uses of third person open up and extend our understanding of the uses of such narration.

From that standpoint, epic fantasy has a lot to say about third-person narration. As James Gifford has argued, fantasy, through depictions of magic, explicitly engages in issues of agency and subjectivity. Gifford sees this strain in fantasy as coming from the influence of anarchist writers in the early twentieth century who valued a "personal and inward turn" (72) (that is not found in the Tolkien tradition). This inward turn led to the construction of individual agency in conflict with both conservative traditionalism and the more directive utopian goals of Marxism (which is partly how Gifford accounts for Marxism's rejection of fantasy). Gifford connects this inward turn directly to fantasy's use of magic, as for instance when he discusses Jes Battis's argument about the link between magic spells and language: "the spoken word (spell/speech) operates secondary to the wilful [*sic*] subject finding a position as active agent for change in the world based on recognizing a personal interiority or self to the subject" (79). A form of language (the spell) catalyzes a performative act of reflection, even of self-creation, that distinguishes the self from consensus reality. When described in these terms, it is striking how much this foundational element of fantasy conventions parallels Rancière's argument about aesthetics as a political (dissensual) intervention into a regime of sensibility. This puts characters on the same level as authors—both create worlds using language, both level the hierarchy between authors and characters and suggest to readers the role language plays in shaping perceptions of the world. Magic allows a character to see the world differently, and writers who are sensitive to this feature of the fantasy world can potentially harness this effect within the forms of their narratives to reflect on how narrative perspective can accomplish a similar "magic." As we shall see, whether tending toward "omniscient" narration (as in the McKillip example) or a limited narration embedded in characters (as in the Abercrombie example), epic fantasy often finds in third-person narration a freedom from exclusionary hierarchical regimes of perception.

Breaking Open the Police Regime in Donaldson's "The King's Justice"

While Stephen R. Donaldson's fiction tends to use focalized narration, like McKillip he uses a limited number of narrators with more touches of omniscience than is the case in the more deeply embedded perspectives of someone like Abercrombie or Bakker, who use far more free indirect discourse. For example, in the following passage from *The Wounded Land* (1980), Donaldson focalizes the narration through Thomas Covenant but allows for observations that seem to exceed Covenant's likely knowledge base: "Covenant whirled. Grief burned like rage in him. He wanted to howl at the Despiser, What have you *done*? But both Linden and the old man were staring at him. Linden's eyes showed concern, as if she feared that he had slipped over the edge into confusion. And the old man was in the grip of a private anguish" (74). Donaldson seems to want the reader to know what everyone is feeling simultaneously, but he is constrained by Covenant's point of view, so he signals that we are still in Covenant's perspective with words like "showed" and "as if," but even these markers are absent in the final sentence, so that the reader can only assume that Covenant's knowledge of the old man's "private anguish" is speculative, based on his reading of surface cues. Nonetheless, the narration remains somewhat distanced—the narrator tells us what Covenant is thinking in indirect discourse rather than free indirect discourse. The Abercrombie passage I cited above would likely have omitted the phrase "he wanted to howl" and simply presented the thoughts "What have you done, Despiser?" in a free indirect fashion. This type of narration is typical throughout the Covenant novels, Donaldson's best known and most characteristic works, and as we saw with McKillip, it is also fairly typical of much third-person fantasy narration.

This passage closely resembles a passage by Donaldson that I discussed in Chapter 1, and while there I emphasized how this style relates to empathy, here I want to point out how this style helps us reconceptualize the "omniscience" of third-person narration. Genette called moments such as the one I cite from *The Wounded Land* "double focalization" and tried to explain them as a "'concurrence' between a "subjective' hero and the 'objective' narrator" (209), as though an omniscient narrator is stepping in to clarify what the character sees. However, what appears to be omniscience or shifting perspectives could in fact be seen in a different way. Nicholas Royle has suggested the term "telepathy" to replace omniscience, noting that knowledge of others' internal states can be attributed to some form of careful perception of the other, and that this model for narrative agency better describes what is "both thematically and structurally at work in modern fictional narratives, and calls for a quite different kind of critical storytelling than that promoted by the religious, panoptical delusion of omniscience" (261). Royle draws his metaphor from the fantastic, which should not be surprising as I have argued that seeing into others' heads is precisely the kind of affordance most readily available in fantasy, which promotes the growth of empathy. Moreover, such passages blur the lines between Covenant as a character (low on the hierarchy of agency and knowledge) and the narrator (higher on that narrative hierarchy). Covenant seems magically to take on exceptional perceptual abilities to narrate others' internal states. It hovers somewhere between a fully embedded third-person limited narration and a truly omniscient narration, largely limiting to one character but allowing a bit more freedom through that character's presumptive observations to cite the interiority of multiple characters. Thus, Donaldson illustrates in his typical practice how the most common style of epic fantasy third-person narration works to level the hierarchical distinctions implied by the authority-driven assumptions of the author-narrator-character hierarchy.

However, in "The King's Justice," Donaldson experiments with a different voice that even more overtly reveals the affordances of his typical style of narration. In that novella, an omniscient narrator freely "head hops" from character to character in a way much more like what Virginia Woolf does in *Mrs. Dalloway* than what Donaldson does in most of his other fiction. Donaldson has explained that he chose this voice partly because he dislikes omniscient and present-tense narration, both of which he uses in this story, presumably as a narrative challenge (Donaldson, personal interview). Thus, early in the story, Donaldson describes his protagonist, Black, with sentences like the following: "Shrouded by the deluge and covered by his dark gear, he looks as black as the coming night—a look that suits him, though he does not think about such things. Having come so far on his journey, and on many others, he hardly thinks at all as he rides" (3–4). Here the narrative voice is explicitly external, going so far as to even point out that the description of Black could not be focalized through Black himself as he "does not think about such things." As a consequence, the story frequently jumps abruptly and at times jarringly from one character to another, as when Black meets a magically gifted child and tells her mother to prevent the child from using her gifts. First, Donaldson says, "He knows now that this child *can* heal him. [...] The girl is indeed precious. But she is too young to suffer the cost of what she can see and do" (14), and then the next sentence begins, "The mother feels sudden tears in her eyes. She has been troubled for her daughter" (14). This type of abrupt jump from one perspective to another without transition is frequent throughout the story and often discouraged by writers and editors as one of the reasons to avoid the omniscient perspective. It might be tempting, then, to dismiss this story as an experimental exercise by a writer uncomfortable with the narrative voice he has chosen.

I would argue that something more interesting is happening here. Due to the conventional genre expectations about third-person limited narration, and the frequent focalization of the narration through Black (despite the passages I cited above), the character of Black often overlaps for the reader with the omniscient narrator. (Note that although I am arguing that narrative "omniscience" is better understood—particularly in this text—as "omnipotence" or "telepathy," and that distinguishing between narrator and author merely perpetuates the hierarchical model of narration that this style undermines, I will continue to use the more familiar terminology of "omniscient narration" in order to highlight how its conventional logic—and reader expectations about how it works— are unsettled by its deployment in this story.) Furthermore, Black exercises quite a bit of agency within the story, observing and intuiting details he has no direct knowledge of (as part of his law enforcement role as the

King's Justice), often magically coercing characters into reveries and expositional narrations and even actions—acting in many ways as the author or narrator of the story. That is to say, the narrative voice (at least as experienced while reading) is not purely omniscient, but a quasi-meta-narrative voice that mixes authorial and character control, breaking down the hierarchical distinction between the authority of author and characters, and between "major" characters (like Black) and minor characters (like the girl's mother). The use of the omniscient narration in the story makes visible the authorial manipulation of the third-person point of view, the *shaping* of narrative (the word for wizards in this world is Shapers), in a way that gets to the heart of what Donaldson's third-person limited voice has always been about: the leveling of distinctions and humanistic valuing of diverse voices, a rejection of the exclusionary practices of what Rancière would call the police order.

I would therefore describe Black as a "writerly narrator," a term I am adapting from Roland Barthes' influential distinction between "writerly" and "readerly" texts. Barthes makes this distinction in order to separate two broad categories of texts: what we might think of as reader-friendly (readerly) which make few demands on the reader and can be enjoyed as finished, coherent works without any reader involvement, and writerly texts that require reader engagement to construct an understanding of what is happening in the text, to write (or re-write) the text for oneself. (We may think of writerly texts as those like James Joyce's *Ulysses* or Thomas Pynchon's *Gravity's Rainbow*, which require far more reader involvement to connect the dots, so to speak, than Jane Austen's *Pride and Prejudice* or George Eliot's *Middlemarch*.) According to Barthes, readerly texts are problematic because they "divorce" the producer of the text from its consumer (in other words, their model of art is too hierarchical), and thus the reader is merely passive: without "gaining access to the magic of the signifier, to the pleasure of writing, [the reader] is left with no more than the poor freedom either to accept or reject the text" (4). Note that the issue here for Barthes is one of agency—freedom—does the text grant freedom to the reader or not? On the other hand, the writerly text "make[s] the reader no longer a consumer, but a producer of the text" (4). By extension, though, we could also consider whether narration allows such freedom to its characters. While obviously characters cannot literally shape the text they are in, is it possible to write a text in which the characters' voices become "writerly," where they appear as producers of the text, breaking down the distinction between producer and product? While perhaps this can obviously be done through metafiction, a more interesting version of this question might ask whether we can do this without metafiction, still allowing the characters to be fictional characters? I would contend that

Black is just such a narrator, or at least that he gestures toward the possibility of such narrative freedom. In making this claim, I must clarify that epic fantasy texts like "The King's Justice" would largely be categorized by Barthes as readerly, but I am arguing that by containing narration and characters with a writerly quality, the text is still degrading that hierarchical separation, just in a different fashion from what Barthes describes. The text is manifesting the link between magical plot actions and the production of text.

Black's writerly features are numerous. Even the story's present tense narration supports this reading, as Barthes suggests that the temporality of the writerly text is a "perpetual present" (5), by which he means that the text always feels (to the reader) like it is in the process of being produced as it is being read and not that it has been "plasticized by a singular system" (5) at the time of writing, which occurs prior to the reader's access to the text. The use of present tense narration supports this feeling of a story in process, being created in front of us, and Black's role as not just a directed product of that text but a free producer is suggested from the very first paragraph. As Donaldson describes the rain Black rides through, we are told, "Ahead it blinds him [Black] to the road's future. But he is not concerned. He knows where he is going" (3). This, of course, literally only speaks of his immediate destination, the town of Settle's Crossways, but the passage invokes the tropes of life (or story) as journey and twists the epic opening of Dante's Divine Comedy (where Dante begins lost in a dark wood "midway on life's journey") to suggest a larger sense of control which contrasts sharply to the feeling of a contingent, unfolding present. Black is not the wandering sinner but the godlike creator.

Beyond this teleological temporality that suggests Black shapes his own future (an idea I will return to), Black also takes a strong narratorial role by his manipulation of the other characters. In plot terms, this is a part of the magic he has been given by the king, who has engraved his body with sigils which Black can touch to call upon power to shape the actions of those around him. While Black uses these powers in the service of solving the mystery of a child's murder in the town, he often does so by spurring the townsfolk to narrate their experiences. Certainly, the interrogative narrative structure comes from the story's detective fiction elements, and we could read this as an act of policing, a disciplinary intrusion supporting a hierarchy. However, while Black's interactions with the townsfolk develop over the course of the story, even from an early stage in the narrative, his narratorial interactions suggest his ability to project himself into other characters' minds, an act of empathy, not just an act of control. For instance, when questioning Jon Marker, the man whose child has died, Black demonstrates an ability to "head hop" much like an omniscient narrator. Marker tells Black about the death of his wife and his attempts to raise his son, Tamlin, alone. When he pauses, Black says, "Your love was enough. You saved him. His love saved you. Tell me" (26). Black here suggests an ability to narrate Marker's inner life that goes beyond the facts Marker has given him, an act of empathy rather than magic. Yet his demand "Tell me," repeated multiple times throughout this section, prompts Marker to *narrate* his story (not simply to answer questions). Similarly, Black orders exposition from a tavern's patrons earlier in the story and from the caravan leader Blossom later in the story. Blossom's narration in particular sounds much more like a narrative voice than like naturalistic dialogue, as when she gives Black (and the reader) the first description of the murderer, the sorcerer Sought: "Altogether he resembled a hierophant who had given his life to the worship of a desert god" (66). Just as Black sees into Jon Marker, Blossom sees into Sought and is able to speculate about his interiority based on exterior evidence. It is a moment of omniscience-tinged narration from a character, which has been ordered by a character who has in many ways been serving as an author-substitute within the story. Black is able to order omniscient narration from Blossom just as Donaldson does from Black.

Thus, the story is structured through much of its length as a series of expositional reveries demanded by Black. I should note here that this is much like the structure that Mendlesohn describes as typical of the portal-quest fantasy. Mendlesohn argues that, in response to the high level of superficial visual detail demanded by fantasy world building most authors counterbalance this externality by revealing characters through a strategy she calls "the *reverie*," which she defines as "that moment when the protagonist [...] meditates on his own character" (9). This is precisely what is happening in "The King's Justice," with one caveat: reveries or flashbacks in this story are not demanded by an omniscient narrator but by a character (Black) acting as the omniscient narrator would. This should make an enormous difference to how we evaluate the significance of this narrative structure, as Mendlesohn's conclusion is that portal-quest fantasy, through its focus on the visual, essentially causes the text to resort to stereotype (we judge characters by appearances),[4] and a rigid denial of polysemous interpretation. Yet by incorporating the "omniscient" narrator within the text in the form of Black, Donaldson enables an effective answer to these assumptions about epic fantasy narration. Black reveals this activity of seeing into someone else's interior not as an act of stereotyping or rigid categorization but as an act of observation and imaginative empathy. Black enables Blossom and Jon Marker (and others) to tell *their* stories in *their* words, just as Donaldson as the true omnipotent narrator of the story enables Black to do the same. Seeing this type of narration as a creative choice—an aspect of agency—rather than an external limitation mandated on the text, truly does open up the text by dramatizing a much more "writerly" role.

Black continually dramatizes narration as an act of creative imaginative projection. For instance, when he investigates the deaths of a band of brigands in the forest, Black gives us a retrospective reverie of a scene he did not *see* but only imaginatively experienced through observation: "The crime is old, but its age does not prevent him from *imagining the scene*" (37, emphasis added). The passage continues with a full paragraph "flashback" to what happened when they were attacked. Furthermore, Black's narrative manipulation of the world around him often takes the form of identifying other characters' needs and attempting to meet them. For instance, Black identifies that Arbor, the girl with the healing gift, has a need to exercise her healing, and that Jon Marker has a need to be healed, and thus he suggests to Arbor's mother Rose that "It would be a great kindness to befriend him" (59). Black's agency thus extends beyond narration and interiority into designing—plotting—the exterior actions of the characters around him. Black in many ways serves as the diegetic proxy for the omniscient/omnipotent narrator.

However, despite Black taking on these narratorial roles, he is clearly *not* the narrator of the story. In fact, the narrative frequently head hops to characters other than Black. Nonetheless, the reader will likely often read these perspectival excursions as still being focalized through Black, first because the most familiar conventions of epic fantasy involve such third-person limited narration, and second because Black's exceptional observational skills often make the apparent point-of-view shift explainable as observational deduction. For instance, the first significant deviation from Black's perspective occurs as he approaches the town and encounters a group of guards. Immediately prior to this shift, the reader is given a series of observations about the town that are marked as focalized through Black but which extend insights into the town beyond Black's immediate knowledge: "*This tells Black* that Settle's Crossways is indeed prosperous" (6, emphasis added), and "[the guards'] presence *tells Black* that Settle's Crossways is now anxious despite its habit of welcome" (6–7, emphasis added). In the context of Black's insightful observations, the following apparent perspectival shift occurs: "The guards watch Black suspiciously as he approaches, but their suspicion is only in part because he is a stranger who comes at dusk. They are also suspicious of themselves because they are unfamiliar with the use of weapons" (7). The point of view here is ambiguous: it could be that the omniscient narrator has jumped into the guards' heads to tell us why they are suspicious. However, in context, I would argue that most readers would not notice this as a point-of-view shift and instead assume that Black is observing how they hold themselves, how they are dressed, and making deductions based on the situation.[5] If that is the case, this is a definitive example of narration as "telepathy" rather than "omniscience," which in this case clearly explains narration in terms of imaginative empathy, using the external cues to transcend physical limitations and see inside other people. While the narration gives a direct description of their interiority, Black could possibly know (or deduce) the facts about the guards, and the magical fantasy context makes this "telepathic" quality of narration even more visible. Such perspectival ambiguity is frequent throughout the story, and as a result, Black experientially feels like the focal character even when the narration is omniscient. This instability breaks down the boundaries between characters, suggesting rather than a hierarchy of knowledge a free passage of information between them.

Yet Black remains a human character and thus limited in his knowledge, not a metafictional proxy author. Instead, features of metafictional narrator and even allegorical narrator collide in this text, unsettling the distinction between author and character. As a character, he is frequently limited in what he sees and even incorrect in some of his assumptions. At one point, while he examines the scene of a crime, he even narrates aloud, "unaware that he speaks aloud" (31). Donaldson the omnipotent narrator makes him speak much as he makes the other characters speak. The narration also at times explicitly departs from Black's sphere of knowledge. After he tells Rose to befriend Jon Marker, he leaves her, and we are told, "Rose follows the stranger with her eyes until she loses sight of him. She hardly feels Arbor tug at her hand. She hardly hears her daughter" (60). Clearly, he is unaware of the exchange between Rose and Arbor if he is out of sight of them, and this passage illustrates how the story continually insists on the limitations of characters' knowledge, as Rose herself is "hardly" aware of her daughter, just as when the narrative jumps back to Black, Donaldson writes, "*She does not know* that Black has already put her from his mind" (60, emphasis added). In fact, at this point, near the middle of the story, Donaldson returns to the road metaphor from the first paragraph to emphasize how Black's formerly godlike view of the future is becoming increasingly limited, as he is now "traveling a road to a destination he cannot see" (60). This insistence upon limited knowledge contrasts sharply with the godlike narratorial control seen elsewhere in the story. Again, this blurs the lines rather than establishing a clear hierarchy. Despite Black's occasional godlike narratorial abilities, he is a human, a character in the story, and as such this shifts his role from the all-seeing disciplinary eye to the empathic participant who shares experience with others. In other words, in this story we can see Donaldson shifting the grounds of narration from the omniscient perspective to a character—god becomes a human, but a human with agency and choice, a wider perspective that allows a wider range of action in the world.

This is why I refer to Donaldson's use of third person narration as humanistic. The power of individual choice is a repeated theme in his fiction, as he shows in the concept of "the necessity of freedom" that recurs with so much importance in the Thomas Covenant books. In that series, the Creator of the Land cannot intervene in its workings and instead must rely on Covenant as a free agent outside of its laws to fix its problems. Christine Brawley argues that "the power of choice, free will" is "essential for the condition of being human" in Donaldson's fiction (84). Thus, this blurring of hierarchical lines and providing agency to all individuals is a defining feature of Donaldson's work and, it would seem, a condition of social reclamation for him. I would suggest that third-person narration with its touches of omniscience is the narrative form taken by the freedom and agency Donaldson wants for his characters. This plays out dramatically in "The King's Justice" through Black's character arc, as he begins as a nearly godlike abstraction, almost an allegorical figure embodying Justice and the police order, and he must be increasingly humanized (without losing his agency) across the narrative.

Black's character arc is crucial to this humanizing of the narration. His title, "King's Justice," suggests an allegorical role: he does not think about things until they demand his attention, and he refuses to dwell on the past. All of these features suggest a flat character who represents an unchanging verity. Perhaps initially, this would seem to account for the distant narration. Yet as he interacts with the people of the town, Black becomes more human, shows increasing uncertainty, and increasingly empathizes. At the climax of the story, Black's narratorial control seems to fade. At the conclusion of his final confrontation with Sought, Black exerts himself to a degree that he expects to be fatal. Here the scene ends with what sounds like the story's last lines: "Black smiles for the last time. But this smile threatens no one. It is glad and grateful, and it is all that he has left. When he falls himself, slumping into the embrace of dark and bright beside the fissure, he is not afraid" (102). While this sounds like the final lines as a solitary hero comes to peace with himself, the story continues and reveals that these assumptions are incorrect as Black survives. In fact, the next section begins by emphasizing the limitations of Black's knowledge: "He does not know that time passes. He does not know how long he is unconscious" (102). He awakens in a bed, uncertain how he has survived, knowing only vaguely that "Someone has cared for him" (103). In this context, we can look back at those final lines of his climactic battle and realize that the plot resolution they suggest—"Black smiles for the *last* time"—is

Black's narrativization of events. This is the teleological perspective Black has claimed for himself since the beginning of the story, the ability to see the future. Yet here Black's ability to see the future is compromised; the narrative he creates for himself ends but his life continues. Moreover, his life continues precisely because of the actions of other individuals acting *outside* of his agency (but not outside his sphere of influence).

In a final act of retrospective narration, the priest of darkness tells Black "how you came to be here" (107). However, he tells the story not under compulsion (as so many other characters have), but because "I have no other gift to give" (107). The word "gift" implies free choice, but also one made in acknowledgment of some form of social debt or obligation. (Jon Marker also narrates here out of a feeling that "he is in Black's debt" and "owes Black some acknowledgement" [109].) The story of how Black's life is saved is also the result of free individuals acting in ways that are the consequences of their earlier interactions with Black: Blossom the merchant goes out of her way to find his body and deliver him to the priest, Rose is present because the priest was introducing her to Jon Marker as Black instructed, and her daughter uses her healing magic to heal Black. Black's actions earlier in the story have enabled a community to form a support system that re-writes the tragic-heroic ending that he wrote for himself, once again blurring the line between who has the author-creator power and who is simply a character. Black's "characters" break free of his narration. Acting as agents of their own narration here cements this free role, and in this final section, the narration jumps rapidly between characters but no longer seems motivated by Black's knowledge and narrative needs. Instead, we see other characters "reading" Black as Black "read" them earlier in the story: Father Tenderson, the priest, "does not understand what has transpired. He has imagined—But he sees Black relaxing. After a moment, he is sure that Black now breathes more easily. Black's faith is stronger than the priest's" (106). This is one of the first times in the story that another character "sees into" Black the way he has been seeing into them. The final line above, like much of Black's narration, seems to be focalized through the priest but imparts information about Black's interiority. Thus, if Black has been taking on the role of omniscience or telepathy throughout the story, at its climax that role is shared out to the other characters, suggesting that this empathic group connection is an affordance of the third-person narrator's role, not a power portioned off to an elite few.

In this final section, the frequent leaping between characters has finally revealed its true purpose. Now no longer an exercise of power, it is an act of social connection and empathy. In the final pages, point of view changes with almost every paragraph, but it is no longer motivated by Black's needs, just as his actions are no longer motivated by the hierarchical demands of the King's Justice—he *chooses* to return to his role serving the King because "He needs his purpose as much as it needs him" (113). All of the characters are placed on an equal footing as the narrative style is revealed as based on freedom, agency, and choice. For Donaldson, "omniscient" third-person narration is not an exercise in godlike hierarchy but a diffusion of power and a sharing of interiority between characters enabling greater social cohesion. Black declares his independence from his king (while still choosing to serve him) and from his author (while still serving as a character in a story).[6] The omniscient narrator becomes a character (Black) to give that character agency "independent" of the author or reader. To read the story in this way is to read the entire story as a literalized metaphor of how narration works, with the goal of creating a narrative voice devoid of hierarchy.

Third-Person Narration and Programmed Subjectivity

Whereas for Donaldson, human subjectivity is defined by choice and agency, R. Scott Bakker, an author of epic fantasy with a degree in philosophy and an interest in neuroscience, sees matters quite differently. Bakker's thought is best characterized by his Blind Brain Theory (BBT), which posits that "Conscious metacognition is not only blind to the actual structure of experience and cognition, it is blind to this blindness" (Krašovec and Bauer). Put more informally, your brain is not conscious of how it works, nor are you typically aware that you lack such awareness. This theory therefore questions the concept of intentionality. According to BBT, intentionality (and therefore agency) is an illusion the brain creates. Desire and will are programmed into the neurons of the brain, not a property possessed by some immaterial subject or soul. Ultimately, when Bakker discusses consciousness, he frequently discusses "programming" and "button pushing," most of which happens below the threshold of awareness.[7] Bakker is primarily concerned with the ease with which these buttons may be pushed, and therefore the extent to which behavior can be mechanistically programmed by outside actors. A simple example would be the bots that select YouTube videos to recommend or advertisements to put on a Facebook page. These bots use trial-and-error algorithms to find the most likely combination to stimulate the desired response (in this case, clicking on the suggested link), and, perhaps most importantly, while bots have been created to facilitate advertising, the bots themselves are a self-evolving artificial intelligence that acts without agency to push buttons in human subjects. Thus, an entire system of semantic meaning-making is shaped without agency or conscious choice. Bakker would contend that, ultimately, this is how all human society functions. Thus, when he describes something like what I have been calling "empathy" (the ability to "see into" another's brain, to see as they see), he describes it in this way: "What I am doing is cueing an assumption on your part which you report, which cues an assumption on my part and back and forth and so on. There is no actual peering into one another's brains, what we are doing is simply working through a kind of social algorithm where you're one half and I'm the other half" (Krašovec and Bauer). Nonetheless, despite Bakker's perhaps pessimistic use of words like "programming" or "social algorithm," something like "empathy" does occur, it is crucially based on perspective, and it fills an important role in the "programming" of brains.

In other words—to connect Bakker's philosophy to his aesthetic practice—if consciousness is a matter of programming, then literature can be an engine for programming perspectives in the "right" ways. (I am bracketing the issue of how, within Bakker's system, we determine what the "right" ways are.) In "The Skeptical Fantasist: In Defense of an Oxymoron" (2006), an essay published while he was still developing the BBT, Bakker addressed the question of why a skeptical materialist such as him would choose to write in such an "unscientific" genre as epic fantasy. His answer is, essentially, evangelical. He argues that mainstream literary fiction is largely written to a social group that already has scientific literacy and values critical thinking, while genre fantasy tends to be popular with a wider range of readers, including many who would be resistant to empirical worldviews, such as "religious literalists" who "have an affinity for anthropomorphic worldviews. They love fantasy" (37). Clearly Bakker makes a number of problematic assumptions: his argument has its own form of elitism, he blatantly stereotypes the audience of epic fantasy without providing empirical proof, and he fails to recognize that many religious fundamentalists are suspicious of fantasy and would never approve of his brand of gory, dark fantasy. Setting aside these problems, though, we may note that his reasoning here resembles his description of empathy above. He argues that entering a conversation requires a common ground, some form of consensus-building: "We cannot honestly debate beliefs we do not think debatable—it really is as simple as that. And this makes the prospect of reaching rational consensus between disparate believers [...] all but impossible" (35). Fantasy, therefore, becomes an algorithm for establishing common ground before introducing new concepts to an audience; it is "an opportunity to speak out, to use the frequency of shared interests to communicate different values, different perspectives, to people engaged in their own ingrown conversation" (37). Thus, Bakker writes fantasy in order to re-shape perspectives, finding a social algorithm that has enough consistency to sway his audience to consensus with the kind of skeptical critical thinking that he believes is most valuable for human behavior.

If writing fantasy is all about shaping perspective, then we may expect that his use of perspective in the Prince of Nothing trilogy will demonstrate just the sort of "interpretative pluralism" (38) that he calls for in this essay. Thus, he uses the same type of third-person limited perspective rapidly shifting between focalized narrators as so many contemporary fantasists use. However, with Bakker, the changes in focal point happen much more rapidly than is typically the case, often with several different shifts of narrator per chapter, a narrative approach found more often in epic fantasy than in other narrative forms (Erikson and Esslemont, for instance, use similarly frequent shifts in narration in the Malazan books). Certainly, this style of narration could be attributed to the world building of epic fantasy: having many different voices gives readers a broader perspectival map of the narrative world. However, Bakker's heightened use of third-person limited narration functions much like Donaldson's quasi-omniscient third person (if for different reasons) by breaking down barriers between characters and blurring the lines between narrative omniscience (which appears in some passages in Bakker's trilogy) and the consciousness of various characters. Ultimately, if all consciousness is the result of programming and button pushing (and characters in fiction are all programmed by the author), then they are all in the same boat and share the same access to these algorithms, regardless of their place in the social hierarchy. In a sense, all perspectives are the same perspective, and they are all the author, as they are all the result of social programming. As a result, characters are constantly "reading" each other, narrating the interiority of others "telepathically" in ways that blur boundaries. However, whereas in Donaldson the outcome of this effect was an optimistic impression of human agency and choice, here what the characters share is a negative knowledge, the lack of control and self-awareness that Bakker sees as the foundation of human subjectivity.

While examples of this style of narration appear throughout Bakker's trilogy (and its sequel, the four-book Aspect-Emperor series), I will focus on the final volume of the original trilogy, *The Thousandfold Thought*, which includes a number of particularly useful examples. The Prince of Nothing trilogy overall tells the story of a holy war clearly modeled on the Crusades. The Inrithi (a religious group comparable to the medieval Catholic Church in its religious and political power) form an army to liberate the sacred city of Shimeh from the pagan Fanim hordes. However, the holy war gets hijacked by a man named Kellhus, a monk from an isolated sect called the Dûnyain who have trained him for total rational control of himself and his surroundings. Kellhus is, in a sense, the programmer and button-pusher, able to read and identify the motives of those around him and shape their behavior. Kellhus turns himself into a messianic figure for the holy war, the warrior-prophet, and uses the army to allow him to infiltrate Fanim territory to confront his father Moënghus, who has been using his own Dûnyain training to manipulate events throughout the world for years. (In fact, it is revealed that Moënghus essentially staged the entire holy war to bring Kellhus to him.) On a plot level, the series is clearly filled with examples of people having their thoughts "programmed" for them, and any narrative focalized through Kellhus is likely to have that quasi-omniscient quality as Kellhus "reads" the other characters. While Kellhus and his father provide perhaps the most obvious examples, another good example can be found in Achamian, the sorcerer who travels with Kellhus, befriends him, and ultimately recognizes him as the forerunner of the Second Apocalypse that his order (the Mandate) has been dreading for centuries. The Mandate's founder, a sorcerer named Seswatha, fought in the first Apocalypse. In order to ensure that the Mandate did not lose their urgency in preparing for the Second Apocalypse, Seswatha created a sorcerous ritual that transfers his memories of the Apocalypse to the Mandate sorcerers, who have nightmares based on Seswatha's memories every night. This sort of detail dramatizes Bakker's central concept of subjectivity, as it suggests that the extent to which the Mandate sorcerers want or desire to fight the Second Apocalypse is "programmed" into them by Seswatha's memories.

However, these boundaries between characters are erased not just on the level of plot but on the level of style through Bakker's use of perspective. First, Bakker frequently makes the characters' lack of self-awareness—the "blindness" of their brains—evident in their narration. For instance, when Sompas, one of the holy war's generals, kills a sorcerer while being mentally manipulated, the passage focalized through Sompas begins as follows: "When the sorcerer slipped away to relieve himself, Sompas found himself joining him. He was not quite willing things to happen anymore—they just … happened. *I have no choice*" (270–1). In the course of a few sentences, the narration gradually pushes inward, starting with a relatively distant third-person perspective, shifting to free indirect discourse (the ellipsis in "they just … happened" suggests Sompas' mind searching for a word), to direct discourse (the final sentence in first person, delivered in italics to indicate it is a voice other than the narrator's). Ironically, this transition to interiority is contrasted by the content of the passage, which denies Sompas' agency. The more deeply the narration embeds in his perspective, the less control Sompas has; instead his behavior is portrayed as automated. Similarly, Sompas' killing of the sorcerer is described as follows: "It had quite possessed a soul of its own. Rising and falling with nary a glimmer. Such a naughty knife. Sompas cleaned it on the twitching man's leggings, then joined his men, his glorious Kidruhil, about the fire. Them he could trust to understand—enough of them, anyway. But a sorcerer? Please. He had no choice. It simply *had* to happen" (271). Overall, two features of this entire scene are particularly characteristic of how narration throughout the book presents this programmed automatism. For one, the central action is elided and described after the fact ("it *had quite possessed* a soul of its own"), as though the knife strikes so fast that it happens without conscious thought. Sompas does not cognize the killing until after it has happened and consequently Bakker does not even provide a sentence describing the moment of action. Second, the passage begins with the sentence construction "Sompas found himself," also implying action that happens automatically that is only cognized after the fact. Bakker uses this construction—"found himself" or "found herself"—with unusual frequency. It appears 91 times just in *The Thousandfold Thought*. By way of comparison, Abercrombie's *The Blade Itself* uses that construction just 14 times; Steven Erikson's *Forge of Darkness* just 17 times; and Ian C. Esslemont's *Assail* a mere 11 times. Each of those books is substantially longer than *The Thousandfold Thought* (which is around 150,000 words; Abercrombie, the shortest of the three comparative examples, is over 190,000). In fact, in my brief survey, the only book I was able to find with a comparable total is Brandon Sanderson's *The Way of Kings*, which uses the "found him/herself" construction 89 times in a novel that is over twice as long (395,000 words). Bakker's characters are constantly becoming aware of their actions after they have taken them, to a degree that far exceeds the agency other writers attribute to their characters.

Yet regardless of these differences in assumptions about agency, Bakker's use of third-person narration is often quite similar to Donaldson's—despite the limited perspective (and ironically despite the lack of *self*-knowledge), his characters frequently claim knowledge of the interiority of the other characters. The barbarian Cnaiür illustrates this in a war council scene early in the third book. This passage is filled with the internal politics of the holy war, as Conphas, one of its leading generals, is being chastised for his failure to participate in previous battles. Cnaiür does not join in the conversation but nonetheless serves as the focal narrator. Bakker indicates fairly clearly that we are limited by Cnaiür's knowledge in passages like, "At first the answer escaped Cnaiür" (50). While much of the passage is constrained to factual descriptions of Conphas, Cnaiür (presumably) offers subjective commentary after a description of Conphas' appearance, "Among all those assembled, he alone seemed unmarked, unscarred, as though mere days had passed since [the Council that started the war]" (50). The source of the word "seemed" is unclear—while it may be that this description is simply Cnaiür's interpretation, he seems to be putting into words the feelings of the entire council in its hostile response to Conphas, but it is still expressed only as *Cnaiür's* observation. This telepathic narration continues throughout the scene, as when "It seemed that Conphas sensed, for perhaps the first time, the impossible dimensions of the Dûnyain's authority over the men surrounding him" (51). While the perfunctory "it seemed" still clearly embeds us in a limited perspective, this passage otherwise reads like an omniscient narration that is able to telepathically register everything happening in Conphas' head. (How exactly does Cnaiür derive this complex realization of Conphas' from observing external, visual evidence?) In terms of narrative authority, the passage gives no reason to doubt Cnaiür's assessment of what Conphas thinks here. This pattern continues, as, despite frequent reminders that we are in Cnaiür's point of view, many phrases exceed the authority of that limitation, such as "The Warrior-Prophet nodded sceptically [sic]" (51) (is a "skeptical" nod visibly different externally?) and "The sound of weeping filled the room, the weeping of other men who'd recognized themselves in the Warrior-Prophet's words" (52) (the contraction is suggestive of free indirect discourse, but the sentence insists that Cnaiür knows what is happening in their heads). Such voicing of others' thoughts may seem excessive, even by the externally visualizing standards of epic fantasy narration, which allegedly support stereotyping. However, the conclusion of the passage suggests a different possibility: "once more Cnaiür found himself watching them with two sets of eyes" (55). Cnaiür is both outsider and insider, able to observe Kellhus's manipulations from outside because he himself is being manipulated (and aware of being manipulated—note that he "found himself" watching, again suggesting the lack of agency). What is happening here is a form of empathy, but it is the "empathy" of recognizing the programming without being able to rise to the position of programmer oneself. Such narration is not necessarily unusual in third person limited, but its frequency here, in the context of a fantasy work, helps us understand its function as something other than an error.

In such passages, I would describe the narration as "third-person-plural" narration. The focalized narrator sees the self in the other in moments that blur the lines between the narrating consciousness and others in their field of view. The perspective of different characters blends together, suggesting that the third-person perspective in general is characterized by a lack of distinction between various agents. It may be worth considering here, when arguing that this lack of distinction is a form of empathy, that empathy has been linked by some theorists to narcissism. Psychoanalyst Heinz Kohut, for instance, argues that "primary empathy" begins in infancy in the child's assumption that the mother is part of the self, which "prepares us for the recognition that, to a large extent, the basic inner experiences of people remain similar to our own" (Kohut 85). Kohut thus considers empathy a "mature" form of narcissism.[8] While this presumption that erases otherness is certainly problematic (particularly from a post-colonial perspective, as I discussed in Chapter 2), what is at work here, in Bakker's terms, may be the "cuing of a social algorithm" to recognize the self in the other, a finding of consensus that enables communication. This third-person-plural narration happens in some of Bakker's more omnisciently narrated moments, as in a passage where demons are summoned to fight against the Inrithi late in the novel. While the passage is ostensibly narrated omnisciently (it is not even clear whether the demons are sentient creatures), the narration nonetheless continues to take on the qualities of third person limited and free indirect discourse, even when using the plural "they," as in "They sensed the mortals, loping like monkeys down murky streets, raping, murdering, warring.... Would that they could devour it all" (325). The last sentence here is particularly striking, as it clearly sounds like free indirect discourse voicing the thoughts of a character, yet "I" is replaced not with "he" but with "they." Here the narration transparently creates the illusion of consciousness, as beings without intentionality (they are magically compelled to kill based on the orders of their summoner) are given the same type of third-person narration as the human characters, while still denying them individual subjectivity by using the plural "they."

This transparency about how narrative perspective creates the illusion of consciousness may also be at work more subtly in passages that blur the lines between focalized narrators. Interspersed between segments describing this final battle, Bakker places a dramatic scene between Achamian and his ex-wife, Esmenet, a former prostitute who has become a concubine of Kellhus. The chapter containing this scene (chapter 15 of the novel) is a good extended illustration of the multi-voiced narrative method, as there are 30 separate point of view sections in a 38-page chapter, cycling rapidly between a number of characters and plots. Such rapid shifting may already be jarring and easily lead to confusion about perspective. Furthermore, the scene frequently creates uncertainty about narrative focalization between the characters, as it often switches between their perspectives and disguises shifts in perspective between narrative segments. However, the third-person-plural character of the narration is most evident in two odd sentence fragments used to end two different sections of the scene. At the end of the second section (focalized through Esmenet), Achamian approaches Esmenet and asks her to go with him. When she does, the final words of the section are a sentence fragment, punctuated as its own paragraph, "Always following" (314). Structurally, this could be a moment of free indirect discourse, with Esmenet reflecting critically on her lack of agency with respect to the men in her life, yet her self-awareness about this issue is ambiguous, and in fact this criticism of her character is more typical of Achamian. Thus, the source of this statement is unclear: is it a critical interjection by an omniscient narrator? A shift to Achamian? It seems to float free of any perspective and be applicable to all of these, a third-person-plural comment.

The intersubjectivity of the narration reaches its climax when Achamian and Esmenet reconcile sexually in a passage near the end of the chapter. While the passage is focalized through Achamian, it begins with an emphasis again on lack of agency: "He *found himself* clutching her hand" (331, emphasis added). Both of them are caught up in their programming here, so agency and perspective do not matter. The final line of the passage again shifts to a murky, shared perspective: as Achamian cries out Esmenet's name in passion, we are given the line, "Such a strange name for a harlot" (335). This refers to an ongoing observation by other characters that Esmenet's name comes from the holy scriptures of Inrithism. When Bakker first introduces their relationship in the first book of the series, Achamian thinks, "A strange, old-fashioned name for a woman of her character, but at the same time oddly appropriate for a prostitute" (*Darkness* 83). While it might seem odd to have such reflections in the middle of sex, it is doubly odd that his thought has changed form— he once thought the name "appropriate for a prostitute." Thus, we might see this latter sentence as being influenced by social sentiments about her now that she has a more public position. Furthermore, in the immediate context of this chapter, it is not Achamian who has been thinking about her name, but *Esmenet*. Her introduction in Chapter 15, before she even encounters Achamian, involves her thinking about her name: "Would they call her Esmenet-allikal, or 'Esmenet-the-other'? […] Or would she simply be the Prophet-Consort" (313). Thus, oddly, at the conclusion of this scene, Achamian seems to be thinking back to *Esmenet's* reverie from the beginning of the scene. This moment blurs narrative perspective and introduces third-person-plural perspective that levels out all subjects as essentially the same subject because of their shared features as programmed entities.

Thus, Bakker's narration in this series suggests that the distinctions between various types of third-person narration are largely illusory (as is, in fact, the first-person perspective). From omniscience to free indirect discourse, from one character to another, at all levels these are simply manifestations of programming. While this may still be described as a form of emancipating characters from hierarchy, it is a rather negative emancipation (as even the "omnipotent" author is not exempt from this programming). This blurring of lines between omniscience and free indirect discourse can best be illustrated by an examination of the climactic encounter between Cnaiür and Moënghus. Moënghus is Cnaiür's former gay lover, and Cnaiür hates him and intends to kill Moënghus for seducing him and making him a pariah from his tribe. Cnaiür finds him in the catacombs beneath Shimeh after Moënghus has received a mortal wound in a final confrontation with Kellhus. From the beginning of the encounter, Cnaiür's lack of agency is emphasized in ways that should by now be familiar: "Blinking, he [Cnaiür] saw the notched blade in the air before him, though he had no recollection of drawing it" (386). Moënghus continues to manipulate him—programming him—calling upon their love, apparently intending to draw him closer and somehow siphon off Cnaiür's life energy to sustain his own. As he succeeds in reaching Cnaiür emotionally, the narration becomes oddly distanced: "The sword dropped from the stranger's senseless fingers, rang like something pathetic across the floor. His face broke, like a thing wrapped about twitching vermin. The sobs whispered across the pitted stone. And Moënghus was holding him, enclosing him, healing his innumerable scars" (387). To this point, the passage has been closely focalized through Cnaiür, even using moments of free indirect discourse. Suddenly, and confusingly, Cnaiür is referred to in the most distant possible terms as "the stranger." Other small touches distance Cnaiür from himself—"the sobs" rather than "his sobs." Within the limited focalization of Cnaiür (perhaps even within free indirect discourse), Cnaiür is experiencing a "third-person" distancing from himself, a sort of third person within third person. This type of framing within framing exposes the self at the center as an illusory construct; thus, the narrative style reflects the lack of agency at the center of subjectivity, which Cnaiür is dramatically experiencing.

The passage continues to blur the lines in narrative style, alternating between free indirect discourse and omniscient narration in confusing or misleading ways. As Cnaiür thinks back to his past relationship with Moënghus, he gives the reader a fragmented reverie of multiple voices, not a coherent reflection of a unified self: "He loved him ... this man who had *shown* him, who had led onto the trackless steppe. [...] Abandoned him. Forsook. He had loved only him. In all the world ... *Weeping faggot!*" (387). As in the example from Sompas above, this passage starts with an external description ("He loved him") and then pushes deeper through free indirect discourse (the fragments "Abandoned him. Forsook.") before ending with direct discourse, italicized to indicate the intrusion of outside voices. What is intriguing about this example, though, is that the outside voice saying "*Weeping faggot*" is unclear. Is it the voice of his father, his tribe, or himself (socialized by his father and his tribe to hate himself)?

It is impossible to say definitively, and of course, it is not a question that needs an answer, because the point is that it does not matter which. All of these voices have blended together in programming his consciousness.

Finally, Cnaiür and Moënghus embrace in what Cnaiür seems to assume will be a sexual encounter (Moënghus seems to intend some sort of vampiric magic to prolong his life). However, for much of the series Cnaiür has been wearing a Chorae, a magic object that kills sorcerers on contact. As they embrace, Cnaiür inadvertently kills Moënghus with the Chorae in another passage with blended levels of narration: "Moënghus gasped, jerked, and spasmed as Cnaiür rolled the Chorae across his cheek. White light flared from his gouged sockets. For an instant, Cnaiür thought, it seemed the God watched him through a man's skull. […] But then his lover fell away, burning as he must, such was the force of what had possessed them" (387). The passage starts with a misleading moment, as Moënghus' actions (gasping, jerking, spasming) could easily be associated with sexual ecstasy. The reader's uncertainty, though, is exceeded by Cnaiür, who clearly does not understand what is happening (he assumes that Moënghus burns with "the force of what possessed them," i.e., passionate love, and in the subsequent passage he asks, "How could you leave me?"). Clearly, Cnaiür does not intend Moënghus' death, yet the clause "as Cnauir rolled the Chorae" makes Cnaiür the subject and uses an active verb that implies he is an agent. Moreover, it is not clear if Cnaiür even realizes the Chorae's role in killing Moënghus; if he is indeed unaware, this sentence could only come from an external, omniscient (authorial) point of view. The entire sentence stages the artificiality of consciousness, as Cnaiür's unintentional murder of Moënghus is described in language that implies intentionality. Yet while these first sentences seem to use a distant narrator (even using direct discourse—"Cnaiür thought"), the last sentence seems perhaps to be using free indirect discourse. I particularly want to focus on the phrase "burning as he must," as it is a focus for the perspectival ambiguity of the passage. For Cnaiür, Moënghus "must" burn because he is literalizing the metaphor of their passionate lust; from a literal, objective perspective, Moënghus "must" burn because of the physical laws that govern the operation of Chorae; from an aesthetic, narrational perspective, he "must" burn as the Chorae is uncovering his lies and manipulations, a moment that is set up earlier in the scene when Moënghus himself says to Cnaiür, "It is *truth* that burns" (386, Bakker's italics). Thus, the phrase "burning as he must" floats free of narratorial subjectivity and authority: who is narrating here? Cnaiür? Bakker? The narrative seems to have been emancipated from this hierarchy of author and character, in this case revealing the effect of narrative as a tool for creating the illusion of consciousness.

Bakker's rich novels deserve a more complete analysis than I have space for here, but to clarify how they connect to my argument, I will confine myself to a few concluding observations. First, despite Cnaiür's programmed subjectivity, despite the way that the narration argues for the illusions of consciousness, the story still generates an emotional connection to the character, a feeling of empathy. Cnaiür is certainly not a sympathetic character through much of this series; he is in some ways a stereotypical barbarian who repeatedly rapes a woman (whose life he initially saved) in order to prove his control over her and violently pushes away other characters. Yet this final moment, in its insight into how these behaviors have been programmed into him, these behaviors that readers have likely deplored, allows an emotional connection to the pain felt by a character who is (most likely) far removed from the experiences or psychology of the reader. Third-person narration may be transparently dramatizing that consciousness is an illusion, but that simply makes it a more powerful algorithm for finding common ground, for breaking down the usual hierarchy of the police order and generating a feeling of common humanity, a feeling we might recognize as empathy. Cnaiür is not reduced to an object of punitive discipline.

Second, it may be possible to object, based on the evidence I have presented above, that the Dûnyain seem to stand outside the illusions of consciousness, that Kellhus and Moënghus exist outside the system, and that their manipulations represent a sort of police action, an intervention that reinstates the hierarchy of inside and outside. I do not have space to consider the thematic structure of the Prince of Nothing trilogy more extensively here, but Kellhus in particular is not immune to being programmed, despite his apparently more "enlightened" position. After a Christ-like martyr death and rebirth at the end of the second volume, Kellhus begins hearing voices that he attributes to God. When he describes this to Moënghus, he says, "Thoughts come. I know only that they're not mine" (340). Kellhus's experience in this series, then, still falls within Bakker's definition of human subjectivity.[9] We may actually consider Kellhus to be something of an author substitute in this regard (rather like Black in "The King's Justice"). Bakker seems to consider himself to be in a position to be better informed about the workings of consciousness than the average person is, but like Kellhus, he is not immune to being part of that system.

Finally, one could observe that many of the examples in this chapter, particularly from Bakker's novels, are actually fairly mundane instances of what we often find in third-person narration, not much different structurally from the examples I opened this chapter with. I would reiterate, as I do elsewhere in this book, that this is actually the point. What Donaldson and Bakker show us about the use of third-person perspective is not unusual (or even unique to fantasy), but the epic fantasy context reveals these features as more than just errors or lapses in limited perspective. Bakker and Donaldson—and their disparate worldviews as embodied by their fantastic worlds—suggest that an affordance of third-person narration is the creation of a model of consciousness, an absorption of self into other not as an act of hegemony but as a blurring of boundaries between selves that allows for recognition and communication. Third-person narration constantly negotiates the boundaries between self and other, whether that means (as it does for Bakker) overtly manifesting how consciousness is, for all of us, a programmed illusion, or whether it means (as it does for Donaldson) finding models of the other's mind to project ourselves into and enable a wider range of choices. Epic fantasy models third-person narration as a way to make everyone visible, as an engine capable of working toward egalitarian empathy.

CHAPTER 4

First-Person Epic Novels

Metafantasy and Fluid Perspective

There is a legendary romance in this. And most fascinating to me, most frightening, is that *it isn't over yet.*
—N. K. Jemisin, *The Hundred Thousand Kingdoms*

To pick up on a question that I posed at the beginning of Chapter 3, why are so few epic fantasy novels written in first person? A number of fantasy critics have undertaken an answer to this question, often landing on similar answers. W.A. Senior, for instance, answers that "Most fantasy novels are written in a third-person voice because the first person would often remove the sense of wonder and distance required to produce fantasy" (136). While I will return to the concept of a "sense of wonder" in my next chapter, this argument about "distance" runs throughout the criticism. Colin Manlove calls "distance [...] between the writer and his material" "the basic condition from which the overt concern with wonder in all its forms is generated" (Manlove 14). Rosemary Jackson explains the reason for the necessity of distance: because "the narrative voice is frequently a 'he' rather than an 'I,'" a reader cannot "dismiss" the story "as peculiar to that individual mind or subjectivity" (31). In other words, third person provides an external authority that prevents the reader from chalking up the fantastic occurrences as hallucinations on the part of the narrator. To modern readers in particular, the first-person voice is always a bit suspect, as we expect a "subjective" perspective to be incomplete or mistaken (i.e., unreliable); thus, in a genre that already trades in the unlikely, readers are more likely to buy into what they are reading if the narrative authority is bolstered by a seemingly "objective" third-person narrator (even though, as I have already discussed, that authority may not be as firm as it first appears).

However, Jackson is more concerned with "real world" fantasies (what Mendlesohn would classify as "intrusion" fantasies). When specifically considering epic fantasy, we may find the issue of narrative distance heightened by an aspect of the genre's name, *epic* fantasy. The narration may rely on distanced narration due to the genre's relationship to the style of ancient epics, and this in turn may provide an entry point into the intersection between narrative style, genre, and ideology. As I have already discussed in my section on "Depth of Time" in the introduction, literary critics like Mikhail Bakhtin and Georg Lukács define the temporality of epics and novels in such different ways that the attempt to combine them will result in a conceptual collision. As Bakhtin explains in "Epic and Novel" (1941), the narrative world of the epic exists at a distance from the contemporary reality of the narrator or writer. Even to the audience of the *Iliad* or the *Odyssey*, the events of the story take place in a distant past; certainly, this is manifestly true for Milton's *Paradise Lost* which tells a story of the beginning of human history. Therefore, epic time is complete and unchangeable, its possibilities exhausted: "the epic past is absolute and complete. It is as closed as a circle" (16). The epic exists at an absolute distance from the fluid, incomplete, changing present—what Bakhtin refers to as "the developing, incomplete and therefore re-thinking and re-evaluating present" (17)—and this temporal, hermeneutic distance is registered in the epic's distant formal style. In the ancient world, the epic was exclusively written using formal, distanced (heterodiegetic) narration while first-person (homodiegetic) narration was reserved predominantly for the more emotional and personal genre of lyric poetry.[1] In contrast, the changing, inconclusive contemporary world is the subject of the novel (even when it is written about events in the past). Lukács describes this difference in terms of "totality." The epic maps a totalized version of reality, where meaning is immanent and everything has a defined place. For something to be a "novel," it must assume the absence of this totality and instead be written from a worldview where meaning is not pre-given but always in process. In other words, the epic envisions an unchanging static totality, an essentialist world where everything is defined and nothing changes. The novel must attempt to *create* totality out of the changing, subjective perspectives of everyday life. Consequently, "objective" narrative distance is crucial for the epic, whereas the shifting "subjective" viewpoint (more commonly associated with first-person perspective) would seem a better fit for the novel.

From that standpoint, we might observe a fundamental tension in the nature of epic fantasy itself, namely that such fantasy attempts simultaneously to be both "epic" and "novelistic." Initially, many of the foundational writers of epic fantasy, such as Tolkien, embraced an epic style, and negative critiques of Tolkien's writing (particularly those from Marxist critics) often focus on features that are more epic than novelistic. Carl Freedman, for instance, calls Tolkien "anti-historical," saying he created a "thin and impoverished world: it is miles wide but only inches deep" (263). Yet this is precisely the point: in emulating the ancient epics, Tolkien is *not* creating the "real historical society" that Freedman values (263) but a closed, totalized world. Freedman wants fiction presenting a fluid world of change and conflict, but Tolkien, like the epic, locates his story in a distanced past. However, as the genre developed, writers increasingly began to mix novelistic elements with the epic in fluid, constantly changing hybrid combinations. Perhaps nowhere is this more evident than in narrative style, where first-person narration has become more common, while still being relatively unusual. Many contemporary fantasists, while still interested in maintaining the epic quality of fantasy, show much more influence from modern and postmodern views of narrative perspective than Tolkien does. Modernist writers such as Virginia Woolf and Ernest Hemingway often expressed discomfort in omniscient third-person narration as they felt it implied a God-like perspective and an essentialist view of the world.[2] Tolkien, the Catholic medievalist, would have no problem using a narrative style that implied a distanced, god-like perspective, but subsequent fantasy writers often reveal their modernist and postmodern influences in their attempts to destabilize essentialist views of identity and language even as they still use an epic plot framework. This is not to say that first-person narration is different in fantasy—more "subjective," perspectival, or transgressive—nor is it to say that first-person narration always serves a deconstructive purpose in epic fantasy. In fact, because of the constraints of the epic form, epic fantasy often has difficulty fully undermining essentialist world views. However, first-person epic fantasy is well-positioned to use narrative voice to deconstruct the subject-object binary that serves as the foundation of the ideology of epic essentialism, as doing so exploits a fundamental collision of forms within the genre itself. Rather than creating worlds that keep modern subjectivity at a distance from the objective, unchanging epic world, these writers show how the fluidity of subjective perspective spills over and infuses the "objects" and "facts" within the seemingly epic world. While the stable, unchanging view of history remains present in some form, the epic narrative tools used to cement that view are simultaneously subverted through the use of narrative style. A totalizing narrative is used to question totalization.

To illustrate the fissures and tensions in epic fantasy as a genre, I will examine how two writers' use of first-person narration particularly exposes and deconstructs epic essentialism. A curious effect of first person in epic fantasy is that it often transforms these narratives into "meta-fantasies," fantasies that reflect on the status and use of the fantasy genre itself. First-person perspective tends to be highly subjective, and therefore it raises problems related to the interior and personal nature of fantasy.

The highly individualized meaning of "fantasy" (as unreliable dream) constantly threatens to replace the stable, enclosed world-creation of the epic. The novels I have chosen particularly draw on this self-reflective quality of first-person fantasy to question the possibility of an enclosed, hegemonic epic world view. My examples also illustrate two areas fundamental to first-person narration which epic fantasy is particularly useful for deconstructing: subjectivity/agency and temporality.[3] Close analysis of the narration in Glen Cook's *The Black Company* (1984) will provide a useful overview of how first-person narration underwrites a postmodern deconstruction of the subject-object binary and therefore the construction of a coherent narrative subject, particularly as it questions the distinction between "objective fact" and "subjective impression" on which historical narration (and novelistic mimesis) are based. On the other hand, N.K. Jemisin's *The Hundred Thousand Kingdoms* (2010) more specifically strikes at epic temporality itself by using the shifting of first-person perspective to create a fluid temporality at odds with a hierarchical epic narrative that is being used to freeze this fantasy world in a static form. In both, a static epic history is placed in conflict with a fluid, subjective perspective via the use of first-person narration, yet at the same time the epic narrative structure provides some form of determinate, fixed historicity that prevents the narrative from fully embracing a constructivist position. Thus, these novels demonstrate the collision between "epic" and "novel" within the structure of epic fantasy. My analysis below will focus primarily on the deconstructive potential within these novels, as that dimension of epic fantasy is largely overlooked. Significantly for my purposes, this potential is activated not only by plot construction but also by sentence construction. For each novel, I will examine first how the overarching plot structure mixes epic elements with modern first-person subjectivity. Then I will examine how this subjectivity is registered on the level of style through specific formal patterns: sentence fragments and elisions in Cook and dislocation of sentence elements in Jemisin. Each novel uses the format of epic to subvert epic essentialism from within on both the narrative and sentence levels.

Theoretical Interlude:
First-Person Narration and Unreliable Narrators

Before diving into these texts, though, I would like to briefly clarify a foundational assumption I am making about first-person narration, namely that it is highly embedded in an individual perspective and thereby, to a large degree, what we may consider "unreliable." In each of the examples below, I will argue that the first-person narration is placed in conflict with presentation of "objective fact" or "historical truth" or some similar formulation, yet, to a certain extent, epic fantasy requires the reader to accept the narrator as a reliable source of information. Otherwise, suspension of disbelief collapses, and the narrative becomes perhaps surrealism or dream fiction or something other than epic fantasy (and indeed, both of these novels ultimately suggest stable, reliable histories). So it will be necessary to briefly address to what degree first-person narration is inherently unreliable.

While first-person narration is obviously embedded deeply in a single individual subjectivity, this need not make the narration inherently unreliable. Yet a convincing argument has come from cognitive accounts of reader response to literature that first-person narration *is* fundamentally unreliable, at least in a late twentieth-century reading context. Building on Ansgar Nünning's research on how the framing of reader expectations leads readers to label a narrator as "reliable" or "unreliable," Bruno Zerweck has argued that historical reading norms have a strong influence on this evaluation. Starting with early twentieth-century modernism, unreliable narration became much more common in mainstream literary fiction "[d]ue to growing epistemological skepticism" (161). In fact, as twentieth-century epistemology developed into postmodernism, which questions any certainty or consensus, Zerweck finds the label "unreliable narrator" to be inaccurate: "It could be argued that the representation of narrators' illusions and difficulties of 'making sense' of their fictional worlds is not unreliable at all, but a *reliable* presentation of the highly problematic human position with regard to cognitive, epistemological, and even ontological certainties" (163). In other words, contemporary readers are likely to find any "subjective" perspective to be "unreliable" in the sense of lacking certainty about truth (because such lack of certainty is an accurate presentation of human consciousness).

Ironically, because epic fantasy writers often feel a need to ground their work in a real-seeming world, they tend to avoid this "unreliability" by avoiding the first-person perspective. In fact, this lack of presenting the "difficulties of 'making sense'" of the world may be why critics like Mendlesohn find "portal-quest" fantasy's world building so thin. Contemporary readers expect human consciousness to be uncertain and truth to be polysemous, and therefore if the story seems to be written from a position of certainty, this ironically seems like a less "reliable" or "realistic" portrayal of human subjectivity. Therefore, I would suggest that during and after the latter half of the twentieth century (during the entire period when genre fantasy rose to popularity), first-person narration has been considered inherently "unreliable" to a certain extent (although I agree with Zerweck that "unreliable" seems like an inaccurate way to describe this, as it is not placed up against a universally accepted standard of truth that would be more "reliable"). This, in itself, may explain why any secondary world fantasy would avoid first-person narration.[4] Epic fantasy often uses the conventions of literary realism to ensure suspension of disbelief in the fantasy world, and like Victorian realist fiction (which also showed a marked preference for third person over first person), this requires a solid, consistent epistemological foundation that is at odds with the highly perspectival nature of first-person narration. Intriguingly, though, that consistent epistemological foundation shares the stable temporality of the epic, yet that stability is fashioned using the subjectivized tools of the novel. Thus, a first-person fantasy novel is in a particularly good position to exploit the fissures already present in this generic mash-up of epic and realist fiction and present "fantasy" not as a rigidly static, essentialist worldview but an epistemologically uncertain one steeped in the creative (and personal) imagination.

The Historical Subject as Fantasy Construct in Cook's *The Black Company*

Glen Cook's *The Black Company* perhaps best illustrates how first-person epic fantasy subverts epic essentialism from within. To begin with, Cook's novel is a jarring combination of stylistic elements. On the surface, it certainly fits the requirements for the epic: it is a sweeping narrative that follows an army of soldiers (in this case a mercenary company) in fights that span a continent in a battle that could be described as being between good and evil. Yet even at this mostly superficial level, the narrative details break down these essentialist categories. The Black Company actually works for the Lady, a powerful sorceress who leads a domineering empire with the help of a group of wizards known as the Taken (or as "the Ten") whom she forcibly controls. In essence, our "heroes" are fighting on behalf of "Sauron" against the rebel forces. The narrator, Croaker, sums up the moral ambiguity in his occasional reflections: "I am haunted by my suspicion that we are furthering the cause of something that deserves to be scrubbed from the face of the earth" (193). The Company itself are ambiguous heroes, as they at times rape and pillage after battles, and Croaker admits, "I still try to avoid looking at the worst. [...] They are complete barbarians, living out their cruelest fantasies" (143). Here we can already see the effect of the first-person narrative to highlight the distance between the unchanging surface of the epic and the subjective ambiguity of modern consciousness. Narrative is manipulated by the narrator for a purpose; Croaker's narration borders on propaganda. The essentialist categories of good and evil are created, in retrospect, by storytellers. The Lady is attempting to control that narrative by having Croaker write the history: "She knows how history rewrites itself. She doesn't want that to happen to her" (317). The moral certainty of Tolkienian epic fantasy is undermined by relativistic ambiguity here.

Yet all of these contradictions exist on the level of plot. Cook is not even attempting to be particularly subtle here, as he has Croaker overtly comment on the theme of moral relativism: "If one chooses sides on emotion, then the Rebel is the guy to go with. He is fighting for everything men claim to honor: freedom, independence, truth, the right.... All the subjective illusions, all the eternal trigger-words. We are minions of the villain of the piece. We confess the illusion and deny the substance" (108). Croaker identifies the values typically associated as the stable cultural truths of epic and epic fantasy as "subjective illusions," making us painfully aware that we identify with the Black Company not because we share their values but because the story is presented from their perspective, and that one is not a villain from one's own perspective. This perspectivism is also the subject of the Lady's commentary later in the novel: "Evil depends on where you are standing, pointing your indicting finger" (281). The Lady is specifically contrasting her "evil" to the even greater "evil" of her husband, the Dominator, whose return from the dead she is fighting against. Here, Cook is able to have his epic fantasy cake and eat it too by critiquing the moral relativism of heroism while still providing a traditionally heroic situation for the Black Company to fight within.

Dennis Wilson Wise, in one of the rare scholarly analyses of Cook, points to this conventional structure as one of three factors limiting Cook's fully deconstructing epic certainties: "group and individual identities" (337), the internal narrative consistency of the Company's Annals (i.e., nothing radically destabilizes our belief in their facts) (338), and "Cook's alignment between narrative climax and two epic fantasy Dark Lords" (the Dominator in the initial trilogy, Kina in the subsequent books) (338). Thus, by structuring the plot in the form of an epic fantasy, Cook ultimately creates a stable history despite his deconstructive tendencies elsewhere: "Although history might *feel* meaningless to people like Croaker, the reader nevertheless grasps the cosmological significance of Kina and the Dominator's downfalls. [...] History therefore has a *direction* [...]. Despite flux and randomness, despite the apparent randomness of it all, a truly nominalist vision of historical change continues to evade Cook's reach" (339). Despite this limitation, the reader is constantly having the Black Company's position relative to "good" and "evil" reframed: first, we assume they are the heroes (as the protagonist of an epic fantasy is, by convention, heroic); then Croaker tells us they are the "minions of the villain"; then a larger villain is introduced to make them heroic once again. The plot structure thereby supports the notion that the positions of "good" and "evil" are relative to the perspective from which they are viewed, or written about, which is in turn supported by the epistemological uncertainty of the first-person narration. These two positions (modern fluidity and epic stability) are in constant collision in the series.

In the style of that narration, the novel is just as suffused with contradictions. Although the narrative content echoes epic fantasy, the writing style derives much of its structure from Vietnam War fiction such as Tim O'Brien's. In a cover blurb for the 2007 Tor edition of the original trilogy, Steven Erikson has described reading Cook as like "reading Viet Nam war fiction on peyote." Wise has identified several formal features of Vietnam War fiction used by Cook, such as its "band-of-brothers theme" and "common man" perspective (334). However, the link to Vietnam War fiction comes primarily through the first-person perspective: "Vietnam War literature's most important legacy is arguably the *Black Company's* rampant subjectivity and perspectivism. [...] Vietnam War literature often possessed a journalistic, even memoirist, quality. It emphasizes subjectivity over objectivity, the observer over the observed. It is a literature that *bears witness* in a highly personal way" (334). Wise notes the relationship of the narration to journalism and memoir, which is a crucial collision of forms both in Vietnam War fiction and *The Black Company*. Vietnam War fiction tends to build on this conflict between the voice of objective journalistic fact and the voice of the subjective memoirist reporting how things felt. Tim O'Brien's "The Things They Carried" illustrates this conflict by constantly contrasting objective facts (the weight of the items the soldiers carry) to the subjective emotions that are what truly made the soldiers' lives difficult, and yet which many Vietnam War veterans felt were not being acknowledged by the culture they returned to after the war.

Croaker, who writes the Annals of the Black Company, embodies this same conflict between journalistic fact and memoirist subjectivity. He narrates in a voice that emphasizes the sparse, direct detail of journalism rather than the elevated diction of epic. Furthermore, despite using terse, factual descriptions without excess adjectives (as we might expect from journalistic accounts), Croaker's narrative priorities do not accord with our expectations of which events are important, either based on the conventions of historical fact, journalism, or the epic. Instead, Croaker focuses on the bathos of everyday life rather than the universal events of the epic or the politically or socially significant events found in historical or journalistic narrative. Ironically, the terse factual language contributes to this feeling of subjective priorities, as important battles are often dispensed with in brief passages, such as the following: "So we went and did it. We captured the fortress at Deal, in the dead of night" (72). The climax of the final battle in the book, after 60 pages of set up, is summed up in just two words: "She [the Lady] won" (303). Yet multiple times in the book, several pages are devoted to the magical prank battles between the company's feuding mages One-Eye and Goblin, while Cook seems to delight in silly details that deflate his characters. At one point, the frightening villainous patron of the Company, Soulcatcher, arrives at a fortress in the following way: "Soulcatcher came over the wall via the [snow] drift. He fell, nearly vanished in the loose snow in the forecourt. Hardly a dignified arrival for one of the Ten" (110). Cook's bathos highlights what may be a fundamental affordance of novelistic discourse. Bakhtin argues that bathos, the mockery of high genres, is the birth of the language of the novel: "The present, contemporary life as such, 'I myself' and 'my contemporaries,' 'my time'—all these concepts were originally the objects of ambivalent laughter. [...] The 'absolute past' of gods, demigods and heroes is here [...] 'contemporized': it is brought low, represented on a plane equal with contemporary life" ("Epic" 21). Thus, Croaker subverts epic conventions by explicitly parodying mythic subjects, undermining our expectations of what is significant or important by instead injecting a novelistic strain of everyday normality. Despite the superficial appearance of journalistic reportage of objective fact, the unexpected choice of details reminds the reader that the reported facts are always chosen by a subjective consciousness.

Thus, Croaker's first-person perspective noticeably mediates "facts" and determines their significance for the reader, undermining the subjective/objective binary on which epic distance and journalistic objectivity rest. Moreover, the novel explicitly erases the distinction between subject and object in fantasy by introducing a level of "meta-fantasy" through Croaker's romantic fantasies about the Lady (fantasies that are "romantic" in both senses of the word), which suggest the degree to which all "facts" are staged and performed based on individual fantasies. As the Lady, the Company's employer, is absent for much of the book, Croaker is obliged to rely on his imagination in order to report on her. The result is that he begins to write "an exercise in which I tried to characterize her" which then "degenerated into a romantic fantasy" (57). While we largely have only Croaker's summary descriptions of his fantasy about the Lady, one brief section is mockingly read aloud by another soldier who comes across it: "She stands in the Tower, gazing northward. Her delicate hands are clasped before Her. A breeze steals softly through Her window. It stirs the midnight silk of Her hair. Tear diamonds sparkle on the gentle curve of her cheek" (104). The style here is markedly different from the rest of the novel, as the romance is written with an omniscient third-person perspective, an attention to descriptive details, and a density of modifiers and figurative language ("delicate hands," "midnight silk," "Tear diamonds"). These elements are, of course, being parodied here, as the soldiers mock Croaker's florid prose ("Tear diamonds" is particularly singled out for laughter), but Croaker defends his fantasy not on the grounds of style but on the grounds of narrative authority: "for all they know, my inventions may be on the mark. [...] Who knows if she is ugly, beautiful, or what?" (104). Fantasy here is transparently a product of first-person subjectivity, which constructs reality, but Croaker wants to maintain the illusion of mimetic authority (both through his third-person style and his rationalizations).

Later in the book, the relationship between fantasy and fact becomes even more complex when Croaker finally meets the Lady. To this point, his romance has appeared occasionally in the book as Croaker tries (largely unsuccessfully) to gather accurate, factual information about the Lady which he can report. However, when he does meet the Lady, he cannot see past his own fantasy version of her to a "factual" truth about her. During his first meeting with her, she is surrounded in "fiery glory" that prevents him from seeing her appearance accurately (184). He responds, though, with conventional courtly etiquette quite out of character in comparison to the rest of the book: "I stared till my eyes ached. And dropped to one knee [...] like a knight doing homage to his king" (184). While the bright light literally prevents him from seeing her, it is his romantic image of her that truly obstructs the possibility of "clear" vision: "for one foolish instant I was totally in love. But I could not see Her. I wanted to see what She looked like" (184). That his fantasy distorts his vision of her is further reinforced when she appears to him in a dream later in the novel. When she appears, Croaker describes her by first quoting verbatim the entire passage from his romance of her (as I have quoted it above). Then, he adds, "My own words, written more than a year before, came back. It was that scene, from that romance, to the last detail. To detail I had imagined but never written. As if that fantasy instant had been ripped from my brain whole and given the breath of life" (250). Here, fantasy not only occludes "facts" but shapes the form they take, as Croaker's fantasies fuel the Lady's performance of her identity.

However, by this point, Croaker has started to distinguish between his fantasies and the material world, as he "did not believe it for a second, of course" (250). Over the course of the novel, Croaker certainly becomes aware that his fantasies do not necessarily match up to reality. After his first experience with the Lady ends with her violently punishing one of her rebellious lieutenants, he rejects his fantasies in a crucial transition point for himself and the entire Black Company: "I do not think that I will be writing any more cute, romantic fantasies about our employer. I have been too close to her. I am not in love now" (193). Croaker's romantic fantasies about the Lady have been shaping his understanding of her, allowing him to act in support of her, just as it takes a direct experience of her violence to re-shape his understanding. In both cases, though, his evaluation is shaped by his perspective (in the latter case, his personal experience of her violence), not "objective facts." Fantasy *is* individual perspective, and it is what shapes and enables behavior, for better or worse.

At the same time, there is a pragmatic side to fantasy's perspectivism, which we can see from the Lady's use of Croaker's fantasies to present herself to him. Fantasy is thus linked to a performance of identity, and in some places in the book, to outright propaganda. Just like when the Lady performs her identity when appearing to Croaker in a dream, the Taken each stage elaborate performances of their identities in order to shape the perceptions of those around them. Soulcatcher, the Taken who most often works with the Black Company, speaks in a variety of voices (presumably the "souls" she has "caught") and wears an outfit that seems designed self-consciously to invoke stereotypical images of dark lords and their minions: "Soulcatcher's slight body is always sheathed in black leather. He wears that head-hiding black morion, and the black gloves and black boots" (110–1). Soulcatcher's construction of a menacing identity also indicates the limited perspective of the narration, particularly Croaker's insistent use of the pronoun "he" despite the "feminine" shape of her body (and later in the novel, it is clearly indicated that Soulcatcher is the Lady's sister). Thus, performance and propaganda go hand in hand with this limited, subjective perspective. Croaker repeatedly claims a straightforward, fact-based soldier ethos ("We shed no tears and told one another no lies" [42]; "Plain-spoken. Straightforward. Simple. Just our style" [117]), yet he must constantly confront the extent to which these "facts" are constructed or performed. His annals themselves (as I have already pointed out) often have an apologetic rhetorical purpose, and the Black Company's missions are often as much about constructing a narrative as they are about accomplishing military objectives.

The novel shows the construction of "facts" most clearly in its handling of a common epic fantasy trope: prophecy. Prophecies, of course, have a reputation as a particular offender in guaranteeing stable epic temporality, as they implying a teleological approach to history. Yet this novel opens by mocking this narrative convention: "There were prodigies and portents enough, One-Eye says. We must blame ourselves for misinterpreting them. One-Eye's handicap in no way impairs his marvelous hindsight" (7). The following paragraph is an epic catalog of all of these portents, providing a parodic excess of omens, after which Croaker sums up, "But that happens every year. Fools can make an omen of anything in retrospect. [...] the best augurs are those who divine from the portents of the past" (8). Croaker presents prophecies as constructs projected onto the past in retrospect—prophecy here is actually the complete, retrospective epic time, which our narrator in the lived present stands in contrast to. Prophecy is only meaningful in retrospect, when we interpret the present as inevitable. The comparison to historical narrative both introduces history as a competing, more scientific discourse than prophecy, and undermines history as another exercise in retrospective petrification of past inevitability. This fluid blending of "historical fact" and "constructed prophecy" continues throughout the book in the handling of the central prophecy about the White Rose, the reincarnated hero who will lead the revolt against the Lady. Rather than treating this as an inevitable outcome of fated history, the Company's take on the prophecy is much more pragmatic and constructivist: "It hangs together in a certain elegant illusion of hope [...]. It's hard to lose when you *know* fate is on your side" (75). Ultimately, the prophecy will come true not because it forecasts the future but because it will provide them motivation to keep fighting even when they lose, "And because of that they'll fulfill their own prophecy" (76). The Company ends up leaving the Lady's service and following a child who seems to be the prophesied White Rose, but the novel's handling of prophecy (and the limited perspective of first-person narration) suggest not that the prophecy has predicted the future but that they have constructed a narrative of the world around them and worked to make that narrative come true. Fantasy and fact are too closely interwoven to separate them, and the interpretation of events shapes the narrative of what happened and why.

Thus, the novel's narrative structure consistently uses first-person perspective to erase the boundary between fact and fantasy, between subject and object. This erasure also manifests syntactically in a key trait of the novel's style: narrative gaps and sentence fragments. On the plot level, I have already indicated how the novel leaves gaps where we might expect major conflicts to be described. Yet these gaps are even more pervasive throughout the text, ironically eroding the distinction between the authoritative narrative consciousness and the reader as outside observer. As I have discussed in Chapter 2, Wolfgang Iser argues that narrative gaps play a crucial role in involving the reader in the text by "stimulat[ing] the reader into filling the blanks with projections" (168). While Iser is particularly interested in how this motivates narrative engagement, it also suggests that part of the narrative facts that we see in a story are constructed *by the audience*. Thus, we might expect that a narrative that more overtly leaves such gaps will more transparently indicate the extent to which facts are constructed, that these facts live in the fantasies and imaginations of readers, undermining the clear subject/object distinction. In *The Black Company*, the reader is drawn into supplying fantasies to supplement absent "facts" in the same way that Croaker is. While this happens to a certain extent with all fiction, the frequency with which Croaker's limited first-person narrative leaves gaps for the reader to fill accentuates the degree to which this world is not presented as a seamless epic totality but a world in flux, being constructed by multiple subjective consciousnesses (including the reader's).[5] Perhaps the most blatant narrative gap occurs during the climax of the Company's plot to kill the rebel general Raker in the third chapter. Croaker and the company's newest member, Raven, track Raker down and confront him. At the climactic moment, Croaker writes, "I charged. Raven arrived at the same instant. [A blank line indicates a narrative transition.] I looked at the body. 'Now what?'" (129) The climax of the battle is literally elided from the narrative. While this may be a symptom of the subjective narration, where combat takes place too fast to be mentally processed (and narrated), it also forces the reader to supply the rest of the scene, calling attention to how facts are subjectively constructed by point of view.

At the syntactic level, this structure of gaps appears in the frequent sentence fragments in the novel. The novel's style can be described as choppy, informal, and conversational (clearly the opposite of epic elevation). Many of these descriptors arise from Cook's abundant use of sentence fragments. Fragments in narrative often index the consciousness of the character—we are in the character's head, and that is why we are not given polished, finished prose. In *The Black Company*, these fragments are more frequent than usual, and like the narrative itself, they are often built on gaps and elisions, particularly elided subjects. While this could be illustrated from almost any part of the book, these fragments appear in greater numbers around moments of high emotion or difficult decisions, marking more clearly the subjective narrative point of view. In the climactic conflict, Croaker is accompanying the Lady as she chases Soulcatcher, who has become a traitor. Croaker's feelings are mixed, as Soulcatcher, of all the Taken, had seemed most relatable and had treated him humanely. After the Lady kills Soulcatcher in an encounter that implies they are sisters (another narrative gap—the Lady never says so directly), Croaker thinks, "Second time, if Catcher could be believed. Second sister. This deserved no allegiance" (299). The key decision point for Croaker, when he decides the Lady should no longer be served, is marked by substantial elisions. A complete sentence might read "[This was the] second time. [The Lady had killed her] second sister." The key details involved in his decision to revoke his allegiance to the Lady are elided from the sentence, engaging readers in supplying those elements themselves. My main point here is that even through its style, the novel involves the reader in constructing the "facts" of Croaker's reasoning, which supports the constructivist undermining of the subject/object binary found throughout the novel's first-person form, but it is also worth noting in the context of my larger argument that moments like this also engage a type of empathy in the reader, as the must "see into" Croaker's head and supply the missing links in his fragmentary logic. (In this sense, Cook's unconventionally minimal style could also have been part of my argument for Chapter 2.) Nonetheless, the prevailing style of the novel ultimately undermines the seemingly objective authority of narration. While the novel misleadingly seems to use a factual, journalistic style, a surprising number of key moments take place only in the reader's head, never on the page. The climax of the book reveals that a little girl who first appears early in the novel fulfills the prophecy of the White Rose, yet even this key moment for the series is never stated directly at any point in the book. (It is also not clear, at least at this point in the series, how seriously the reader should take it, as the prophecy is only substantiated in Croaker's imagination.) Ultimately, then, *The Black Company* reveals all facts, all truths, all subject positions— from "hero" and "villain" to "author/authority" and "reader"—as fantasy constructs. While the larger structures still follow a traditional epic narrative (the fight against the Dark Lord, for instance), the language of the novel, as the result of the first-person perspective, collides with those affordances. In the style, despite the appearance of reportage, readers are *made to construct* the "facts" in their imaginations, and the use of imagination is itself questioned through the metafantasy components of the novel. Cook uses the framework of the epic to deconstruct the unbroken, static epic surface and reveal history and narrative as constructs with no fundamental essence.

Epic Temporality as Fantasy Construct in Jemisin's *The Hundred Thousand Kingdoms*

While *The Black Company* undermines narrative authority and reveals the narrating subject as a fantasy construct, Jemisin's *The Hundred Thousand Kingdoms* looks to temporality itself. Certainly, the questions of who is narrating and when they are narrating are inseparable, but Cook reveals how the narrator's motives shape an understanding of the world rather than simply revealing the world "as it is." While Jemisin also deals with problems of subjectivity, she particularly focuses on the time of narration, establishing a fissure between static epic continuity and personal (and thus fragmented) memory. The novel tells the story of Yeine, the mixed-race daughter of an Arameri princess and a Darre prince. The Arameri have been the rulers of this world for thousands of years, and they have invited Yeine to Sky, the Arameri's capital, ostensibly to name her as heir to the throne, but practically speaking she is expected to die in a three-way power struggle with the king's two children, revealing which of those two will make the stronger ruler. However, these court politics are complicated by the involvement of the gods. The Arameri derive their power from their service of the god of light, Itempas, who won a war thousands of years earlier with the two other gods, Nahadoth the god of darkness, and Enefa, the goddess of twilight and balance. Itempas murdered Enefa and enslaved Nahadoth, in addition to enslaving Enefa's children, the other godlings. They now serve the Arameri, to whom they are known as the Enefadeh. However, Yeine is the subject of the Enefadeh's scheme to end their enslavement and return Enefa to life, as at Yeine's birth, she was implanted with a seed that carries the remains of Enefa's soul. Thus, Yeine (and her first-person narration of the story) is split between two cultures—Arameri and Darre—and two temporalities—Enefa's past and her present within the human woman Yeine.

As with Cook, the larger narrative structure here still holds traces of epic essentialism, as the mythic history of the world, once revealed, is never genuinely questioned. (In fact, to a certain extent, Yeine has privileged access to the past due to her dual identity.) However, on the level of style, the first-person narration constantly undermines this essentialism, illustrating the same collision between "epic" and "novel" as the Black Company series. The complex plot situation leads to a complex narration, with fragmentation, dual-voicing, and temporal fluidity all appearing before the reader is given enough information to understand why. Ultimately, we learn that the majority of the novel is apparently narrated by Yeine to herself (or to Enefa's soul within her) in a few moments during which she is dead after being killed at the succession ceremony, before she is reborn as the new goddess of twilight, a new being combining the memories of Enefa and the life experiences of Yeine. Clearly, this situation is useful for breaking down binary oppositions and questioning historical narratives. Yeine's narration constantly reminds the reader that the epic past is not separate from the ongoing changeable present, as Itempas and his priests would like it to be in order to protect their power. Instead, epic continuity bleeds into the changeable present as Yeine notes when she learns the details of Itempas, Nahadoth, and Enefa's relationship in the past: "There is a legendary romance in this. And most fascinating to me, most frightening, is that *it isn't over yet*" (226). The clear separation between epic temporality and the present, which Bakhtin saw as crucial to genre definition, is here erased.

Just as the plot breaks down binary oppositions, the narration fragments the subject/object distinction, much as Cook does. Jemisin seems to delight in playing games with the narrating "I."[6] The introduction of the narrator is a familiar convention of first-person novels, as in the famous opening of Herman Melville's *Moby-Dick*, "Call me Ishmael." Yet Yeine introduces herself in a context of fluid identity: "I forget myself. Who was I, again? Ah, yes. My name is Yeine" (2). Yeine is a forgetful first-person narrator struggling to hang onto her sense of self as she fuses with another subjectivity, but this explanation of events will not become clear to the reader for hundreds of pages, so this initial introduction unsettles the sense of a coherent narrating self. Later in the novel, she begins having dreams which are memories that clearly do not belong to her (as Yeine), but which continue to be narrated in the first person. Chapter 5 narrates one such flashback, calling attention to how the narrating "I" is separate from the "I" which is Yeine, who apparently comments in parentheses: "(It is not the Sky that I know. [...] I am not me)" (49) or "(I do not think I like this other me)" (50). Outside the parenthetical commentary, the voice is clearly that of the person whose memory Yeine occupies, typically without an indication of Yeine's presence: "I make myself smile [...] I have surprised him. It gratifies me to realize that I can" (50), "I finally realize my error" (52), and "The nearby capital ... oh. Oh, no" (53). This last example suggests an immediate reaction similar to free indirect discourse. In fact, the entire passage is double-voiced, much like free indirect discourse (which joins narrator and character),[7] yet both voices are in first-person. This double-voicing troubles the subject/object distinction in first-person narration, where the separation between narrator and other characters is presumably much clearer than in free indirect discourse. First-person narration is conventionally considered to be highly subjective; thus, if the reader is unsure of who that subject is, the narration becomes unstable.

This absorption of an external voice into the narrating "I" is one way of breaking down the subject/object distinction, while in another passage, Jemisin does so by having Yeine narrate Enefa's past in third person (even though Enefa is, in fact, part of her), thus seeing a part of herself as a distanced object. This passage repeatedly calls attention to the artificial narrative construction of the past, beginning first with a repetition of the familiar storytelling formula:

> Once upon a time there was a
> Once upon a time there was a
> Once upon a time there was a
> Stop this. It's undignified [139].

This unexplained transition into the story (it starts the chapter and is otherwise unlinked to the previous chapter) and the sentence fragments are typical of the novel's fragmented style, as is the intruding voice that says "Stop this," a voice that is never identified. It may be Yeine talking to herself, or it may be Enefa, who appears to break in at other points in the narrative. The point, though, is that it fragments and disperses the narrative "I," as the reader does not understand the status of the narrator, and even the story that is being given to explain the narration is manifestly artificial. Yeine (or perhaps Enefa) also interrupts the story to point out, "This is an approximation, you realize. This is what your mortal mind can comprehend" (139). When the story ends, before shifting back to the present, there is a brief return to first-person narration, and the narrator says, "Mortals have no words for what *we gods* feel" (143, emphasis added). Again, the narrator is unclear here, and perhaps more importantly, at this point in the novel the reader has not been clearly told that Enefa's soul resides in Yeine. This chapter happens in the middle of that revelation, but before it is clearly explained in expository prose. Thus, the reader is not likely to conclude that the "I" in this section is anyone other than Yeine, and her identification with "we gods" and her knowledge of "what *your* mortal mind can comprehend" are disorienting. At the same time, as Enefa *is* part of Yeine, the "I" has not actually shifted to a new character here, and the reader's assumptions (confusing as they may be) are accurate. In any case, the fragmentation of the narrating "I" disrupts the unified, coherent sense of pure identity, just as Yeine represents a third position outside of binary oppositions with respect to her mixed-race identity and Enefa breaks down the neat binary of light and dark in the book's cosmology. Even though this uncertainty is ultimately clarified by the conclusion of the novel, it does not change that experientially the reader goes through hundreds of pages before achieving that tenuous clarity about who the narrating "I" is. This disruption of unified identity in some ways goes further than Cook, who used the "I" narrator to disrupt epic "objectivity." Jemisin even disrupts the "I" narrator itself.

However, what distinguishes Jemisin's handling of first person is not her disruption of subjectivity but her disruption of the temporal dimension: not just "who is the self" but "when is the self?" How is the self related to history? The novel begins with the sentences, "I am not as I once was. They have done this to me, broken me open and torn out my heart. I do not know who I am anymore" (1). This clearly establishes the identity fragmentation in the novel as related to history. The sentence "I am not as I once was" has a complex temporality, as it introduces a fissure between the "narrating I" and the "narrated I." This fissure also plays out in the plot of the novel as Yeine must frequently compare her memories of Enefa's past to the official story enshrined in the Arameri's history. While Ene-fa's memories do ultimately provided a privileged, stable historical truth (in conventional epic fashion), the process of arriving at these memories is marked by substantial fluidity. Through her use of the temporality of the narration and even the syntax of her sentences, Jemisin unsettles our certainty about history by constantly placing the "fixed" past in the narrator's shifting present through constant games with time. To illustrate how this works, I will discuss three structures that Jemisin uses to unsettle the temporality of narration: fluid temporality, as the narration circles back on itself and frequently plays with sequence; artificial immediacy, where retrospective narration is performed as though it is happening in the immediate present; and grammatical dislocation, where sentence structures themselves require readers to sustain awareness across the time of reading by displacing elements of the sentence to the beginning or end (or into separate fragments).

First, predominantly on the level of plot construction, Jemisin frequently has Yeine circle back on her own narration, narrating events out of sequence. This is, of course, a common element of first-person narration,[8] and it has the effect of reminding the reader of the distinction between the temporal experience of events and their artificial ordering into a narrative. Furthermore, in this novel, it constantly reminds the reader to connect the past to the lived, changing present and therefore to see the past in the same changing light as the present. Many chapters begin with the narrator's out-of-sequence, proleptic commentary on the story, presumably from her standpoint at the end after she has died. Chapter 7, for instance, begins with the statement, "How strange. I have only now realized that this whole affair was nothing more than one family squabble pitted against another" (72). While this comment has the bathetic effect of reducing the epic struggles of gods and monarchies to "family squabbles," temporally it reminds the reader of the overall status of narration—the narrative "past" is part of a fluid present moment where the narrator is still capable of re-thinking and re-interpreting. These chapter structures build on the frequency of other proleptic comments throughout the narrative, such as "Only later would his words disturb me" (79) and "Later I would understand that I had already begun to love Sieh, possibly in that very moment" (84). Prolepsis often implies destiny or a fixed form to history. Much like prophecy, proleptic flash-forwards define the present as heading toward an inevitable future endpoint. Intriguingly, though, these comments almost always have the opposite effect by reminding readers that the past moment of narration is subject to constant reinterpretation and revision. This places the past in the same fluid uncertainty as the present, which becomes quite clear when the narrator expresses overt uncertainty, as in lines like, "I will remember later why this is relevant" (99). Thus, when the novel actually changes the sequence of events by telling them out of order, it reminds us of the fluid subjective temporality that is constantly interpreting the past. The continual circling of the narrative, caused by the first-person narrator's perspective, prevents any simple separation of static past from the fluid present.

Yet despite these continual reminders that events are being narrated from a retrospective position, Yeine regularly stages an artificial immediacy to the narration, as though it is happening in the present moment. This becomes particularly evident in structures that register surprise or distress in response to events. One such simple moment occurs when Yeine visits her mother's old room in the palace and begins to get lost in childhood memories: "I remembered sitting in bubbles with her, giggling as she piled her hair on top of her head and made silly faces—No. None of that, or I would soon be useless" (112). As this scene is being narrated in retrospect, it seems odd to narrate this moment with immediacy, instead of giving a more direct, distanced description of her emotions, such as "I had to stop remembering or I would have been useless." The future tense verb ("would soon be") seems particularly artificial in this retrospective moment.

The best illustration of this performed immediacy happens when Yeine is attacked and asks Nahadoth to defend her, which he does by turning her attackers into diamonds, effectively killing them, a consequence Yeine did not intend. As she tells the story of the attack, she again presents the moment with emotional immediacy by interrupting her sentences: "I had an instant to decide whether to dodge or reach for my knife—And in that sliver of time, I felt the power around me coalesce, malice-hard and sharp as crystal. That this analogy occurred to me should have been a warning" (243). This last sentence is yet another example of retrospective commentary, a reminder of the narrative situation that comes so quickly on the heels of the performed immediacy of the interrupted sentence that it blatantly identifies the artificiality. The metalinguistic comment about her analogy has a similar effect, as the figurative language "malice-hard and sharp as crystal" might initially be credited to the retrospective narration (who has time to think of metaphors like this in the moment while being attacked?), yet Yeine not only suggests that the analogy occurred to her in the moment, but she also credits it as the source of Nahadoth's choice of punishment for her attackers (turning them into diamonds). Is this a retrospective interpretation? A narration that seeks to justify why events happened as they did? Or is it an instance of figurative language becoming magically literal? The artificial, performative narration leaves this unclear. Then at the end of the attack, she describes her emotional response:

Through it all I remained still and kept my face impassive.
[section break]
He shouldn't have tried to hit me. He deserved what he got. He shouldn't have tried to hit me.
And the man who tried to help him? What did that one deserve?
They are all my enemies, my people's enemies. They should not have … they should not…. Oh, gods. Gods.
The Nightlord cannot be controlled, child. He can only be unleashed. And you asked him not to kill.
[section break]
I could not show weakness [245].

Here Yeine creates a clear distinction between the past tense retrospective narration that flanks this passage with an objective description of her external appearance and the internal dialogue presented as an emotional response in the moment. The choppy paragraphs, the incomplete sentences, the ellipses, the exclamations, the incoherent rambling—these are markers of stream of consciousness, much in contrast to the distanced position of the retrospective narrator. To present the passage in this way can only be an artificial performance of the past. This passage even contains another circling back, as the lines "the Nightlord cannot be controlled. He can only be unleashed" (239) call back to a warning she gives herself earlier in the chapter (although the addition of the word "child" here suggests identity fragmentation, as though an external voice is now reminding or cautioning her). Such repetitions break the immediacy of the passage with reminders of careful structure, and at the same time they continue the pattern of uniting past and present within the moment of narration. In fact, overall, this performative immediacy has that same effect: we might read it as a function of memory—Yeine is remembering the moment she is narrating and so she experiences the powerful emotions as though they are happening now, but this response is thus another reminder of how the first-person perspective breaks down temporality. The subjective experience of temporality breaks apart the unified form of the chronicle; instead, we are left with the subjective experience of time and memory.

This process of circling back, uniting past and present, correlates to a syntactic pattern in the novel, a structure similar to Cook's use of fragments. In this case, Yeine's narration frequently displaces elements of the sentence to phrases at the beginning or ending, at times into separate fragments, which forces the reader to constantly recall the past within the sentence, to unite the present syntactic moment and the past. In formal grammatical terms, a "dislocation" occurs when the subject of a sentence or argument is placed before a sentence (called a left dislocation) or after (a right dislocation), in order to emphasize the topic, as in a sentence like, "The line of succession, that is what we are here to discuss." There are a fair number of such dislocations in *The Hundred Thousand Kingdoms*, perhaps more than are typical in a novel (outside of character dialogue, as this is predominantly a feature of spoken English). These often occur at key moments, particularly clustering around Yeine's death and transformation into a god, as in the description of transitional states between light and dark immediately before her death: "From the instant the sun sinks out of mortal sight until the last light fades: that is twilight. From the instant the sun crests the horizon 'til it no longer touches earth: that is dawn" (361). However, I am extending the term to also include adjectival phrases and other sentence elements that are displaced from the main clause of the sentence, requiring the same mental process of "bringing together" elements that are temporally sequential. Unsurprisingly, while this type of structure can be found throughout the book, it occurs most in this climactic section, which is thematically about the bringing together of a fragmented world. As she describes her own body as she is re-forming it with her divine powers, Yeine employs multiple dislocations: "My hair wafted in, shining. My gown swirled about my ankles, an annoyance" (384). Her metaphorical descriptions often split off adjectives, dislocating them to the right: "like the petals of a great flower, scintillating" (389) and "like metal spun into curls. Beautiful" (391). She also dislocates the description of emotions: "I felt tears sting my eyes. Foolishness" (356) and "I lowered my eyes, pained" (356). Even the final sentence of the story contains a dislocated fragment: "So we [Yeine and the other gods] passed beyond the universe, and now there is nothing more to tell. [section break] Of this tale, anyhow" (395). This sentence dislocates the final prepositional phrase not only into a separate fragment but past a blank line on the page into its own section. Yet this fragment ironically suggests continuity, as the story will continue on. The story is not finished or set in an unchanging epic past. Just as the reader must mentally unite this fragment to the preceding sentence, the temporality of this entire book is linked by this clause to the ongoing, ever-changing temporality of the present, as embodied by the subjective perspective of the first-person narrator. Given the narrative structure of the book, this would be an appropriate ending even if it were not the first book of a series.

However, to bring home the ideological stakes of this syntactic pattern, I will conclude with one final example of dislocation. This example occurs in one of the out-of-sequence commentaries at the beginning of a chapter (which could already be considered a larger structural dislocation). In this instance, Yeine discusses the formal religion of Itempas promulgated by the Arameri, specifically how the priests tell the story of the gods' war: "The priests do mention the Gods' War sometimes, mainly as a warning against heresy. Because of Enefa, they say. Because of the Betrayer, for three days people and animals lay helpless" (186). After further description of the horrors wrought by the war, she again says, "Because of Enefa, the priests say. They do not say, because Itempas killed her" (186). In both instances, the official cause espoused by the priests in their static epic of the past is dislocated from the sentence, "Because of Enefa." Here the dislocation is particularly functioning to create a fissure between the official, smooth, orderly temporality of the priests and Yeine's revisionist interpretation, where she supplements their history with what "they do not say." Throughout the book, Yeine is battling the received history that supports the hegemony of the Arameri, supplementing that fixed chronicle with the personal narrative that comes from the first-person memories she shares with Enefa. Thus, the dislocation also suggests the supplementary, revisionist nature of the entire narrative. She breaks off the causation of the priests' narrative and replaces it with a different one. She does this again at the end of this section: the Arameri "saved as many as they could of the survivors. For a price. The priests don't mention that, either" (187). The price, of course, is servitude to the Arameri. The reader is required to break off an old version of the narrative and fuse a new explanation of events onto the story. Thus, the temporality of Yeine's fractured first-person narration specifically deconstructs the hegemonic epic stasis of the seemingly totalizing priestly narrative.

Conclusion

I should clarify that I do not mean to suggest that any epic fantasy that does not explicitly undermine "epic essentialism" is participating in it. Even writers who are not consciously intending to do so may destabilize the epic worldview simply due to the affordances of novelistic structures. Nor am I suggesting that epic fantasy engages in a full-blown deconstruction of essentialism that has somehow been missed by countless critics: as I have pointed out, both of my sample texts exhibit a collision between that deconstructive impulse and some degree of ultimately stable temporality. However, I *am* suggesting that epic fantasy affords a unique opportunity to undermine the essentialism that often attaches to the epic and other static historical ideologies. On an experiential level, the use of language that so sharply contrasts conventional epic essentialism calls attention to issues of temporality and historicity: the uncertainty of reading Jemisin is a more memorable effect of the novel than the fixity of Enefa's history. Even though this criticism of epic essentialism can be carried out in mainstream fiction, epic fantasy is capable of subverting essentialism from within by combining elements of the epic with features of the novel, presenting epic subject matter in a subjective fashion through the first-person point of view. Furthermore, *The Hundred Thousand Kingdoms* take us beyond the more straightforward critique found in *The Black Company* to suggest something more positive about fantasy's social role: Yeine is able to reconstruct the world by constructing a new narrative in which the Arameri do not have control. The consequences of this reconstruction are not simple, as subsequent books in the series explore problems that arise within these new social formations, but this only serves to highlight how the narrative is not merely replacing one epic stasis with another. In other words, the epic view is incomplete. Jemisin uses the metafantasy potential of first-person epic fantasy to suggest that the rational, static world needs fantasy and imagination to transform it, and due to its complex collision of structures, no literary form is better positioned to make this argument, perhaps, than thoughtfully written epic fantasy.

SECTION III

Wonder

CHAPTER 5

Spoiler Alert

Twists, the Sense of Wonder, and Narrative Transcendence

"Yes, it is indeed wonderful," [Ozma] agreed. "Not all fairies know that sort of magic, but some fairies can do magic that fills me with astonishment. I think that is what makes us modest and unassuming—the fact that our magic arts are divided, some being given each of us. I'm glad I don't know everything, Dorothy, and that there still are things in both nature and in wit for me to marvel at."
—L. Frank Baum, *Glinda of Oz*

In the climactic sequence of *The Hundred Thousand Kingdoms* by N.K. Jemisin, the last text I discussed in the previous chapter, Yeine, the first-person narrator, is killed (temporarily) by being stabbed with a knife from behind, which is described using a sentence structure typical throughout epic fantasy: "There, poked through the bodice of my ugly dress, was something new: the tip of a knife blade" (362). This is another example of what I described (somewhat loosely) in the previous chapter as displacement, and it would fit my argument there quite well. However, here I want to emphasize a different aspect of the syntax, the structure of delay. By displacing the crucial, telling detail—the knife blade that kills her—to the end of the sentence, Jemisin delays as long as possible giving the key information. Consequently, the reader is engaged in a process of discovery and surprise by the structure of the sentence. The structure of delay occurs quite commonly not just in epic fantasy but in many genres that use suspense as a key component of their effect. Essentially, the sentence leaves the reader hanging, waiting to find out what exactly is happening, until everything clicks into place with the final detail. I will be arguing in this chapter that this, and similar structures, are a key formal component in generating what is often described as the "sense of wonder" in epic fantasy.

I must emphasize, then, that my example illustrates how "sense of wonder" is actually a formal quality of the text's style. I argue this in contrast to the perhaps more common supposition that a sense of wonder, as Istvan Csicsery-Ronay suggests, "resists critical commentary" and "short-circuits analytic thought" (71). In order for "wonder" to exist, the audience must experience the emotional rush as the result of some form of breakthrough, but that breakthrough must be constructed in a formal way that conforms to rules and patterns. There is nothing to transcend if there is not first a rational groundwork, and this transcendence is rarely effective when wholly arbitrary. Texts frequently construct this sense of wonder by establishing a set of defining rules for the world and then breaking those rules. This rule violation brings with it an experience of freedom, of magic, of transcending the system, yet it is not a chaotic denial of that system but the discovery of a higher order system. In that way, "wonder" here is tied to the process of scientific rationality, which may be a bit of a surprising link, given that fantasy is most often associated with the irrational and the supernatural.[1] Yet by combining irrational, intuitive leaps and transcendent breakthroughs with the discovery of rational, coherent systems, epic fantasy is instilling the mental flexibility which, I have been arguing, is at the core of epic fantasy's affordances. While my argument in this chapter will not be directly about empathy, as so much of this study has been, this mental flexibility is at the core of the empathy I have been describing, so the sense of wonder is still closely related. As I have described it, empathy is a process of stepping out of one's own subjectivity to match it with the subjectivity of another, a process which opposes the rigidity of seeing the world in terms of pure, essentialist categories. By breaking through categories to see larger order connections, the sense of wonder performs a similar operation. It erodes complete confidence that a universe of stable categories can ever be mastered, and instead encourages curiosity and exploration.

Wondering about Wonder

Before examining the textual construction of wonder, we should examine what this elusive term means. As Csicsery-Ronay points out, it seems difficult to analyze an affect like "wonder." Thus, most "historical or cognitive" theories of the genre "do not have much to say" about wonder (71). Yet Csicsery-Ronay links "wonder" to two long-running categories of discussion in aesthetic philosophy, the sublime and the grotesque. In the sublime, a consciousness is confronted with an expansion of the world beyond its boundaries, while in the grotesque, the boundaries that distinguish separate categories are collapsed by something that partakes in elements of multiple categories. While I will discuss these (particularly the sublime) in a bit more detail below, the important detail here for a definition of wonder is that "in both cases the response is to suspend one's confidence in knowledge about the world, and to attempt to redefine the real in thought's relation to nature" (Csicsery-Ronay 71). In other words, they require mental flexibility in redefining reality. Thus, wonder is an experience of transcending the mundane world, what Csicsery-Ronay describes with phrases like "translation from the mundane" and "sense of liberation from the mundane" (71), yet at the same time, both the sublime and the grotesque (and thus wonder) "are related to scientific reason" (79). This may seem odd, but if we consider the dramatic narrative of scientific discovery, it involves the mind encountering phenomena that are unaccountable (from the odd biology of the platypus to the behavior of quarks, to use Csicsery-Ronay's examples) and being motivated by curiosity to investigate how this disruption of the known world occurs. For Csicsery-Ronay, who writes specifically about science fiction, this scientific narrative of curiosity and discovery motivated by wonder finds a parallel in the wonder of science fiction. This perhaps accounts for why he uses words like "translation" and "liberation" which avoid the spiritual/religious connotations of words like "transcendence" that I have chosen to use. Yet he nonetheless recognizes that wonder itself crosses traditional category boundaries by fusing concepts from the scientific and the spiritual. He particularly points this out through his discussion of the grotesque, which "introduces mythic thought in a nonmythic context, 'contaminating' the pure aspirations of rational thought with the fluctuating, metamorphic, class-defying world picture of the sacred" (78).

If science fiction injects the mythic into the rationalistic, epic fantasy is capable of doing the opposite: mixing the scientific into the mythic. With its basis already set in a mythic mode, the injection of "wonder," if we take it to be associated with rationalistic discovery and the feeling of a breakthrough, would then add a rational flexibility to the seemingly static mythic system. To make this claim does go contrary to many knee-jerk assumptions that have been made by critics of epic fantasy. Darko Suvin has perhaps most infamously made this argument that fantasy fails to inspire critical thinking. In *Metamorphoses of Science Fiction*, Suvin claimed fantasy, when it does not create a tension between the supernatural and the empirical world (as in intrusion fantasy), is just a "subliterature of mystification" (which would therefore include much that I define as epic fantasy) (9). Science fiction, in contrast to fantasy's "anti-cognitive laws" (8), "develops [a hypothesis] with totalizing ('scientific') rigor" (25) but at the same time estranges us from the familiar world. By simultaneously including cognition and estrangement, SF allows for an effective critique of the material world, whereas fantasy at best is a nostalgic allegory "for a world where goods are not commodities and people are not alienated by the omnipervasive machinery" (Suvin, "Considering" 238). Similarly, Farah Mendlesohn calls the sense of wonder "superficial" and sees it as playing a part in "shut[ting] the protagonist out of real engagement with the world" (136). She argues that portal-quest fantasy makes the world static and comprehensible by an accretion of excess detail, that it works not by defamiliarization but by "familiarization," "creating a world through the layering of detail, and making that detail comprehensible" (9). Both Mendlesohn and Suvin, then, see epic fantasy creating a static world, familiar and not estranged, the "wonder" merely superficial mystification. Yet these statements seem logically at odds: if wonder combines the cognitive and the emotional, if it spurs a curiosity about a world that exceeds perception, how can epic fantasy both be about a sense of wonder and a fixed, static world? Clearly, Mendlesohn is defining "wonder" somewhat differently than I am, and Suvin is so invested in the cognitive that he fails to note the affective dimension of "estrangement," as Csicsery-Ronay does. If epic fantasy can be shown, then, to contain the formal structures of a sense of wonder, it would then follow that it may accomplish the cognitive benefits of defamiliarization and its attendant mental flexibility.

Literary critics who write about fantasy do typically take this sense of wonder as given, but so much so that, much like Csicsery-Ronay observes about science fiction, what wonder is and how it functions are rarely analyzed in detail.[2] Brian Attebery addresses wonder at some length in more than one study of fantasy. In *The Fantasy Tradition in American Literature* (1980), Attebery defines wonder as "making the impossible seem familiar and the familiar new and strange" (3) (a definition that neatly encompasses both the defamiliarization valued by most critics and the familiarization criticized by Mendlesohn), but he locates wonder as an experience *outside* the text: "the experience is extraliterary because it depends on the needs, expectations, and background of the reader. It defies analysis under any system of literary values" (155), an assumption that seems fairly common and is likely the cause for so little critical attention. In *Strategies of Fantasy* (1992), his view seems to have evolved. While still linking wonder to defamiliarization (via Victor Shklovsky and Bertolt Brecht), Attebery more closely follows Tolkien's notion of "recovery,"[3] the idea that fantasy re-infuses meaning into a modern world that has been stripped of its significance: fantasy "offers the possibility of generating not merely a meaning but an awareness of and a pattern for meaningfulness. This we call wonder" (*Strategies* 17). Now Attebery credits this feeling to a property of the text, specifically its artificiality, which enables wonder because wonder is dependent on "seeing things not so much as they are but as they might be or ought to be" (128). Thus, fantasy has "a certain contrived or constructed quality" (129) that marks it as idealized and therefore capable of infusing the world with meaning: "Fantasy, *by its structure*, emphasizes the difference between fiction and life [...] so that our own tribal storytellers can resume their proper function [...] and recapture the modern world for the imagination" (141, emphasis added). However, Attebery only generally identifies what these structures are beyond the broad discussion of generic artificiality. This idea that fantasy returns a sense of meaning to the world is a theme throughout the criticism, from Katherine Hume who talks about how fantasy writers (C.S. Lewis, specifically) attempt "to reimpress us with the wonder of it all" (Hume 118) to Chris Brawley, who argues that fantasy writers are attempting to create "a new mythology in order to infuse readers with the sense of the transcendent which is no longer accessible, for many people, in religion" (9). Yet all of these critics still tend to associate wonder largely with emotion, particularly Brawley who replaces "wonder" with "the numinous" and (speaking specifically of mythopoeic fantasy) says, "these feelings [...] are non-rational and cannot be directly explicated by words" (15). Thus, the critical discourse on wonder shares a feature with the larger critical discourse on the aesthetic: both its detractors and its defenders share the view that wonder is a non-cognitive state and thus shy away from identifying specific structural components of it. Indeed, if one believes wonder is an emotion that is beyond language, one would not expect to find it in language.[4]

Wonder tends to be analyzed far more in the related field of fairy tale studies, where we can find more effective definitions for countering assumptions that wonder merely mystifies feelings and emotions. Christina Bacchilega's discussion of a "politics of wonder" in fairy tale adaptations is particularly enlightening in this regard. Fairy tales, much like epic fantasy, have a reputation for reinforcing hegemonic ideology, such as capitalist consumerism, yet Bacchilega is quick to point out that this is not the whole story, that "wonder" affords audience participation, which makes the audience an active producer and not just a consumer; thus, "we can imagine different choices and endings, and we do" (3). A key to her definition of wonder is the concept of transformation, which refers to something that happens literally in fairy tale plots (and most epic fantasy plots) but also has political connotations for what it means to tell these stories and to adapt them. Furthermore, her definition of wonder specifically calls for an active response from the reader. As she defines wonder through a reading of the Grimm fairy tale "The Golden Key," she emphasizes the active participation and curiosity of the story's protagonist: his knowledge of the world "opens him up to being in awe" and "his knowledge, curiosity, and openness to the world are part of this boy's survival kit" (191). While Bacchilega's definition of wonder as "re-enchanting" a world where magic has gone stale falls in line with many of the definitions above, her emphasis on participation and curiosity sounds much more like Csiscery-Ronay's account of wonder as a scientific motivation, and the "staleness" of magic that she describes is precisely the Marxist critique of consumerism and mystification in fantasy. In other words, true "wonder" recognizes such ideological manipulation and resists it by actively seeking meaning, attempting to break through to greater understanding, what Bacchilega calls stories "calling for our own active—and, even more so, activist—responses to and participation in the process of storytelling and interpretation" (194). While the case is obviously a bit different in epic fantasy, where the plots are not adapted from traditional stories quite so transparently, the attempt to infuse the reader with awe and curiosity in a way that involves them in seeking out truth and going beyond the traditional restrictions of genre formulae are certainly comparable.

Yet this definition still does not give us a rhetoric of stylistic devices that achieve wonder. For that, I will be examining examples from Brandon Sanderson and Michael Moorcock, certainly a disparate pair of writers philosophically, politically, and theologically. Yet in both I find that plot twists and structures of delay and surprise lead to the sense of breakthrough that I am calling narrative transcendence—a narrative structure of moving beyond set limitations that creates a sense of expansion and extension that spurs a participatory curiosity and awe in the audience. In this definition, I am somewhat drawing on the aesthetic history of the sublime, as Csiscery-Ronay does. As the sublime was developed particularly by Edmund Burke and Immanuel Kant, it is not just an emotional response but a synthesis of perception and cognition. An object is sublime when our perception of it exceeds our ability to cognize it. In simple terms, it is too "big" for us to process (this, of course, does not need to mean physical size). Yet this leads to a feeling of expansion of the self, because as we imagine this "large" object, we paradoxically contain it within our mind. The result is a feeling of breakthrough, of going beyond the limitations of the self. In a sense, the experience of the sublime teaches the mind to see the world differently. (This is particularly true of the Burkean sublime, which Vanessa Ryan, perhaps semi-facetiously, refers to as Burke's "theory of psychological hygiene" [276].) It is perhaps not surprising that fantastic wonder would participate in the sublime: Csicsery-Ronay calls the sublime "an unambiguously heroic domain" (72) because it elevates the participants and emphasizes totalization (that is, it relies on "the infinite expansion of an idea that is so integral, so impossibly unified, that it not only contains, but annihilates all multiplicity within it" [Csicsery-Ronay 83]). For this reason, he seems to prefer grotesque wonder, although I am not convinced that the drive toward unity in the sublime needs to "annihilate multiplicity." In fact, by cutting across traditional ways of seeing, it instills a greater flexibility. I might adapt Csicsery-Ronay's summary statement about the grotesque—"Sf spectacle is based on the creation of grotesque effects to demonstrate the fluidity of the real" (80)—to say something similar about the sublime in fantasy: epic fantasy spectacle is based on the creation of sublime effects to encourage the mind to be fluid in transcending our rigid expectations about "reality."

In saying this, I am actually less influenced by the discourse of the sublime than I am by the literary history surrounding the concept of surprise. All of the structural figures that I will be examining as sources of wonder—twists, delays, suspense—rely on some element of surprise. This seems like a superficial, experiential element of the text, which has led to some critical disdain (or apathy) for such apparently gimmicky devices as twists, deus ex machinae, and suspenseful delays of information. In this critical climate, it might seem odd to so thoroughly associate wonder with surprise, but there is actually a long tradition of doing so in aesthetic philosophy. Christopher Miller, in an extended analysis of the history of surprise in literature, traces the concept back to Plato, who considered "wonder (*to thaumaston*) [...] an essential condition of philosophical inquiry" (17), and Aristotle, whose ideal plot "involves both a reversal of fortune (peripeteia) and the hero's recognition of that development (anagnorisis), and both are said to turn upon surprises" (17). Writing primarily about the eighteenth century and the development of the novel as a genre, Miller argues for the dual nature of surprise as both a stressful experience the reader must recover from (as it disrupts expectations) but also a positive opportunity for learning. Surprise is both pleasant and unpleasant, largely because it disrupts mental routines. Aristotle described this as an "experience of being blindsided or jolted out of oneself," which is instructive as long as it maintains "the element of rational cognition" (Miller 18). Joseph Addison argued that surprise was instructive—"As a sudden blow against the routine or familiar, the experience of surprise was presumed to focus the attention and leave a more indelible mnemonic impression" (Miller 7)—while Descartes says, "to be in a state of wonder is to be in a mode of articulate receptivity" (Miller 20). Far from being passive or purely emotional, all of these thinkers associate surprise with mental flexibility as it shakes us out of our mechanistic ways of thinking and forces us to consider alternative views of the world.

It may be surprising that surprise and wonder are not entirely pleasurable. The title of this chapter is a reference to the primacy placed on surprise in popular culture, to the extent that many readers fear that "spoiling" the surprise will in some sense "spoil" the experience of the text. One might therefore think of surprise purely as part of the *pleasure* of narrative, but this is not the case. As surprise and wonder disrupt homeostasis, they can actually be uncomfortable experiences. As they essentially tell the audience, "your cognitive models for the world are wrong," they actually damage our pride in our own view of the world. (Cognitive scientists refer to this as "prediction error.") In fact, one noteworthy UC San Diego study suggests that readers actually enjoy stories *more* when the surprises are spoiled for them ahead of time (Lehrer), and these findings are corroborated by dozens of anecdotal accounts, not to mention by the advertising conventions of major films. While viewers frequently complain that movie trailers spoil major plot points, these trailers are constructed based on the assumption that more people will see a movie if they know what to expect.[5] The very structure of advertising presumes that surprise is not a comfortable experience. If this is so, then why do audiences still value surprise so much? Does this contradict assumptions about the importance of wonder?

Perversely, I would suggest the opposite: that this confirms that wonder (and surprise) are formal, cognitive, rational experiences. The answer, oddly enough, may be found in Adam Smith dealing with the question of whether the experience of surprise can be repeated. Many audiences assume that surprise is an experience that can only be had once (with regard to the same stimulus), and thus, for instance, movies like *The Sixth Sense* that are built around a single, crucial twist are not valued as "rewatchable" films. This accounts for the concern with spoiling the surprise. Without surprise, this line of thinking goes, there is no wonder, and without wonder, we miss the effect of that wonder (whether it is pleasure or a salutary flexibility in perspective). Theorists who write about surprise have largely made similar assumptions, but Smith

> argues that even with repeated exposure to a novel or poem, the reader can "enter into the surprise and admiration which it naturally excites in him." [...] The startling implication is that feelings of surprise and admiration are renewable resources—funds of emotional energy always available to the reader. More profoundly, the phrase "enter into" suggests how that energy is to be used: through an imaginative act of sympathy [Miller 30].

This is part of Smith's theory of sympathy (a term that in the eighteenth century was used largely like I have been using "empathy" in this study). By imaginatively entering into another person's feelings, we can re-experience the moment of surprise (the *anagnorisis*, or character's revelation) and re-enter our earlier experience of reading the work, an act of imaginative sympathy both with the character and with our past selves.

The implications for my argument about wonder are profound. If surprise or wonder is a repeatable experience, that implies it has a formal structure, and by entering into that formal structure the reader is "inhabiting another consciousness" (even if it is their own "unspoiled" consciousness, or a character's surprised perspective), which is an act of empathy. Thus, even a viewer who does not enjoy surprise and has the ending of *The Sixth Sense* "spoiled" can still enjoy the film and experience the moment of breakthrough on a cognitive, formal level, by recognizing the structure of surprise that generates the sense of wonder. Certainly, anecdotally, I would confirm that re-watching a film or re-reading a book with a well-structured surprise still gives me that feeling of breakthrough, of wonderment, that we usually associate only with the initial surprise. (This chapter partly grew out of my contemplating that phenomenon upon rereading Sanderson's Mistborn Trilogy.) Consequently, I will analyze the "feeling" of transcendence as a formal structure, generated by texts, that imparts the "magical" sense of mental flexibility, of reframing the world and breaking through to a higher order of meaning. In the following pages, I will primarily look at narrative and syntactic delays and plot twists as methods by which writers involve the reader cognitively in a sense of breakthrough that leads to the response we usually call "wonder." Brandon Sanderson's Mistborn Trilogy, particularly the final revelations in the last volume *The Hero of Ages* (2008), demonstrate clearly how narrative twists use cognitive breakthroughs to achieve a feeling of transcendence that rewards curiosity and openness. Because this example relies significantly on an analysis of plot structure, I will follow it up with a section focused on syntax to examine the style I alluded to in my introduction, a syntax that delays key details to create a suspenseful buildup of information. This delay involves the reader in the rational process of deducing the solution, which then results in either a satisfying sense of confirmation or the breakthrough of surprise. While such syntactic structures are fairly common in fantasy, I will examine a few especially revelatory examples from Michael Moorcock's paradigmatic heroic fantasy in the Elric series. Despite the differences in these writers—Sanderson approaches wonder spiritually, Moorcock secularly; Sanderson writes in established genre conventions, Moorcock at a time when genre conventions were being established—these examples nonetheless show surprising continuities. Thus, they demonstrate that wonder is an experience structured into texts, and that the effect of narrative transcendence, rather than simple mystification, is an invitation to curiosity and transformation based on increasing levels of understanding.

Narrative Transcendence
in Sanderson's Mistborn Trilogy

Brandon Sanderson is an excellent starting point for this study of wonder, as his entire narrative method is built on revelation and breakthrough. He is also particularly useful for this study, as he falls in line with a key element of the history of fantasy that is often used as a source of criticism against it: Sanderson, like Tolkien, is a religious writer, although (also like Tolkien) Sanderson does not explicitly write "religious" fiction. Sanderson is a Mormon and many of his stories both explicitly and implicitly involve religion.[6] As religion is often stereotyped as anti-rational and unscientific—in Marxist terms it is typically linked to mystification—it may be tempting to assume that Sanderson's emphasizing of narrative surprise and wonder reinforces the argument that fantasy relies on a simplistic, nostalgic ideology of good vs. evil rather than a critique of the complexities of the material world. However, analyzing the narrative structure of Sanderson's novels reveals that they derive their effects from the gradual, carefully controlled revelation of information that inspires a feeling of transcendence in the reader. Sanderson structures these novels to give narrative pleasure through understanding *why* the world works by incrementally unveiling a set of rational rules; thus, he links that seemingly religious feeling of transcendence to the rational thought process associated with the scientific mind. This is fantasy as a collision of scientific form and spiritual form—fantasies for a scientific era.

Sanderson counters simplistic mystifications by using rationalistic narrative structures, namely a structure of revelation. I deliberately use words like "revelation" and "transcendence" rather than simply describing "plot twists," as Sanderson himself sees religion and science, spiritual and rational thought, as fundamentally linked.[7] Mormon theology itself supports the value of scholarship and intellect, and Sanderson's fiction is saturated with scholar-heroes. The Mistborn novels include such examples as Emperor Elend who responds to religious debates in a "rational, scholarly" fashion (*Hero* 163), and the even more important scholar-hero, Sazed, who will be discussed in more detail below, but every Sanderson novel contains multiple examples of heroes who use their brains more than their weapons. A particularly revealing example of this pattern can be found in the first novel of Sanderson's The Stormlight Archive, *The Way of Kings*. (Even the title of the novel fits this pattern, as each novel in this series has a title that comes from a scholarly text in its world.) The particular scholar-hero in this novel is Jasnah Kholin, an infamous atheistic heretic who is also a famously brilliant scholar who discovers important secrets about her world. Jasnah is part of an order of scholars called Veristitalians, who "tried to find the truth in the past. They wished to create unbiased, factual accounts of what had happened in order to extrapolate what to do in the future" (523). Jasnah represents the value of rational scholarly endeavor, of seeing the world as it is rather than as we wish it, and in a speech to her ward she discusses this specifically in reference to religion: "It strikes me that religion—in its essence—seeks to take natural events and ascribe supernatural causes to them. I, however, seek to take supernatural events and find the *natural* meanings behind them. Perhaps that is the final dividing line between science and religion. Opposite sides of a card" (1225). Jasnah explicitly identifies her project here as demystification. Interestingly, though, she also presents religion and science as opposite sides of the same card, as fundamentally linked discourses. For Sanderson, religion has no value if it does not help us understand the world *as a rational system*. While literary criticism may prefer a clearer acknowledgment that this truth is entirely textual and not transparently conveying the essence of reality, nonetheless Sanderson attempts to achieve transcendence in his work not through mystification, but through narrative structures that help us understand the *textual* world *as a rational system*. In so doing, he appeals to the reader's curiosity through a consistently transformative understanding of the world that suggests how the world exceeds our capacity to encompass it even as Sanderson encourages us to construct a rationalistic, scientific, ever-evolving understanding of that world.

Brandon Sanderson's Mistborn Trilogy is thus structured in constantly widening circles of understanding, with the reader regularly breaking through to a higher level which casts previous reading in a new light. In the first Mistborn book, Sanderson introduces a culture dominated by the Lord Ruler, a seemingly immortal, all-powerful evil dark lord whose dictatorial rule and rigid class hierarchy mark him as an enemy of freedom. Against him, Sanderson sets Vin, a street urchin who learns she has the magical ability to "burn" metal she has consumed for various effects, making her a rare Mistborn. She is trained as a Mistborn in the magic called allomancy by Kelsier, a messianic figure who leads a resistance against the Lord Ruler. At the same time, a scholar from the enslaved Terris race, Sazed, teaches her about a different form of metal magic, feruchemy, which enables the storage of attributes in external sources of metal, usually worn as bracers or earrings. Throughout the book, a series of chapter epigraphs tells the story of the Lord Ruler's rise to power in a struggle against an ancient evil, a story which includes the narrator (assumed to be the Lord Ruler himself) worrying about the loyalty of his Terris packman, Rashek. These epigraphs, we learn, are excerpted from a document the resistance recovers and studies later in the novel. In the climactic sequence, Vin confronts the Lord Ruler and in a moment of revelation, realizes that the Lord

Ruler is Rashek, not the writer of the journal. Furthermore, this revelation means that the bracers he wears on his arms are the key to his power, through feruchemy, not allomancy. This allows her to remove his bracers, thereby defeating him. In the second book, *The Well of Ascension*, Vin and her husband Elend seek out the titular Well as a source of magic power to help end a conflict in the kingdom, only to discover that the Well was the prison for Ruin, the being the Lord Ruler had defeated and had been keeping imprisoned for centuries. In fact, all of his social restrictions were motivated by a desire to protect the world from this force of cosmic destruction. Each of these developments is marked by structures of surprise as the reader gradually gains further knowledge that forces a reinterpretation of previous events.

This pattern of plot twists, or revelations, in his novels, has an experientially spiritual component, but it is achieved through a rational means. This may be easier to understand by creating a distinction between kinds of narrative revelations. To be sure, most popular narratives build suspense around patterns of mystery followed by revelation. In fact, this could be said to be fundamental to the concept of narrative suspense. However, we must distinguish between "what" revelations and "why" revelations. Sanderson's plots do not merely surprise readers by revealing new information (telling us "what" is happening). Any plot that is driven by revealing what happens to characters is using "what" revelations. In fact, "what" revelations explicitly mystify events, as essentially the only explanation they offer is essentialist—that's just the way it is. Martha Wells's *The Death of the Necromancer* (1998) contrasts Sanderson by relying heavily on "what" revelations. Wells uses a classic mystery story structure set in a secondary fantasy world, and the plot is even more inspired by heist narratives and detective stories, to the point of including an obviously Sherlock Holmes-inspired detective named Ronsarde (with his own Watson, Doctor Halle). Like Sanderson, Wells frequently delays revealing key information to the reader, but this information largely relates to *what* is happening, as in this early scene: "Madeline shouted 'Get back!' Nicholas ducked as a shot exploded behind him. [...] Nicholas looked at Madeline. *She stepped forward, holding a small double-action revolver*" (37–8, emphasis added). To this point in the novel, the existence of guns in this fantasy world has not been established (although it has established a roughly nineteenth-century level of technology), and the delay in identifying the gun seems to be a deliberate choice (Wells does not begin "As she drew her gun, Madeline shouted...") that initially causes the reader to misidentify what is happening as magic. The orientation here is toward stabilizing our understanding of the world, not expanding it—it simply explains the confusing explosion in a surprising way. It may be possible that the affordances of detective fiction are colliding with fantasy in this case. Both fantasy and detective fiction are structured around breakthroughs and revelations, but where fantasy tends toward the flexibility of wonder, detective fiction more commonly results in the restoration of order, the reasoned structuring of a known universe.[8] On the other hand, Sanderson's plot structures function differently; they explain *why* things happen as they do. The carefully structured release of information in Sanderson's novels is designed to gradually give an improved understanding of *how the world works* to the reader. The revelation that Rashek is the Lord Ruler helps the reader understand why he acts as he does and why Vin is able to defeat him. Incomplete information gives way to more complete information, a rationalistic pattern. By structuring his novels as a series of discoveries, Sanderson reinforces the scientific excitement of finding out why unexpected events happen. By taking advantage of the endorphin rush we feel when learning new information, Sanderson is appealing to readers' desire to understand the world, not a desire to mystify it.

This pleasure in increased understanding is also the source of the feeling of transcendence created by his novels. "Transcendence" here means the feeling of attaining a standpoint outside the rules of a system from which one can observe the entire system (and take pleasure in the feeling of mastering the system). Of course, the narrative does not actually take us outside the system because that system is generated by the text itself, yet it *creates the feeling* of getting outside the system from within the system of language—it gives the reader an almost spiritual feeling of transcendence as a linguistically constructed form. The pattern works like this: a set of rules (often a magic system) establishes the parameters of the world; characters seem to break those rules, suggesting the ability to escape the system; new information reveals these rule violations are not arbitrary but are part of a higher-level system behind them, which the reader has the pleasure of uncovering. Just as the sublime is the perception that the mind is capable of encompassing a force that is beyond the self, in the same way, I would argue, this ever-escalating sense of rule violation followed by re-establishment of the new rule system creates the sublime effect that I am calling "transcendence." Significantly for the purposes of this argument, though, it is a feeling of transcendence grounded in the discovery of the rational, orderly rules of a world, not the mystification of those rules.

Two significant examples from the Mistborn Trilogy should effectively illustrate this narrative transcendence at work: a minor example regarding Vin's ability to pierce "copperclouds," and the more significant one about Sazed and the prophecy of the Hero of Ages. In the world of Mistborn, allomancers burn different metals for different effects.

Bronze allows one to sense when another allomancer burns metals, thus tracking them down as though by radar. Copper, on the other hand, creates a "cloud" that blocks this effect, allowing allomancers to operate without fear of detection. These rules are established early in the first novel in the (perhaps overly expository) training Vin receives. However, Vin inexplicably develops the ability to "pierce" copperclouds, sensing allomantic pulses even when copper is being burned. This might initially seem like an irrational inconsistency in the plot, and as Sanderson seems to be setting Vin up as the prophesied savior figure (the "Hero of Ages" in this series), anyone familiar with fantasy tropes might initially write this off as a sign that she is the special, prophesied hero—a sign of fantasy's promotion of an irrational, anti-cognitive world view that actually stifles curiosity by answering "why" questions with "just because." However, late in the series we learn of another form of metal magic, hemalurgy, which allows one to steal an allomancer's ability if a piece of metal soaked in that allomancer's blood is embedded in one's body. Usually this metal appears in the form of large spikes imbedded in the bodies of the fearsome Inquisitors (most notably in their eyes). However, from the beginning of the first novel, Vin has worn an earring given to her by her mother, who put it in Vin's ear while apparently going insane and killing Vin's sister. When it is revealed in the third novel that Vin's earring is not only a piece of jewelry but a tiny hemalurgic spike, a number of details throughout the series come together. Vin's ability to pierce copperclouds is explained because her ability to use bronze has been boosted by hemalurgy (apparently her infant sister would have had this ability had she lived). Furthermore, the disembodied villain of the series, Ruin, is able to manipulate people with hemalurgic spikes in their skin, which is why the Inquisitors act as his agents throughout the series. Thus, Vin having such a spike in her body explains a number of her actions, including the voice of her dead brother that she sometimes imagines hearing in her head: it is actually Ruin speaking to and manipulating her. In retrospect, upon receiving this revelation, the reader can note the carefully controlled release of information, going back to the very earliest chapters of the series.

It even explains what initially may have appeared to be plot holes or concessions to fantasy conventions. In Vin's climactic encounter with the Lord Ruler, Vin is about to be killed by the Lord-Ruler when she inexplicably "drew upon the mists" (*Mistborn* 630) to give her the power to defeat him. At the time this is unexplained, as this world's ever-present mists seem to be simply a feature of the climate, not a magical source of power. Although she has broken the rules and exceeded what seemed to be her capabilities, it is noteworthy that this moment does not generate the same wonder as the later revelation. However, after learning about the earring, a small detail from that earlier fight with the Lord Ruler gains importance: "He slammed her with another of his powerful Pushes, blasting her backwards [...] and her mother's earring ripped free of her ear" (*Mistborn* 626). While this moment is not underlined in the first book, in the third book, after the reader has learned that the mists are inimical to Ruin and that hemalurgy would prevent Vin from channeling them, this moment finally makes sense. The mists are the last remains of Ruin's god-like rival Preservation, and Vin can only draw on his remaining strength when she is free of Ruin's influence (in the form of the earring/spike). It is *that* moment of looking back across nearly three books and rationally fitting together the pieces of the narrative that makes the twist work, that imbues it with the experience of breakthrough and transcendence. By understanding more about how the world works, the reader can now understand *why* events have happened as they have.

To compound this transcendent feeling of mastery granted by greater knowledge, Sanderson structures the revelation scene about the earring to lead the reader through the process of making the connections, rather than presenting it as an announcement from a transcendent god-like narrator. The scene takes place in the middle of a climactic confrontation, as another character realizes what the earring is and removes it, at which point Vin is able to tap into the mists again, win a seemingly unwinnable battle, and literally transcend her own body to become a disembodied spiritual power. It begins from the perspective of Marsh, a former ally, Kelsier's brother, now an Inquisitor serving Ruin. As he fights her on Ruin's behalf, he resists Ruin's control and presents a series of reminders of minor character-building scenes from earlier books in the series: "His hand moved up to her collarbone. And then he saw it. A single bit of metal, glittering in Vin's ear. Her earring. She'd explained it to him once. *I don't remember it*, Vin's voice whispered to him from the past" (637). The action pauses for Marsh to recall details from this seemingly minor scene from the first book in the series. Now, though, after the discoveries about hemalurgy in this volume, the odd details are highlighted; most noteworthy, her insane mother killed her infant sister but only gave Vin an earring. Marsh recalls something an ally had written in a letter after learning about hemalurgy: "*Don't trust anyone pierced by metal.* [...] *Even the smallest bit can taint a man. The smallest bit*" (637). Then he examines the earring itself: "As he looked closer, the earring—though twisted and chipped—looked almost like a tiny spike" (637). Then Marsh resists Ruin's control for one small action: "Summoning all the will he had remaining, Marsh reached out. And ripped the earring from Vin's ear" (637). There are two things to note about the construction of this scene. First, Sanderson carefully leads the reader through a series of details that have been planted throughout the series, from the first book to the third, making it clear that this narrative design has always been present (it is not an improvisation at the last moment), and that in fact a careful, attentive reader could have reasoned this out just as Marsh has. Apparently contradictory details are now absorbed in a higher order system that has always been present, and the reader may feel the sudden expansion of knowledge as a metaphorical lift to higher vantage point from which to see more of the design of the world. Yet this affective "lift" has been designed through a rational process.

Second, the style of the passage repeatedly delays the key details as long as possible, allowing the reader the opportunity to make those connections independently before dramatically presenting them as realizations—breakthroughs—being made by Marsh. When Marsh first sees the earring, "it" is separated in its own sentence and only vaguely identified. An inductive description of details ("metal," "glittering") proceeds the final identification of the object itself (an "earring"), again giving the reader the opportunity to piece together what Marsh is looking at and (even if we have already figured it out or have read the passage before) simulating Marsh's emotional response of abrupt realization with the final, punchy revelation of information. This pattern continues throughout the passage: *"even the smallest bit. The smallest bit"* and "the earring—though twisted and chipped—looked almost like a tiny spike" both highlight the key revelatory detail by separating it at the end of the sentence either by repetition or be delaying it with an interrupting phrase. His climactic action in the scene is similarly delayed by being pushed into a separate sentence fragment: "And ripped the earring from Vin's ear." This syntactic pattern of delay is particularly pronounced in epic fantasy, especially around moments of revelation, awe, and wonder. It is *the* signature syntactic figure of wonder in epic fantasy. For my argument about Sanderson, though, I particularly want to emphasize the multiple levels of transcendence or breakthrough occurring here. Literal transcendence within the narrative (Vin actually transcends her body at the end of the passage) is matched to the feeling of transcendence inspired in the reader by the surprise twist revealing a new level of information and design in the world, which is matched by syntax that expresses the feeling of surprise in Marsh—a structure of feeling that can be re-experienced upon re-reading. Ultimately, the pleasure of rational explanation is mirrored by the pleasure of additional rule violations, in this case the winning of an "unwinnable" battle as Vin defeats Marsh and then abandons her physical body.

However, this late moment in the series is matched by a further revelation in the final pages, a violation of the conventional fantasy hero tropes that brings together all of the narrative patterns I have discussed in the character of Sazed, who most thoroughly represents the fusion of the religious and the scientific discourses in Sanderson. Sazed appears in the first book of the series as an ally of Kelsier who functions as another teacher and mentor for Vin. He is another scholar-hero because his primary job is to preserve the knowledge of his dying race, the Terris. He does this using the third type of metal magic, feruchemy, which allows him to store attributes (most notably knowledge or memories) in metal in order to access them later, making him a kind of fantasy computer through his use of the bracers he wears as storage devices on his arms. His primary area of study is religions, and he loses faith in religion after the woman he loves dies. He is a thoroughly unconventional fantasy hero, in that he is quiet, bookish, and emasculated (quite literally as he is a eunuch). Thus, the series' most surprising revelation is that he, and not Vin, is actually the "Hero of Ages." When Vin dies in the final battle of the novel and the world seems to be coming to end, it once again seems to break the conventional rules—isn't the hero supposed to save the world? However, as Sazed witnesses her death, he (and the reader) realize that the prophecies that have been repeatedly quoted and applied to Vin throughout the book have been misinterpreted: "*The prophecies always used the gender-neutral* [...] *perhaps because they referred to a hero who wasn't really either [man or woman]? [...] The hero would be [...] not a warrior, though he would fight. [...] the words of the prophecy [...] say that the Hero will bear the future of the world on his arms. Not on his shoulders. Not in his hands. On his arms*" (714–5, italics as in original). This moment of revelation follows the same pattern as Marsh's revelation above, as it pulls details that have been discussed since the beginning of the series (the "on his arms" prophecy is on the first page of the first novel of the series) but introduces them in a context that allows the character and reader to reinterpret them. It also uses the same structure of delay to highlight key details: Sazed's realization about the phrase "on his arms" is pushed off into a sentence fragment that is delayed by two structurally similar fragments ("not on ... not in ..."), as he realizes the prophecy could refer to the feruchemical bracers on his arms. It is fascinating that the climactic moment in an epic fantasy trilogy full of action-adventure would involve a scholar (and the reader) *reinterpreting a text* in order to better understand how the world works. Certainly, it may be problematic that this scene reinforces the notion of prophecy as teleology, that the essence of the world is fixed and hierarchical and merely there to be discovered. While other texts handle this conflict between essentialism and constructivism in more nuanced ways, it is nonetheless significant that the reader has been enmeshed in the same "prediction error" as the characters with regards to their expectations about the hero. The structure of the narrative encourages reinterpretation, awareness that prior interpretations may be incorrect, perhaps even an awareness of the textuality of meaning in the world. This final twist is a goad to curiosity, to the flexible awareness that our assumptions may be wrong and need to be continually reinvestigated. That expansion of the awareness of possibilities is the moment of sublime perception.

As the scene proceeds, Sazed seizes Vin's power and uses the knowledge of science stored in his metal bracers to fix the world. Again, the content and the form go hand in hand here, as knowledge—science—saves the world, and the reader's increased knowledge of the world creates narrative pleasure through the revelation. In fact, despite his growing doubts about religion, the knowledge that Sazed has gathered of world religions proves to be essential to his role as savior of the world: "And, in a moment of transcendence, he understood it all. He saw the patterns, the clues, the secrets. [...] Gems, hidden from Ruin in all the religions of mankind" (716). One religion had seen mapmaking as a sacred duty, while another had studied the stars. This astronomical and geographical data allows him to adjust the planet's orbit and structure to fix the destructive effects of Ruin's interventions. Again, this is both a moment of structural transcendence, as the reader recognizes that a pattern of character development throughout the book has a larger purpose, and a moment of literal transcendence in the narrative as Sazed goes beyond his earlier limitations to achieve a moment of cognitive breakthrough. This final twist also follows the classic Aristotelian model, as Sazed's final revelation is essentially about his own identity, an *anagnorisis*, and thus even upon re-reading a reader can imaginatively re-experience Sazed's own realizations as an act of imaginative sympathy. Finally, as in the example of Vin above, Sazed transcends his humanity at the end of the scene: "It wasn't until that moment that Sazed understood the term Hero of Ages. Not a Hero that came once in the ages. But a hero who would span the ages. A Hero who would preserve mankind throughout all its lives and times. Neither Preservation nor Ruin, but both. God" (718). It is a bold move to not only have the scholar be the hero, but to actually have him become the God of his world at the end of the story, and that boldness is highlighted by yet another sentence structure of delay, as "God" is, once again, in a fragment at the end of the passage after another delaying fragment.

While Sanderson could be faulted for a somewhat essentialist worldview in his use of prophecy here, nonetheless, in both plot and narrative structure the climax of the Mistborn series derives its power and narrative pleasure through the application of rational, orderly thinking, not through mystification. But in doing so, Sanderson achieves an almost religious, spiritual, transcendent effect. Thus, Sanderson embodies the ideological

link between the discourses of science and religion, which both aim to explain the world from a transcendental standpoint. At the same time, he demonstrates that the pleasure of fantasy might be linked as much to rationalistic demystification as it is in any other more self-consciously "literary" form.

The Wonder of Delayed Syntax in Moorcock's Elric

In Sanderson, the broader level of narrative structure echoes the syntax to create the sense of wonder. The final revelations about Sazed's identity use the same syntactic pattern of delay that I noted in the introduction and in the passage about Vin's earring: the phrases "on his arms" and "God" have the same dramatic revelation of key information delayed by inductive lists of details that lead the reader to that abrupt conclusion. Many sentences split off key moments into separate fragments or sentences beginning with the conjunction "and," as with "And, in a moment of transcendence, he understood it all," again representing Sazed's feeling of wonder at the revelations. This structure allows the reader to experience that wonder as well, after first building to it through a mass of evidentiary details that the reader has an opportunity to construct for themselves, and thus readers also have the epiphany on the basis of their own rational efforts. I have already called this delayed syntax the signature syntactic figure of wonder in epic fantasy, and so to justify that description, I will conclude by examining how Michael Moorcock uses the same structure of wonder in his Elric series.

The anarchist Michael Moorcock's frequent deployment of such expansive structures in the Elric series indicates quite clearly why structures of delay are so common in fantasy, and why (in spite of the tinge of essentialism in Sanderson's deployment of them) these structures couple so nicely with what James Gifford describes as a "liberation-driven" politics (Gifford 73). Certainly, one of the most intriguing aspects of this structural similarity is that it appears in such different writers. Many fantasy writers are non-religious, and Moorcock's atheistic cultural materialism is about as far-removed from Sanderson's Mormonism (or Tolkien's Catholicism) as we might imagine. Nonetheless, they use similar stylistic structures of transcendent wonder, suggesting a secular component to this structure of wonder. Again, this is evidence of the degree to which epic fantasy structures are the result of collisions of forms, in this case the collision of a rationalistic (scientific) desire for a transcendent relation to the world and a religious one. Sanderson might approach transcendence from the religious end and Moorcock from the rational materialist, but both arrive at similar places through the collisions within the experience of wonder.

Another contrast between these writers that demonstrates the extent to which the structure of wonder underlies fantasy is the different eras in which they are writing. Sanderson writes at a time when epic fantasy has definitive parameters and set conventions. Moorcock creates Elric at a time when those labels are just being established, and it is worth pausing briefly to consider why Moorcock's Elric books (and his Eternal Champion cycle more generally) fits into the epic fantasy tradition when it is more commonly defined as "sword and sorcery." To be sure, as Mark Scroggins details, Moorcock's influences for the series tended to be writers like Poul Anderson and Fritz Leiber rather than Tolkien, who had little influence on Moorcock (31), and Moorcock developed Elric when an editor asked him for "some Conan-type stuff" (qtd. in Scroggins 24). However, Moorcock clearly thought of what he was doing in this series in epic terms—he even suggested "epic fantasy" as a name for the genre in his 1961 essay "Putting a Tag on It," and his body of criticism of epic fantasy (collected in the volume *Wizardry & Wild Romance* [2004]) indicates Moorcock's association of heroic fantasy with the epic tradition. More importantly, once Moorcock gets past the earlier serialized Elric short stories, the later books (late both in series chronology—such as *Stormbringer* [1965]—and in composition—such as the prequel *Elric of Melniboné* [1972]) grow to the scale more often associated with epic fantasy. *Stormbringer* ends in a battle that literally transforms the world. Prior to this final battle, Elric travels through a portal to what appears to be a version of our real world and visits the tomb of the hero of French epic, Roland, who is introduced as another manifestation of the Eternal Champion, placing Elric (and Moorcock's other avatars of the Eternal Champion) distinctly in the epic tradition. Thus, Moorcock takes an intriguing place in fantasy history in intertwining the threads between "epic" and "sword and sorcery," an issue I will consider at more length in Chapter 6, particularly in relation to one of Moorcock's influences, Fritz Leiber. However, whereas Leiber, as I will show, imports elements of epic parodically, Moorcock plays it straight with the scale and style of the epic.

Moorcock's Elric stories were rapidly written, originally largely to finance Moorcock's avant-garde science fiction magazine *New Worlds*, and they are deliberately formulaic. Yet Moorcock uses the formulae intelligently and thoughtfully to reflect on the function of the narratives themselves, as Colin Greenland notes: "Moorcock is the first sword-and-sorcery writer to build the psychological function of reading fantasy into the work itself. Enlarged and simplified, the hero is a symbol of the reader" (125).

In a romantic form such as fantasy, Moorcock argues that the goal is not to portray realistic psychology but to distill meaning in striking images: "The romance's prime concern is not with character or narrative but with the evocation of strong, powerful images; symbols conjuring up a multitude of sensations to be used (as mystics once used distorting mirrors, as romantics used opium or, latterly, LSD) as escape from the pressures of the objective world or as a means of achieving increased self-awareness" ("Foreword" 20). The political value of this lies in the shaping of perception, which can enable a "self-perception" that liberates the self from ideological determination (Gifford 69). These powerful images portray a "chaotic, infinitely malleable but totally undependable" (Greenland 128) reality that places the burden on human perception to create meaning. As Greenland puts it, "it was the search for a new standpoint that was most important" (128)—in other words, the point of fantasy is to create new ways of perceiving reality that give it meaning and purpose.

Thus, for Moorcock, fantasy entails a shift from the emphasis on character to the emphasis on image, and the creation of what I have been calling "wonder" is linked to the shaping of perception in a way that lines up with the argument in the aesthetics of surprise ranging from Aristotle to Adam Smith. Furthermore, Moorcock's emphasis on formula demonstrates that this wonder is formally constructed, at least in part by the style of writing. In an interview with Greenland, Moorcock describes the style of his popular fantasy work as conscious, disciplined, formulaic but somewhat overblown: "You want a slightly elevated prose style, with a certain amount of purple in it, but at the same time it must never get in the way of the narrative" (9). Specifically, he cites using rhythm and rhyme to echo the King James Bible, and "using a lot of *ands* to begin sentences … to keep the whole thing shifting forward all the time" (10). This last detail is particularly intriguing, as Brandon Sanderson tends to do the same in many of the examples cited above, such as in the dramatic conclusion of Marsh's epiphany: "And ripped the earring from Vin's ear." As I have noted in Chapter 1, beginning sentences with "and" has the paradoxical effect of extending connections while highlighting separation. "And" should be connecting ideas, so why create the hard separation of the sentence or paragraph divide? In Sanderson's case, as well as Moorcock's, it again marks this syntax of delay that dramatically emphasizes the wonderful revelation. Moorcock offers a good example in *Elric of Melniboné* with the arrival of a ship which magically sails on land: "And then they saw something emerge from the forest and the land itself seemed to ripple. It was something which glinted white and blue and black. It came closer. 'A sail,' said Dyvim Tvar. 'It is your ship'" (247). Not only does this passage start with "and," but the preponderance of "ands" within the passage gives a rhythmic sense of continuous forward momentum, yet this rhythm all serves to delay the revelation of what Elric (and the reader) are seeing. The surprising, wonderful detail is initially referred to vaguely as "something" and "it" (twice), with small evidentiary details building up in increasingly obvious ways (the rippling land, the glinting colors, the sail) before finally naming the object itself—a ship sailing where it should not be. Once again, this involves the reader in constructing in their imaginations something which should not exist, rationally deducing the existence of the irrational. This experience of that-which-exceeds-perception existing within one's mind causes the perception-expanding experience typically called the sublime, here serving the purpose of instilling greater mental flexibility.

Notably in relation to Csicsery-Ronay's argument about grotesque and sublime wonder, Moorcock's fantasy is particularly known for its grotesque imagery, and he frequently uses the same structures of delay for the grotesque as well. Elric himself is physically a grotesque character, his appearance marked by the dissolute features drawn from nineteenth-century degeneration theory, reminiscent of the "living dead" imagery of classic vampire stories like *Dracula* or *Nosferatu*. To set up these images, the initial description of him in *Elric of Melniboné* is filled with inverted sentences that delay naming what exactly is being described: "It is the colour of a bleached skull, his flesh; and the long hair which flows below his shoulders is milk-white. From the tapering, beautiful head stare two slanting eyes, crimson and moody, and from the loose sleeves of his yellow gown emerge two slender hands, also the colour of bone" (169). The first sentence in particular uses a right dislocation to place the tenor of the metaphor *after* the vehicle, thus obscuring the reader's ability to visualize Elric: we picture a skull before we realize we should be picturing a head with flesh, a moment of grotesque hesitation.[9] Furthermore, the entire passage delays naming who is being described—only after several pages of description is the object of this description identified by name as Elric. Once again, the style of the text invokes a sense of wonder through its dramatic delay, although in this case more through the perceptual confusion of the grotesque, yet still involving the reader in a rational deduction process. After all, the novel is titled *Elric*, so the reader should likely deduce who is being described before the artificially dramatic reveal.

Finally, Moorcock particularly reveals the epic roots of this stylistic device through its connections to the temporal extension and vast scale of the epic. This becomes particularly clear in the climactic Elric novel (though not the last one written), *Stormbringer* (1965). Toward the end of this novel, Elric and the warring armies the book has been about to this point become merely the tools of the Lords of Law and the Lords of Chaos as they battle to determine the future shape of a reborn earth. The Lords of Law enter the battle tangibly at the end of a chapter after Elric blows the Horn of Fate in a scene clearly designed to invoke awe and wonder. The chapter ends: "The note took long moments to fade and, when it had at last died away, there was an absolute hush over the world, the milling millions were still, there was an air of expectancy. And then the White Lords came" (421). At this point, the features of delay should be so familiar that I need not belabor the commentary, but the description of this entry is further delayed by a chapter break, and the following chapter begins with, essentially, an epic simile:

> It was as if some enormous sun, thousands of times larger than Earth's had sent a ray of light pulsing through the cosmos, defying the flimsy barriers of time and space, to strike upon that great black battlefield. And along it, appearing on the pathway that the horn's weird power had created for them, strode the majestic Lords of Law, their earthly forms so beautiful that they challenged Elric's sanity, for his mind could scarcely absorb the sight [421].

By beginning with an extended simile, this passage suggests that the syntax of delay has its roots in the history of the epic simile. If we consider the function of these similes, they often attempt to convey a powerful or dramatic image by conferring an extended quantity of language on it, and they frequently do so by placing a lengthy description of the metaphor's vehicle *before* the description of the tenor, thus dramatically delaying its appearance. Many of Milton's epic similes follow this pattern, as in his description of the angels fallen into hell in Book 1 of *Paradise Lost*: "[Satan] stood, and called / His legions, angel forms, who lay entranced, / Thick as autumnal leaves that strow the brooks / In Vallombrosa [...] or scattered sedge / Afloat, when with fierce winds Orion armed / Hath vexed the Red Sea coast, whose waves o'erthrew / Busiris and his Memphian chivalry [...] *so thick bestrewn, / Abject and lost, lay these*, covering the flood, / Under amazement of their hideous change" (I.300–313, emphasis added). The structure should be familiar by now: in order to create a picture of the vast extent of the angelic army lying destroyed, Milton pauses to create a double metaphor, first of leaves, then of the Egyptian army drowned after Moses crossed the Red Sea, before finally circling back to a long delayed but now contextually much expanded description of the original tenor, the "abject and lost" fallen angels. These dramatic delaying structures are, in Moorcock's hands, the legacy of the epic simile and serve a similar function in *Stormbringer* to confer a transcendent sense of elevation to this battle, a sense of universe-historical import.

This temporal extension is also on display in the final pages of the book, after the new earth has been created, as Elric is killed by his vampiric sword Stormbringer. Throughout the series, Elric has been a flawed, abject hero constantly bemoaning his lack of agency in service to the sword which sucks the souls from his enemies in order to give him the supernatural strength to be a hero. While there is much to be said here about the sword as a metaphor for drug abuse or the abuse of power, in these final moments when the sword turns upon its bearer, Moorcock uses a delaying syntax in order to create the sublime sense of the extended eternity in which Elric's soul will now be tormented by being part of the sword:

> [H]e felt the icy touch of the blade against his heart, reached out his fingers to clutch at it, felt his body constrict, felt it sucking his soul from the very depths of his being, felt his whole personality being drawn into the runesword. He knew, as his life faded to combine with the sword's, that it had always been his destiny to die in this manner. [...] And, as he died, he wept again, for he knew that the fraction of the sword's soul which was his would never now rest but was doomed to immortality, to eternal struggle [433].

Here the rhythmic parallelism extends the first sentence, seemingly endlessly—it has *five* verbs in parallel form. The passage, unsurprisingly, concludes with a sentence beginning with "and," which then delays the main idea (that his soul "would never rest") behind several other clauses before ending with yet another repetition of parallel clauses. The entire passage is, on a content level, about the extension of his tormented existence, and on a formal level, it continually extends itself so that it seems to expand beyond the boundaries of the short time it takes to read. As the concept of extended time is so essential to epic fantasy, this passage clearly demonstrates why these figures of delay are such an important part of the transcendent wonder generated by epic fantasy, as are Elric's concerns with agency in the passage, the relationship between history and the individual. In the Elric stories, this wonder is used in a conventionally structured way to expand the reader's perception of possibilities, to make the reader feel the depth of time as Elric feels it but also to recognize how the universe exceeds a human's cognitive limitations.

Just as Bacchilega reminds us by talking about the "politics of wonder" and associating it specifically with transformation, these authors demonstrate how epic fantasy uses wonder to transform our view of the world. As Moorcock's "powerful images" transform perception and Sanderson's expand perception, wonder is not merely an affect tacked on by the reader but a linguistically constructed function of style, which largely serves to expand cognitive flexibility and transform our fixed, stable worldviews.

CHAPTER 6

The Mundane Fantastic

Stylistic Magic and Genre Collisions

"The last time I stood beside an Earl of Dros Delnoch in battle, we carved a legend," [Druss] said.

"The odd thing about sagas," offered Rek, "is that they very rarely mention dry mouths and full bladders."
—David Gemmell, *Legend*

Late in David Gemmell's influential novel *Legend* (1984), in the midst of one of many battle scenes as the Drenai protagonists defend the fortress walls of Dros Delnoch from the Nadir hordes, a small detail indicates how Gemmell's stylistic ambiguities undermine the magical performance of language with mundane reality. As Gemmell introduces the antagonist for an action set piece in combat with the hero Druss, he pauses for a paragraph of description, starting with the following sentence: "Below the walls, among the Nadir, was a giant called Nogusha" (295). As the reader knows we are in a fantasy novel, the immediate picture conjured by the word "giant" is likely to be a towering monster, something akin to a frost giant or a character out of "Jack and the Beanstalk." This dramatic buildup is supported by the structure of the sentence, which uses prepositional phrases to delay the giant's introduction. This structure of delay appears to follow fantasy's stylistic conventions for generating wonder (as I described in Chapter 5), and thus builds the reader's expectations. Thus, in this context, the final sentence of the paragraph comes as a surprise: "An inch over six feet, Nogusha was the tallest warrior in the Nadir ranks and the most deadly" (295). While the entire paragraph has staged the impressive stature of Nogusha, the effect here is almost certainly going to be one of diminishment, almost bathos. Gemmell deflates the anticipated effect of wonder, replacing it with the merely mundane. The enormous monster suggested by the word "giant" is revealed to be substantially shorter than the average professional basketball player, "giant" only relative to those around him. This moment forces readers to re-orient their imaginations, unmasking the fantastic expectations as the readers' projections on the text and re-grounding the audience in the mundane, largely rational world that has been typical throughout this novel. If the wonder discussed in my last chapter is, in Csicsery-Ronay's phrase, the "sense of liberation from the mundane" (71), then this passage reads almost as an explicit rejection of wonder. This moment of uncertainty, of re-orientation when the reader vacillates between the fantastic and the mundane, most characterizes the style of *Legend* and other fantasy novels that make up the mundane fantastic. While structurally similar to wonder, here the uncertainty leads not to a new understanding but to a return to a familiar, everyday understanding of the world. This different use of uncertainty is crucial to both the novel's unmasking of "legends" as projections constructed by language and the ultimate assertion that such legends are necessary. I am referring to this as stylistic magic, as the novel contains little literal magic (that is, diagetic magic) and is largely set in a rational world that seems to come out of the history of the real world, yet the language of the novel—sometimes playing with genre expectations, sometimes simply playing with words in ways that emphasize precision and category formation—creates a sense of mystery and uncertainty that generates the affect of magic and instills an awareness of the constructed nature of that affect.

Gemmell's tendency to downplay and deflate magic is linked to an overall philosophy that favors pragmatic, physical action over abstract representation. In a 2007 interview with Stan Nicholls, Gemmell makes a curious distinction between being a writer and being a storyteller. For Gemmell, the writer can become paralyzed with concern over abstractions, while the storyteller is concerned with physical action. Throughout this interview, Gemmell repeats this preference for direct action, which he seems to see both as more pragmatic and more truthful. When Nicholls observes that problems are resolved with direct action in Gemmell's books, Gemmell agrees that this reflects his personal philosophy: "Problems that come up I tend to headbutt, go straight at and kick out of the way. It's the only way in which I'm political."

It may seem puzzling for a writer to disclaim "writing" and reflection in favor of direct action, but there are clearly political stakes in championing action over rhetoric. As I have already discussed, too much distrust of complexity and rhetoric might work in favor of fascist or totalitarian leaders that seek to dominate an unthinking populace,[1] but the case is perhaps more complex than that. Gemmell's muscular, masculine philosophy of action over paralyzing reflection, of sincere, direct honesty over posing and artifice, has a dual literary genealogy: the heroic tradition in epic myth and historical narrative, and cynical twentieth-century war fiction that subverts the ideology of heroism and glory (ranging from Hemingway to Tim O'Brien to Gemmell's fantasy contemporary Glen Cook, as discussed in Chapter 4). In this way, Gemmell's writing embodies the core principle of collision at the heart of the style I have been investigating throughout this study. Particularly in his influential and characteristic first novel *Legend*, Gemmell's writing struggles to contain multiple incompatible traditions: the plot—built around an extended siege in a key battle in an immense war—invokes heroic legendary narratives from the *Iliad* to Thermopylae that often valorize cultural ideals of glory, honor, and sacrifice, yet despite this epic set up, the novel commonly uses the deflating irony of realistic war fiction. The central hero, Druss, appears as the noble, idealized hero intended as a pattern for the reader, yet the novel's unadorned language and emphasis on direct portrayal of action is much more reminiscent of the style of popular pulp heroics as in Robert E. Howard's Conan stories. *Legend* emerges at the tumultuous overlap between competing forms, simultaneously holding Druss up as a paragon of heroic courage and yet distrusting such ideological abstractions.

In its position at a crossroads between literary forms, Gemmell's writing shares intriguing affinities with another author writing at a transition in genre history, Fritz Leiber, whose stories about Fafhrd and the Gray Mouser span what Jamie Williamson describes as an important hinge moment between the pregenre popular pulp period and a unified definition of a "fantasy genre." Prior to this defining period ranging from the mid–1960s to mid–1970s, Williamson describes two general bodies of writing that fed into the fantasy genre (and retroactively were grouped as fantasy), a literary group of writers (such as Dunsany, Eddison, and Tolkien) who published books with "reputable" publishers and sought to imitate the *form* of historical narratives (such as the epic), and a popular group of writers (such as Robert E. Howard and Clark Ashton Smith) who published in the pulps for a popular audience, only superficially imitating the *content* of historical narratives in a simple, direct, action-oriented prose.[2] Early in his career, Leiber clearly belongs to this latter category, and the first Fafhrd and Gray Mouser stories in the 1930s and 1940s fit into this pattern. However, Leiber is one of a small number of writers whom Williamson shows disrupting any too simple reading of this history. In fact, the majority of the Fafhrd and Gray Mouser work "dates to the genre period" (178) and Leiber himself is a "connecting thread" between the pregenre and genre periods (186). In fact, Leiber's creation of a "fully secondary world" "perhaps recalls Cabell and Eddison rather than Howard," and "The sophistication of Leiber's controlled, varied, often heavily ironic (if not notably archaized) prose also to some degree recalls those writers rather than Howard" (178). In other words, while still being very much influenced by the pulp ancestry, Leiber's *style* came to resemble that of the "literary" writers, the more elaborate and distanced style that I have described throughout this book as typical of epic fantasy. This may indicate Leiber was adapting his creations to new genre norms, or perhaps even that he is openly parodying these genre norms, distrusting their idealization from the position of the everyday workingman.

Thus, Gemmell and Leiber arrive at similar formal collisions from opposite directions: Gemmell begins with a larger epic structure which he undermines through a plain, action-oriented style reminiscent of the pulps, while Leiber begins with roguish pulp heroes and then parodically applies a style associated with epic idealization. Both work at a collision point between epic fantasy and other subgeneric forms. In light of my argument from the previous chapter that the affect of wonder defines epic fantasy style, these writers illuminate what happens when fantasy de-emphasizes sublimity and wonder in favor of the mundane, the everyday, pulling toward a form of fantasy more commonly called sword and sorcery. While my definition of epic fantasy (see the introduction) is broad enough to include texts often classified as "sword and sorcery," the distinction becomes analytically significant, I believe, in relation to this point. The latter subgenre label is associated with a refusal of idealization, with heroes such as Conan who are often selfish and engaged in activities on a personal rather than national or global scale.[3] This, to some degree, weakens the communal associations that I have described as an affordance of the epic by undermining the abstractions that allow us to generalize to a group identity. This is not to say that empathy and communal identity are absent, but they are not foregrounded to the same degree. Gemmell and Leiber are particularly fascinating as they both seem to be caught in contradictory impulses—the impulse to undermine and deconstruct, and the impulse to generalize and make communal connections. In consequence, they are particularly useful writers for thinking through the impact of the contradictory formal influences at the core of the fantasy genre.

In this way, they parallel a more canonical literary figure caught in a similar collision of contradictory formal impulses: Joseph Conrad. Because a more substantial body of critical literature exists to comment on Conrad, it will be useful to consider briefly how Conrad's core concerns come from a similar conflict. Early in his career, Conrad was seen as writing in the tradition of adventure fiction that included Rudyard Kipling, Robert Louis Stevenson, and Rider Haggard (Watt 43). Many of these same writers influenced the early popular pregenre fantasy writers that eventually developed into sword and sorcery, particularly Haggard whom Williamson calls the beginning of a "bridge between this nineteenth-century nonfantasy and [Robert E.] Howard" (173) and whose influence Williamson cites frequently among many pregenre fantasy writers. Despite

Conrad's professed disdain for Haggard, numerous critics have seen Haggard's work as an important context for Conrad's and suggest that he may have even been attempting to draw from Haggard's audience even in major works such as *Heart of Darkness*.[4] In keeping with the adventure tradition (and much like Gemmell in particular), Conrad values physical activity, especially physical labor, over abstraction and idealization. Ian Watt, for instance, argues that Conrad contrasts his cynical, practical narrator Marlow in *Heart of Darkness* to the "idealising abstractions" favored by most other characters, "a language that has very little connection with the realities either of the external world or of their inner selves" (245). Yet despite this favoring of physical activity over rhetoric, Conrad's style is known for elaborate syntax, broad vocabulary, and lists of adjectives (sometimes descending into abstraction rather than concrete, physical detail). In this sense, Conrad's more baroque stylistic approach is akin to Leiber's, a style appropriate for reveries and subjective perspective rather than the clear delineation of action. Thus, Conrad is also caught between a distrust of idealization as an artificial fantasy structure and a literary tradition that focuses on abstract interiority.

In Conrad's case, this may be motivated by the urgent need, as an immigrant and cultural outsider, to use language to connect to a community, even as this experience makes him aware of language as an artificial performance of values.[5] However, what makes Conrad particularly valuable as a point of comparison to Gemmell and Leiber is his compromised awareness of the *need* for idealizations, even if ideals are simply illusions (or fantasies). Conrad's attitudes towards language and community share surprising affinities with those of anarchist thinkers at his time, despite his criticism of anarchism in novels such as *The Secret Agent*, and it may be worth noting here as well James Gifford's argument about the role anarchists played in shaping the fantasy genre.[6] Paul Hollywood explains the connection between Conrad and the anarchists: "Both needed to attack the political language of their time, to construct a theory of language as expression rather than representation" (247). For both, language only expresses the internal subjective view of the speaker, but while for anarchists, this freeing view of language demolishes ideology and hegemony, Conrad distances himself from anarchists in his belief that, while constructivism is fine for artists, it is dangerous in politics because it seems to "absolve man from the responsibility of telling the truth directly" (249), claiming to represent the "real" while deluding people about what was "real." However, despite being potentially destructive, ultimately these abstractions are necessary because they give us the illusion of order that is necessary to function in a world with no inherent order. Thus, Conrad's art is built upon a fundamental collision: Conrad disliked the artificial fantasies that ordered people's lives and created the political and personal chaos he criticized in his fiction, yet nonetheless he did not want to "break the spell and 'connecting power' of language, the 'saving illusions' and 'tyranny of forms,' which is 'all we have got to hang on to'" (Hollywood 262), a utilitarian vision as Conrad refuses to falsely resolve the conflict between language as artifice and as precise representation of "reality." Conrad starts with the form of "adventure fiction," a form appropriate to his preference for direct action, yet refuses to accept its simple illusions, which he nonetheless sees as necessary.

Transforming "adventure fiction" in the sentence above to "fantasy fiction," Gemmell and Leiber are doing something similar to Conrad—and fantasy is perhaps a genre even more suited to engaging with this problem as it is overtly about illusions. In the last chapter, I examined how writers use form and structure to actively create the sense of wonder in epic fantasy, an illusion of magic that is often described with terms like "suspension of disbelief." However, writers like Gemmell and Leiber try to have it both ways, creating the absorption of wonder while consistently undermining it. For instance, *Legend*, as the title suggests, is concerned about the intersection between realism and "legend," the unclear middle ground where the romantic and magical are nonetheless pragmatic because of how they affect behavior, in this case by motivating the courageous defense of a fortress against a seemingly undefeatable enemy army. Both Gemmell and Leiber are strikingly postmodern in this regard, with their awareness of the artificially constructed nature of fantasy side by side with a pragmatic argument about its use value. By consistently deflating epic idealization, they illustrate even more sharply the collision at the core of genre fantasy between constructivist awareness and pragmatic absorption. Thus, despite the seeming focus on the rational, mundane world and the preference for direct simplicity that this suggests, Gemmell and Leiber also reveal through their style an affordance of epic fantasy to demonstrate the practical value of the irrational, the legendary, perhaps even the spiritual. Epic elements collide with other more skeptical influences to forge a fascinating liminal style.

Furthermore, these two writers form a striking contrast in styles that seems to arrive at similar places from opposite directions. Gemmell writes with a direct, unadorned, rationalistic style of war fiction that he consistently undermines with touches of irrational uncertainty, while Leiber uses an elaborate style suited to epic elevation that he lampoons from a more grounded perspective. Thus, *Legend*, while superficially simple and direct, incorporates a number of noteworthy types of ambiguity or unclear writing, varying from the level of syntax to the temporal or perspectival structure of the narrative. In a sense, the uncertainty raised by these structures provides the stylistic "magic" that is sometimes lacking from the plot. If, as I argued in the last chapter, the seemingly irrational sense of wonder has at its root a rationalized expansion of cognition, here Gemmell demonstrates the inverse: even at its most mundane and "rational," fantasy introduces a significant non-material, spiritual dimension to its politics.[7] At the same time, in contrast to Gemmell's predominantly spare and reportorial style, Leiber indulges in a parodic excess of romanticized language. His characters seem to expect the world to conform to the rational rules of our real world and find themselves surprised by the fantastic world they live in, and their cynical rationality often starkly contrasts the elaborate flourishes of Leiber's writing.

An important implication of this argument is that magic, often the most identifiable element of epic fantasy, indicates neither an essentialist view of language nor an ahistorical, nostalgic desire for the pre-industrial past. In arguing that a fantasy writer's focus on the mundane, rational world comes from a distrust of language, I am specifically linking the linguistic philosophy of fantasy not to some form of nostalgic medievalism but to its modernist and postmodern roots, not to an essentialist desire for credibility in fantasy but to a constructivist impulse. In this context, we may see a distrust of idealization at the heart of the formation of a genre that seems devoted to idealization. The focus on the mundane in Gemmell and Leiber signals their awareness of the spell cast by language to shape our perception of the world. They hesitate to use this power, and yet nonetheless they recognize the need for its "saving illusions" to form social bonds for political action (both on the individual level—what I have referred to as empathy throughout this study—and on the level of large-scale social change). That they do so in such different ways—Gemmell using simple, direct language marked with various reminders of linguistic uncertainty, Leiber using a parodic excess of genre markers—reveals the range of possible stylistic tools available to the fantasy writer.

Stylistic Magic in Gemmell's *Legend*

The passage with which I opened this chapter is characteristic of Gemmell's *Legend* and his overall approach to fantasy and language. Gemmell deflates the wonder of fantasy, continually reminding the reader that this wonder is the product of unreal expectations produced by legendary stories. The magic of fantasy is not the literal magic of a power that changes the world but the "magic" of the subjective filter of language that shapes how we interact with that world. This unmasking of the artifice of fantasy, legends, and language itself is one of Gemmell's avowed objectives in his fiction, as Gemmell described himself as writing about the "true nature of heroes" (Priest), suggesting that heroes are often unreliable. In comments such as this, Gemmell seems as much influenced by twentieth-century war fiction—the ironic realism of writers like Ernest Hemingway and Tim O'Brien—as he is by the ancient tradition of heroic narrative that clearly influences the superficial plot structure. The collision of these two influences helps to found a new subgenre of fantasy, often called "military fantasy," which has been a significant influence in late twentieth- and early twenty-first-century fantasy. In fact, several writers represented in this study can be connected to some degree with military fantasy, writers like Gemmell's contemporary Glen Cook or later writers like Erikson, Bakker, and Kuang. Gemmell taps into a fundamental tension throughout recent fantasy writing between epic idealization and cynical realism through an attitude that starkly separates the rational, mundane world and the ideal-istic projections that are expected out of myths, legends, and the fantasy novels inspired by them; thus, understanding how this tension manifests in Gemmell's use of style is crucial for understanding the development of epic fantasy style over the past three to four decades.

On a plot level, the theme of unmasking heroism appears often in *Legend*, particularly through the pairing of the legendary Druss and the primary point-of-view character, the everyman warrior Rek. When Rek is first introduced, we find him preoccupied with his failure to live up to the masculine heroic ideal. In drunken conversation with a friend reminisc-ing on a past battle, he says, "'I didn't hesitate. Straight in with my sword raised, didn't I?' 'Yes.' 'No, I didn't. I stood for two minutes, shaking. And you got cut'" (9). Rek wants to write his own story as the unhesitating hero who lacks fear, and he is haunted by his failure to live up to that ideal. At this early stage in the novel, Gemmell contrasts Rek's fantasy of heroism with the psychological reality that he seems to be suffering from PTSD, as we see him, for instance, dreaming about past battles where he "cried and begged" to escape (9). Later, on the walls with Druss preparing for the Nadir's attack (after Rek marries the daughter of the earl of Dros Del-noch and then becomes the earl himself), Druss says to him, "The last time I stood beside an Earl of Dros Delnoch in battle, we carved a legend," and Rek replies, "The odd thing about sagas [...] is that they very rarely men-tion dry mouths and full bladders" (221). Rek constantly reminds read-ers of the mundane realities of combat that underlie the "golden lies" of heroism, in much the same way that the novel itself, through much of its middle section, focuses less on glorious combat than on the details of pre-paring for a siege, such as the digging of latrines.

Yet despite all of these frequent reminders of the artificial nature of legends, the novel also suggests the need for these legends, what we might call the "saving illusion," to borrow Conrad's concept. The novel argues for the importance of self-consciously crafting legends, being aware of the pragmatic power of the illusions that language and narrative create. Ulric, the Nadir leader, reflects on this on the eve of winning the siege, after killing Druss, realizing that even if he wins the battle he has lost the narrative due to Druss's heroism: "'your heroics have made me the dark shadow.' In all legends, Ulric knew, there were bright heroes and dark, dark evil. It was the very fabric of each tale. 'I am not evil,' he said. 'I am a warrior born, with a people to protect and a nation to build'" (313). Ulric recognizes that the conventional fantasy formula of good and evil is an artifice laid over a more complex historical reality, yet he also recognizes that this formula has power to shape future actions. Similarly, Druss and Rek defend Dros Delnoch to create a legend of courage and resistance that will fuel future actions. It may be futile and irrational, but such legends function pragmatically to create necessary illusions of heroism.

However, these examples only show this constructivist attitude toward language in the content of the novel, in its plot, but the core of my argument is how this attitude manifests in the style of the novel. For much of the book, the language could be described as reportorial, seemingly transparent. There are very few rhetorical fireworks and many direct sentences without excessive subordination, much more like the style Williamson associates with pulp fantasy than the more baroque stylings of Donaldson and Erikson discussed in Chapter 1, or those of Leiber discussed later in this chapter (or even a writer like Le Guin, despite her strategic use of minimalist passages). The following typical example from the beginning of Chapter 2 creates a good contrast to those I discuss most frequently elsewhere in this book:

> Rek watched in silence as the groom saddled the chestnut gelding. He did not like the horse; it had a mean eye, and its ear lay flat against its skull. The groom, a young slim boy, was crooning gently to it as his shaking fingers tightened the girth [15].

The sentences are each relatively short, as are the clauses, leading to an almost choppy feeling as the short sentences are joined with the parataxis of "and" or a simple semicolon. While there is more adjectival modification than in something like Hemingway's style, the writing is predominantly direct and factual without figurative flourishes, ostentatious parallelism, or apparent alliteration. While this is not consistently true in every paragraph of the novel, this is the prevailing style, and its spare feeling of reportage fits with the distrust of idealizing rhetoric I have been pointing out in the novel's themes and Gemmell's own statements.

However, given this prevailing style, any disruptions of that style stand out even more noticeably. Just as I discussed with the example of the word "giant" above, the mundane, rational surface of reportage often breaks down under the weight of various strategies of stylistic ambiguity or linguistic quibbling, strategies which pull at the seams of the novel's construction, hinting at the irrational magic beneath the surface, ultimately indicating its artifice. While these strategies are interconnected, I will discuss them as three separate features: qualifiers, banter, and unclear syntax.

Qualifiers

While the term "qualifier" has several grammatical meanings, here I am referring to phrases that modify other descriptors (adjectives, adverbs, other descriptive clauses), framing those descriptions in a way that makes the reader (at least briefly) aware that the descriptive phrase may not accurately correspond to reality. (In the previous sentence, "at least briefly" serves as a good example of such a qualifier.) A typical example in *Legend* occurs in a long description as Rek enters a forest controlled by an outlaw named Reinard. Rek rehearses to himself the legend of Reinard's history, which the outlaw uses to frighten off interference: "Reinard. Sired by a prince of hell, born to a noblewoman of Ulalia. *Or so he told it.* Rek had heard that his mother was a Lentrian whore and his father a nameless sailor. He had never repeated this intelligence; he did not, *as the phrase went*, have the guts for it" (17, emphasis added). We might note here an increase in the use of figurative language, as compared to the paragraph about saddling his horse, but that figurative language is always framed by a qualifier. First, Reinard's legend is presented in dramatic fragments but immediately deflated by the qualifying phrase "or so he told it," which undercuts the authority of the legend and compares it to the mundane reality in the following sentence. The second qualifier in this passage is perhaps even more revealing, as here Gemmell (or Rek) seems self-conscious that the figurative language he uses is a dead metaphor, an overused cliché, and rather than saying it directly he points out that this is a common phrase used by others. Figurative language in this novel is usually marked by this type of self-consciousness, attributing it to others, or at least to a particular consciousness other than the author. For example, a few paragraphs before this passage, Rek metaphorically describes the historical events taking place: "But the sun was rising, *Rek knew*, on the Nadir. For the Drenai it was the dusk on the last day" (16, emphasis added). Gemmell ensures that the reader knows this metaphor, also a bit overused, comes from Rek's perspective. Gemmell is able to simultaneously use and disclaim figurative language by making us aware that individual subjectivity is projecting it onto the world—typical of the novel's strategy of holding on to idealization while simultaneously being cynical of it.

This frequent qualification suggests a struggle for the most precise descriptive language, often a failed struggle as language comes up short. Rek must resort to clichés and made-up stories because these are the only tools language presents to express reality. This often manifests as an uncertainty about the categories language creates. For instance, Rek describes the face of Virae, a young woman he has just saved (and will eventually marry) as follows: "It was beautiful. Not in any classic sense, he knew, for the brows were too thick and thunderous, the chin too square, and the lips too full" (26). This sentence actually stages a performance of qualifying language. Gemmell chooses to have Rek first think a simple, absolute sentence ("It was beautiful") and then qualify it ("not in any classic sense") rather than taking a more direct approach (such as "While her face was not classically beautiful, it possessed a strength …"). The reader is thrust into the dramatic process of Rek struggling with linguistic categories to classify her face, rather than simply presenting directly the results of that process. This struggle for precision is repeated in qualifiers throughout the novel, sometimes from the narrator and other times in dialogue, in phrases like "his voice gentle, sad even" (44), "his eyes burned brightly—feverishly—in dark sockets" (101), "You're among friends … mostly" (154), "when a woman is beautiful, she comes to expect a certain—how shall I say?—a certain reverence from men" (193), and "The day had been a nightmare—more than a nightmare—for the bald-one-eyed surgeon" (235). In each case, a moment of hesitation calls attention to language's lack of precision for representing lived experience.

Even when Gemmell invokes traditional epic concepts such as fate, he does so in a qualified way. Bowman, an outlaw who joins the defense, tries to say something about Rek's role in fate or destiny, but ends up simply guessing at the best way to say what he wants to say: "But I do believe that you were merely the instrument of … who knows? … a law of natural justice, perhaps" (262). The reader sees Bowman inventing word-labels to apply in a haphazard attempt to describe a reality beyond the limits of language. These moments of linguistic uncertainty lie behind the qualifications throughout the novel, as characters attempt to match language precisely to reality, but in doing so they call attention to how these numinous categories are *applied to* lived experience, creating the meaning.

Banter

An entertaining popular narrative often requires clever dialogue as a way of engaging audiences and making characters relatable. This is

certainly not surprising. However, in *Legend*, much of the bantering dialogue centers on precise language just as the qualifiers discussed above.
An exchange between the mystic warrior Serbitar and Rek late in the novel
clearly illustrates this link between qualifiers and banter:

> [Serbitar:] "You are seldom boring, my friend."
> [Rek:] "Seldom? 'Never' is the word I was looking for."
> "I beg your pardon. 'Never' is the word I was, of course, seeking. [...] The
> stars are bright tonight [...] Though I suppose it would be more accurate to say
> that the angle of the earth makes visibility stronger."
> "I think I prefer 'the stars are bright tonight'" [279–280].

The banter here explicitly quibbles over the most accurate use of language,
which adverb to use or the scientific accuracy of a common turn of phrase.
Interestingly, Rek favors the less rationally accurate but more socially conventional (and perhaps poetic) turn of phrase here. Their bantering dialogue calls into question the accuracy of language and, significantly,
allows for the pleasure of the non-cognitive, aesthetic response.

The inclusion of humor here (as we will see in Leiber as well) is arguably another anti-epic element of the style. (Certainly, in the ancient
world, epics were expected to be serious.)[8] Humor theory generally supports the idea that humor often unsettles our certainty regarding the representational capabilities of language. By engaging multiple meanings and
breaking down rigid category distinctions laid down by syntax and diction, humor reveals the polysemous instability of language.[9] Gemmell's
use of banter—particularly banter that centers on wordplay and shifting
frames of meaning—contributes to the same deconstruction of the representational power of language. Banter questions the reliability of language,
undermining the reader's certainty in linguistic authority and suggesting
the liberating magical possibility that "anything is possible," that any turn
of phrase may be surprisingly upended. This effect is visible in one important pattern in the novel's banter, the inversion of figurative and literal language. Whether it happens intentionally or accidentally, this simple frame
substitution frequently destabilizes a fundamental poetic device typically
used to elevate the importance of epic action. This type of banter happens
repeatedly in Rek and Virae's relationship (borrowing from the tropes of
romantic comedy, which require humorous misunderstandings early in a
romantic relationship). For instance, shortly after they first meet, they discuss a rabbit they cook for supper:

> [Virae said,] "You'd better not ruin that rabbit. I don't like killing things at the
> best of times. But at least there's a purpose if one can eat it."
> "I'm not sure how the rabbit would respond to that line of reasoning," said
> Rek.

"Can they reason?" asked Virae.
"I don't know. I didn't mean it literally."
"Then why say it? You are a strange man" [45–6].

This case involves both ideas about violence (Rek violates the conventions of rugged masculine heroes by opposing the killing of defenseless animals) and rationality (as they quibble over an animal's ability to reason), both of which are areas where we have seen the novel introduce instability elsewhere, but most significantly we see the substitution of a figurative script (the hypothetical situation of rabbits being told why they are being killed) for a literal one (rabbits cannot reason, so explaining it to them would not matter). Communicating with figurative language is difficult as it is not always clear when language is literal and when it is not. A similar situation occurs a few pages later as Rek muses about whether they will "always" be together (another quibble about language, as he argues that "always" for them is relative to the length of the siege of Dros Delnoch):

> [Rek said,] "'Never' and.5 'always.' I had not thought about those words much until now. Why didn't I meet you ten years ago? The words might have meant something then."
> "I doubt it. I would only have been nine years old."
> "I didn't mean it literally. Poetically" [47].

Gemmell's banter, like his qualifiers, often centers on a self-consciousness about using figurative language. Rather than embracing the high poetry of style which might elevate the material to an epic status, he repeatedly indicates that "poetic" meanings are highly subjective and unreliable, even as they may be better at communicating certain subjective, personal, irrational truths.

Unclear Syntax

The misreading of scripts that suggests the unreliability of communication need not always be humorous. In other conversations, Gemmell includes scenes that are set up like those above, where a character responds to a different script than intended, revealing the instability of language, but which do not play for laughs. For instance, as Druss tours the walls on the night before battle, he encounters a farmer-turned-soldier named Gilad: "'Why did you come here, Druss?' asked Gilad, meaning to ask why the axman had chosen to interrupt his watch. But the warrior misunderstood. 'I came to die,' he said softly [...] 'To find some spot on the battlements to make a stand and then to die'" (186). Here, the code switch (hinging on the ambiguous word "here") results not in a humorous misunderstanding but a confessional moment. This indicates that the affect associated with this "bantering" structure need not be so joyous and liberatory, that failures of communication also open a space for deeper emotional connections. However, Gemmell's prose mirrors this effect not just in dialogue between characters (where the intended meaning is overt) but in descriptive statements placed in such a way that ambiguities are unclear to the reader as well. Thus, the novel does not just dramatize the potential miscommunications of language; its own language creates that instability through unclear syntax that injects mystery into the otherwise mundane, rational narrative.

This instability can be caused by one of the simplest grammatical structures in the English language, noun phrases beginning with "the." This may be particularly striking, as Mandala cites noun phrases as a grammatical tool to "normalize fantastic events" (116). Mandala discusses deictic noun phrases, phrases where, as speakers, we "are assuming that our hearers already know something of what we are talking about" (99), using as her principle example a passage from early in George R.R. Martin's *A Game of Thrones* where Bran refers to "*the* Night's Watch." This phrasing, without any additional modification, implies an already accepted, given element of the world, when in fact this is the first time the reader encounters it. Mandala argues that "In this way, readers are cast, linguistically at least, as already believing the incredible" (100–1), thereby increasing the credibility of the text. That use of noun phrases differs significantly from the following description of Druss being ambushed: "Something swished through the air. Light exploded in his eyes as *the club* hit him" (139, emphasis added). Here, rather than increasing credibility and the illusion of a stable world, the deictic noun phrase generates confusion, or at least a momentary hesitation. Calling it "the club" and not "a club" implies that it is already a given element of the world, but it has only been identified vaguely before as "something" and is not established as a club until this moment. This passage is reminiscent of what Ian Watt calls delayed decoding,[10] which Watt describes as a technique Joseph Conrad uses to accurately represent the process of perception, as rapid events initially confuse our senses but are eventually "decoded" (Watt 175). Oddly, the moment of decoding here ("something" becomes "a club") introduces a further ever-so-slight instability through a linguistic presentation that suggests the new information is old information.

This pattern repeats elsewhere in the novel, most significantly in a passage describing the death of one of the primary antagonists, Ulric's shaman Nosta Khan. Throughout the novel, the occasional passages from Ulric's point of view often feature his interactions with Nosta Khan, who is tracking the Drenai's psychic allies known as the Thirty. This buildup might suggest a climactic clash coming late in the novel, but Nosta Khan's actual death undermines such dramatic expectations. After a scene where Ulric sends Nosta Khan on an unexplained mission, the story enters Rek's point of view, as his dreams are invaded by horrifying monsters. Other than the juxtaposition, this scene has no clear links to Nosta Khan's mission; however, after Rek slices the monsters up with a sword, he awakens to be told by Serbitar that he has been "the victim of Nosta Khan" but held him off (292). A delayed explanation has clarified the chaos, but this all sets the context for the moment that starts the following section: "In the tent of Ulric the candles flickered. The warlord sat transfixed, staring at *the headless body* on the floor before him. The sight was one that would haunt him for the rest of his days. One moment the shaman had been sitting in trance before the coals, the next a red line had been drawn across his neck and his head had toppled into the fire" (292, emphasis added). Again, new information is introduced in a deictic noun phrase. In fact, Nosta Khan's fate is in no way indicated in the entire Rek section of narrative (and furthermore is not even a rationally anticipated outcome, as the reader has no reason to expect that killing the dream monsters will kill Nosta Khan, certainly not that it will affect his physical body). Thus, it is not even entirely clear initially to whom "the headless body" belongs, and the use of "the" generates further uncertainty with its implication that the reader *should* already know, or at least expect, this body. That Nosta Khan's death runs counter to conventional expectations further generates confusion, as the reader likely does not expect such a significant enemy to die so abruptly. The entire scene is disorienting, perhaps reflecting Rek's perspective as he understands little of what is happening to him, and the syntax supports this effect by not orienting the reader clearly. Notably, this is one of the rare "magical" scenes in this novel. Much of the novel's action occurs in the physical, mundane world, far more "sword" than "sorcery," and when magic does occur even the certainties of syntax break down. If, as James Gifford suggests, magic in fantasy gives us a look at the novel's view of subjectivity, then subjectivity in *Legend* is confused and chaotic.

In fact, the magic that actually exists in the diegetic world of the novel is largely telepathic in nature, as the Thirty's psychic powers entail the blending of consciousnesses. Intriguingly, the blending of perspectives is also one of the primary ways the novel's syntax is unclear. Often, moments of syntactic ambiguity occur at a fulcrum point where perspective between characters is changing without that change having been clearly signaled. For instance, a passage discussing preparations for the siege is told largely from the point of view of Orrin, who is leading the efforts: "A deputation had visited Orrin, begging for demolition to cease. Others found that the sight of the clear ground between walls only emphasized that Druss expected the Nadir to take the Dros. *Resentment grew*, but the old warrior swallowed his anger and pushed on with his plan" (117, emphasis added). While this entire paragraph is largely from Orrin's perspective, the beginning of the quoted passage briefly shifts to a summary of the deputation's position, while the latter part clearly shifts back to a description of Orrin's emotional state. In the middle of this, the phrase "resentment grew" sits unclearly—whose resentment? It may be referring to the people who want the work to cease, but the remainder of the sentence also suggests that Orrin ("the old warrior") feels his own resentment at the uncooperative responses his plan is receiving. "Resentment" is the subject of the sentence and is not attributed. Furthermore, as it is singular and not plural, it seems as though it should refer to one party or the other, not both (as Orrin and the deputation would seem to be resenting separate things). Thus, as it sits at a fulcrum moment between two perspectives, the phrase seems to float free of an established perspective and vacillate between possible sources.

At the same time, both parties in this example share a similar feeling of anger and resentment, so the ambiguity emphasizes what they share. Unsurprisingly, these fulcrum moments tend to appear in similar moments of shared feeling. For instance, when Rek mourns Virae's death, the passage is written from Rek's subjective point of view for a number of paragraphs. Then Druss arrives and attempts to comfort Rek in a passage that the reader likely assumes still describes Rek's point of view. However, it ends with the following sentence: "For a long while Druss stood silently in the doorway, *his heart aching*" (284, emphasis added). Only at the end of the sentence does the perspective shift become clear, as only Druss (or a distant, omniscient narrator) would know the state of his own emotions. Somewhere in this passage, the narrative has shifted from one mind to another rather like the Thirty using their psychic powers. (Again, Nicholas Royle's metaphor of telepathy to replace the term "omniscient narration" seems appropriate, as discussed in Chapter 3.) The reader may again experience here a moment of hesitation and reorientation. Thus, despite the surface mundanity of the narrative, the syntax unsettles that appearance of rationality, but it does so in a way that suggests a blending of minds, the parallels and connections between people.[11]

This social connection created by the magic of words sums up the novel's attitude toward language. Linguistic illusions are necessary to create stable group identities, a sense of community and empathy. This comes through clearly in the novel's ambiguities surrounding the Drenai's motives for fighting. Many times, characters question why they are engaging in such a futile defense. Druss even tells Ulric how much he admires him (he has "the mark of greatness" [255]), and Rek concedes that "It may be that a Nadir empire will prove vastly beneficial to the world" (317).

Certainly, many characters point out that the siege will inevitably fail and that the conquest of the Drenai cannot be stopped (a "fate" that the novel unsettles, as Ulric is forced to abandon the siege and dies before he has a chance to return). What, then, are their motives? The answer is one Conrad would likely understand, a necessary illusion. Irrational behavior still has a psychological purpose for generating group identity. Gemmell communicates a similar idea when Caessa—one of the defenders who has formed a close relationship with Druss—is driven insane in battle shortly before her death and, insisting that her mother is out on the battlefield, begs Druss to help save her: "he saw her madness. He could not understand it, for he knew nothing of her life, but he sensed her need. With an effort that tore an agonizing scream from him, he bunched up his legs beneath himself and stood [...] 'Come on, little Caessa, let's find your mother'" (307). This moment mixes epic heroism and personal scale in a way that seems to sum up the entire book: Druss goes to great, heroic lengths to push himself to fight for an irrational reason, but he does so out of empathy, a desire for social connection, because someone else needs it. Ultimately, Gemmell concludes that while language may create illusory ideals, that it may not correspond to the rational, mundane world, that illusion is necessary in order for us to exercise (heroic) agency in the world.

Leiber's Ironic Density

While Gemmell starts with an Iliadic plot that he undermines with mundane reality, Leiber works from the opposite direction. Leiber begins with the world of sword and sorcery, smaller in scale, with shorter narratives about events of individual significance, yet he relates these adventures in a style more typical of epic heroism. Thus, like Gemmell, Leiber works on the borders of fantasy subgenres, illuminating the tensions at the core of the fantasy genre. While there are certain similarities between Gemmell and Leiber (both former journalists with an interest in history and with a reputation for writing rationally grounded fantasy), stylistically they could not appear more different, with Leiber embracing figurative language and seeming to take delight in writing elaborate, dense sentences and using archaic linguistic flourishes. Where Gemmell tends to take his narratives very seriously, Leiber's are frequently told with a lightly ironic touch. Intriguingly, though, Leiber's tales of Fafhrd and the Gray Mouser did not always use this style. As Williamson notes, Leiber's sword and sorcery writing splits between stories written in the 1940s and early 1950s and his return to the characters in the mid–1960s and later. Leiber is one of the writers Williamson calls "a bridge between the pregenre and genre periods" (186), and Williamson constantly seems unsure of how to classify Leiber's style in relation to the split between the simpler pulp style and the mannered complexity of the literary tradition. (For instance, Williamson describes Leiber's fellow "bridge" writer, Jack Vance, as "the only popular writer [*possibly excepting Leiber*] whose prose carries the deliberately crafted artificiality of the early twentieth-century literary writers" [185, emphasis added].) This may be because Leiber's style itself shifts markedly from early stories like "The Jewels in the Forest" (1939) with its pulpy action-adventure directness to "Ill Met in Lankhmar" (1970) with its elaborately textured and frequently parodic style. In fact, it is tempting to attribute that shift in style to a shift in the marketing and general conceptualization of the world of Newhon where Fafhrd and the Gray Mouser live. Leiber returned to fantasy in the 1960s, following the sword and sorcery revival (Williamson 186). Then, following the "Tolkien boom of 1965–66" (Williamson 186), the Fafhrd and Gray Mouser stories were collected in book form (rather than the pulp short story form in which they had previously appeared) in the late 1960s. When the stories begin to be published in books, as a sustained ongoing adventure, with increasing appearance of the apparatus of epic fantasy such as maps, Leiber's style turns to this increasingly elaborate form. It is perhaps not too great a stretch to note that while the world was originally created in the pulp, action-adventure mold, the shift in style corresponds with a re-branding of the series more along the lines of new conventions of the fantasy genre. Perhaps Leiber was attempting to shift the scale of the narrative.

However, regardless of his (or his publisher's) marketing intentions, Leiber clearly sits at a crux point in the formation of the genre, and thus he also shows another example of the collision at the heart of fantasy between epic idealization and mundane, everyday rationality. Like Gemmell, Leiber both uses the magic wonder of fantasy and distrusts it, but his approach is the mirror image of Gemmell's: the artifice of fantasy manifests in an ironic abundance of mannered style. In his case, we do find wonder (rather than its deflation), but it still lies behind a screen of irony. A tension between the rational and the mysterious defines these stories. Even in his wildest fantasies, his characters approach the world with the same rational consistency we would expect of anyone in the real world. In fact, Fafhrd and the Gray Mouser are often as skeptical of the possibility of magic (and as bewildered when it actually occurs) as any modern cynic might be. However, as I will argue here, despite this difference from Gemmell, Leiber also displays an awareness of how language constructs reality while nonetheless gesturing toward the need for the irrational mystery to create a sense of community—the conflict that lies at the heart of the genre.

This ironic contrast between the skeptical characters and fantasy frame of the story goes back even to the first Fafhrd and Gray Mouser story, originally titled "Two Sought Adventure" (1939) and later retitled "The Jewels in the Forest." In this story, the two heroes search for treasure in an ancient tower in a mysterious forest—certainly a conventional setup for a folk tale or fantasy story. However, this early story (definitively in the pulp era) is primarily written in a straightforward style, with the reflections on language and storytelling conventions primarily coming at a plot level. Fafhrd and (particularly) the Mouser approach the legends and warnings about the tower's monstrous guardians with a strikingly rational modern sensibility, assuming the world around them is mundane and everyday in contrast to the dire warnings. The Mouser responds to the archaic and stylized warnings of a local girl more as a modern anthropologist among "superstitious" natives: "Imagination was such a rare commodity with them [peasants] that this girl unhesitatingly took it for reality" (36).

The protagonists' attitudes condition the reader to seek out rational rather than magical justifications for events throughout the story. Much of the story is built around the interpretation of a riddle in a note that reveals the location of a treasure of jewels. The phrasing of the riddle implies to the skeptical mind that the magical dangers it describes do not exist, that they are merely inventions to frighten away treasure hunters. However, the conclusion of the story provides a rational explanation for the riddle that is simultaneously an irrational, magical occurrence beyond easy comprehension: the entire building where the jewels are housed is a guardian, some sort of magically living structure, and the jewels themselves seem to be its mind. In a sense, the entire story is structured to trap the skeptical reader. Thus, like the story's heroes, we are startled by a conclusion that is actually fantastic and outside the seemingly rational framework. The story is structured to make us aware of the distinction between our "objective" standpoint and the one that would be necessary to anticipate that conclusion. Language is reliable (and interpretable) only insofar as the subject possesses the requisite frame to comprehend it. In other words, the "magical" conclusion here is fully in keeping with the skeptical, rationalist story preceding it, and not a rejection of it. Thus, Leiber's mundane fantastic is the inverse of Gemmell's: Gemmell suggests a fantastic world and deflates it with mundanity; Leiber teases with a mundane world and then upends it with the irrational fantastic. Yet the effect is much the same: magic comes from subjectivity, and that subjectivity is constructed through the interpretation of language.

However, this story reads largely as an adventure tale with a magical twist, and in the language of this early story, Leiber has not yet developed the full ironic density of style that we will find elsewhere. Later in his

career, as Leiber returned to a genre now being more coherently defined as
"fantasy," in stories like "The Bazaar of the Bizarre" (1963) and particularly
"Ill Met in Lankhmar" (1970), Leiber would evolve a style of ironic density
that parodied its own subjective romanticism while simultaneously cele-
brating the need for experiences that exceed our subjective frames of experience. I describe that style as "dense" because Leiber seems to attempt
to load as much meaning as possible into every sentence through hyphenation, coined verbs, interrupting phrases, and lengthy complex sentences
filled with subordination. The effect is one of high detail yet also of being
old-fashioned, at times Latinate, with a humorous subtext that seems to
parody the style of older literary fantasists even as it relishes that style.[12] As
I could start with nearly any sentence in these stories, a good illustration
is the very first sentence of "Ill Met": "Silent as specters, the tall and the
fat thief edged past the dead, noose-strangled watch-leopard, out of the
thick, lock-picked door of Jengao the Gem Merchant, and strolled east on
Cash Street through the thin black night-smog of Lankhmar, City of Sev-
enscore Thousand Smokes" (122). This sentence compresses entire clauses
into hyphenated adjectives; for instance, instead of "the door whose lock
they had picked," he writes "the lock-picked door." This compression, the
shifting around of lexical units, breaks apart and reshapes the conventional units of language, creating a sense that words are constantly shifting
categories. The effect is a gratuitous excess of language, but also a playful-
ness as words cross from one part of speech to another and appear in odd
and surprising forms.

    This style pervades the entire story, with numerous hyphenations—
"Slivikin [...] gray-lightninglike leaped a long leap to the floor and down
an inky rathole" (168); "They hop-shuffled into Cheap Street" (158); "no
head-choppings whatsoever tonight" (151)—coined verbs—"They upped
the two worn steps" (159) (as a verb, not typically used in the sense of
going up stairs)—and alliteration, a staple of Anglo-Saxon poetry that
adds to the old epic feel of the style—"Although fired—and fuddled—by
fortified wine" (159) and "the Mouser and Fafhrd merely exclaimed in
mild, muted amazement at the stars, muggily mused as to how much the
improved visibility would increase the risk of their quest" (154). Nor is
this style unique to this story, as "Bazaar of the Bizarre" can supply many
similar examples: "all this mad merchandising [...] Merchants are ever an
evil mystery" (234); "low and loutingly" (223), "servile and sinister" (223).
"Bazaar" also contains frequent examples of hyphenation as well: "a sour
lifted-eyebrow look" (228); "As for the quaintly clad slim girls in their
playfully widely-barred cages, well, they were pleasant pillows on which to
rest eyes momentarily fatigued by book-scanning and tube-peering" (231).

    While a modern reader may find such excess self-evidently parodic (or unintentionally funny), these stories also more overtly satirize the artifice of romantic conventions, indicating that the style too should be read, at least in part, as parody. "Ill Met" details the first meeting of Fafhrd and the Mouser, and their romantic partners Vlana and Ivrian. As such, the story contains quite a bit of dialogue as the new friends tell their stories to each other, but Leiber makes it clear that the "facts" they narrate are shaped by the conventions of storytelling: "It was clear to Fafhrd that while he and the Gray Mouser had idly boozed in the Eel, Vlana had been giving Ivrian a doubtless empurpled account of her grievances and the Guild and playing mercilessly on the naïve girl's bookish, romantic sympathies and high concept of knightly honor" (147). While there is certainly a gendered component here, as Fafhrd assumes that naïve, romantic idealism is a feminine trait, we should not fail to notice that Fafhrd could also be describing this story, with its "empurpled" style and narrative that ultimately involves Fafhrd and the Gray Mouser taking revenge on the Guild, who insult their "knightly honor" by assassinating Vlana and Ivrian. Furthermore, when Ivrian calls Fafhrd a coward for not already getting revenge on the Thieves' Guild to defend Vlana's honor, Fafhrd's response mockingly implicates him in the same "empurpled" and "romantic" discourse:

> He sprang to his feet, face flushed, fists clenched at his sides, quite unmindful of his down-clattered mug [...] "*I am not a coward!*" he cried. "I'll dare Thieves' House and fetch you Krovas' head and toss it with blood a-drip at Vlana's feet. I swear that, witness me, Kos the god of dooms, by the brown bones of Nalgron my father and by his sword Graywand here at my side!" He slapped his left hip, found nothing there but his tunic, and had to content himself with pointing tremble-armed at his belt and scabbarded sword where they lay atop his neatly folded robe—and then picking up, refilling splashily, and draining his mug [149–150].

This passage itself uses many of the stylistic traits I have noted elsewhere in the stories—alliteration ("...feet, face flushed, fists...," "brown bones"), hyphenation ("down-clattered mug," "tremble-armed"), archaic diction ("blood a-drip"), and words shifting lexical category ("scabbarded sword"). In fact, some of these examples are spoken by the narrator and some by Fafhrd, whose oath also uses the same elaborate, interruption-filled syntax as the rest of the story. Yet Fafhrd is clearly being mocked here: his oath is motivated by heroic masculine romanticism (the accusation of being a coward), and the slapstick moment when he is unable to find his own sword and has to point at it from across the room as he makes his dramatic oath portrays the language here as the result of drunken hubris. The effect is heightened by the contrast between the silliness of the final sentence and the elaborate high style that it continues to use, continuous with Fafhrd's style in his oath. The entire scene serves to deflate the heroic high style that the story itself uses, revealing that style as a pose used to perform a form of aggressive, and irrational, masculinity.

Thus, "Ill Met in Lankhmar" mocks its own elaborate style as a way of expressing distrust in the constructivist nature of heroic rhetoric. The dangers of rhetoric are even more pointedly dramatized in "The Bazaar of the Bizarre," a story that functions as a satire of both advertising and the romanticized worldview of heroic narrative itself. In this story, a race of interdimensional merchants known as the Devourers sell "trash" by magically deceiving their customers into believing this trash is beautiful and desirable. As Fafhrd and the Gray Mouser's patron sorcerer Ningauble explains, "The method of the Devourers is to set up shop in a new world and first entice the bravest and the most adventuresome and the supplest-minded of its people—who have so much imagination that with just a touch of suggestion they themselves do most of the work of selling themselves" (233), and once these heroes are imprisoned, the Devourers may sell to the rest of the population without interference. The satire of capitalism and consumerist ideology is overt here, and perhaps needs little comment, but significantly, Leiber focuses on the role played by imagination and fantasy in advertising. Leiber here shows a keen understanding that advertising creates demand, rather than simply responding to demand, perhaps even an early understanding of what are today referred to as "influencers" (in this case, the "adventuresome" ones who are targeted first because they "have so much imagination" that they "do most of the work of selling themselves").[13] This critique coincides with the distrust of heroic idealization I have been observing throughout this chapter, as the magic of the Devourers makes literal something that occurs more abstractly in the real world—the Gray Mouser gets ensnared in one of their shops because he literally sees the junk there as beautiful, magical objects.

However, Leiber goes a step further in this story by specifically implicating the language of heroic narrative itself in the generation of the manipulative ideology of consumerism. Consider, for instance, how Ningauble and his comrade Sheelba first explain the problem of the Devourers to Fafhrd. First, Ningauble, speaking in "his most sugary-priestly tones," says,

> "Let me put it as a hypothetical case. [...] Let us suppose, My Gentle Son, that there is a man in a universe and that a most evil force comes to this universe from another universe, or perhaps from a congeries of universes, and that his man is a brave man who wants to defend his universe and who counts his life as a trifle and that moreover he has to counsel him a very wise and prudent

and public-spirited uncle who knows all about these matters which I have been hypothecating—"

"The Devourers menace Lankhmar!" Sheelba rapped out [232].

Ningauble's verbose, pretentious explanation is interrupted by the simple, urgent description of Sheelba, yet here again we may see Leiber mocking the excess of his own story, as Ningauble's style, with its complex syntactic delays, alliteration, and obscure diction, more closely resembles the style of the rest of the story than Sheelba's verbal directness, yet the target of the joke here is clearly Ningauble's use of language. The language of fantasy, it would seem, by appealing to the imagination with its elaborate style, allies itself more with the Devourers than with the direct simplicity of Sheelba.

Leiber particularly targets the language of heroic narrative through the way the Gray Mouser suffers from the Devourers' illusions. In many instances, the Gray Mouser projects his imagination specifically while reading books, even to the point of having the scripts used to print the words in the books appear as a fantasy object: the Mouser reads "scripts that looked like skeletal beasts, cloud swirls, and twisty-branched bushes and trees—but for a wonder he could read them all without the least difficulty" (230). Fafhrd, his eyes covered with a magical cobweb that allows him to see things as they actually are, later flips through these same books and finds nothing but blank pages. The Mouser imagines language *as* magic here. Moreover, even when the Mouser is not reading, Leiber connects his enticing visions to the dense linguistic devices used in this story. Parallels between the description of the Mouser's visions and Fafhrd's view of reality suggest that what the Mouser sees is figurative language made literal. The Mouser, for instance, sees beautiful women kept in cages throughout the store, beckoning seductively to him. While this certainly calls attention to the use of sexual desire and the objectification of the body in advertising, a particularly odd detail Leiber focuses on is the castanets the women hold: "she rattled golden castanets in a most languorously slow rhythm, though with occasional swift staccato bursts" (237). The reason for this detail becomes clear later in the story when Fafhrd sees reality through the magic cobweb: these "women" are actually alien monstrosities: "It had pale legs and a velvet red body and a mask of sleek thick golden hair from which eight jet eyes peered, while its fanged jaws hanging down *in the manner of wide blades of a pair of golden scissors rattled together in a wild staccato rhythm like castanets*" (250, emphasis added). Fafhrd uses golden castanets here as a familiar metaphor to help imagine the alien anatomy—a common use of figurative language in general that is particularly necessary in fantasy—but the Gray Mouser literally *sees* the metaphor. This suggests the danger of figurative language, as it is the

Mouser's inability to distinguish the literal from the figurative that puts him in danger. The inability to distinguish fact from fantasy is explicitly linked here to the use of figurative language and the difficulty of discerning when language is figurative or not.

The Mouser also mistakes fact for fantasy in a situation that calls to mind one of the most common conventions of epic fantasy and heroic narrative more generally, a fight scene. Fafhrd finds himself fighting a magic iron statue that is defending the shop in what Leiber describes as "a conventional longsword duel" (246), a phrase that self-reflexively calls attention to the genre. This "conventional" fight (mundane but also "deadly") is seen as highly amusing by the Mouser, who takes pleasure in it like the presumptive reader of a fantasy story: "[Fafhrd] suffered some feelings of hurt and irritation when the Mouser [...] grinned hugely at the battlers and from time to time laughed wildly and shouted such enraging nonsense as, 'Use Secret Thrust Two-and-a Half, Fafhrd—it's all in the book!'" (246). The Mouser is, of course, referring to one of the books he read in the shop, which he imagined describing advanced fighting techniques. He confuses this imagined "nonsense" for reality and takes pleasure in what, to him, seems an unimportant, low stakes duel: "lacking Sheelba's cobweb, what the Mouser saw was only the zany red-capped porter prancing about in his tip-curled red shoes and aiming with his broom great strokes at Fafhrd [...] The Mouser had never suspected Fafhrd had such a perfected theatric talent, even if it were acting of a rather mechanical sort, lacking the broad sweeps of true dramatic genius" (247). The Mouser fails to see the true significance because he is distracted by the pleasure of the performance, which he ironically deems inferior to the "true dramatic genius" of a real performance (it is "inferior" and "mechanical" because, of course, it is real and not staged for entertainment value). The Mouser, like a caricature of a reader, expects the conventions of entertainment and is disappointed if reality does not measure up to the simulation. Furthermore, again the scene is described with the elaborate style Leiber has associated with the fantastic throughout, the elaborate syntax and hyphenated adjectives (e.g., "tip-curled shoes"). Fafhrd, on the other hand, more simply and directly thinks, *Sheelba's cobweb has shown me the Gray One in his true idiot nature*" (247). If this is a metafictional reflection on the dangers of fantasy tropes to readers, it seems to be a damning one.

Thus, while magical events happen in the story, the point still seems to be to privilege the mundane over the artificial fantastic, as in the other examples of the mundane fantastic. Yet, in the final analysis, the story does not rest definitively on the value of mundane reality, of seeing things "as they are." After saving the Mouser, Fafhrd decides to keep the magical cobweb so he can continue to see behind the misleading appearances into the true nature of things: "He would peer at the Mouser more closely and at every person he knew. He would study even his own reflection! But most all, he would stare Sheelba and Ningauble to their wizardly cores!" (251). Immediately after he thinks this, the two mysterious sorcerers appear to abruptly take the cobweb back. While, of course, the threat of being seen to their "wizardly cores" is their motive here, this ending suggests the need for mystery and imagination—perhaps it is not best to always see things as they are. To see his friend's "true idiot nature" might rob them of that friendship. Leiber suggests that a completely rational worldview loses something important. However, that mystery is not merely mystification, as "Bazaar" actually argues quite strenuously against mystification. Instead, I would suggest that this mystery is needed in order to facilitate the imaginative social bonds that form communities.

In the Fafhrd and Gray Mouser stories, the social bond formed by linguistic artifice is particularly illustrated through the connection between the two heroes, and the conclusion of "Ill Met in Lankhmar" offers a virtuosic illustration. After completing their revenge against the Thieves' Guild, Fafhrd and the Mouser leave Lankhmar together in a moment of shared identity that happens without language but is described in a massive sentence of 280 words that contains all the hallmarks of excess found throughout the story:

> With no more word than they had exchanged back at the Mouser's burned nest behind the Eel, but with a continuing sense of their unity of purpose, their identity of intent, and of their comradeship, they made their way with shoulders bowed and with slow, weary steps which only very gradually quickened out of the magic room and down the thick-carpeted corridor, past the map room's wide door still barred with oak and iron, and past all the other shut, silent doors—clearly the entire Guild was terrified of Hristomilo, his spells, and his rats; down the echoing stairs, their footsteps speeding a little; down the bare-floored lower corridor past its closed, quiet doors, their footsteps resounding loudly no matter how softly they sought to tread; under the deserted, black-scorched guard-niche, and so out into Cheap Street, turning left and north because that was the nearest way to the Street of the Gods, and there turning right and east—not a waking soul in the wide street except for one skinny, bent-backed apprentice lad unhappily swabbing the flagstones in front of a wine shop in the dim pink light beginning to seep from the east, although there were many forms asleep, a-snore and a-dream in the gutters and under the dark porticos—yes, turning right and east down the Street of the Gods, for that way was the Marsh Gate, leading to Causey Road across the Great Salt Marsh, and the Marsh Gate was the nearest way out of the great and glamorous city that was now loathsome to them, indeed, not to be endured for one more stabbing, leaden heartbeat than was necessary—a city of beloved, unfaceable ghosts [190–191].

Here they find identity with each other beyond language ("with no more word"), community without representation ("a continuing sense of their unity of purpose"), finding connection through common actions rather than words. This empathy of action would seem to be the ideal for one who distrusts idealizing abstractions as Gemmell or Leiber seem to, a moment that would transcend language, yet ironically it is narrated to us in a way that calls attention to its linguistic construction. We see many of the features that should by now be familiar in Leiber's style: the interrupting clauses (introduced by dashes in this case, particularly the long descriptive clause starting "not a waking soul in the wide street"), the hyphenated adjectives ("black-scorched," "bent-backed"), the archaic diction ("a-snore and a-dream"). However, the excessive syntax itself draws the reader into community with the characters. The main clause—"they made their way"—occurs early in the sentence, and it unifies them through a collective action so that each of the remaining details in the sentence is a collective description, two people acting as one (from posture—"shoulders bowed"—to emotion—the city was "now loathsome to them"). A long sequence of prepositional phrases calls attention to the continual sequence of identical actions ("out of ... down ... past ... and past ... down ... down ... past under ... and so out"), which is then followed by a sequence of parallel participle phrases ("turning ... and there turning ... yes, turning"). Mandala has pointed out that prepositional phrases do significant work in "establish[ing] an orientating link with the reader, turning descriptions of place into dramatized reflections of character emotions" (116). Rather than simply being a list of details, the prepositions orient the reader relative to those details, making them a meaningful sequence, but they also serve to dramatically delay the conclusion of the passage, creating an emotional buildup to the final description of the city itself as now invested with the irrational emotional meaning of past experience, "a city of beloved, unfaceable ghosts." The sentence thus places the reader alongside the characters in the physical and emotional journey away from the city, performing that community in its own elaborate structure. Elsewhere, Leiber is seemingly critical of the artificial idealization of language, its failure to correspond to reality, its creation of a substitute reality. However, we could not have this moment of identity through action without the excessive style of this sentence. Language may construct ideology, but it also provides the illusions necessary for collective action.

Thus, both Leiber and Gemmell extend a crucial affordance of fantasy that I am examining in this section—while epic fantasy may be criticized for its focus on the unreal or irrational, it actually requires a cognitively consistent grounding in the rational, mundane world for a sense of wonder to occur. Yet what they add to this is an understanding of the relationship between linguistic constructivism and the practical needs of society. Fantasy reveals the illusions created by its conventions as a social necessity. By operating on the fringes of subgeneric distinctions, both Gemmell and Leiber are able to use one set of conventions (cynical war fiction and sword and sorcery action-adventure, respectively) to comment on another (epic idealization). Consequently, at foundational moments for the fantasy genre, writers like Gemmell and Leiber create a language for fantasy out of a fundamental tension: a self-consciously artificial "magic" which nonetheless forms social bonds, a necessary foundation for any form of social progress.

Narrative Frames

CHAPTER 7

Narrative Frames

*Paratexts, Blurred Boundaries, and
the Deconstruction of Essentialist Narrative*

> The magical phrases (*voces mysticae*) quoted through-
> out the novel are real. I don't mean that they really sum-
> mon magical powers; personally I don't believe that
> they do. But very many men and women *did* believe in
> the power of these words and used them in all serious-
> ness to work for good or ill. Individuals can make their
> own decisions on the matter, but I didn't pronounce any
> of the *voces mysticae* while I was writing *Lord of the Isles*.
> —David Drake, "A Note to the Reader," *Lord of the Isles*

David Drake's fantasy novel *Lord of the Isles* (1997) contains little of
the textual apparatus usually associated with epic fantasy, other than a
modest map. It has no epigraphs, chapter titles, section titles, glossaries,
appendices, or illustrations. Yet Drake opens the novel with an intriguing "Note to the Reader" in which he admits to "stealing" the poetry in
the book from Homer, Horace, and various medieval poets and concludes
with the passage I have quoted above (ix). What is most fascinating about
this opening is that at the outset of his fantasy novel, Drake blurs the
boundary between "real" and "fantasy." As I discussed in my introduction, the fantasy genre is partly defined by the reader's expectation that it
is non-referential: it creates its reality rather than referring to the existing, consensus world. Yet Drake's entire note serves as a reminder that
this is not the case in every way, that even fantasy novels reflect reality to
some extent. Then, he concludes by suggesting a basis in reality even for
the novel's magic—presumably its least "realistic" element. Rather than
stating in a straightforward fashion that the magic phrases are "stolen"
from history, just as he did with the poetry, Drake chooses a different rhetorical tack: first making a seemingly bold statement (the magic is "real")
and then hedging it ("I don't mean..."). This technique, similar to saying "don't think of an elephant," plants an idea even as it denies it. Drake

continues along the same lines by denying the legitimacy of magic ("personally I don't believe they do") but then seeming to affirm it through his actions ("I didn't pronounce any of the *voces mysticae*"). Thus, Drake both denies and affirms the legitimacy—the reality—of the magic in his world. Is that magic real in the primary world or not? Moreover, that magic is specifically linked to presence in language—it is not merely a question of whether or not magic exists, but of whether certain *forms of language* can bring about a change in reality, whether these words should cross the boundary to the material world by being voiced.

Drake's con-man, carnival-barker rhetorical gesture here is characteristic of the paratextual material in epic fantasy, which tends to blur the boundary between fictional and real by simultaneously denying fantasy's importance (because this material is trivial and artificial) and insisting on that importance. Similarly, Jack Vance opens his fantasy trilogy *Lyonesse* (1983) with a "Preliminary" history which "may be neglected" by "impatient readers" (ix), while Gene Wolfe begins *The Knight* (first book of *The Wizard Knight*) with a list of characters, about which his first-person narrator says, "You would be wasting your time to read this now. It is just to look the names up in" (ix). As with Drake's note, these paratexts are each placed at the beginning of the text, implying their primacy and importance, and yet they deny their necessity. Vance simultaneously legitimates his fantasy by giving it a historical narrative and yet inverts the priority by giving primacy to the fictional story. Wolfe does something similar, calling attention to a convention of the fantasy text (the glossary) and yet denying its centrality to the narrative at the same time. These examples overtly call attention to a formal affordance of fantasy paratexts: by fictionalizing the threshold framing the fiction, they blur clear-cut category boundaries in a way that enables a greater awareness of constructivism, polysemy, and textual openness, even when this awareness may operate against more essentialist elements of the text.

While this may seem like a surprising claim to those unfamiliar with the genre, I have already discussed briefly how fantasy critics like Brian Attebery make this metafictional effect a central element of fantasy. Moreover, even a writer often treated (by me as well as by others) as the paradigmatic fantasy essentialist, J.R.R. Tolkien, reveals this boundary-blurring potential in his use of paratexts. Vladimir Brljak has pointed out that Tolkien's fictitious textual history for *Lord of the Rings* draws from the "found text" tradition that legitimizes the "authenticity" of a fictional text by purporting that it is a historical document. Accordingly, the "dominant view" of critics has been that these paratexts create a "validating and authenticating" frame (5). However, Brljak argues that in Tolkien's attempts to make the text seem as much as possible like an actual ancient historical text such as *Beowulf*, he consistently "went out of his way to undermine the (intra-fictional) authenticity of the narrative we find ourselves reading" (14). Tolkien was well aware that historical artifacts do *not* provide unmediated access to the past, but instead remind us of how distant and alienated we are from that past. In attempting to generate that feeling of a distant past, he created a world where "the historiography of this fictional world is exposed to all the 'provisionality and indeterminacy' which actual-world historiographic metafiction raises" (21). While Tolkien certainly does not appear to intend to undermine belief in absolute truth, the form of his text results from a collision with a much more postmodern sensibility than would initially seem to be the case. To the extent that the epic fantasy tradition of paratexts has been borrowed from Tolkien, we may expect to find this postmodern affordance within fantasy surprisingly common, even when at odds with the writer's other values.

Each of the above examples is an instance of what Gérard Genette has termed "paratexts," elements that surround the main text, connected to it but not fully part of it. Paratexts include such elements as prefaces, notes, dedications, epigraphs, chapter titles, and even the book's title (all of which make up the peritext), while also including elements of marketing and publicity, such as the publisher's cover blurbs, promotional interviews, and other materials "outside" the text being discussed (the epitext). According to Genette, the function of the paratext is to serve as a "threshold" to the text, helping readers to transition from a place outside the text to a place inside the text in a way that the author (and publisher) desires. He calls it "a zone between text and off-text, a zone not only of transition but also of *transaction* [...] at the service of a better reception for the text and a more pertinent reading of it" (*Paratexts* 2). With this description of paratext as threshold, it perhaps makes sense that epic fantasy would make greater use of paratextual materials than other genres, as the transition from primary world to secondary needs to be carefully managed lest the illusion of the fantastic world be lost. Thus, as many fantasy critics have noted, the genre is characterized by widespread appearance of elements not typically found in mainstream fiction throughout much of the twentieth century: maps of the fictional world, glossaries of characters and terms, pronunciation guides, historical prefaces and appendices, and explanatory notes describing fictional social practices and magic systems. Even elements conventionally found in contemporary fiction are present to a greater degree in fantasy: chapter and section divisions are still fairly standard in all fiction, but fantasy is far more likely to use chapter and section *titles* than the typical Booker or Pulitzer Prize winner. Epigraphs certainly appear in mainstream novels, but many fantasy novels will have multiple epigraphs, not only at the beginnings and endings of books, but also at the start of sections and even at the start of every chapter. The proliferation of such elements is sometimes lamented or parodied. Diana Wynne Jones mocks it in *The Tough Guide to Fantasyland* (1986), where she facetiously starts every section of the book with a quote from "Gnomic Utterances," even including an entry on them that says, "The Rule is that no Utterance has anything whatsoever to do with the section it precedes" (113). (In fact, the entire book is structured as a glossary or appendix, perhaps parodying another typical fantasy paratext.) This excess of paratextual materials occasions frequent comment in both scholarly writing and informal discussion of fantasy,[1] yet paratexts are rarely the subject of extended critical analysis, despite their clear centrality to the form and structure of epic fantasy.

A closer examination of fantasy paratexts reveals a key feature: while paratexts are meant to serve as a transition, a threshold that eases entry to the text and provides an authoritative context in which to receive that text, fantasy texts are constantly fictionalizing that threshold. Epigraphs, for instance, my primary focus for much of this chapter, typically provide authority to the text, connecting the author's text to the cultural capital of another text (without requiring that author's permission). Yet in epic fantasy, epigraphs are often themselves fictional texts from within the secondary world. Stefan Ekman notes this destabilizing aspect of fantasy paratexts in one of the only extended analyses of fantasy paratexts, his thorough analysis of fantasy maps, *Here Be Dragons: Exploring Fantasy Maps and Settings* (2013). Ekman notes that in many ways fantasy maps serve to create a stable, coherent world, citing other critics who refer to a map as an "authenticating device" (Ekman 14) that exists to "stabilize the fantasy" (qtd. in Ekman 16), but Ekman observes that the situation is more complicated than that. In a sense, fantasy maps are not even real maps, as they do not *represent* a world but instead *create* a world that does not exist. Yet, extending Ekman's comments, we might observe that in some sense, this is what representation always does—creating an orderly stable world, not merely "representing what's already there." Thus, as a threshold for a fantasy text, a map occupies a strange space between "real" and "constructed": "The map blurs the distinction between representation and imagination, suggesting that the places portrayed are in fact representations of existing places" (Ekman 21). Perhaps Ekman's most interesting example, relative to my argument, comes from Russell Kirkpatrick, who presents maps in *The Right Hand of God* (2005) with a copyright credited to a cartographer in his fictional world: "it becomes part of that world, a product of it," and thus, "Examining the map is not a question of entering the story; the fictional world has already been entered" (Ekman 31). I find this last observation crucial, although I would take it a bit further than Ekman, who uses this to distinguish between a paratext (as a threshold to the text, something separate from the world) and a doceme (a part of a text, such as a map that is a part of the textual world). I would point out that the reader initially approaches paratextual materials with the conventional assumption that these materials are a threshold, and *only discovers after the fact* that "the fictional world has already been entered." The outside is therefore revealed as already inside, blurring the boundary between "real" and "fantasy" much as David Drake does in his note to the reader. This blurring of the threshold between the material world and the imagination creates a rich affordance for postmodernist constructivism and ideological critique.

The legitimating function of the paratext (and consequently its subversive potential when fictionalized) is perhaps most visible with the epigraph. Genette identifies several functions for epigraphs, yet a recurring thread is that each of these functions grants authority to the text not through the content of the epigraph but simply through its existence by being attached to the text. One function is "commenting on the text" (157), but frequently "the commentary is puzzling" and seems to be there only to test the reader's hermeneutical capacities, to encourage the creation of meaning. Thus, the epigraph, by its very existence, involves the reader in a process of constructing meaning, rather than "representing" meaning (much as fantasy maps do not "represent" a landscape). Furthermore, the epigraph is an attempt to gain authority, because quoting from a prestigious source offers "the sense of indirect backing" (159). Moreover, the most powerful effect of an epigraph is "due simply to its presence, whatever the epigraph itself may be: this is the epigraph-effect" (160). Genette describes this effect as the "consecration" of a text by linking it to a "prestigious filiation" (160). To give a historical example, "People have rightly seen the epigraphic excess of the early nineteenth century as a desire to integrate the novel, particularly the historical or 'philosophical' novel, into a cultural tradition" (160).

From this standpoint, it should not surprise us that genre novels such as epic fantasy so frequently reach for this consecration, as certain writers often see themselves as a minority fighting for a legitimate voice in the literary market. (In fact, the Gothic novel is one of the few genres that used epigraphs as frequently as epic fantasy, with Ann Radcliffe and Matthew Lewis often including epigraphs with each chapter [Genette 146].) Many fantasy writers would seem to follow this pattern in their use of epigraphs: Samuel Delany and R. Scott Bakker both attempt to connect their fantasy fiction to a larger academic conversation by including epigraphs from scholarly and philosophical sources such as Foucault and Said (Delany), or Nietzsche, Kant, and Adorno (Bakker). Others such as Scott Lynch follow this convention more ambivalently, blurring boundaries between high and low literature. Lynch's *The Lies of Locke Lamora* (2006) includes epigraphs at the start of each section: two from Shakespeare, a figure with much cultural capital, but Lynch chooses one of his lesser plays (*Henry VI Part III*); one from Rousseau's *Emile*; and one from contemporary popular culture in Major League Baseball pitcher Mitch Williams ("I pitch like my hair's on fire"). This last is surprising and ironic in light of the other three, being more informal and raising questions about the "legitimating" function of the epigraph. Nonetheless, while Lynch demonstrates that such epigraphs may still have a boundary-blurring effect, epic fantasy far more commonly uses epigraphs taken from fictional writers and texts in the secondary world: in addition to the examples I analyze in detail below, a quick scan of epic fantasy writers finds examples of fictional epigraphs in books by Steven Erikson, Tad Williams, Alan Campbell, Janny Wurts, David Eddings, David Farland, Gregory Keyes, N.K. Jemisin, and more. This raises serious questions about the "legitimating" function of the epigraph. How can a manifestly fictional epigraph confer narrative authority? Genette certainly allows for the case of invented epigraphs, citing Walter Scott and F. Scott Fitzgerald as authors who have written their own epigraphs. (Fitzgerald actually attributes the epigraph of *The Great Gatsby* to a character from his earlier novel, *This Side of Paradise*.) Yet this fictionalizing of the epigraph seems not to have a significant bearing for Genette on the function of an epigraph, which is largely based on its *form* which *seems* to grant legitimacy to a text, an appearance which is always to some extent fictitious. (For instance, I may associate Delany's novel with Foucault due to the epigraph, but Delany did not need to get Foucault's approval or authorization to use his epigraph—thus, the legitimacy it grants is illusory.) However, by using an overtly fictional epigraph, one that calls attention to its artificiality because it *cannot* be anything other than an authorial construction, fantasy makes the reader aware of this game, at the same time as it still formally functions as an epigraph to grant its illusory historical/philosophical authority to the text. It makes visible how authority comes from formal convention and not from the essence of History or Nature.

This is, of course, an important point, as I have already discussed how epic fantasy is too frequently associated with discourses of naturalization, essentialism, and static triumphalist views of history. Farah Mendlesohn, for instance, associates the "trend for maps" in portal-quest fantasy (which she attributes to Tolkien) with just this type of hegemonic, monologic discursive practice: "This form of fantasy embodies a denial of what history *is*. In the quest and portal fantasies, history is inarguable, it is 'the past.' In making the past 'storyable,' the rhetorical demands of the portal-quest fantasy deny the notion of 'history as argument' which is pervasive among modern historians" (14). As I have been arguing throughout this study, while the epic form may tend toward the totalization of fixed narrative, its hybridization with the novel form affords a much more flexible awareness of history than Mendlesohn credits it with here, an awareness of the intermingling of "factual history" and "constructed fantasy" that is ripe for postmodern exploitation. The paratextual materials, significantly, place this awareness on the edges of the text. In other words, regardless of whether the content of the text embraces a postmodern awareness of historical constructivism or a traditionalist nostalgia for a fixed idealized past, the reader's awareness of the text's artificiality *at the point of entering the text* works against the notion of a "fixed narrative." While I do not intend to enter the sociological arena of fan studies in any great way here, one need only look at fan fiction, fan "theories" (how can you have a "theory" about an "inarguable" narrative?), and debates about canonicity to realize that at the intersection point between text and reader these texts are anything but fixed, that they do not foster a simplistic historicist thinking. In this chapter, I will argue that the paratext is the place where the polysemy of the epic fantasy text can be analyzed in formal, structural terms. In the use of these glossaries, appendices, epigraphs, and other similar materials, we can analyze how the text blurs the boundaries between what is "fact" and what is "artificial construction," indicating the perspectival nature of all such "facts."

While there may be an entire separate study in looking at how these paratexts reflect back on reader activity in fan communities, I will only touch on that lightly in the following pages. In keeping with the focus of this study, I will instead examine how the paratexts intersect with various elements of the style of the main text of the novel. How does the presentation and the style of the paratext inflect the reader's understanding of the main text? How does the main body of the text reflect (or work against) the construction of the paratexts? This analysis will require close reading of the paratexts themselves and of selected passages of the main text to see how these interact to blur the boundaries between History and histories, or the boundaries between self and other. The remainder of this chapter will be divided into two parts. First, I will start with a broader overview of how paratexts have a metatextual effect of blurring boundaries, most notably in the case of Brandon Sanderson who makes paratexts an integral part of his narrative method. Then, I want to dive more deeply into a case study specifically about epigraphs. While I will not be able to discuss epigraphs in the same detail as Ekman covers maps, epigraphs are especially useful as a salient feature of much epic fantasy, more robust for analysis than chapter titles, more consistently used than prefaces. They are also more likely the result of authorial crafting than introductions, prefaces, cover flap text, or even maps.[2] Publishers and editorial decisions often factor heavily into the crafting of other paratextual materials. Thus, epigraphs will be particularly useful for this argument, as many fantasy writers deliberately use them in ways that significantly interact with the main text, thus blurring the boundary even between what is threshold and what is text. To best illustrate the *affordance* of this practice, I have selected a text where the ideology of the main text might be at odds with the polysemy of the paratext, Robert Jordan's Wheel of Time series, a narrative with heavily essentialist leanings. Ultimately, this example will indicate how the form of epic fantasy paratexts unsettles and troubles essentialist assumptions, at times even working against them.

Cosmeres, Multiverses, and Blurred Thresholds

While all fantasy paratexts potentially blur boundaries between fictional and real, Brandon Sanderson's fiction makes the most thorough and visible use of this effect, making his fiction a good starting point for analysis. In Sanderson's fiction, nearly any paratext may reveal that "the fictional world has already been entered" (much as Kirkpatrick's map), from the epigraphs to the maps to illustrations in the text to the appendices to even the dust jacket cover blurbs. This is particularly the case in The Stormlight Archive. Conventionally, the text on the dust jacket of a book is used to convey plot information from the perspective of the publisher in order to persuade potential readers to buy the book. However, the back of the dust jackets for the hardcover editions of The Stormlight Archive contain text that is clearly written from an in-world perspective. For instance, dust jacket text of the first book, *The Way of Kings*, opens with "I long for the days before the Last Desolation" and continues with lines like "The world became ours, and we lost it." This text is not simply a quote from within the book (which is a bit more conventional for dust jacket text), nor does it provide any locus from within the text to attribute it. Thus, while this paratext serves some of the expected functions of the dust jacket text (plot summary, identification of major characters, etc.), it is also partially absorbed into the story world. There could be no clearer example of the threshold already being absorbed into the fictional world. That this text sits side-by-side with real-world blurbs praising Sanderson's books only heightens the boundary-blurring here. In personal appearances, Sanderson has confirmed that these cover blurbs are written by a fictional character (Chaos, "Re: Back Cover Flaps"), but his refusal to spoil the identity has led to fan speculation on message boards, attempting to decipher clues from these texts to determine the identity. One discussion post comment, for instance, even refers to the "storybook" tone and the writer's "flare for the dramatic" as evidence about the writer's identity (Numb, "Re: Back Cover Flaps"). While such debates may seem superficial, they are evidence of the effect that such boundary-blurring paratexts have, as readers are invited to import the fictional stakes of the narrative into real-world debates and practice what is essentially a form of textual analysis of historical documents. "History as argument" may or may not be practiced within the text, as Mendlesohn desires, but it is certainly being practiced on the margins of the texts by readers.

The dust jackets are far from the only place where Sanderson fictionalizes the paratextual frames of his novels. He also does this with the appendices, or "Ars Arcanum," which give an overview of the magic systems in his books. All of these summaries are written not from a distanced editorial or authorial perspective, but again by an in-world character—in this case, a named character, Khriss, a scholar from the world Taldain who has appeared in Sanderson's *White Sand* series of graphic novels. Khriss's authorship of the appendices has significant implications: rather than being presented as authoritative and final, the Ars Arcanum is contingent: the tone is often speculative, the definitions are the result of research, and over the course of a series, the Ars Arcana evolve as the characters' (and readers') knowledge of the world evolves. In the Mistborn Trilogy, the appendix gives a list of each of the metals used in allomancy and its effects, but the list grows from the first volume to the last as more metals are discovered. Furthermore, in the Ars Arcanum to *The Alloy of Law* (2011), a sequel to the Mistborn Trilogy, Khriss admits to inventing some of the terminology ("end-positive, according to my terminology" [390]), having her own motives for prioritizing information (hemalurgy is "of greatest interest to me" [392], suggesting a larger reason for gathering this information), and even prefaces some of her comments with phrases like "I'm certain" (389). Ironically, framing her information by insisting on her certainty has the opposite effect, introducing the possibility of *un*certainty, subjectivity, exploration, and incomplete knowledge into a textual apparatus that one would assume should secure meaning. Finally, rather than being textually self-contained and recursive, the text of the appendix often points *outside* itself to knowledge a reader would need to find elsewhere or which does not appear in the books at all. For example, Khriss uses key terms related to the functioning of magic without defining them, like "Investiture" (391), which appears in the text of enough of Sanderson's novels that a reader may be able to put together a meaning, or "spiritweb" (390) which is not defined at all and, in all Sanderson's fiction, appears only in the Ars Arcanum of *The Alloy of Law* (at the time of its publication) (stormlightarchive.

fandom.com only cites this appearance of the term in the text—all other citations are from personal appearances by Sanderson). Again, this means that to understand the Ars Arcanum, the reader must go *outside* the text and search for answers. It refuses to foreclose meaning but instead opens up curiosity and exploration. Ironically, the glossary needs a glossary, which in itself is an excellent thumbnail definition of such post-structural concepts as the web of textuality and deferral. As in my analysis in Chapter 5, I am not suggesting that Sanderson is attempting a Derrida-inspired deconstruction of fantasy but that his approach to the paratextual materials resonates strongly with postmodern, deconstructive thinking about language and knowledge, even though he is writing quite traditional, mainstream epic fantasy.

It may also be apparent from the description above that Sanderson has tied together much of his epic fantasy within a larger framing narrative: Mistborn, *Elantris*, The Stormlight Archive, *White Sand*, and several others are all standalone stories on different worlds with different magic systems, but they all exist within the same universe that Sanderson calls the Cosmere. The paratexts are one of the ways that Sanderson uses to communicate this larger metatextual framework for the series. The story collection *Arcanum Unbounded: The Cosmere Collection* provides the most complete published explanation of this framework story. (The structure of this collection in itself is intriguing in its blurring of boundaries: it is organized into sections featuring each different Cosmere world; each section is prefaced with a solar system map for that world [created by Khriss's traveling partner Nazh] and a descriptive introduction to the system written in the voice of Khriss, while each story has an authorial afterword written by Sanderson [as himself] explaining the genesis of that story and that particular storyworld.) In the novella "Mistborn: Secret History," Khriss appears as a character in the story and explains the history of the Cosmere to the story's protagonist: a god-like being named Adonalsium was killed by sixteen people, and when he shattered into Shards, each of those killers absorbed a Shard and ascended to godlike status themselves, each controlling a different essential aspect of the universe. This is why the primary "dark lord" figure in the Mistborn series is Ruin, while the comparable figure in The Stormlight Archive is Odium. Despite some essentialism in the construction of this story (while Odium is a historical personage, he in some degree represents the essential concept of "hatred" or "passion"), this metastory captures a conventional element of epic fantasy—the serialization and formulaic repetition of similar elements—and connects it to a larger narrative that rationally justifies the repetition and interconnection between stories.

In this regard, Sanderson's Cosmere is similar to Michael Moorcock's

Multiverse. Moorcock created a number of similar, popular fantasy heroes like Elric and Hawkmoon on essentially formulaic principles, but he tied these heroes together as separate manifestations of the archetypal Eternal Champion, who fights endlessly across parallel universes in the battle between chaos and order. The larger metastory thus absorbs the publishing conventions of endless repetitive fantasy series *into the fantasy world itself.* The concept of the Eternal Champion is, in many ways, an author's (perhaps embarrassed) justification for writing formulaic fiction. The repetitions became not just part of the formula but a structural and thematic principle. Mark Scroggins describes the multiverse as Moorcock's "scientific (or science-fictional) rationalization for the thematic continuities of his created worlds" (22). Sanderson's Cosmere has a similar effect, although it starts from a more readerly position rather than a writerly one. In his preface to *Arcanum Unbounded*, Sanderson describes the genesis of the Cosmere in his teenage reading experience, where he would imagine a character named Hoid whom he projected into the books he was reading (11). Thus, for Sanderson, the seed of the meta-story is not the awareness of publishing conventions (as it seems to be for Moorcock), but the experience of the reader whose somewhat arbitrary experience of gathering texts to read can be shaped into a coherent pattern through the imagination. Just as Genette describes how epigraphs can make meaning through sheer juxtaposition (rather than authorial intention)—a meaning that is "often the most stimulating or most rewarding" (158) because it is generated by the reader—Sanderson recognizes that readers create synergistic connections by juxtaposing the texts that they read. He therefore consciously makes this part of his writing practice by building that connection into his texts: Hoid actually appears in some form in nearly every Cosmere novel. At the same time, Sanderson has kept the details of the Cosmere largely in the background, as the readerly pleasure comes from its appeal to the imagination. In the preface, he writes, "I would guess that most people who read my works don't know that the majority of the books are connected, with a hidden story behind the story. This pleases me" (11). Instead he works through clues and "hints" (11) that allow readers to build the story in their imaginations and encourage the type of exploration, discussion, and debate that mimics scholarly debate—the same debate that the Ars Arcanum described above provokes. While certainly this is not a postmodern deconstruction of epic fantasy, as all of these debates occur in the context of a promise of eventual transcendental understanding of the meta-story to be revealed by the authoritative author, at the level of reception of the text, the finality of the text is not foreclosed, and this lack of stable, final meaning is *built into the design* of the text, bringing out an affordance of the paratextually framed narratives found throughout epic fantasy.

This spurring of the reader's curiosity and open exploration remains a consistent feature throughout Sanderson's work. I have already discussed, in the context of the sense of wonder, the contingency of Sanderson's narratives, the way they shape reader expectations by setting up a misleading structure, where readers likely misinterpret evidence set before them, only to have a moment of revelation unveil new information that casts the old in a new light. This plot structure fits consistently with the larger structure of the Cosmere and the paratexts—there is always more to be discovered, and so meaning never seems final, as one's understanding of events might at any time be overturned by new information. Furthermore, Sanderson specifically accomplishes these structures of surprise through his use of boundary-blurring chapter epigraphs in the Mistborn Trilogy. In each volume of the series, every chapter begins with a portion of a historical text from an initially unidentified author. Each epigraph's narrative, argument, or (in some cases) sentence continues directly from one epigraph to the next, and the content of those epigraphs frequently does not correspond to the content of the chapters they open. For instance, in the second book, *The Well of Ascension* (2007), the epigraphs of two consecutive chapters read as follows: "The others call me mad. As I have said, that may be true" (526), "But must not even a madman rely on his own mind, his own experience, rather than that of others?" (539). Neither of these chapters are particularly about madness or reliable witness. Furthermore, if the conventional function of the epigraph is to confer cultural capital and authority upon a text, this questioning of the reliability of the epigraph's writer further undermines its typical function. Thus, these epigraphs instead invite the reader into the process of interpreting hints and evidence from historical documents, trying to relate those hints to events in the main body of the narrative to determine their relevance (a process that is eventually echoed by the characters, who discover the document from the epigraph and attempt to interpret it themselves). Sanderson is not merely piling on expositional historical data. In Chapter 5, I discussed how a series of epigraphs in the first book sets the reader up to expect that the Lord Ruler is the epigraph writer, Alendi, when in fact it is the mutinous Terris porter Rashek whom Alendi mentions briefly in a few of the epigraphs (204, 589) who actually turns out to be the Lord Ruler. While this twist has significant plot implications, I want to focus here primarily on the effect on readers, for at this point in the text, our understanding of history *changes* as we realize that for the entire book *we have been wrong* about what happened. Thus, in retrospect, our interpretation of the epigraphs changes as we now see them as setting up the twist, the revelation that the Lord-Ruler is Rashek, by subtly introducing the character. If viewed from a synchronic perspective at the end of the text, this might of course seem to confirm an essentialist, teleological narrative of history. But when viewed from the process of reading chronologically through the narrative, we find a different story: the reader is engaged in a process of historical enquiry, comes to faulty conclusions, and then must revise and re-interpret those conclusions based on new information. Having learned this pattern, can a reader ever be certain that they have achieved final, fixed knowledge about this world?

Thus, by blurring the lines between text and paratext, the Mistborn novels undermine the legitimating function of epigraphs. Epigraphs instead become an in-world text open to constant revision, a text continually subject to interpretation and debate. On the other hand, this use of epigraphs to set up plot surprises simultaneously reconfirms the epigraph's authoritative function, as the epigraph *is* a source of knowledge for understanding plot (ultimately, there is a "correct" understanding of history, once we reach it). Sanderson's practice never wholly escapes this essentialism, the need for an answer that at least appears to be final, but this contradiction between open form and closed content more compellingly demonstrates the collision between postmodern textual openness and stable history that forms the core conflict within epic fantasy, regardless of the philosophical or ideological position of the text. Other fantasy writers, often operating on the fringes of epic fantasy, tend to take fuller advantage of the metafictional possibilities for fictionalizing the threshold of the fantasy text. For instance, M. John Harrison's Viriconium sequence begins as a traditional dying-earth quest fantasy, but by its third volume, *In Viriconium* (1982), the quest elements have degraded from heroic world-saving battles to an artist's futile and occasionally absurd attempts to save a woman trapped in a plague zone in the city. The book uses obvious parallels to the plots of earlier books in the series, and the degraded plot is echoed by a theme of degraded art within the world itself. Harrison seems to be critiquing the fantasy form itself as a degraded version of the epic, and he highlights this metafictional reflexivity by giving each chapter an epigraph related to these themes, some from characters in Viriconium, others from the real world (such as Jessie Weston's famous essay on the "Waste Land" which inspired T.S. Eliot's poem). Similarly, Jeff VanderMeer's *City of Saints and Madmen* (2001) incorporates paratextual elements like Sanderson's. The second edition, published by Prime Books, includes a story written by an in-world character on the dust jacket. VanderMeer's name and the title of the book appear in the text of the story and are highlighted on the cover so that the story also serves the traditional cover-function in identifying the author and title. Furthermore, even the "about the author" blurb is incorporated into the fictional world, as it mentions VanderMeer's disappearance, a reference to the story "The

Strange Case of X" that appears in the book. Like all of the stories in *City of Saints and Madmen*, "The Strange Case of X" is written by a character in the world (some of these stories are fiction-within-the-fictional world, some are historical texts). This story is a case study by a psychologist in the fictional city of Ambergris studying a patient who believes himself to be a man named Jeff VanderMeer who wrote a book about a fictional city called "Ambergris," a book titled *City of Saints and Madmen*. This fictional VanderMeer eventually enters a portal which takes him to that city. In contrast to Sanderson, these metafictional narratives much more overtly and subversively examine the relationship between imagination, historical narrative, and fantasy narrative.

While it would be profitable to analyze such overtly subversive fantasy narratives in more detail to reveal how they exploit paratextual materials, that is not my intention here. Instead, I would like to end this chapter with a detailed analysis of a more conventional, popular epic fantasy series: Robert Jordan's Wheel of Time. If paratextual boundary-blurring is an affordance of the form, and not simply a thematic idea overlaid by a writer with a critical consciousness, it will be more productive to a examine text that thematically engages in a more essentialist, totalizing view of history. For this purpose, Jordan's Wheel of Time series serves as the primary example of a fantasy text that deploys various essentializing modes of thought, in its content, at least, but where the paratextual structure cuts against the grain.

Clashing Styles in The Wheel of Time

In the 1990s, Robert Jordan's The Wheel of Time prefigured what George R.R. Martin's A Song of Ice and Fire has been to the early twenty-first century, a seemingly endless popular epic fantasy series that has extended into media beyond the original books. Jordan anticipated Martin in that the series overstayed its welcome, leading to audience fatigue at later volumes that appear to put off final confrontations and extend infinitely rather than moving toward a narrative conclusion. Jordan, in fact, died after the eleventh book was published without completing the series, and it took replacement Brandon Sanderson (in a career-making fill-in role) three lengthy volumes to wrap up all of the plot threads. Thus, Jordan is one of the paradigmatic figures of popular, commercial epic fantasy, and many of the negative scholarly accusations about epic fantasy seem fair when directed at Jordan. In particular, the construction of his world betrays a strong tendency toward essentialist thinking, rigid race and gender roles, and a teleological, monologic view of history. Nonetheless, the fictionalized epigraphs he uses in The Wheel of Time unsettle the essentialism and cause destabilizing collisions within the ideology of the series as it unfolds, providing a demonstration of the boundary-blurring affordances of epic fantasy paratexts.

The title of the series itself is suggestive of a static view of history, with its overtones of historical repetition, history as a script that the present is doomed to repeat. The main plot of the series reflects this, as it tells the story of Rand al'Thor, a young farmer who learns that he is the Dragon Reborn, a mythic figure who is the reincarnation of an ancient hero who defeated the dark lord Shai'tan at the cost of "breaking" the world—causing massive social and technological upheaval. Rand is therefore fated to repeat this pattern, saving the world from Shai'tan but once again breaking it. Thus, the end of the story, the trajectory of the plot, is inscribed in its past, and the excessive proliferation of prophecies predicting future events in the series underscores this view of history: ancient prophecies about the Dragon Reborn (from multiple cultures), modern prophetic dreams from at least two of Rand's friends (Perrin's wolf dreams and Egwene's dreams), and one of Rand's girlfriends (later, one of his wives), Min, who sees cryptic prophetic images in auras around people. (To illustrate the frequency of these prophecies, I would cite an index of Min's viewings that appears on a fan website, which lists 89 such viewings in the eleven volumes written by Jordan ["Min's Viewings"].) To be sure, with so many competing prophecies, it would be possible to create a climate of polysemous uncertainty, but more often all of these prophecies point in the same direction and, even when they are cryptic, eventually pay off with a clear resolution later in the series.

Jordan also relies far too heavily on stereotyping to develop his characters and cultures. While protagonists are allowed a bit more complexity, minor characters (and many significant characters who are not protagonists) are entirely defined by their culture, which is usually developed as one or two stereotypical features. Everyone from Cairhien is obsessed with social class and political intrigue. The Aiel are desert warriors, and everything they say or do is defined by this. However, even the protagonists are often defined by reflexive, repetitive tics. For instance, Rand's frequent companion Nynaeve tugs on her braided hair obsessively, an action described frequently throughout the series (Stubby the Rocket, "How Many Times Does Braid-Tugging..."). While there is certainly some value in archetypal simplicity, in a narrative of this scale which attempts to encompass an entire world, reducing so many characters and cultures to a few superficial traits does flatten out the world and suggest identity is rigidly defined by essence.

Something similar happens with the magic system, where the magic channeled from the One Power is divided into two parts, *saidin* and *saidar*, which are only available to men and women respectively. This gendered magic system is then explained in terms that reinforce conventional gender roles, as for men, *saidin* is wild and uncontrollable. Men must actively "fight it to make it do what I want, fight it to keep from being eaten up" (*Shadow Rising* 153). It is a raging torrent that resists control, and so men must wrestle with it. *Saidar*, on the other hand, is gentle. It requires patience and openness to master it. For a woman to exercise *saidar*, she must learn *not* to strive for control but instead to passively open herself like a flower: "I surrender to it, and by surrendering I control it" (*Shadow Rising* 152). When being trained to use magic, women magic-users (the Aes Sedai) are taught to think of themselves as a flower being filled with the light of *saidar* or as the river banks with the river of *saidar* flowing through them. This binary magic system codes male magic as active, female as passive; male as the assertion of will, female as the removal of will (or more accurately, the subtle shaping of will); male as aggressive, female as gentle and nurturing (or, more negatively, cunning). All of these are fairly traditional gender role stereotypes. Moreover, *saidin* was "tainted" by Shai'tan when he was defeated by the Dragon, causing any men who use it to go insane. Thus, a central responsibility of the Aes Sedai is literally to capture and emasculate men (disempowering them by cutting off their access to the Source). So while this world does create an empowered space for women, it is nonetheless still steeped in rigid, conventional gender roles. Powerful women are suspect—the Aes Sedai are never wholly trusted. The power itself, embedded in the essence of the world, is linked to gender roles, implying that those gender roles are also part of the essence of the world, not a product of social construction.

The series is long enough that mitigating factors to these concerns can certainly be found, but my purpose is not to engage in full analysis of the world building of the Wheel of Time but to use this problematic essentialism as a background against which to examine Jordan's use of paratexts, particularly epigraphs, and how they interact with the style of the main text. In discussing this, I will be focusing on the books written by Jordan, as in many ways, the final volumes written by Sanderson bear more hallmarks of his writing than Jordan's. For the most part, the primary function of Jordan's paratexts seems to be exactly what one would expect out of a threshold, a "friendly" introduction to the world that eases the transition from "real" world to "textual" world. In fact, the books constantly use the paratexts to signal to the reader what to expect. Chapter titles already do this to a certain extent, but the chapters in the Wheel of Time also begin with an introductory image that foreshadows the point of view or narrative content of the chapter: a harp indicates the involvement of the gleeman (traveling minstrel) Thom Merrilin and a stylized sun tells the reader this chapter will involve the strict warrior society known as the Children of Light. The glossary at the end of the book includes a pronunciation guide for the unusual names and places, which is a further level of assistance beyond what most such glossaries offer and suggests a rigid attempt to control the reader's perception of the world (there is a "right" way to pronounce the names of the characters—an instance of a paratext generating a fictitious sense of "authority" for the text). None of these features by itself conveys this essentialism—R. Scott Bakker also provides a pronunciation guide for character names in a series that, as I have already discussed, is quite heavily constructivist. However, working in concert with the world design of the series, these paratexts strongly reinforce a monologic, static view of history. History is incontestable, not open to interpretation, simply "right" or "wrong."

On first view, the epigraphs in the series share this welcoming and legitimating function. While Jordan does not use chapter or section epigraphs as Sanderson does, each book begins with it at least one and sometimes two epigraphs, and all books after the first end with a closing epigraph. Starting with book four, *The Shadow Rising*, each of these opening epigraphs serves the traditional function of explaining the title of the book (with the exception of book seven, *A Crown of Swords*, where the title is explained in the closing epigraph instead). Again, this could be linked to both a "welcoming" and a "legitimating" function. The first three books in the series have titles that identify specific, important events or settings in the story: *The Eye of the World* (book 1) is the setting where the story's climax takes place; *The Great Hunt* (book 2) reflects the quest structure of the book as the entire novel is the "hunt" for a magic relic; *The Dragon Reborn* (book 3) simply takes its title from a central element of the series. However, in book 4, the series makes a structural shift from self-contained books with a single narrative thread to more open, ongoing narratives with parallel narrative threads. This shift is echoed by titles that are less grounded in the plot and more evocative of theme or atmosphere: *The Shadow Rising* (book 4), *Lord of Chaos* (book 6, despite appearances, not a character in the story), *The Path of Daggers* (book 8, despite appearances, not a place that appears in the narrative), or *Knife of Dreams* (book 11, despite appearances, not a magic relic in the novel). Thus, a reader might be tempted to see such titles as authorial comments ("Jordan is saying something thematic about chaos") or advertising gimmicks ("the publisher thinks *The Path of Daggers* sounds dramatic and will sell more books") which would break the immersion of the world by intrusively marking the title as imposed on the story world (rather than an entrance into it). Consequently, the epigraph provides "legitimacy" to the title by marking it as proceeding from the story world. For instance, *The Path of Daggers* cites two in-world sources of a saying about the dangers of interacting with powerful people: "Who would sup with the mighty must climb the path of daggers," credited as an "Anonymous notation found inked in the margin of a manuscript history (believed to date to the time of Artur Hawkwing)" (xi). The title is therefore given backing from History (conceived here as an authoritative source) in the fictional world. However, despite this function of conferring legitimacy on the title, what is happening here is still a blurring of boundaries. The epigraph is gaining its "authority" from a fictitious source, and thus the "authority" it grants is manifestly artificial. (Furthermore, the title itself, as a threshold, is located on the blurred boundary between inside and outside the text.) These small cracks in the novel's essentialism unsettle its overall effect.

Furthermore, the construction of the epigraphs is deliberately archaic, which evokes through style the same age and historical authority that the attribution does. The phrase "who would sup with the mighty" as subject sounds Latinate or medieval, grounding this world in an epic past. This is also part of the legitimating, welcoming function of these epigraphs, as many of the epigraphs are taken from prophecies about the Dragon Reborn, prophecies that use this "old-fashioned" style to signal their legitimacy as prophecy and also prepare the reader for some of the more stilted, narratively distant stylistic moments in the main text. This continuity between archaic style in the epigraph and in the main text is most evident early in the series. In *The Eye of the World*, the first epigraph is from a text called *The Breaking of the World* (author unknown), and largely uses the type of elaborate style I discussed in Chapter 1 of this study, full of parallelism, repetition, and paratactic connections using "and":

> And the Shadow fell upon the Land, and the World was riven stone from stone. The oceans fled, and the mountains were swallowed up, and the nations were scattered to the eight corners of the World. The moon was as blood, and the sun was as ashes. The seas boiled, and the living envied the dead. All was shattered, and all but memory lost, and one memory above all others, of him who brought the Shadow and the Breaking of the World. And him they named Dragon [xv].

The rolling, repetitious rhythms feel like the style of the King James Bible, appending that historical/religious authority to the prophecies of this text. At the same time, this also prepares the reader for this style appearing in the main text, a style which might otherwise seem out of place in a late twentieth-century novel. In fact, the second epigraph cements this connection between paratext and text by ending with an image of wind, "Let the Dragon ride again on the winds of time" (xv) (an image quoted frequently throughout the series and in its promotional materials), which is immediately picked up in the first paragraph of the main text:

> The Wheel of Time turns, and Ages come and pass, leaving memories that become Legend. Legend fades to myth, and even myth is long forgotten when the Age that give it birth comes again. In one Age, called the Third Age by some, an Age yet to come, an Age long past, a wind rose in the Mountains of Mist. The wind was not the beginning. There are neither beginnings nor endings to the turning of the Wheel of Time. But it was *a* beginning [1].

This same opening (with variations on the geographic source of the wind) appears as the opening paragraph of every book in the series, and here it ties both to the repetitious parallelism and the wind imagery from the epigraphs.

Thus, the opening paragraph serves as a sort of bridge from narrative past to narrative present, retaining the archaic style while only gradually easing the reader into the more novelistic narration of the bulk of the book. However, this book retains much of the stylistic flavor of these epigraphs throughout. The text is marked by more narrative distance and less free-indirect discourse or slangy, informal reveries using the characters' language than is commonly the case in contemporary epic fantasy. The style of the epigraph is to some extent maintained in the first chapter even as the narrative shifts to follow Rand's point of view as he travels from his farm into town: "The wind howled when it rose, but aside from that, *quiet lay heavy on the land. The soft creak of the axle sounded loud by comparison. No birds sang in the forest, no squirrels chittered from a branch.* Not that he expected them really; not this spring" (2, emphasis added). Phrases like "quiet lay heavy on the land" carry on the sonorous rhythm of the epigraph, as does the parallelism of "no birds sang [...] no squirrels chittered," a stark contrast to the final sentence fragment with its abrupt, direct, informal style reflecting Rand's thoughts. This jarring of modern conversational (some critics might say "bland") prose against the rich, historical style continues throughout the book, but it is prepared for and justified by the epigraphs, which suggest then that this book shares a status as chronicle of historical past with those epigraphs. Yet, ironically, this legitimating function of the epigraphs' style simultaneously blurs the boundary between epigraph and text as the style of the epigraph seems to seep into the text. The frame is already part of the fictional narrative.

This style remains fairly consistent throughout *The Eye of the World*. As a result, it seems perfectly appropriate when Rand defeats one of Shai'tan's lieutenants, Ba'alzamon, at the climax of the book, for him to say the more formally phrased, archaic-sounding, "It is ended" (762) rather than something more informal, such as "It's over." However, as the series goes on, the fissures in the style become more pronounced, as the formal, archaic, or poetic epigraphs start to diverge from the more pervasive use of the "bland" conversational prose found through much of the main text. Book 10, *Crossroads of Twilight* (2003), is often singled out by readers as a low point of the series, primarily for its shapeless plot and lack of narrative progress. However, I would suggest that in this volume the problem is as much a problem of style, as the excessive attention to mundane details and endless character reveries contrasts markedly with the archetypal and archaic framing of the series found in the epigraphs. There are numerous examples, but a passage from the book's 99-page prologue serves as well as any. In one lengthy section, an Aes Sedai named Yukiri wanders through their headquarters, the White Tower, having various encounters with other Aes Sedai. Many of these encounters lead to lengthy physical descriptions of each character she meets, often characters making one of their few appearances in the series, as though Jordan wants to fix each detail in this world as precisely as possible. For instance, as Yukiri approaches two other Aes Sedai who appear nowhere else in the series, she describes them in detail: "The dark stocky Warder [an Aes Sedai's personal guardian] following just far enough behind to give them privacy must have belonged to Pritalle Nerbaijan, a green-eyed woman who had largely escaped the Saldaean nose, because Atuan Larisett had no Warder" (37). This sentence lacks the rhythm of the earlier examples from the first book (or even this book's epigraphs), instead focusing entirely on listing details. The interrupting phrase describing Pritalle, in fact, foregrounds her physical description at the expense of the clarity of the sentence (it sounds as though she "escaped the Saldaean nose" because Atuan had no Warder). Most of these details are superfluous, as these characters have no particular bearing on the plot of this novel or the series as a whole. This sentence functions like a glossary entry embedded in the main text, as a way of establishing authoritatively a particular part of the textual world. We should consider this example in contrast to writers like Sanderson who introduce seemingly insignificant details in order to involve readers in a process of interpretation that opens up the text. Here, it is as though Jordan does not trust the reader's involvement in using their imagination to form the world and instead wants to record as many details as possible to fix them in place the "correct" way. This works entirely at odds with the imaginative nature of fantasy: instead of blurring the lines between creator and reader and establishing flexible connections, Jordan's text pushes toward precisely the type of fixed, static universe for which epic fantasy is often criticized. Unsurprisingly the result is a writing style that is muddied by its attempt to fix every detail in its place. In other words, the style here is at odds with the affordances of the genre.

Crossroads of Twilight highlights this tension between its rigid control of representation and the genre's boundary-blurring affordances because the novel's use of epigraphs still leads to an openness that exceeds the rhetorical attempt to enclose and control every detail. The book's closing epigraph is frequently quoted in the fan community, and it opens up more hermeneutic fissures—both within the text and in its reception—especially in contrast to the monologic control elsewhere in the text. The epigraph itself is a simple quatrain using a storm metaphor to foreshadow the coming conflict and the destruction Rand and his followers will wreak while saving the world: "We rode on the winds of the rising storm, / We ran to the sounds of the thunder. / We danced among the lightning bolts, / And tore the world asunder" (823). Thematically, this is a typical function of the ending epigraphs of the series, building anticipation for future volumes with an atmosphere of impending doom. However, what is particularly intriguing about this example is the attribution: "Anonymous fragment of a poem believed written near the end of the previous Age, known by some as the Third Age. Sometimes attributed to the Dragon Reborn" (823). The Third Age is the era in which the series is set, and thus the attribution is suggesting that this epigraph was written by Rand. In other words, this epigraph suggests a largely invisible narrative frame to the series, with a future epigraphist or editor who *does not have access to definitive, authoritative historical information.* The attribution can only say that it is "believed" and "sometimes attributed."

While this undercuts the authority of the epigraph in a fashion more similar to what we have seen in Sanderson or in Brljak's argument about Tolkien, this fictionalized framing creates an even sharper division. The text itself tends to lack the ironic distancing or uncertainty found in this epigraph, particularly with the much closer, internal narration of the later volumes. In fact, readers may feel better informed, more authoritative, than the fictional epigrapher. Rand only appears in a couple chapters in this volume (one of its glaring narrative weaknesses), but in both cases, the reader finds him contemplating the coming conflict while a literal storm takes place around him. The first of these occurs in Chapter 24, a chapter titled "A Strengthening Storm," which picks up both the metaphor found in the epigraph and the literal storm that opens the chapter. While a reader might forget this scene, as it occurs over 150 pages before that closing epigraph, the epilogue that immediately precedes the poem is nearly identical, opening with Rand contemplating a storm and receiving a report from the leader of his army. The book ends in Rand's perspective, immediately before the epigraph, with these words: "Thunder rolled again for distant lightning" (822). In that context, the final epigraph reads almost as an extension of the text, making a suggestive argument that Rand indeed does compose that poem. Yet the argument is only *suggested* and is to a degree undercut by the uncertainty of the (presumably fictitious) epigrapher. The reader feels more knowledgeable—has greater access to authoritative information—than the epigrapher. In other words, the text pits the reader against the paratextual frame, requiring the reader to make arguments and construct details to form certainties in contrast to the historical uncertainty of the narrator. Such activity is clearly at odds with the stylistic attempts found elsewhere in the text to fix details without need of the reader's imagination.

Rather than just smoothing out the reader's transition into and out of the book by familiarizing its contents, such epigraphs actually serve as invitations to reader involvement in constructing the text. These epigraphs played a substantial role in fan communities at the time the books were being published, providing sources for theories as readers attempted to construct the meaning of past events or forecast the future direction of the series. Many discussions and debates took forms dramatically similar to academic essays studying literature. The closing epigraph of *Crossroads of Twilight* occasioned a surprising volume of such commentary, such as in the essay "The Real Meaning of the Poem" by the user Brother of Battles on theoryland.com. The essay begins by responding to another theory and offers a thesis disagreeing with its premise (the poem refers more to one people group from the book, the Aiel, than another, the Seanchan). Then the essay proceeds with a line-by-line analysis. For instance, the third line of the poem is explained by saying, "The Aiel are the only people that use the phrase 'Dance' as a reference to battle," followed by another supporting citation from book 2, when an Aiel warrior says, "bring your lightning bolts, I will dance among them" (Brother of Battles). In the comments section following the essay, other users express doubts about this theory, presenting alternative interpretations and questioning whether an image as generic as dancing in the lightning can serve as a "poetic fingerprint" (Sugarbullet). While the argument is largely superficial (the stakes in whether the poem refers to the Aiel or the Seanchan or another group are never exactly clear and largely relevant only to an understanding of the plot), the *form* of argumentation here is precisely the kind of introduction of "disputatious sources" (Mendlesohn 14) and contextualizing of evidence (Mendlesohn 16) that critics like Mendlesohn find to be lacking in epic fantasy. Even in a text like the Wheel of Time, which internally seems to lack those features, the paratextual interface with the reader enables an open community of inquiry and argumentation. The text supports the reader's imaginative interaction with and construction of a textualized history. Moreover, the constructed nature of that history is manifestly evident, as the history they are arguing about is never anything other than text—a realization that is enabled by the fictionalization of the authorizing paratextual apparatus itself.

I am not suggesting here that Robert Jordan is deliberately deconstructing fantasy tropes or using epic fantasy to give readers a postmodern awareness of the constructed nature of history. Indeed, to a certain extent, literary history shows us that nearly any text can be read as self-questioning by a reader determined to find such instability. Nonetheless, I would argue that epic fantasy's conventional fictionalizing of the paratextual frame introduces tremendous potential for such instability, particularly at the point of reading the text. Despite Jordan's essentialist tendencies—the attempt to place all details in a rigid regime where everything has a "right place"—the affordance of the forms he is working with push back and cut against those tendencies. Perhaps many of the weaknesses that readers have complained of in the Wheel of Time are the result of this fissure, an epistemological tension in the construction of the text. If this is true, this may actually explain the failings of many problematic epic fantasy narratives, as the problem may not be the genre but those texts' failing to take advantage of its affordances. By presenting narratives as fictional histories of other worlds, epic fantasy is consistently opening up the question of the nature of historical knowledge, and by so thoroughly and overtly absorbing the conventions of narrative authority into that fictional frame, these novels present a powerful opportunity for undermining hegemonic assumptions about the nature of historical truth.

CHAPTER 8

Frame Narratives

Historical Truth, Literal Metaphors, and Epic Irony

> Even when I had sight, to see through a single pair of eyes was a kind of torture, for I knew—I could feel in my soul—that we with our single visions miss most of the world. We cannot help it. It is our barrier to understanding. Perhaps it is only the poets who truly resent this way of being. No matter; what I do not recall I shall invent.
> —Steven Erikson, *Forge of Darkness*

Can epic fantasy be ironic? Throughout this book, I have been exploring ways in which the phrase "epic fantasy novel" seems like a contradiction, and the potential affordances which that contradiction enables. In Chapter 7, I went so far as to suggest that the framing of fantasy as imaginary history reflects back on the discourse of history and therefore has the potential to indicate the extent to which imagination plays a role in constructing history. However, that was merely an analysis of the *implicit* framing of fantasy. When such frames become an explicit part of the narrative structure, the potential for ironic deconstruction of monolithic, hegemonic views of history is amplified. Yet, as I discussed in Chapter 6, when such irony is introduced, some critics might assume that it undermines the epic framework, compromising the narrative absorption fantasy requires. Thus, the question of whether or not *fantasy* can be ironic is central to the consideration of narrative frames in fantasy.

The prevailing critical assumption seems to be that epic fantasy cannot contain large-scale structural irony. The root of this assumption may lie in Todorov's influential definition of the fantastic as a moment of uncertainty between the "real" and the "imaginary," as the reader wonders whether the story being narrated is "actually happening" or the narrator is "the victim of an illusion of the sense": "The fantastic occupies the duration of this uncertainty. Once we choose one answer or the other, we leave the fantastic for a neighboring genre, the uncanny or the marvelous" (25). The logic proceeding from this definition would seem to say that epic fantasy more properly occupies the marvelous than the fantastic because it requires the reader to "suspend disbelief" and accept that the imaginary events depicted are actually happening to the narrators. While the fantastic can effectively undermine existential certainties, the marvelous is typically assumed to be more conservative. Rosemary Jackson, in extending Todorov's schema, describes the following features of the marvelous: "The narrator is impersonal and has become an authoritative, knowing voice. There is a minimum of emotional involvement in the tale—that voice is positioned with absolute confidence and certainty towards events. It has complete knowledge of *completed* events, its version of history is not questioned and the tale seems to deny the process of its own telling" (33). As discussed above, Jackson explicitly links secondary-world narrative to the marvelous (42) and largely avoids analyzing the "better known authors of fantasy works" (such as Tolkien and Le Guin) (9). By her definition, a secondary world is a world that requires belief, which is properly the subject of religious allegory and not skeptical irony. The assumption behind such arguments seems to be that the *form* of epic fantasy makes it ill-suited to irony which might introduce uncertainty and tension, and not that specific writers (such as Tolkien or Lewis) gravitate toward the allegorical due to their own artistic proclivities.

This assumption has taken root and shaped the critical reception of fantasy to such an extent that criticism about fantasy takes as a given its need to generate belief. Ann Swinfen frequently argues for the importance to fantasy of instilling "secondary belief" in its readers, a term borrowed from Tolkien. This secondary belief is made possible through internal consistency, a central tenet of world building in most analyses.[1] Consequently, "An external narrator, looking down and commenting on the secondary world, as it were, from without, destroys the illusion of secondary reality" (75). Swinfen's emphasis on consistency would certainly seem to mitigate against the inclusion of a narrative frame which might ironically contrast or throw into question the reliability of the main narrative (just as, in Chapter 4, I discussed critical assumptions that a first-person narrator destroys epic immersion). As a result, even among critics who analyze epic fantasy, it is frequently faulted for lacking in irony, for being too direct in its themes. Colin Greenland, for example, in writing about Michael Moorcock's Eternal Champion novels, faults them for lacking "subtlety [and] irony" (121). Farah Mendlesohn goes even further, associating the entire "portal-quest" mode of fantasy, in its relation to the epic, to "closed narratives" (5) and claiming that "Fantasyland is constructed, in part, through the insistence on a received truth [...] with a consequent denial of polysemic interpretation" (7). As I have already discussed, Mikhail Bakhtin's influential essay "Epic and Novel" would seem to reinforce these assumptions by arguing that the epic mode, which requires temporal distance from a completed past age, collapses with the introduction of the "serio-comic" ironic mode, which is most appropriate to representation of the "inconclusive" present (39). The novel is defined by irony, yet the epic mode is essentially devoid of irony.

I wish to dispute that this is necessarily the case; irony can coexist with fantasy in the formal collisions that make up the epic fantasy novel. In fact, writers of epic fantasy have used ironic style to great effect in novels that maintain the visceral narrative immersion of the epic while exposing the ideological uses of language. I have already shown how the implicit framing of epic fantasy creates an affordance for the deconstruction of received historical truth, even in texts that otherwise do not fully take advantage of this affordance. Now, I would like to turn my attention to texts which make the frame explicit by including a frame narrative that ironizes the text. While it might be easy to see irony in overtly satirical fantasy (such as Terry Pratchett's fiction), in order to demonstrate that epic fantasy *in principle* can be stylistically ironic while still allowing for the narrative absorption that so many fans of the genre value, I will be examining two novels that use style in an ironic way without completely invalidating it through outright parody. Writers of epic fantasy, by setting their narrative within a frame, have the freedom to use all of the features associated with epic style (elaborate syntax, archaic diction, heightened metaphor) but with an overarching narrative distance that is often thematically significant. Due to the contextual pressures of the frame, any style—any use of language—is potentially ironic as it is a manifestation of character. This irony then reflects on the fashioning of language itself, reflexively drawing attention to its ideological function; by presenting style itself ironically, language is shown to be not a transparent (or transcendent) representation of truth but discourse with a political/ ideological purpose. While epic fantasy enables many types of frames, I will focus particularly on how Samuel Delany and Steven Erikson use "stories within stories" to ironize the stylistic effects within their novels. This technique allows them to demonstrate the instability of reality as our perception is shaped by language, which in turn is shaped by competing ideologies exercising a will to power. Both writers use this narrative frame to create stylistic devices that ironically comment on this relationship between fantasy/ imagination and history, showing the role fantasy plays in constructing historical "truth." I will call these devices literalized metaphor (Erikson) and parenthetical excess (Delany). Thus, in slightly different ways, these writers demonstrate how epic fantasy can provide ironic stylistic tools to reveal "history" as a narrative construct with a rhetorical purpose.

Frame Narratives
and Deconstructing Narrative Truth

Whereas the previous chapter examined more generally how the fantasy text is "framed" for the reader, here I will be examining "frame narratives" as a specific, more limited type of structure. The frame narratives described in this chapter give the main text of the narrative a tangible existence in the diegetic world of the story. This is comparable to canonical novels like *Frankenstein*, *Wuthering Heights*, and "Heart of Darkness," the frame narratives most frequently discussed by literary criticism, where the bulk of the narrative is orally narrated by one character to another character or group within the fictional world. Such is the situation in Erikson's *Forge of Darkness* (2012), where the poet Gallan apparently narrates the entire novel to another poet, Fisher Kel Tath. Similarly, the main narrative may be presented by the frame as a written narrative within the storyworld. In Delany's *Tales of Nevèrÿon* (1979), the text we read is presented as a historical document (or the reconstruction of that document). In contrast, consider Robin Hobb's *Assassin's Apprentice* (1995), where the epigraphs are clearly an in-world document (a history written by Fitz and referred to in the main body of the text), but the main text of the novel has no in-world status. Even though it is presented in first person, the reader can at most *assume* that it is, say, Fitz's personal journal or his internal thoughts, but because it is given no formal status within the world, it is not strictly speaking a frame narrative by this definition. (Otherwise every first-person narrative would be a frame narrative.) My definition of frame narrative—a narrative where the main body of the text has an existence within the diegetic world—may seem a bit backward: technically, the "frame narrative" is the part of the narrative that tells the story of the story being told (the Walton portion of *Frankenstein*, the opening chapters by Lockwood in *Wuthering Heights*). My definition would even allow for dramatic monologues like Robert Browning's poems to be frame narratives, as the entire text of a poem like "My Last Duchess" is framed by a dramatic situation where a character speaks within the storyworld. However, my definition maintains an important affordance of the frame narrative, one which Browning illustrates very well: namely, that the frame creates an ironic tension in the language of the main text. Browning's narrators often reflect in the language they use a disparity between their own judgment of themselves and the author's implicit judgment of them: the Duke in "My Last Duchess," for instance, indicates his intense self-centeredness through his preoccupation with using possessive pronouns ("*My* Last Duchess") and sentence structures using "I" as the subject followed by an active verb.[2] As my analysis below will largely focus on analyzing the style of the *main* narrative, not the frame itself, my definition emphasizes this relationship between the main text and the frame, namely that the frame exerts a pressure that ironically warps the style of the text.[3]

While overt frame narratives of this sort may be comparatively rare in epic fantasy, such structures simply make overt the implicit framing that already exists in the genre. In his essay "Beyond the Pale," John Clute argues that self-referential framing lies at the core of fantasy. To make this argument, he uses a rhetorical reversal: arguing that Joseph Conrad's "Heart of Darkness"—itself a framed narrative—belongs side-by-side with the literature of the fantastic. Clute describes Conrad's novella as a "Club Story," which he defines as "a tale or tales recounted orally to a group of listeners forgathered in a venue safe from interruption" (421), a genre which stretches back at least to medieval story cycles like the *Decameron* and *The Thousand and One Nights*. Including the circumstances for the telling of the tale has the consequence of both "fram[ing] Tall Tales in a way that eases our suspension of disbelief during the duration of the telling" and "surrender[ing] the tale to the judgment of the world once it has been told" (422). In other words, it both generates belief (through the listener's/reader's absorption in the tale-telling) and calls attention to its questionable status as story, which requires judgment (do I really believe your story?). Rather obscurely, Clute says that the primary result of a Club Story is that it "enforces our understanding that *a tale has been told*" (422). Crucially, the tale can only provide itself to authorize its truth value. Thus, it highlights the way story creates and organizes our perceptions of the world. The framing device calls attention to the *telling* of the tale. As Clute points out about "Heart of Darkness," readers have continually focused "upon the highly foregrounded, indeed spectacular way it is actually told, upon the presentness of the storytelling" (420).

In Clute's reading, "Heart of Darkness" is a prototypical fantasy story, with Marlow crossing a threshold into a strange (to him), dream-like world and embarking on a quest that he hopes will give meaning to that world. The structure of the novella calls attention to the role *telling* his quest as a story plays in *constructing* the meaning (or lack thereof) that he finds. While Clute does not explain it in quite this way, Marlow's relation to the story is potentially ironic, as a reader should be wary of any disparity between Marlow's attempts to make meaning through the story and the reader's own reading of the events. Clute then links Conrad's frame tale to the fantasy genre more generally through Tolkien's categories of recovery and escape. Tolkien sees twentieth-century history as fractured, and thus fantasy for him is a "subversive" attempt to write a "counter-story," a "literature of refusal" (430). While we may disagree with the particular form that escape takes in Tolkien, the broader point is that escape from history is subversive because we are escaping from the tyranny of history, exercising our agency through story to re-shape the world. For Clute, the core of fantasy is a "conversation" (432) with what he repeatedly calls the "Ocean of Story." The fantastic is "connection. Touch one story and we touch them all" (432). If we follow Clute on this point (and I have already argued throughout this book that the fantastic is about "connection," ranging from empathy on a personal level to the communal level), then the fantastic is *about* story and the role it plays in constructing reality. In that sense, it implies that the frame and meta-narrative are fundamental parts of the fantastic, that the frame points the reader back to the structure of the story and to considering its purpose.

This may be a somewhat surprising claim to make about fantasy—particularly epic fantasy—but it should not be surprising to claim about frame narratives. Nonetheless, even outside fantasy, frame narratives run the risk of the irony being missed. For instance, Chinua Achebe's landmark post-colonial critique of "Heart of Darkness" largely equates Marlow and Conrad, an assumption that subsequent critics have called into question. C.P. Sarvan responds to Achebe that "This ironic distance between Marlow and Conrad should not be overlooked though the narrative method makes it all too easy" (282). The danger of the frame narrative is that it appears to grant authority to a character's speech—as Marlow does almost all the talking, it is too easy to forget he is a character and overlook the ironies of his self-justifying rhetoric. For instance, Marlow's insistence that his story can be believed because he "hates a lie" is rendered ironic by the climax of the story, when he feels it necessary to lie to Kurtz's Intended about Kurtz's last words. Thus, an unironic reading of "Heart of Darkness" could see Marlow's role as fixing the meaning of the text through his insistence on his authority as a witness, yet the frame subtly ironizes his role, pointing to the larger themes in the text of the "discrepancy between appearance and reality; between assumption and fact; between illusion and truth" (Sarvan 282).

Thus, while the Club Story narrative frame may show a character striving to deny impurity, assert authority, and fix meaning by creating a coherent structure,[4] the frame narrative reveals this as ironic by dramatizing the attempt, unveiling the constructed, artificial nature of "storied" meaning. Conrad continues to be a good illustration of this, as his entire artistic method centers on a paradox: his desire to use language to make the reader see material reality and his simultaneous awareness of the futility of this endeavor. Edward Said extensively analyzes this narrative method, one which he points out nearly always uses "the swapped yarn, the historical report, the commonly exchanged legend, the musing recollection" (119) as "stable" narratives in contrast to the instability of seeing.

(Kurtz in "Heart of Darkness" and Jim in *Lord Jim* are both talked about far more than they are seen.) However, his narrators' attempts to insist upon the authority of their narratives implicitly destabilizes their stories: "The reflective narrator is always a narrator preventing the wrong sort of interpretation. His narrative invariably assumes the currency of a rival version" (120). This all leads to "the general loss of faith in the mimetic powers of language" (125). Said suggests here that Conrad's approach to framing narrative ironically calls attention to the role of language itself, that despite his stated goal to privilege the visual over the unsayable of language, his every attempt reminds the reader that language constructs a reality rather than giving us transparent access to the essence of reality, a situation he cannot escape. Thus, Conrad demonstrates frame narratives as implicit ironic metanarratives: he constantly puts his narrators in the same position as himself, attempting to "story" the world in order to give direct access to History and Truth, but ultimately, they are left only with the constructed representation they have made.[5]

Thus, if we accept the contention that epic fantasy is a highly framed genre through its attempts to connect to the "Ocean of Story" that helps us make sense of the world, and further (via the parallel to Conrad) that such attempts to make meaning will run up against the unstable, constructed nature of language, then it stands to reason that epic fantasy has a structural potential to subvert stable hegemonic views of history by revealing stories as ideological constructs that attempt to shape the world. Furthermore, these frames have a particular focus on language, as they call attention to its representational function, and consequently the author's style in writing can be ironically related to the frame to reveal how those uses of language shape reality. Finally, this subversion can be accomplished without fundamentally eroding the experience of absorption, as the "Club Story" frame calls for belief even if it subtly undermines the basis of that belief. In other words, epic fantasy frames once again embody a productive collision of forms: credible belief (the fixity of meaning Mendlesohn laments in epic fantasy) and constructivist self-awareness. Epic fantasy can simultaneously have both irony and immersive, visceral narrative. I will focus predominantly on the ironic, deconstructive effect, as it has gone largely undiscussed in epic fantasy. As I will show, frame narratives are highly useful for epic fantasy writers who are especially reflective about the nature of the genre in which they are writing.

Erikson's Literalized Metaphors

Without its narrative frame, Steven Erikson's Malazan prequel *Forge of Darkness* could on superficial reading appear to be a straightforward example of the supposed stylistic excesses of epic fantasy. Throughout the book, the style is frequently formal, elevated, baroque, perhaps archaic. Many characters, especially ones of legendary or heroic stature, often speak in language reminiscent of Shakespearean heroes. For instance, in a key moment in the story, two such legendary figures, the heroic Anomander Rake and his brother Andarist discover the body of Andarist's fiancée after she has been raped and murdered. Anomander swears vengeance in an almost mythic moment that one can imagine appearing in an epic poem or a romanticized Hollywood film: "I am awakened to vengeance, and so shall this weapon be named. Vengeance" (480). Andarist responds with a passionate but reasoned and temperate speech that seems less an example of realistic psychology than narrative invention: "Vengeance deceives. When you see its road to be narrow it is in truth wide. When you see it wide the path is less than a thread. Name your sword vengeance, brother, and it will ever claim the wrong blood. [...] Who is to blame for this? The slayers who came to this house? Those who commanded them? [...] Vengeance, Anomander, is the slayer of righteousness" (480). The reader could be forgiven for finding Andarist a bit distant at the death of his fiancée here, as he shows a great deal of concern with philosophical questions of agency and responsibility, while his metaphor of the wide and narrow paths seems to suggest more time for reflection than is likely for a speech in the moment. This is clearly not a style of psychological realism, but a heightened one, and taken out of context the passage might appear to be wallowing in a nostalgic view of honor-based cultures in an escape from present realities.

Yet when we consider that the entire novel is framed by the narration of an in-world character, we will see that the overall narrative context renders these Shakespearean speeches ironic, allowing Erikson both to use the familiar elevated epic style and at the same time make a more sophisticated comment on the use of language and narrative to construct identity and history. While this novel is a prequel telling the story of the Tiste peoples (the Andii, Liosan, and Edur) who play a central role in Erikson's Malazan Book of the Fallen, it is not presented directly as "history." Instead, the story is framed as a narrative by the poet Gallan, a Tiste Andii who was alive at the time of the events, to a human poet contemporary with the later series (thousands of years later). It is not just an origin story, but a story about origins and about how the narrative of origins is a construct created for ideological purposes. In the Prelude that introduces this frame, Gallan emphasizes both the political nature of narrative and its ideological use value. Narrative is shaped by the perspective of the storyteller, and perspective is something a blind man like Gallan particularly understands: "Even when I had sight, to see through a single pair of eyes was a kind of torture, for I knew—I could feel in my soul—that we with our single visions miss most of the world. We cannot help it. It is our barrier to understanding. Perhaps it is only the poets who truly resent this way of being. No matter; what I do not recall I shall invent" (xxi–xxii). Gallan emphasizes that the story he tells is "my memory […] my creation" (xxii), not to be confused with the events themselves. Imagination and invention are necessary supplements to "truth" as they are the only way to achieve the multiple perspectives that would transcend the narrow, limited box of individual perspective. At the same time, however, Gallan reminds us that the ensuing narrative is carefully crafted to serve his purposes—in fact, it reminds us that all narrative is shaped and that history itself is a narrative shaped to ideological purposes. In this light, the speeches above can be seen more ironically as the inventions of a poet who is idealizing these key historical figures and placing in their mouths words that are weighted with the knowledge of events that are yet to happen in the narrative. The frame enables a doubleness in the style, in that it functions both as enthralling epic narrative and as an ironic reminder of the narrativity of history.

Erikson's framing, however, is subtle. He simply provides the Prelude, which perhaps an incautious reader could easily forget, but he continually provides oblique traces of Gallan, evidence making the invisible presence of the poet narrator palpable throughout the novel. Gallan himself never appears in the narrative, although other characters talk about him, reminding the reader who is actually telling the story. For instance, the painter Kadaspala refers to finding Gallan "who sings unheard and walks unseen by any" (641), a moment that is both thematic (the character here is referring to how the wisdom of artists is unheeded) and a meta-joke (Gallan is literally invisible in the novel). Further, the poet's voice is subtly present in the style everywhere in the novel, particularly through the figurative language which is far more pervasive than we might typically expect from a novel. Many chapters are constructed around specific recurring patterns of images which often tie into the thematics of those chapters, demonstrating how the language constructs meaning. In Chapter 13, for instance, Kadaspala has an extended point of view section that focuses on a motif of colors and paints. After a number of point-of-view changes, the chapter ends with the following image: "The sun's light was hard and strangely harsh, as if every colour was paint, and every hue and every shade held in it, somewhere, a hint of iron" (401). Such a structural tie to the dominant motif of the chapter is good construction, of course, but what is striking here is that the point-of-view character is not Kadaspala the artist but the warrior Ivis who has had no contact with Kadaspala. The only tie between the two is the narrator. Such subtle moments reinforce the narrator's shaping control of the narrative and call attention to how everything we see is "colored" by his intentions.

From the perspective of literary theory, such moments have a particular resonance, as they take the organic unity so valued by the New Critics and make it not just a conveyor of irony but a source of irony. The unified structure is itself ironic. The text reveals that the consistent, unified, organic structure imposes artificial order on the chaos of events, but at the same time it offers precisely that much-sought aesthetic unity. Erikson unifies these motifs across characters on a scale that crosses not just chapters but the entire novel. The book ends with a very brief return to the framing narration of Gallan. The narrative has just finished with an image of Hood (whom long-time readers know will eventually become the god of death) grieving the death of his family by declaring a crusade against death itself. Then the narration shifts back to the frame, with Gallan saying, "I did not walk among them, Fisher kel Tath. Would that I had. He raised a banner of grief, and this detail waves my intent, but Lord Anomander, at this juncture, was not ready to see it. They were too far away. They were caught in their own lives" (661). This passage once again insists on Gallan's absence from events (regretfully, in this case), and also uses his distance from events to argue for his better position from which to see the narrative organization of their lives. Yet the metaphor he uses, the "banner of grief," betrays the extent to which he is actively constructing the unity he sees: despite not literally walking among them, he is present in shaping the narrative we are reading because this banner image is a unifying motif that crops up at key points in the book. Often, as is the case with the "banner of grief," the banner referred to is both a literal object (a flag raised over an army) and a figurative one (a representation of what unites a group of people): "They raise high banners of faith" (405); "Touch lips to no banner I raise" (457); "they ride out to meet us, assuming they have the courage to face the challenge of our banner" (595).

One key scene links the banner metaphor significantly to the consciousness of the soldier Narad. Narad is part of the military unit responsible for the brutal rape at the center of the political conflict in the book, an unwilling participant carried along by the pressure of the mob mentality. In reflecting on the violence and moral decay of his unit, he considers his ugliness—the result of a disfiguring beating he received earlier in the novel—as a metaphorical externalization of the moral ugliness of the soldiers, a metaphor he expresses specifically through the image of a banner: "He walked with his ugliness for all to see, and perhaps this relieved the others since they imagined that they could hide the ugliness they had inside. Instead, he was their banner, their standard, and if they haunted

him, surely he must haunt them as well" (550). Narad starts to see himself, like a banner, as an emblem physically symbolizing the abstract interiority of the other soldiers: "His was the face of war. His was the body that
raped the innocent [...] and he moved through it like a standard, a banner
awaiting the rallying cry of killers" (551). Narad's metaphor seems singu-
larly appropriate because in an almost medieval, allegorical sense moral
interiority becomes physically reflected in his exterior. A banner is itself
a metaphor, a representation meant to unify a group of people into a single identity, and by seeing himself as that metaphorical banner, Narad creates a double-layered metaphor that reveals the hidden interior that unites
the soldiers in ways they would rather hide. Yet Gallan's use of the same
metaphors ironically suggests that this metaphor is a bit too perfect—the
image is not any more psychologically realistic than the dialogue. Narad,
the violent, poorly educated caravan-guard-turned-soldier probably lacks
the self-awareness or linguistic capability to craft such perfect metaphors.
Here Gallan betrays the extent to which the unity of imagery and meaning
in this book is as carefully crafted and open to ideological analysis as the
esprit de corps that a banner is meant to create.

This use of the frame to render style ironic has its zenith in a central
stylistic feature of the novel that I call "literalized metaphor." Narad's banner metaphor is a good example of how this figure functions, as it takes
something abstract (the soldiers' moral ugliness), expresses it through
a metaphor (physical ugliness), but then makes that metaphor a literal,
embodied part of the story world (Narad is literally ugly). Conventionally, the vehicle of a metaphor is not literally present. However, in a literalized metaphor the line between figurative and literal becomes blurry, as
the literal events become reflected in the metaphors and the metaphors
themselves seem to literally change the world of the narrative. By meld-
ing narrative invention and the ideological use of language, a literal metaphor shows how language has concrete consequences by shaping the world
around us, just as Narad's ugliness becomes a self-fulfilling prophecy that
explains for him (if not justifies) his involvement in the rape. The reverse
of this process also happens, as the language of the narrative becomes
shaped by the literal events. The best example of this occurs when T'riss,
a powerful being connected to the fundamental essence of reality, visits
Mother Dark, the leader of the Tiste who has been establishing a religious
cult around herself in place of the old worship of the river god. T'riss's
arrival re-awakens the river god, and the rising river starts flooding the
streets of the Tiste capital Kharkanas and Mother Dark's temple. As the
world around them is literally transformed by T'riss's entrance, Mother
Dark's high priestess Emral realizes what is happening: "All at once comprehension arrived, a flood in her mind" (259). The literal water becomes

metaphorical water—the transformation of the world has leaked into the language of the novel, transforming that as well. This seepage between literal and figurative language continues throughout this key scene. A few pages later, "relief was flooding through Emral" (261). Then, while debating who should follow T'riss into her audience with Mother Dark, one character says, "The two of us together twice drowns the threat and what needs drowning twice?" (261). T'riss herself, in her audience with Mother Dark, says, "I come to stir the waters" (268), and when Mother Dark warns of an impending schism and civil war, she says, "In matters of faith, waters will part" (271). All of these metaphors are clearly derived from the situation itself, and either the characters are cleverly punning in a crisis, or the shaping hand of the narrator Gallan is reaching through here to remind us of how he is transforming these materials just as the world of the characters is being transformed.

This interpenetration of the metaphorical and the literal happens throughout the novel. Even Andarist's naming of his sword when Anomander swears vengeance for the rape (in the passage I discussed at the start of this section) illustrates a metaphor becoming literal. Andarist names the sword "Grief" rather than "Vengeance," saying to Anomander, "You will take my grief, Anomander, or never again shall I look upon you, or call you brother, or know your blood as mine own" (481). When Anomander refuses to take this name from him ("It has no strength, no will. Grief? Upon iron, it is rust" [481]), his brother Silchas exhorts him, "Take his grief, Anomander! Upon your blade, take it!" to which Anomander replies, "And so dull every edge, Silchas?" (481). The entire passage puns on the name of the sword, shifting between references to the physical object (named "Vengeance" or "Grief") and the emotional state it is named for: Andarist calls out, "Will no one share my grief?" (481) and Kadaspala, also present at the scene, says "I am not the one wielding vengeance" (482). The language surrounding the use of the sword becomes cleverly entangled in the emotions to which its use is linked, these metaphors functioning both to ironically suggest the shaping hand of the frame narrator and the role figurative language serves in justifying the characters' various reactions to violence.

On a larger scale, the central plot of the novel involves a metaphor that is made literal: namely the religious schism surrounding Mother Dark. T'riss's visit is an important turning point in the novel because she consecrates Mother Dark, turning her skin as black as the darkness she has metaphorically represented and also turning black the skin of her followers, such as Anomander, creating a separate race called the Tiste Andii. Ultimately, the blackness of their skin becomes a literalization of all the metaphorical meanings that darkness has in this culture. When T'riss tells Anomander, "Night will claim your skin. Before your eyes, darkness will be revealed" (268), she initially seems to be speaking metaphorically. However, moments later, Mother Dark observes of him, "You are no longer blinded by darkness, and all who come to me will receive this blessing. Even now [...] I see Night come to your skin" (271). Allegiance to Mother Dark ("all who come to me") jumps from a metaphor to a literal, physical sign. Before this point, the darkness has functioned largely as a myth or symbol. Several characters tell a myth of primordial unity, when all was darkness before the emergence of light: "the stars were but holes in the fabric of night, a thinning of blessed darkness; and [...] in ages long past there had been no stars at all—the dark was complete, absolute [...] when harmony commanded all and peace stilled every restless heart" (131). Mother Dark seems to have initially aligned herself with this worship of the darkness to connect herself to this mythic discourse of peace and harmony. However, despite this promise of unity, like any symbol, darkness is polysemous and characters frequently debate its meaning. Mother Dark's darkness is often associated not so much with "ignorance" as mystery, the willingness to accept uncertainty and thus difference. However, a number of characters question the validity of this interpretation. Kadaspala, when observing the aftereffects of violence, thinks of darkness in terms of denial, an artificial attempt to impose unity on the psyche: "In the world of night promised by Mother Dark, so much would remain for ever unseen. He began to wonder if that would be a mercy. He began to wonder if this was the secret of her promised blessing to all her believers, her children. *Darkness now and for evermore. So we can get on with things*" (374). Such criticism suggests that the false unity of not seeing difference covers up potentially damaging realities. Ultimately, darkness presents the danger of mystification, covering up the workings of power beneath an unquestionable naturalness.

Thus, when characters' skin becomes literally dark as a sign of loyalty, it is like Narad becoming a physical emblem of the moral ugliness of the soldiers. The body becomes a metaphor with ideological consequences, an artificially imposed unity that matches the symbolic unity the darkness allegedly represents. Ultimately, these metaphors have very real political consequences. Skin color becomes used as an index of faith in Mother Dark. When Scara observes that Silchas's skin is not changing, he says, "I see your skin still resisting the caress of Mother Dark," and asks "And you are without doubt?" (450). The problem with the metaphor of darkness is that it implies a conflictual model. The rhetorical separation in this political power struggle, like all such power struggles, is often represented as a good-and-evil, black-and-white binary: if there is dark, there must be light. This model is built into the origin myth, according to which the original, harmonious darkness was destroyed by the appearance of light in the form of stars: "The sun opened its eye and so slashed in two all existence, dividing the worldly realm into Light and Dark [...] without one the other could not be known to exist—they needed each other in the very utterance of defining their states, for such states existed only in comparison" (89). Thus, the metaphorical binary thinking creates the need for opposition—darkness cannot be a uniting force if there is nothing to unite. In a very Derridean way, the promise of wholeness requires an absence, a rupture, at its center. In a sense, the linguistic construction of this metaphor of darkness *creates* the conflict at the center of the book. Thus, at the same time as Mother Dark is turning her loyal followers black, the rebellious priestess Syntara becomes pure white, "bloodless, white as bone" (271), and starts to lead the revolt against Mother Dark's rule. The metaphorical binary becomes literal as skin colors change to match the sides in the conflict. The logic of opposing Mother Dark is often couched specifically in terms of the necessity for this type of binary thinking: "The purity of your skin is now a symbol—the light within you is a power. [...] in darkness there is ignorance. In light there is justice" (275). Throughout the novel, the forces of light (the Tiste Liosan) are focused on justice, hard and fast rules that can be clearly seen, in contrast to Mother Dark's emphasis on mystery.

In summary, then, both in relation to the forces of "light" and those of "dark," the metaphor shapes the terms of the conflict—how one interprets the meaning of "light" and "dark" shapes how one behaves in the conflict—and the shaping power of this rhetoric is made literal in the plot as it reshapes the bodies of the characters. The literalized metaphors indicate how language shapes reality. Justice appears "natural" because symbols, myths, and other artificial constructions make it *seem* natural and right. At the same time, we should remember that this neat metaphorical explanation for historical events is framed by the invisible hand of the narrator just as the other patterns of metaphor we have seen elsewhere in the novel, calling it into question as yet another interpretation of history. This is fantasy that reflects back on the whole genre, as the myth-making function of fantasy is precisely this same use of language-as-metaphor to give structure to reality. Through the frame narrative, Erikson is able to reflect ironically on such uses of language by presenting those metaphors as the constructions they are, in a narrative that is also about how the uses of such metaphors have the magnified consequences of literally leading to war. The cumulative effect of this ironic style, then, is to destabilize the binary of fact/invention or of literal/metaphor, showing how history is shaped by ideology and language just as much as poetry is.

Delany's Parentheticals

Erikson subtly gestures at an affordance of fantasy's framing, namely that epic fantasy's pre-built frame is ready-made for ironies involving language and the ideological representation of history. While *Forge of Darkness* shows how that potential can be used without completely collapsing fantasy's narrative function, I will conclude by considering what happens when the theoretical component of fantasy representation is emphasized. Samuel Delany overtly makes that the subject of his Return to Nevèrÿon series, particularly in the first volume *Tales of Nevèrÿon*. Delany's Nevèrÿon does not tell a coherent single narrative. Instead, it is fragmented, more a collection of short stories and expository theoretical prose set allegedly in the very earliest days of human civilization. Many of the stories revolve around a slave revolt led by Gorgik, who is Delany's theoretically sophisticated version of Conan the Barbarian as the psychosocial product of a rich prehistoric environment. However, the revolt (and presumably the epic action) is rarely at the center of the narrative. In Delany's case, narrative frames are everywhere, distancing the reader in multiple ways. First, the entire series is framed as a fictional re-writing of an ancient text called the Culhar' fragment or Missolonghi Codex, allegedly the oldest extant example of writing. This academic frame is explained in appendices over several volumes through a debate between several translators and academics, raising the issue of origins—where our stories come from and what their purpose is. On top of this, Delany writes an introductory essay by a fictitious "real-world" scholar named K. Leslie Steiner who interprets and analyzes Delany's fictional text. At times, Steiner's description of the main text includes playful (self-)deprecation, as when in a riff on the tendency of fantasy to be too verbose, Steiner cites a description of the narration of the book as like taking a tour of a museum with a well-informed friend "who you only wished [...] would shut up" (15).

By framing the fantasy narrative within an academic debate, Delany intentionally deconstructs the distinction between academic discourse and myth. Unlike many texts above, Delany's process has been well-documented by literary criticism. Kathleen Spencer has argued that Delany's use of philosophical appendices "serves to challenge the readers' expectations about the form or nature of fiction" (64) as the academic essay becomes part of the text itself. Spencer lists a number of ways in which the Nevèrÿon cycle consistently disappoints reader expectations for sword and sorcery, such as the lack of linear progression or the relative absence of a central hero (Gorgik appears sporadically and is rarely depicted taking action). However, perhaps the most important disruption comes from the frame itself, in the blurring of exposition and narrative, or as Sylvia Kelso summarizes it, "it is no longer clear where 'fact' becomes 'fiction,' an effect intensified because the 'factual' Appendix is fictional" (290). In fact, Kelso builds on Spencer's argument by pointing out that Delany treats "Theory-as-praxis" (290), making theory the content of the fiction rather than a marginal supplement. This boundary blurring ranges from his inclusion of epigraphs from Derrida and Foucault to his characters giving long philosophical disquisitions on semiotics and Marxist theory, as in "The Tale of Old Venn" or the conclusion of "The Tale of Dragons and Dreamers." The text is constantly shifting between academic discourse and narrative. Delany thus reveals (even more transparently than the examples discussed in Chapter 7) the political dimensions of fantasy's blurred frames. As a gay African American writer of SF (itself a marginalized genre), Delany sought to deconstruct such binaries as black/white and gay/straight in order to open up a space for marginal identities, and his use of gay identity and SM motifs in the series has been well-documented.[6] Succinctly, Delany's goal seems to be to "create a fictional space and shatter the ossification of tradition, custom, and oppressive worldly paradigms" (Danylyshen 164). While I have argued that this destruction of "ossified tradition" is the outcome of much of the epic fantasy discussed above, Delany's particular goals and politics give a concrete grounding that makes epic fantasy visible as political action—an appropriate place to conclude my analysis of epic fantasy.

However, because this political context has been thoroughly discussed by other critics, rather than reiterating those arguments, I will be focusing on Delany's style, particularly how the irony provided by the framing enables this deconstruction of tradition. In the preface, Delany (as Steiner) calls the series "an intricate argument about power, sexuality, and narration itself" (14). While the first two items in this list have been thoroughly analyzed by critics, the last—"narration itself"—has not been covered with quite the same close attention to detail. Most critics recognize it and discuss it briefly. (Georgia Johnston, for instance, argues that "Delany challenges stereotype and assumption at the level of discourse. [...] He changes the dominant controlling discourse rather than oppose it" [236].) However, rarely is there much close reading of the mechanisms Delany uses to reflect on narration, namely the irony that allows him to reflexively create narrative authority while questioning the practices that create that authority. This irony derives principally from the framing of the stories. For instance, while the academic framing essays undermine the boundaries of the text simply by being included, Delany often parodies the very academic discourse he is using. He does this in obvious ways with his self-deprecating analysis through the fictional K. Leslie Steiner, but he also does this in subtler ways through his characterization of the scholar S.L.

Kermit who writes the appendix, whom Delany presents as condescending and patriarchal. For instance, when Steiner refers to a non-gendered narrator as "she," Kermit calls this "a quaintly feminist aberration" (257). Later, he reacts to her theories (such as that the child-ruler in the text is a girl) with "smiles [of] intrigued indulgence" (259). By presenting Kermit's "objective" academic discourse as smugly patriarchal, Delany reveals academic discourse as a contest of personalities just as much as narrative, and by doing so, he breaks down discourse categories between narrative and academic analysis.

By calling attention to personalities and motives involved in academic interpretation, the text enables its critique of fantasy as a narrative of origins. As Kermit puts it elsewhere in the appendix to *Tales*, "If some writer were actually to put down these stories, just what sort of reflection might they constitute, either of the modern world or of our own past history" (259–260). The metafictional reference to the book in the readers' hands (these tales *have* been put down in a single volume) makes it clear that the tale of origins is always a tale about the present, about "us," a point that Steiner makes more bluntly in the preface: "all we are really learning about is our own age's conception of historical possibility" (19). The academic frame *is* the story because it shows us how the narrating of history is an attempt to stabilize it, to suggest that "History […] has already been negotiated, so that beyond a certain point any attempt to know more is at best error and at worst sedition" (16). While Steiner presents this last statement as only one side of the dialectic of history, it is the direction that any closed historical narrative tends. Thus, awareness of the constructed nature of that History saves us from falling into that trap because we see how the language itself constructs meaning. Consequently, by offering a fantasy story that self-consciously reflects its creation process in language, the novel fashions a new myth by deconstructing the artificial categories that have previously been created to separate people.

Yet further frames within the stories themselves continue to structure the book in ways that parallel the shaping, myth-making hands of Delany, Kermit, and Steiner. Even within individual stories, there are often narrative frames and stories-within-stories. In the fourth story in *Tales*, "The Tale of Potters and Dragons," we follow a hero from an earlier story, Norema (an agent of a merchant in the city of Kolhari) and Raven (an assassin) as they seek out the mysterious Lord Aldamir who apparently controls lucrative rubber plantations. Norema and a naïve young apprentice named Bayle have been sent to open up trade with him, while Raven has been sent to assassinate him. The mission becomes dangerous as they are attacked and must go into hiding. Yet even these moments that would conventionally be emphasized in such an action-oriented genre are instead re-framed, as "action" becomes "discourse." For instance, when Norema is attacked in her sleep by an assassin and saved by Raven, the action occurs while Norema sleeps and is only narrated retrospectively by Raven: "'When this one here climbed up into your window with a knife in her—in *his* teeth and a garrote cord knotted around his wrist, I was up behind and—' Raven made the jabbing motion Norema supposed would sink a sword in a kidney" (197). Delany steps back from any seemingly transparent presentation of the action and instead presents it as *story*, a story Raven tells (even performs) for Norema about what just happened. As Raven and Norema then reconstruct the events around them, they realize that this entire encounter has been engineered by the monastery they have visited so that Bayle will carry a *story* back to Kolhari: "the youngster returns by the next boat with tales of the absent Lord [Aldamir]'s might, given over to him throughout a day of entertainment by a host of drunken, garrulous priests [...] Now Bayle will carry the tale of Lord Aldamir back to Kolhari" (201). The story we are reading is a story about the fabrication and transmission of story, one that is overtly *storied* for us by the characters themselves.

Raven and Norema choose to flee instead of returning to Kolhari. Then, rather than continuing to follow their narrative and providing resolution, the story is framed by a concluding chapter that returns to the city and a conversation between Norema's employer and Bayle's employer (the potter of the title) as they speculate about what happened to their missing employees. The story that we were reading *becomes* the story that is being told by these other characters. We may be reminded here of Delany (as Leslie Steiner) commenting in the intro, "something about these stories defers origins—not to say endings—in favor of fictions" (12). Instead of being given a direct, conventional climax, we only see the stories that are told about them. They are turned into narrative, which has a purpose, in this case to perpetuate racial, national, and gender stereotypes. The potter assumes that Bayle ran away because it was "easy [...] in the barbaric south, with no supervision and no constraints" (211). Norema's master bases her assumptions about Norema's fate on gender stereotypes, as she assumes Norema was set upon by "evil men, sensing the weakness of a woman" (212). Finally, the potter sums up the "moral" of the story for them with an Orientalizing rhetorical gesture: "Truly the south is a strange and terrible land, where every evil we here in civilized Kolhari can imagine of it comes reflected back to us" (212). The story here emphasizes the constructed nature of reality, especially in light of stereotypes and assumptions made about the other.

This framing structure is rendered particularly ironic due to a detail I have thus far omitted: Norema and Raven discover that "Lord Aldamir" does not actually exist—he is an invented identity created to safeguard the power of the rich in Nevèrÿon, to keep competition from accessing the lucrative rubber plantations in the south. The many stereotypes and warnings the readers have heard of the savage south throughout the story have been legends designed to keep people away so they do not discover this fabrication. As Raven points out when explicating the plot to have Bayle carry back his tales of Lord Aldamir, "The one thing that the rumor will not make them doubt is Lord Aldamir's existence" (201). Thus, the entire story, with its many inset stories within stories, reflects on the creation of legends and their ideological uses. By the time the reader sees the employers' conversation in the final chapter, we already know more than they do, and so we are simply witnessing the creation of a legend that reinforces existing ideology.

While this thematic reflection on the ideological construction of reality through story is present in the formal structuring of the story, it also manifests in the stylistic figure most characteristic of Delany, the use of parentheticals. While I am using the term "parentheticals" here loosely to include any phrase that interrupts the main clause of a sentence with additional information, many of Delany's parentheticals are in fact in parentheses. This style of writing allows Delany to suggest multiple simultaneous levels of meaning, opening up the possibilities within his sentences and unmasking the hierarchies that structure society (and also unmasking that these hierarchies are themselves structured through language). Georgia Johnston has noted that Delany frequently uses such play with linguistic form in a fashion derived from Derrida, who provides Delany with an image of texts written in parallel columns to express the possibility of bringing in marginalized voices. Johnston argues that "Using the column, he is able to articulate narratives for his experiences that are parallel to, simultaneous with, but invisible in narratives of the dominant white and straight culture. By using the column form, Samuel Delany makes readers aware that there are more narratives, though they were heretofore invisible, outside available, acceptable discourse" (220). While Johnston applies this argument to Delany's autobiography (and Delany primarily uses the *image* of writing in columns rather than actually doing so), the frequent parentheticals in *Tales* seems to accomplish much the same purpose. In fact, Delany himself has written that language has a multi-level structure, which communicates on two levels: "one, at which the author intends to communicate, and two, at which the language itself, both by its presences and absences, frequently communicates things very different from, or in direct opposition to, that first level" (*Jewel-Hinged Jaw* 107–8). While Delany seems to be expressing a broadly poststructuralist view of language here, fantastic fiction in particular sets about combining language into unexpected meanings, which makes it a particularly effective place to make the reader aware of these multiple levels within language.[7] Thus, his parentheticals operate side-by-side with the frame narrative, as both serve to make the reader aware of how language and narrative construct and organize reality.

The book is full of these parentheticals, almost obsessively so, making much of the text stylistically dense as most sentences and paragraphs present a hierarchy of information of varying relevance (an appropriate style for the very organized, hierarchical society being represented). Many of the descriptions in the first story, "The Tale of Gorgik," confirm this relationship between hierarchy and Delany's multi-level syntax. As this story introduces the reader to the fantasy world, much of the exposition describing the city of Kolhari uses complex sentences laced with parentheticals to describe the class and race hierarchies of the city:

> Along the upper end, where the road dipped down again to cross the Bridge of Lost Desire, male and female prostitutes loitered or drank in the streets or solicited along the bridge's walkways, many come from exotic places and many spawned by old Kolhari herself, most of them brown by birth and darkened more by summer, like the fine, respectable folk of the city (indeed, like himself [Gorgik]), though here were a few with yellow hair, pale skin, gray eyes, and their own lisping language (like Miese) bespeaking barbaric origins [30].

While the simple inversion of the class hierarchies of modern America (here dark skin is "normal," white skin "barbaric") is a fairly conventional way of signaling the artifice of racial hierarchies, the layered complexity of the sentence also reflects the linguistic construction of hierarchy. In order to place all of these elements in relation to each other, a speaker must use subordination, separating more "important" information from less important. In this passage, general categories are given primacy while specific examples (Gorgik, Miese) are relegated to literal parentheticals. Yet in a passage that is *about* racial hierarchy, this pattern of privileging general over individual can easily be read ironically.

In fact, the language of this story closely parallels the academic discourse in Kermit's appendix, suggesting the extent to which hierarchical imposition is a function of the academic, scholarly mindset Kermit represents (and is, of course, part of his patriarchal mindset as well). Such is the case in this passage describing the fictional history of the text:

> The fragment known as the Culhar' (or sometimes the Kolharē Text)—and more recently as the Missolonghi Codex (from the Greek town where the volumes, now on store in the basement of the Istanbul Archeological Museum, were purchased in the nineteenth century, and which contain what is now considered to be one of the two oldest versions of the text known)—not only has a strange history, but a strangely disseminated history [247].

The stylistic similarity here, with the lengthy interruptions deferring the end of the sentence with less important information, foregrounds how language constructs these levels of meaning. Such moments reinforce William Schuyler's argument that the "frame" of this text is not even genuinely a frame: "At the same time, the stories must not be taken to be set somehow within a frame consisting of the other material. As parts of the books, they function at the same hierarchical level as the 'Remarks.' [...] The books call into question by their very form our notions of what counts as narrative and exposition" (68). The hierarchy between narrative and theory in fiction is undermined even as the sentences themselves insistently organize information hierarchically. By ironically blurring the boundaries between narrative and exposition (a parallel between text and paratext similar to those discussed in Chapter 7), the text is undermining the very linguistic construction that it seems to create through its hierarchical syntax.

The extent to which this hierarchy is structurally a function of language is further emphasized (and deconstructed) in "The Story of Gorgik." As Gorgik moves from his lower-class city background to his enslavement in the royal household, the story frequently reflects on the different discourse registers he encounters: "*Their* language [the nobility's], polished and mellifluous, flowed, between bouts of laughter in which his indelicacies were generously absorbed and forgiven (if not forgotten), over subjects ranging from the scandalous to the scabrous" (47). The core of the sentence is "Their language flowed over subjects," yet it is interrupted twice for long additional phrases, and the second interruption is interrupted at a secondary level by a parenthetical phrase. In fact, these interruptions emphasize the nature of the language itself ("polished and mellifluous") and the distinction between superficial action and deeper consciousness (in the phrase "forgiven (if not forgotten)"). Thus, the sentence about different discourse registers calls attention to its own multiple levels while describing language and placing that language in a relational, social context. The remainder of this passage emphasizes how these differing discourse registers are related to social hierarchy by noting that Gorgik's "blunt" language follows the "narrow range" laid down by the "slaves and thieves, dock-beggars and prostitutes, sailors and barmaids and more slaves—people, in short, with no power beyond their voices, fingers, or feet" (47). This final reminder of their lack of power is located syntactically within a parenthetical, a subordination within a subordination within the sentence. In such moments, Delany uses the dialogic complexity of his sentences to break the superficial hegemony of a single voice by reminding the reader of the many other marginalized levels of voices.

The point here is that the hierarchizing tendency of language is artificial, that it actually *creates* history and tradition rather than merely *reflecting* tradition. A highly formulaic genre deeply associated with a sense of the past—a genre such as epic fantasy—can therefore play a significant role in shaping the imagination either in an "ossified" hegemonic way or, conversely, re-shaping the imagination to be aware of language's shaping role. The most overt reflection on this use of formula occurs in the final story in the collection, "The Tale of Dragons and Dreamers." Here, in perhaps the most viscerally "action-oriented" story, as Gorgik and his friend and lover Sarg liberate the slaves in a castle, we see a further function of the parentheticals: they are a way of indicating repetition across time and thus generating a sense of "tradition." The second chapter of the story begins with the sentence "And again Small Sarg ran" (221), picking up in the middle with "and" as though the reader knows already what is going on. The transition here implies continuity with the past, with tradition, with a repeated ritual, even though the reader does not yet know what is being repeated. As the reader proceeds through the events of Sarg's rescue, the parentheticals constantly inform us of how this is similar to (or different from) other rescues: "he shoved away a curtain of leaves [...] to reveal the moonlit castle. (How many other castles had he so revealed ...)" (221). He knows where to go to find an unlocked door because "(as he ran, he clawed over memories of the seven castles he had already run up to; seven side doors, all unlocked ...)" (222). Even the physical action in this scene, Delany's nod to genre conventions, is rendered in this complex, layered style: Sarg "jabbed his sword into the shoulder of the guard who'd started forward (already hearing the murmur behind the wooden slats), yanking it free of flesh, the motion carrying it up and across the throat of the second guard (here there was always a second guard) who had turned, surprised; the second guard released his sword (it had only been half drawn)" (223). Along the way he registers both similarity (always two guards) and difference (the second guard only half draws his sword). Note also that Sarg anticipates the sound of the slaves he is saving, as we see clearly a few lines later: "Behind the boards and under the screams [of the guards], like murmuring flies, hands and faces rustled about one another. (Seven times now they had seemed like murmuring flies)" (223). This moment of poetic imagery is anticipated in the middle of the action sequence—multiple levels of temporality converge in one complex moment of action.

This emphasis on repetition and continuity seems to be a direct comment on the often repetitious, formulaic quality of epic fantasy or sword and sorcery action (similar to the response to serialization in the construction of the Eternal Champion or the Cosmere, as discussed in Chapter 7). The scene is familiar to the fantasy audience: readers have seen a brute with a sword cut an enemy's throat in a thousand fantasy stories, but this story acknowledges the repetition and emphasizes how it is part of fantasy's link to tradition, not in the sense of a simple nostalgic return to the past but by ironically calling attention to how narrative repetition creates a sense of tradition and historicity. Furthermore, this scene—one of the only directly presented scenes of physical action in the entire book—is consistently treated ironically. While Sarg claims to be "liberating" these slaves, the slaves actively question the value of his liberation, even pointing out to him that they are likely to either be recaptured or simply starve because they lack the means to take care of themselves. Joshua Yu Burnett has pointed out that "Small Sarg, in his simplistic narrative of liberation through battle, has failed to take into account the systemic and structural components of slavery, thinking that, simply by uncollaring slaves and letting them run, he can destroy slavery itself" (262). Thus, Gorgik and Sarg, who seem to take on the role of heroic liberators, actually reveal that the heroic narrative paradigm as itself part of the artificial, unchanging form of history that Steiner describes in the preface. As one of the slaves in the castle points out to Sarg, "the natural drift of our nation is away from slave labor anyway [...] Have you considered: your efforts may even be prolonging the institution you would abolish" (228). Heroic forms of "liberation" may, in fact, simply be regressive narratives counter to the development of history, keeping it in a fixed form of "tradition." The whole scene ironically parodies heroic fantasy—in a style that calls attention to how fantasy creates the narrative of history, as enabled by the overall framing device. The epigraph to this story, taken from Foucault's *The Archaeology of Knowledge*, reflects directly on this: "Take the notion of tradition: it is intended to give a special temporal status to a group of phenomena that are both successive and identical (or at least similar) [...] it allows a reduction of the difference proper to every beginning" (215). Narrative repetition is often used to create a false sense of "tradition" that reduces the complex causality of material reality, but by ironically reflecting on that through the narrative framing and parenthetical style, Delany instead calls attention to how formulaic narrative can be used to *create* narrative history for ideological purposes.

Thus, Delany sums up in theory the argument I have been expounding for the past two chapters, one that Erikson indicates more subtly, and that lies in the background of the framework of epic fantasy as a whole: that the tools for an ironic consideration of historicity and the ideological uses of narrative are fundamental to the structure of epic fantasy. As a form about tradition and about the past, yet also a form that inherently contains a potentially ironic frame (in its distance from the present), fantasy is actually well positioned for postmodern considerations of identity and the constructivist role of language. I might very easily have started with Delany, but my hope by placing him last has been to show that he is not an isolated voice or an edge case. Instead, Delany is giving theoretical voice to a structural feature of the genre itself. Certainly, not every writer takes advantage of these affordances as they often exist in collision with more stabilizing narrative forms; however, the invisible but ever-present framework provided by the formula of the genre may have more progressive potential than is implied in the label "formula."

Conclusion

I have ended this study with issues related to the framing of epic fantasy as they bring us back to a core affordance, the relationship between narrative form and social forms. As a genre that partakes of historical tradition (the epic) and modernist individualism (the novel), epic fantasy is uniquely positioned to exploit some of the central collisions in the novel form and make visible how novelistic form intersects with social forms. Moreover, the language of the text—the style—by structuring the reader's experience, generates these tensions in instructive ways. This language is constantly both constructing and deconstructing worlds, creating the unique affective experience of reading epic fantasy. My goal has been to demonstrate this affordance in as many ways as possible, to show the breadth of tools available to epic fantasy, from syntax to narrative perspective to reflexive self-awareness. This last constitutes an appropriate end point, as the genre's thematic concern with imagination and story afford a strong perspective from which to reveal the possibilities of narrative form. Thus, despite often being consigned to the fringes of speculative fiction scholarship, epic fantasy has much to offer to our understanding not just of popular culture but literary form in general. As a genre of "big things," epic fantasy amplifies and magnifies. In its use of language, it makes visible many affordances of narrative more generally, helping us understand the "magic" connectivity of language—how it constructs the reading subject and community in ways that lie at the heart of the novel.

Chapter Notes

Preface

1. This article has subsequently been published: "Between World and Narrative: Fictional Epigraphs and Critical World-Building" by Stefan Ekman and Audrey Isabel Taylor (*Journal of the Fantastic in the Arts*, vol. 32, no. 2, 2021, pp. 244-265).

Introduction

1. Dennis Wilson Wise has recently published a similar but far more thorough and developed argument about what he delightfully refers to as Evil Possessed Vampire Demon Swords (EPVIDS) (Wise, "A Brief History").

2. Jamie Williamson's excellent history of the development of the fantasy genre, *The Evolution of Modern Fantasy* (2015), is a perfect illustration of this tendency. Throughout the book, Willliamson frequently mentions the style of the various writers he discusses and builds his argument around crucial stylistic distinctions between different groups of pregenre fantasy writers, but these references to style take the form of generalizations that are rarely backed up with examples or analysis. While such stylistic analysis is certainly not Williamson's goal in the book, this is typical of how style is usually handled in the critical literature on fantasy.

3. Levine offers a clarification between the two terms, pointing out that genre can change over time because it is based on ways of classifying texts that includes "style, theme, and marketing conventions" (13). Forms are context-independent (a sonnet is always a sonnet regardless of audience or when it was written), while genres are "customary constellations of elements into historically recognizable groupings of artistic objects, bringing together forms with themes, styles, and situations of reception" (14). On the other hand, Farah Mendlesohn has argued that fantasy is a form, citing Eleanor Cameron who writes that fantasy is "a very special category of literature that compares with fiction as a sonnet compares with poetry. Either you have a sonnet if you have written your poem in a certain way, or you don't if you haven't" (qtd. in Mendlesohn xv).

4. I am referring to a rhetorical tendency I have noticed in numerous conference papers to use the concept of the "fuzzy set" to rationalize a non-specific definition of key genre terms. Attebery himself actually gives quite specific definitions for the terms he uses.

5. Gifford's *A Modernist Fantasy* discusses Jackson's influence in a lengthy introductory section (16–23), and Mark Bould breaks down her argument about the fantastic "hesitation" by pointing out that even the fantasies she favors, as commodities, are often labeled in advance as fantasy, disrupting the uncertainty in their reception (59).

6. As Brian Attebery notes, "rather than broadening her theory to fit the exception, she concludes that *The Lord of the Rings* is a failed fantasy" (21).

7. While I particularly want to credit Ekman's influence here, I could as easily cite a number of other critics who have discussed the self-reflexive or metafictional qualities of fantasy. Brian Attebery has made this one of the cornerstones of his arguments about fantasy, with a full

chapter devoted to the subject in *Strategies of Fantasy* (1992), and in his more recent essay "Structuralism" (2012), he asserts that "fantasy typically displays and even celebrates its structure [...] fantasies often take on a metafictional dimension" (83). Similarly, Palmer-Patel (2020) argues at length that various repetitive fantasy forms enable a conscious awareness of narrative structure: for instance, the hero's interpretation of prophecies exposes "how the intertextual awareness of their place in a narrative allows for the character to act as reader and construct both the narrative and their own identity" (47).

8. Dennis Wilson Wise makes similar observations in an essay about Glen Cook, "History and Precarity: Glen Cook and the Rise of Picaresque Epic Fantasy" (2019). Wise sees epic fantasy as a literature of totality in the Lukácsian sense, where an "integration between culture, art, life, social institutions, and individual action" opposes "alienation, individual separateness, and reified social relationships" (332). However, Cook's introduction of a picaresque narrative model in his Instrumentalities of the Night series results in an epic fantasy totality "rendered devoid of positive content: a totality emptied of meaning" (347). My argument takes this a step further as I suggest that in epic fantasy, the novel form (with its present-oriented chronotope) collides with the epic form (with its fixed past totality). The result is a form that creates artificial totalities that are fundamentally unstable because manifestly artificial. I would contend that Cook's artistic practice simply takes advantage of this instability already present in the genre.

9. Gayatri Spivak's concept of "strategic essentialism" is a good illustration of the productive use of problematic concepts to enable political action. In an influential interview with Elizabeth Grosz, Spivak argues that it may be necessary (in the context of cultural negotiation) to treat identity categories as essences in order to be able to coordinate political action between heterogeneous individuals who otherwise have shared interests (Grosz 185). (Spivak's particular concern is transnational feminism.) Such "essentializing" of a group of people has "strategic" value, even though her deconstructive

philosophy maintains that such essences are not only artificial but often at the heart of sexist and racist hierarchy. While Spivak later rejected the term as she saw it misused as an anthropological term (see, for instance, *Other Asias* 260), it continues to be influential as a demonstration that unrestrained deconstruction can undermine political action.

10. This generalization about genre characters has been countered by numerous critics, with Mandala's chapter on "Style and Character" offering a counterargument appropriate for my study. Mandala argues that by looking at style we can see in "plain" details how characterization is carried out through language (119–146).

11. An extensive critical literature connects empathy to reading fiction. In addition to those cited elsewhere in this book, a few others have been influential on developing my concept of empathy. Benedict Anderson's *Imagined Communities* (1983) argues that reading (particularly the reading of newspapers and novels) generates a sense of other people out there who are connected to or similar to the reader: "print-capitalism [...] made it possible for rapidly growing numbers of people to think about themselves, and to relate themselves to others, in profoundly new ways" (36). Arjun Appadurai has extended similar arguments about the role of imagination and narrative in creating communal identities in *Modernity at Large* (1996), where he argues that narrative creates "scripts" that help readers both to fashion "narratives of the Other" and shape their own "possible lives" (35–6). Finally, M. Angeles Martínez provides a useful cognitive definition of empathy that lies in the background of my use of the term: "blends resulting from matching features across a particular reader's self-concept and a focalizer's character construct" (119).

12. Williamson makes a compelling case that the fantasy canon was formed based on a retrospective reading of a fantasy tradition starting in the 1960s, which he traces particularly to the Ballantine Adult Fantasy Series and its editorial consultant Lin Carter (3–5). Williamson cautions against "retrojecting" a homogeneous tradition onto texts prior to this period, but "retrojected homogeneity" primarily affects claims about writers

who may be "trying to do the same type of thing" (14). I have therefore attempted to avoid this error in two ways: my study focuses largely on fantasy written since the establishment of the genre, and I analyze the effect of the text rather than the intent of its construction.

13. Linda Hutcheon has defined postmodern fiction specifically through its interest in history as "historiographic metafiction": postmodern fiction's "theoretical self-awareness of history and fiction as human constructs," she says, "is made the grounds for its rethinking and reworking the forms and contents of the past" (5). Thus, by combining extended historical temporality and awareness of constructed story, epic fantasy aligns surprisingly well with a postmodern outlook.

14. Interestingly, Susan Mandala sees the stereotype of SFF style as being the opposite: that it is too simple, unadorned, unthoughtful (see, for instance, Mandala 18). Nonetheless, she also devotes a full chapter on uses of "archaic" style in fantasy, suggesting an overriding awareness that epic fantasy's style is mannered.

Chapter 1

1. Brooks, for instance, describes the work of poets like Donne and Wordsworth in the following way: "the relation between part and part is organic, which means that each part modifies and is modified by the whole" (737).

2. Interestingly, Carver himself says nearly the same thing when arguing against writers overwriting while reaching too desperately for formal innovation: "Someone else's way of looking at things [...] should not be chased after by other writers. It won't work" (Carver 48).

3. It would be overly simplistic to suggest that florid style is the only reason epic fantasy is often ignored. In fact, literary minimalism itself has been the subject of controversy. Robert Clark's *American Literary Minimalism* (2014) sets up its argument in many ways as a defense of charges against minimalism. He notes that in the 1980s, especially, many critics reacted strongly against it. He cites as an example Joe David Bellamy, who writes "some of the so-called minimalists have sacrificed

stylistic richness or sophistication in search of other values. [...] whatever else the newest American fiction might try to do in the years ahead, my hope is that, stylistically and imagistically, it will strive for more robust, more muscular, more ambitious performances—a swing of the pendulum back in the direction of Faulkner and Flannery O'Connor" (qtd. in Clark 20). Nonetheless, the valuing of clear and direct style (if not outright minimalism) continues to dominate the academy and, I think, too often blinds critics to the affordances of more elaborate prose styles.

4. To cite one further example, from roughly the same time frame, Colin Greenland, in writing about Michael Moorcock's Eternal Champion novels, faults them for lacking "subtlety, irony, [...] original and good style, [...] colour, density, depth, and [...] real feeling" (121). The prose, he says, "hobbles its heroes, burying their violent actions under a ton of description" (122), and "heroic fantasy" in general "is the most degenerate kind of fantasy fiction. An indiscriminate mix of elements from ancient literature and legend, distilled from an ever more dilute epic tradition, it is imitative, crude, and rarely more than a reiteration of conventions" (122–3). Again, while this focus on evaluation is commonly challenged on a theoretical level, in practice this principle still guides much of the selection of texts for teaching in literature courses or as objects of academic analysis for publication.

5. I am also drawing here on theoretical work on language, stereotyping, and defamiliarization from Homi Bhabha and Slavoj Žižek. Bhabha explains the role played by stereotyping in creating communal identities. For Bhabha, the stereotype is a "repetitious" and obsessive form of language—stereotypes and clichés are habitual forms of seeing the world that reinforce identity category hierarchies. Such "fixated" forms potentially destroy others in an attempt to maintain identity (as fixed, singular, and pure): the repetition of "the *same old* stories" (77) is an aggressive act that protects the narcissistic ego from any damaging acknowledgement of difference. On the other hand, Žižek opens for us a window on how to repair the damage done by habitual, stereotypical conventions. Žižek argues that fantasy

(in the broader sense of psychological desire) paradoxically both participates in interpellation and resists it: on one hand, "*through fantasy, we learn how to desire*" (fantasy as interpellation), but on the other hand, it is "a defence" against the desires being imposed on us (118). Fantasy "disrupts" rigid designators to allow us to see how they function—it allows for identification rather than division (128).

6. Many Marxist critics, for instance, assert that fantasy literature engages in mystification, which might be termed an attempt to "escape" from the material conditions of history. Darko Suvin infamously dismissed fantasy as "a subliterature of mystification" (9). On the other hand, Tolkien famously defended fantasy in "On Fairy-Stories," writing, "I do not accept the tone of scorn or pity with which 'Escape' is now so often used [...] The world outside has not become less real because the prisoner cannot see it. In using escape in this way the critics have chosen the wrong word, and, what is more, they are confusing, not always by sincere error, the Escape of the Prisoner with the Flight of the Deserter" (79).

7. While my analysis focuses on *Erikson's* style, on the issue of inventing names, I must point out that the Malazan world was co-designed by Erikson and fellow writer Ian C. Esslemont. Thus, to the extent that the rhythm is the result of naming and invented terms, both writers should be credited.

8. It is worth noting two other issues that Mendlesohn does not account for. First, this attribution of knowledge beyond the presumed limitations of a focalized narrator is not a feature of third-person narration unique to portal-quest fantasy narration. In fact, it is a structural affordance of third-person limited narration more generally (see Jonathan Culler's "Omniscience" and Nicholas Royle's *The Uncanny*). Epic fantasy exploits this affordance in particularly revelatory ways, as I shall argue further in Chapter 3. Second, as W. A. Senior argues, questions of knowledge and ignorance are structured into the narration of the series. While Mendlesohn simply sees Covenant's doubts about the fantasy world as a rhetorical trick confirming "that *we* should believe" (41), Senior argues that the narrator's ability to go "beneath the surface" is part of building narrative tension around the very notion of a reliable view of reality: "What is a reliable view here? How is Covenant, or how are we, to balance the opposite views [in prophecies about him] if he himself does not know what to think or how to feel?" (156).

9. Donaldson's style does shift somewhat in the decades between the Second Chronicles and Final Chronicles, a point that Donaldson frequently addresses in the "Gradual Interview" on his website, where he points out that he "made a very conscious effort to preserve the style of the first six [books]" (November 2006) but that changes in his life and approach to writing intervene. However, my focus here remains on broad patterns across the series. An in-depth study of such shifts would likely be instructive, particularly as it may help illuminate the intersection of genre conventions for style with the influence of personal language patterns, a point Donaldson raises elsewhere in the interview: "some patterns are inherent to the way I think, and I can't think my thoughts without them" (December 2010).

10. Consider, for instance, Deke Parsons' description of Tolkien's orcs: "The orcs do not represent lower-class workers, or any other real-world constituency. They have no free will and are suitable only for war and pillaging because they were designed that way by an evil power. They are automatons [...] they are organic robots whose only capacity is for cruelty" (20–1). To illustrate the dangers of this type of characterization, Parsons further suggests that the Peter Jackson film adaptation of *Lord of the Rings* overlays this stereotypical other with the more contemporary other found during the War on Terror that was taking place as the films were released, citing "the overriding theme that the good (Western) people have to stick together and must not allow their differences to cause them to be estranged from each other in the face of Sauron (terrorism)" (54–5). Thus, the stereotypical representation of orcs reinforces racial stereotyping in the sociopolitical sphere.

11. I am indebted to Donaldson himself for pointing out the connection between this passage and Kristeva's category of the semiotic after he heard an early version of

this argument at the International Conference for the Fantastic in the Arts on March 17, 2016.

12. Strunk and White say the following about avoiding "a succession of loose sentences": "An unskilled writer will sometimes construct a whole paragraph [...] using as connectives *and, but,* [...] A writer who has written a series of loose sentences should recast enough of them to remove the monotony" (25–6). Again, Strunk and White refer to specific examples and make allowances for particular aesthetic effects, but they adequately illustrate the general "rule" of good style that opposes stringing together clauses with coordinating conjunctions.

13. Intriguingly, parataxis is a common stylistic feature of the "simple" style of writers like Hemingway. Here, though, Erikson uses it for the accretion of complex detail, illustrating that the affordances of form can be shaped to different uses. The "meaning" of a form comes from an intersection of various factors, not from some essence inhering to the form itself.

Chapter 2

1. This stereotype is not entirely accurate. Brian Attebery, for instance, has argued that women fantasy writers in particular (including Ursula Le Guin) have used the conventional structures such as coming-of-age in epic fantasy to demonstrate "how inherited story structures may be used to question the practices and beliefs that gave rise to them" (88). Of course, implicit in this argument is the point that women have historically been left out of those inherited structures.

2. This history is perhaps too extensive to require documentation, but to give just one supporting example, John Crowe Ransom infamously dismissed women poets like Edna St. Vincent Millay in his essay "The Woman as Poet" in passages like the following that contrast women to male poets: "Man distinguishes himself from woman by intellect [...] He knows he should not abandon sensibility and tenderness [...] but now that he is so far removed from the world of simple senses, he does not like to impeach his own integrity and leave his business in order to recover it" (77).

3. Debra Ferreday's essay, "Game of Thrones, Rape Culture and Feminist Fandom" (2015), is a good start for anyone wishing a more detailed discussion of these issues.

4. I want to make it clear here that based on his statements from interviews, Martin would not approve of a voyeuristic response to the scene. In an interview with *Entertainment Weekly*, Martin says of fan responses to the Red Wedding, "Just as you grieve if a friend is killed, you *should* grieve if a fictional character is killed. You *should* care. If somebody dies and you just go get more popcorn, it's a superficial experience isn't it?" (Hibberd).

5. Farah Mendlesohn seems to credit this reluctance to embrace gaps as the source of the "diegetic overkill" she cites in portal-quest fantasy (9). In a contrasting point of view, China Miéville has argued in his brief essay "On World Building" that gaps are an essential part of fantasy world building: "Histories, laws, cultures, aesthetics—worlds—are colossal, and colossally complex. There is no way you can ever tell the story of a whole world. [...] leave [non-essential details] alone, even if that leaves the reader uncertain. That's fine. In fact, it's good—it's culture shock. Hopefully it communicates a sense that there is a world beyond the book."

6. The elaborate styles of some modernist writers have been described by some critics as a response to the changes in communication caused by technology, particularly the telegraph. John Carlos Rowe, for instance, sees the primary conflict of Henry James's story "In the Cage" being between two style of language common to literary modernism: "connotative complexity and the short and economical style of the telegram" (486). Kuang seems critical of telegraphic style for reasons similar to James, but intriguingly she deploys it ambivalently (and perhaps ironically) rather than combatting it with a self-consciously complex style.

7. For an example of these resources and the reasons readers give for wanting to use them, see Twitter user @readatmidnight's tweet and the following discussion: "For everyone who wants to read The Poppy War but hesitant due to the list of triggers, I made a summary of Chapter 21 (where the most graphic content occurs) here. Read

this instead on your first read through or reread."

8. I use the word "alienation" specifically to gesture toward Marxist theory, although Marxist critics such as Frederic Jameson have frequently taken issue with Le Guin's spiritualized, non-revolutionary politics. See, for instance, "World Reduction in Le Guin," where Jameson describes her world building as a "systematic exclusion, a kind of surgical excision of empirical reality, something like a process of ontological attenuation in which the sheer teeming multiplicity of what exists [...] is deliberately thinned and weeded out through an operation of radical abstraction and simplification" (271), an editorial reduction of reality which Jameson associates with "her predilection for quietistic heroes and her valorization of an anti-political, anti-activist stance" (275).

Chapter 3

1. I have a few reasons to justify this assertion. First, a list of "great" epic fantasy novels likely includes a higher percentage of atypical examples. Second, by basing my list on a user-generated list from a website, I allowed a few first-person entries on the list that many readers would not classify as epic fantasy (which is significant because part of my argument involves genre expectations; thus, reader classification of genre is actually important here)— Kevin Hearne's Iron Druid Chronicles and Deborah Harkness's All Souls Trilogy are both written in first person, the former more commonly classified as urban fantasy and the latter as contemporary intrusion fantasy or even horror. On the other hand, two that I classify as mixed (William Goldman's *The Princess Bride* and R. A. Salvatore's Dark Elf Trilogy) are actually narrated largely in third person with a first-person frame, and Patrick Rothfuss's *The Name of the Wind*, which I included with the first-person narration, actually has a third-person frame, although most of the novel is narrated in first person. Thus, the percentage even from this list could drop as low as 13%, depending on how we classify some of these borderline texts. On top of that, a number of writers only represented on this

list by one series (written in first person) much more commonly write in third person: for instance, Karen Elliott's Spiritwalker Trilogy, which is written in first person, was the only item by her that I included on this list, but this prolific author of at least five other series typically writes in third person.

2. This is largely the argument that Timothy Bewes makes about Rancière in his essay "Free Indirect."

3. It is intriguing here that the paradigmatic example of a Club Story that she mentions to illustrate the narration of epic fantasy is Joseph Conrad's *Heart of Darkness*, as that text contains two *first-person* narrators (the frame narrator and Marlow). While I will address the differing nature of authority and subjective perspective in first-person narration and frame narratives in Chapters 4 and 8 respectively (issues about which Mendlesohn makes a number of puzzling assumptions), here I will simply point out the oddity of conflating third-person narration (even with a generally unwarranted personification of the narrator) with a subjective first-person narrator like Marlow, which I believe leads Mendlesohn to a number of problematic conclusions about narration in epic fantasy.

4. I have already noted this argument in part in her calling portal-quest fantasy "the last resting place of physiognomy" (11). See Chapter 1.

5. Again, this is Genette's "double focalization." Culler notes a similar type of effect in passages from Marcel Proust's *A la recherché du temps perdu*, where the narration diverges from the apparent focus character to give information he could not possibly know. Culler explains this knowledge by analogy to the telephone—just because the narrator is not present does not mean they cannot gain knowledge. It is a device "permitting imaginative recuperation of details of inner and outer lives of the characters. As long as the narrator is imaginative and resourceful, he need not be hindered by physical limitations" (29).

6. While I have compared the narration of "The King's Justice" to Woolf's *Mrs Dalloway*, in regard to this independent quality of the narration, I also find similarities to her story "Kew Gardens," which Frank Stevenson has described as a story

that is an "autopoietic system," which he defines as "a *self-generating* and *selfcreating* system" that emphasizes "the *reflexivity* of both itself and all its parts" (para 28). I would suggest that "The King's Justice" similarly gestures toward the possibility of a story that is "self-generating" and "independent of the author" (para 31).

7. For a more in-depth explanation, see Bakker's definitive article, "The Last Magic Show: A Blind Brain Theory," and more generally his posts on his blog "Three Pound Brain."

8. Mark O'Connell uses Kohut's definition, applied to John Banville, to argue that third-person narration is a way to attempt to imagine others outside the self.

9. In fact, Kellhus's experience resembles a hypothetical situation Bakker describes in an interview: "You may not believe in God, but with enough ingenuity I could wire you up to a transcranial magnetic stimulation machine and give you an experience of God. Which, given that I hooked you up to an apparatus, you would regard as being artefactual, but nevertheless you will have that experience whether you want to or not. Because you are mechanical" (Krašovec and Bauer).

Chapter 4

1. For more on my use of the terms "first person" and "third person" in relation to Genette's categories of "homodiegetic" and "heterodiegetic" narrators, see the introduction to Chapter 3.

2. Barbara Olson has extensively studied how the use of omniscient narration, particularly by modernist writers, has often implied or paralleled certain theological beliefs in *Authorial Divinity in the Twentieth Century: Omniscient Narration in Woolf, Hemingway, and Others* (1997).

3. Agents and time are two of the three areas that Lisa Zunshine classifies as essential to making meaning in narrative. Any narrative, Zunshine argues, contains "source tags" that allow readers to locate the narrative relative to who is involved (agents), where the narrative occurs (place), and when it occurs (time). By undermining two of these three areas, first-person epic fantasy can significantly deconstruct the totalizing function of

narrative. For more, see Lisa Zunshine's *Why We Read Fiction* (2006).

4. It may be objected, of course, that third-person narration could be similarly unreliable, although most research focuses on first-person narrators as unreliable. However, 1) because I am speaking of readers' frames for making meaning, the expectation of "objectivity" in third-person narration requires much stronger markers of unreliability to shake a reader's faith, and 2) many definitions of unreliability, such as Zerweck's, require that unreliable narration be "personalized" (155), and third-person narration is typically impersonal.

5. This is, of course, the essence of Bakhtinian dialogism, as he argues that language is fundamentally intersubjective, lying "on the borderline between oneself and the other. The word in language is half someone else's. It becomes 'one's own' only when the speaker populates it with his own intention, his own accent, when he appropriates the word, adapting it to his own semantic and expressive intention" ("Discourse" 293).

6. These games with narration are a feature throughout Jemisin's fiction, as in the blind first-person narrator of the second Inheritance novel, *The Broken Kingdoms* (2010), or her experiments with second-person narration in the Broken Earth Trilogy (2015–2017). For more on this latter, see Kim Wickham's "Identity, Memory, Slavery: Second-Person Narration in N. K. Jemisin's The Broken Earth Trilogy" (2019). Wickham argues that second-person narration in the series "serves to destabilize the reading process, mirroring [the protagonist's] fragmented identity, while simultaneously creating an empathetic reading experience" (401), allowing readers to identify with the intergenerational trauma of slavery.

7. For more explanation of free indirect discourse as a double voice (joining narrator and character), see, for instance, Roy Pascal's *The Dual Voice: Free Indirect Speech and Its Functioning in the Nineteenth-Century European Novel* (1977).

8. See, for instance, Peter Stockwell on "temporal shifts" in narration, when a narrator steps out of the past-tense narrative to speak in the present, from his or her own "coding time" (Stockwell 78).

Chapter 5

1. It would not be surprising for C. Palmer-Patel, whose *The Shape of Fantasy* (2020) makes a similar argument based on more general narrative structures, that "the structural and narrative patterns of the Heroic Epic" derive from "science, philosophy, and literary theory" (1). This means that fantasy "is not an illogical form" but is "governed by a sense of rules and structure, one that reflects our current understanding of the world and cosmolology" (2). While her argument was published too recently to have been a formative influence on this chapter, she arrives at strikingly similar conclusions to mine based on an analysis of different formal structures (primarily plot and character structure).

2. I have already discussed, in Chapter 4, W. A. Senior's offhand reference to the sense of wonder: "Most fantasy novels are written in a third-person voice because the first person would often remove the sense of wonder and distance required to produce fantasy" (136). This assertion is backed by a similar statement from Colin Manlove that "distance [...] between the writer and his material" is "the basic condition from which the overt concern with wonder in all its forms is generated" (Manlove 14). While both of these statements imply a link between the mental state of wonder and the form of the text, that link is not pursued much beyond the (questionable) assumption that it requires distance.

3. J.R.R. Tolkien, perhaps the most influential voice in defining the genre, identified its effects primarily as "recovery, escape, and consolation." In his essay "On Fairy-Stories," Tolkien metaphorically describes the modern technological world as a "prison" and claims that a primary benefit of fantasy lies in the escape from that prison: "critics [of Escape ...] are confusing [...] the Escape of the Prisoner with the Flight of the Deserter" (79). Given Tolkien's Catholic religious beliefs and reactionary anti-modernity, we should not be surprised that fantasy's appeal has largely been thought to be religious and spiritual rather than scientific and rational. This would then mean that fantasy is a mystification of the world rather than an effective comment on the material world.

4. Susan Mandala does discuss wonder as a component of style, but she does so largely by focusing on how texts walk the line between unfamiliar and familiar, which does not directly address feelings of awe or transcendence implied by the term "wonder."

5. As an example of this mindset, the Mental Floss article "The Reason Movie Trailers Give So Much Away" cites director Robert Zemeckis saying, "We know from studying the marketing of movies, people really want to know exactly everything that they are going to see before they go see the movie. [...] What I relate it to is McDonald's. The reason McDonald's is a tremendous success is that you don't have any surprises" (Rossen).

6. For more on the religious dimensions of Sanderson's fiction, see Weronika Łaszkiewicz's chapter on him in *Fantasy Literature and Christianity* (2018), where she states based on his statements in interviews that while "he wishes to create gripping stories rather than to preach, faith is also a prominent factor at work" (191).

7. While Sanderson arrives at this link between cognition and wonder via a different path, this connection is similar to Jacques Derrida's arguments about the dual origins of religion and its parallels to science in "Faith and Knowledge." As Michael Naas summarizes Derrida's position in *Miracle and Machine* (2012), both religion and science promise to reveal a pre-linguistic essence of the world but at the same time require a linguistically embedded set of social practices to grant authority to that essentialism. While I am not claiming that Sanderson is directly influenced by Derrida, they both recognize structural similarities between religion and science and understand that the experience of "transcendence" is a formal property of social practices embodied in language.

8. James Gifford sums up this difference neatly in relation to his argument about fantasy's anarchically liberating representations of magic: "the radical potential for social change more comfortably finds a companion in the liberation-driven unreality of magic and its wish for agency in the individual than it does in the generically-necessary reassertion and stabilization of the hegemonic norm spun in to the unravelling red thread of a mystery yarn"

(73). While Gifford acknowledges that these are tendencies and not rigid truths about genre, he does effectively suggest how the magic of fantasy may be more revolutionary than the "realism" of detective fiction.

9. Geoffrey Galt Harpham describes the grotesque in terms of a perceptual experience marked by an interval or hesitation, an intriguing description in the context of my argument about wonder and delay: "the interval of the grotesque is the one in which, although we have recognized a number of different forms in the object, we have not yet developed a clear sense of the dominant principle that defines it" (16).

Chapter 6

1. See particularly Adorno's *Minima Moralia*, as I discussed in Chapter 1, as well as my discussions of debates surrounding aesthetics (introduction) and clarity (chapter 1).

2. This general overview can be found on Williamson 1, but I am also drawing on details from throughout his book for this summary.

3. Palmer-Patel helpfully describes the distinction between settings in fantasy as existing along a scale from "localised" to "epic" (meaning "world or multi-universe scale") with the possibility of narratives sliding along the scale at different points in the story (Palmer-Patel 9).

4. See Murray Pittock's "Rider Haggard and *Heart of Darkness*" (1987) for an overview of such arguments.

5. For a detailed explanation of Conrad's attitude toward performance in language, see Ian Watt's discussion of Marlow's distrust of "idealising abstractions" (Watt 245) and Rebecca Walkowitz's *Cosmopolitan Style*, where she argues that Conrad's awareness of his foreign-ness in England made him aware of how British culture is performed, put together by "artful display and tactical performance," "strategically produced," and how "national identities are shaped by conditions of collective experience" (Walkowitz 43).

6. Gifford traces fantasy's roots to the anarchists of late modernity, and what he calls the "personal and inward turn" (72). According to these anarchists, the individual agent has the capacity to change history, and "the personal (a key term for this group) unconscious emerges for them as a genuine agent of change distinct from the deterministic political unconscious that looks via Jameson to the psychoanalytic formulation of the mental apparatus as a manifestation of the mode of production" (70–1). Magic in fantasy expresses this attitude about agency when it represents "the wilful [*sic*] subject finding a position as active agent for change in the world based on recognizing a personal interiority or self to the subject" (79).

7. This also reverses Darko Suvin's influential argument about cognitive estrangement: whereas in Chapter 6, I argued that the magic is actually cognitive, here I will argue that what seems to be cognitive and rational is actually "magic" (i.e., rationality is constructed and provides non-rational emotional/spiritual benefits).

8. This need not be the case, of course, and my working definition of epic draws from Griffiths and Rabinowitz whose account of the epic tradition even includes Joyce's *Ulysses*, certainly a prime example of parody and humor in style.

9. For more on how humor violates conventional social scripts or frames, see Victor Raskin's General Verbal Theory of Humor in *Semantic Mechanisms of Humor* (1985) or Umberto Eco's essay "The Frames of Comic 'Freedom'" (1984). Along similar lines, Susan Purdie has used Lacanian theory to argue that joking marks a "transgression of Symbolic Law" that establishes jokers as "'masters' of discourse" (5). While Purdie indicates that the rules are broken only to be reinstated as an exercise in power, it only takes a small step from her theory, via Kristeva's addition of the semiotic to Lacanian theory (see Chapter 1 for a more complete overview), to realize that this rule violation can also be experienced as a liberating pleasure from the symbolic order, an elating realization that words are not always as fixed in meaning as we may assume.

10. Ian Watt described "delayed decoding" as a technique in Conrad's fiction where there is a temporal lag between the sensory "messages from the outside world" and the narrating mind's "reflexive process of making out their meaning" (Watt

175). Events are happening too quickly to process, so the narrator (and reader) first sees what happens and only figures out how it happened after the fact. In a definitive example from *Heart of Darkness*, Marlow narrates an attack on his boat by first describing in confusion that "sticks, little sticks, were flying about" before later realizing, "Arrows, by Jove! We were being shot at!" (qtd. in Watt 77).

11. The novel's syntax also demonstrates significant ambiguity in its temporality. Peter Brooks' argues in *Reading for the Plot* (1984) that the default tense for narrative is the simple past tense (past preterite), and that tense is "decoded by the reader as a kind of present, that of an action and a significance being forged before his eyes, in his hands, so to speak" (22). Yet Gemmell frequently shifts verb tense between past preterite and past perfect in flashbacks in ways that unsettle a reader's ability to clearly recognize the boundaries between flashback and the "present tense" of the plot. (The opening of Chapter 10, which begins *in medias res* and then flashes back to the immediately preceding events, is a good example.) As the reader typically thinks of any action as unfolding in the present—"a significance being forged before his [*sic*] eyes, in his hands, so to speak" (Brooks 22)—the continual shifting of the actual tense of that action unsettles the sense of temporal stability and the certainty of an unfolding narrative destiny—a further syntactic "magic."

12. E. R. Eddison, a pregenre "fantasy" writer known for his elaborate style, seems to have been a particular favorite of Leiber's. For instance, Poul Anderson describes Leiber's enthusiastic participation in a costume dinner in Eddison's memory (Anderson ix), and Lin Carter cites Leiber's preference for Eddison's villains over Tolkien's (Carter 117).

13. René Girard referred to this as mimetic desire, the concept that people want things that they see others wanting, which he outlined in *Deceit, Desire, and the Novel* (1961).

Chapter 7

1. For instance, David Pringle damns the convention by praising its absence in Phyllis Eisenstein's *Sorcerer's Son* (1979): "It is refreshing to come across a high fantasy novel which begins with 'Chapter One'—and launches you straight into the story. There is no prefatory matter here, and there are no appendages: no maps, genealogies, lists of dramatis personae, or glossaries. [...] there are no divisions into 'Parts' or 'Books,' no chapter titles, no epigraphs. In short, there is no cumbersome apparatus whatsoever—just a good, plain tale written in pellucid style" (193).

2. For instance, in a conference presentation of a portion of Ekman's argument about fantasy maps, Steven Erikson pointed out that the maps appearing in fantasy novels are often the product of publishers and the artists they hire rather than coming directly from the authors themselves. Erikson and fellow Malazan creator Ian C. Esslemont, for instance, worked from much more detailed maps in their gaming and writing of the world (Erikson, session comments). While authorial intention is not an overriding concern of my formal analysis, surely we can expect more stylistic resonance between textual artefacts created by a single consciousness than in cases where multiple (possibly divergent) interests are involved. At the very least, I am not structuring my argument to account in detail for marketing and public relations aspects of a text's publication.

Chapter 8

1. Another example would be Mandala, for whom "construction of plausible other worlds" (29) is central to her argument about style.

2. While I cannot take credit for originating this argument, some form of it can be found in nearly every analytical reading guide for the poem on the Internet. However, as I feel professionally bound to cite my sources, I will speculate that I first heard this argument in a lecture on the poem by Caroline Levine.

3. Although Cleanth Brooks and the New Critics would likely not have credited popular fantasy fiction with irony, what I am describing coincides precisely with Brook's definition of irony in his argument that irony is central to literary language:

"the 'meaning' of any particular item is modified by the context. For what is said is said in a particular situation and by a particular dramatic character" (730).

4. Mendlesohn's argument, for instance, refuses to see the potential for irony in this framing, as she uses Clute's notion of the Club Story as the backbone for her argument that portal-quest fantasy is a "closed narrative," like the epic, which "demands that we accept the interpretation of the narrator" (5). While Mendlesohn's critique of the insular, often sexist and racist, privileged world of the "clubs" from which Clute takes the name "Club Story" is valid, she falls into the same interpretive trap as Achebe in her assumption that the Club Story is marked by "the *unquestionable purity* of the tale," that the "impurity and unreliability [...] must be consistently denied and the authority and reliability of the narrator must be asserted" (7), leading to a "consequent denial of polysemic interpretation" (7). Such an approach fails to the see the potential for irony in the frame narrative.

5. Similar arguments can be made about some of the most influential frame narratives of the past two centuries. Peter Brooks points out that the "nested narrative structure" of Mary Shelley's *Frankenstein* "calls attention to the motives of telling" (369). The case is similar with Emily Brontë's *Wuthering Heights*. Hillis Miller has argued that the novel's famous nested frame narratives expose how each of these characters (and the reader) attempt to construct meaning out of events, a meaning that is constantly deferred (Miller 86). This structural affordance for a deconstructive deferral of meaning may be why frame narratives

have become a particularly popular device among postmodern writers: "The novel of the postmodern era with its ingrained self-reflexivity and tendency to subversion has a special affinity to this device. It is particularly apt to problematise the fiction/reality binary in a quest for 'truth,' taking issues of authenticity, identity and perception centre stage" (Puschmann-Nalenz 50). While it is not as extensively discussed in the critical literature on frame narratives, the frame can also often place ironic pressure on the style of the narrative, as, for instance, in *Wuthering Heights* where Lockwood's "melodramatic language" is his artificial attempt to feel the passion that Heathcliff genuinely feels (Berlinger 187).

6. Joshua Yu Burnett's "The Collar and the Sword: Queer Resistance in Samuel R. Delany's *Tales of Nevèrÿon*" offers a detailed reading of the SM themes of the novel and a thorough overview of previous arguments for further reading. Robert F. Reid-Pharr's "Disseminating Heterotopia" and Georgia Johnston's "From the Margins of Derrida: Samuel Delany's Sex and Race" also discuss the political dimensions of Delany's formal focus on the margins.

7. This is an argument Delany makes more extensively and technically in his analysis of Le Guin's *The Dispossessed*. See, for instance, his claims that the deconstructive effects of placing a signifier into a sentence work in a "particular, unique, and identifying way" in science fiction due to its emphasis on defamiliarization (*Jewel-Hinged Jaw* 140). In "Postmodern Fantasy and Postmodern Biblical Studies," Fred W. Burnett provides a useful overview (250).

Works Cited

@readatmidnight. "For everyone who wants to read The Poppy War but hesitant due to the list of triggers, I made a summary of Chapter 21 (where the most graphic content occurs) here. Read this instead on your first read through or reread: [Dropbox Link]." *Twitter,* 23 May 2018, 12:19 a.m., twitter.com/readatmidnight/status/9991428561398 49728?lang=en.

Abercrombie, Joe. *The Blade Itself.* Pyr, 2007.

Abraham, Nicolas, and Maria Torok. "Mourning *or* Melancholia: Introjection *versus* Incorporation." 1972. *The Shell and the Kernel: Renewals of Psychoanalysis, Volume 1,* edited and translated by Nicholas T. Rand, U of Chicago P, 1994, pp. 125–138.

———. "Notes on the Phantom: A Complement to Freud's Metapsychology." 1975. *The Shell and the Kernel: Renewals of Psychoanalysis, Volume 1,* edited and translated by Nicholas T. Rand, U of Chicago P, 1994, pp. 171–176.

———. "Story of Fear: The Symptoms of Phobia—the Return of the Repressed or the Return of the Phantom?" 1975. *The Shell and the Kernel: Renewals of Psychoanalysis, Volume 1,* edited and translated by Nicholas T. Rand, U of Chicago P, 1994, pp. 177–186.

Achebe, Chinua. "An Image of Africa: Racism in Conrad's *Heart of Darkness.*" *The Massachusetts Review,* vol. 18, 1977, pp. 782–794.

Adorno, Theodor W. *Minima Moralia: Reflections from a Damaged Life.* 1951. Translated by E.F.N. Jephcott, Verso, 2005.

———. "Parataxis: On Holderlin's Late Poetry." *Notes to Literature,* vol. 2, edited by Rolf Tiedemann, translated by Shierry Weber Nicholsen, Columbia UP, 1992, pp. 109–149.

Anderson, Benedict. *Imagined Communities: Reflections on the Origin and Spread of Nationalism.* Verso, 1991.

Anderson, Poul. "Introduction: The Wizard of Nehwon." *The Best of Fritz Leiber.* Nelson Doubleday, 1974, pp. vii–xv.

Appadurai, Arjun. *Modernity at Large: Cultural Dimensions of Globalization.* U of Minnesota P, 1996.

Armstrong, Isobel. *The Radical Aesthetic.* Blackwell, 2000.

Attebery, Brian. *The Fantasy Tradition in American Literature: From Irving to Le Guin.* Indiana UP, 1980.

———. *Strategies of Fantasy.* Indiana UP, 1992.

———. "Structuralism." *A Cambridge Companion to Fantasy Literature.* Edited by Edward James and Farah Mendlesohn. Campbridge UP, 2012, pp. 81–90.

Bacchilega, Christina. *Fairy Tales Transformed?: Twenty-First-Century Adaptations and the Politics of Wonder.* Wayne State UP, 2013.

Bakhtin, M.M. "Discourse in the Novel." *The Dialogic Imagination.* Translated by Caryl Emerson and Michael Holquist, U of Texas P, 1981, pp. 259–422.

———. "Epic and Novel." *The Dialogic Imagination.* Translated by Caryl Emerson and Michael Holquist, U of Texas P, 1981, pp. 3–40.

———. "Forms of Time and of the Chronotope in the Novel." *The Dialogic Imagination.* Translated by Caryl Emerson and Michael Holquist, U of Texas P, 1981, pp. 84–258.

Bakker, R. Scott. *The Darkness That Comes Before.* Overlook P, 2003.

_____. "The Last Magic Show: A Blind Brain Theory of the Appearance of Consciousness." *Three Pound Brain,* 12 April 2012, rsbakker.wordpress. com/essay-archive/the-last-magic-show-a-blind-brain-theory-of-the-appearance-of-consciousness. Accessed 9 July 2020.

_____. "The Skeptical Fantasist: In Defense of an Oxymoron." *Heliotrope,* issue 1, August 2006, pp. 32–38, www. heliotropemag.com/Issue01/pdf/ Heliotrope_pg32–38_Skeptical Fantasist.pdf. Accessed 9 July 2020.

_____. *The Thousandfold Thought.* Overlook P, 2006.

Barthes, Roland. *S/Z,* translated by Richard Miller. Hill and Wang, 1974.

Battis, Jes. *Queer Spellings: Magic and Melancholy in Fantasy-Fiction.* 2007. Simon Fraser University, PhD dissertation.

Berlinger, Manette. "'I *am* Heathcliff': Lockwood's Role in *Wuthering Heights.*" *Bronte Studies,* vol. 35, no. 3, November 2010, pp. 185–193.

"Best Books of the 20th Century." *Good reads.com,* goodreads.com/list/show/6. Best_Books_of_the_20th_Century. Accessed 13 March 2020.

"The Best Epic Fantasy (fiction)." *Good reads.com,* goodreads.com/list/show/50. The_Best_Epic_Fantasy_fiction_. Accessed 13 March 2020.

Bewes, Timothy. "Free Indirect." *Political Concepts: A Critical Lexicon,* 2012, www.politicalconcepts.org/free-indirect-timothy-bewes. Accessed 9 July 2020.

Bhabha, Homi. *The Location of Culture.* Routledge, 1994.

Booth, Wayne. *The Rhetoric of Fiction.* U of Chicago P, 1961.

Bould, Mark. "The Dreadful Credibility of Absurd Things: A Tendency in Fantasy Theory." *Historical Materialism,* vol. 10, 2002, pp. 51–88.

Brawley, Chris. *Nature and the Numinous in Mythopoeic Fantasy Literature.* McFarland, 2014.

Brljak, Vladimir. "The Book of Lost Tales: Tolkien as Metafictionist." *Tolkien Studies,* vol. 7, 2010, pp. 1–34.

Brooks, Cleanth. "Irony as a Principle of Structure." *Literary Opinion in America,* edited by Morton D. Zabel, Viking Press, 1951, pp. 729–741.

Brooks, Peter. *Reading for the Plot: Design and Intention in Narrative.* Harvard UP, 1984.

_____. "What Is a Monster? (According to Frankenstein)." *Frankenstein,* by Mary Shelley, edited by J. Paul Hunter, Norton Critical Edition, 2nd ed., W.W. Norton, 2012, pp. 368–391. Originally published in *Body Work: Objects of Desire in Modern Narrative,* Harvard UP, 1993, pp. 199–220.

Brother of Battles. "The Real Meaning of the Poem." *Theoryland,* 24 Nov. 2004, www.theoryland.com/theories.php? func=5&rec=77&theo=2014. Accessed 24 Aug. 2020.

Burnett, Fred W. "Postmodern Fantasy and Postmodern Biblical Studies: A (Science) Fictive Review of Lance Olsen and Samuel Delany." *Journal of the Fantastic in the Arts,* vol. 8, no. 2, pp. 244–274.

Burnett, Joshua Yu. "The Collar and the Sword: Queer Resistance in Samuel R. Delany's *Tales of Nevèrÿon.*" *African American Review,* vol. 48, no. 3, Fall 2015, pp. 257–269.

Carter, Lin. *Imaginary Worlds: The Art of Fantasy.* Ballantine, 1973.

Carver, Raymond. "On Writing." *Mississippi Review,* vol. 14, no. 1/2, 1985, pp. 46–51.

Chaos. "Re: Back Cover Flaps." *17th Shard: The Official Brandon Sanderson Fan Site,* 25 April 2014, 17thshard.com/ forum/topic/7777-back-cover-flaps. Accessed 24 Aug. 2020.

Clark, Robert C. *American Literary Minimalism.* University of Alabama Press, 2014.

Clute, John. "Beyond the Pale." *Conjunctions,* no. 39, 2002, pp. 420–433.

Conrad, Joseph. *Heart of Darkness.* 1902. Edited by Robert Kimbrough, Norton, 1988.

Cook, Glen. *The Black Company.* Tor, 1984.

Csicsery-Ronay, Jr., Istvan. "On the Grotesque in Science Fiction." *Science Fiction Studies,* vol. 29, no. 1, March 2002, pp. 71–99.

Culler, Jonathan. "Omniscience." *Narrative,* vol. 12, 2004, pp. 22–35.

Delany, Samuel. *The Jewel-Hinged Jaw: Notes on the Language of Science Fiction.* 1978. Revised ed., Wesleyan UP, 2009.

_____. *Tales of Nevèrÿon.* 1979. Wesleyan UP, 1993.

Derrida, Jacques. *Différance.* Frederiksberg: Det Lille Forlag, 2002.

_____. "Faith and Knowledge: The Two Sources of 'Religion' at the Limits of Reason Alone," translated by Samuel Weber, *Religion,* edited by Jacques Derrida and Gianni Vattimo, Stanford UP, 1998, pp. 1–78.

Donaldson, Stephen R. *Epic Fantasy in the Modern World: A Few Observations.* Kent State University Libraries, 1986.

_____. "Gradual Interview." *stephenrdonaldson.com,* stephenrdonaldson. com/fromtheauthor/gi.php. Accessed 19 April 2021.

_____. "The King's Justice." *The King's Justice: Two Novellas.* Putnam, 2019, pp. 1–113.

_____. *The Last Dark.* Putnam, 2013.

_____. *Lord Foul's Bane.* 1977. Del Rey, 1984.

_____. *The One Tree.* 1982. Del Rey, 1983.

_____. Personal interview. 15 March 2019.

_____. *The Wounded Land.* Del Rey, 1980.

Drake, David. *Lord of the Isles.* Tor, 1997.

Eco, Umberto. "The Frames of Comic 'Freedom.'" *Carnival!* Edited by Thomas A. Sebeok, Mouton, 1984, pp. 1–9.

Ekman, Stefan. *Here Be Dragons: Exploring Fantasy Maps and Settings.* Wesleyan UP, 2013.

Erikson, Steven. *The Crippled God.* Tor, 2011.

_____. *Deadhouse Gates.* 2000. Tor, 2006.

_____. *Dust of Dreams.* Tor, 2009.

_____. *Forge of Darkness.* Tor, 2012.

_____. *Gardens of the Moon.* Tor, 1999.

_____. *Memories of Ice.* 2001. Tor, 2006.

_____. *Midnight Tides.* 2004. Tor, 2007.

_____. Personal interview. 17 March 2016.

_____. Session comments. International Conference for the Fantastic in the Arts. Marriott Orlando Airport Lakeside, Orlando. 23 March 2012.

_____. *Toll the Hounds.* Tor, 2008.

Ferreday, Debra. "Game of Thrones, Rape Culture and Feminist Fandom." *Australian Feminist Studies,* vol. 30, no. 83, March 2015, pp. 21–36.

Fike, Matthew A. *The One Mind: C. G. Jung and the Future of Literary Criticism.* Routledge, 2014.

Freedman, Carl. "A Note on Marxism and Fantasy." *Historical Materialism,* vol. 10, no. 4, 2002, pp. 261–271.

Ganiere, Rebekah R. "Writing Wednesday—What's in a Genre? High Fantasy versus Epic Fantasy." *rebekahganiere. com,* 14 Jan. 2015, rebekahganiere.com/ 2015/01/14/writing-wednesday-whats-in-a-genre-2. Accessed 23 July 2020.

Gemmell, David. *Legend.* Del Rey, 1984.

_____. "Stan Nicholls Inteview." *Deathwalker,* 19 May 2007, web.archive.org/ web/20070519114511/http:/www.death walker.co.uk/GCStan.htm. Accessed 14 Aug. 2020.

Genette, Gérard. *Narrative Discourse: An Essay in Method.* Translated by Jane E. Lewin, Cornell UP, 1980.

_____. *Paratexts: Thresholds of Interpretation.* Translated by Jane E. Lewin, Cambridge UP, 1997.

Gifford, James. *A Modernist Fantasy: Modernism, Anarchism, and the Radical Fantastic.* ELS Editions, 2018.

Girard, René. *Deceit, Desire, and the Novel: Self and Other in Literary Structure.* 1961. Translated by Yvonne Freccero, Johns Hopkins UP, 1976.

Greenland, Colin. *The Entropy Exhibition: Michael Moorcock and the British "New Wave" in Science Fiction.* Routledge & Kegan Paul, 1983.

_____. *Michael Moorcock: Death is No Obstacle.* Savoy, 1992.

Griffiths, Frederick T., and Stanley J. Rabinowitz. *Epic and the Russian Novel from Gogol to Pasternak.* Academic Studies P, 2011.

Grosz, Elizabeth. "Criticism, Feminism and the Institution: An Interview with Gayatri Chakravorty Spivak." *Thesis Eleven,* no. 10/11, 1985, pp. 175–189.

Harpham, Geoffrey Galt. *On the Grotesque: Strategies of Contradiction in Art and Literature.* Princeton UP, 1982.

Harrison, M. John. *Viriconium.* Spectra, 2007.

Hartwell, David G. "The Making of the American Fantasy Genre." *The Secret History of Fantasy,* edited by Peter S. Beagle, Tachyon, 2010, pp. 367–379.

Hassan, Ihab. *The Dismemberment of Orpheus: Toward a Postmodern Literature.* 2nd ed., U of Wisconsin P, 1982.

Hibberd, James. "'Game of Thrones' author George R. R. Martin: Why he wrote The Red Wedding." *Entertainment Weekly,* 2 June 2013, ew.com/article/ 2013/06/02/game-of-thrones-author-george-r-r-martin-why-he-wrote-the-red-wedding. Accessed 18 June 2020.

Hobb, Robin. *Assassin's Apprentice*. Bantam, 1995.

Hollywood, Paul. "Conrad and Anarchist Theories of Language." *Contexts for Conrad*, edited by Keith Carabine, Owen Knowles, and Wiesław Krajka, Columbia UP, 1993, pp. 243–264.

Hume, Katherine. *Fantasy and Mimesis: Responses to Reality in Western Literature*. Methuen, 1984.

Hutcheon, Linda. *A Poetics of Postmodernism: History, Theory, Fiction*. Routledge, 1988.

Iser, Wolfgang. *The Act of Reading: A Theory of Aesthetic Response*. Johns Hopkins UP, 1978.

Jackson, Rosemary. *Fantasy: The Literature of Subversion*. Methuen, 1981.

Jameson, Frederic. "World Reduction in Le Guin." 1975. *Archaeologies of the Future: The Desire Called Utopia and Other Science Fictions*. Verso, 2005, pp. 267–280.

Jemisin, N. K. *The Hundred Thousand Kingdoms*. Orbit, 2010.

Johnston, Georgia. "From the Margins of Derrida: Samuel Delany's Sex and Race." *Oxford Literary Review*, vol. 25, 2003, pp. 219–238.

Jones, Diana Wynne. *The Tough Guide to Fantasyland*. DAW, 1996.

Jordan, Robert. *Crossroads of Twilight*. Tor, 2003.

———. *A Crown of Swords*. Tor, 1996.

———. *The Dragon Reborn*. Tor, 1991.

———. *The Eye of the World*. Tor, 1990.

———. *The Great Hunt*. Tor, 1990.

———. *Lord of Chaos*. Tor, 1994.

———. *The Path of Daggers*. Tor, 1998.

———. *The Shadow Rising*. Tor, 1993.

Keen, Suzanne. *Empathy and the Novel*. Oxford UP, 2007.

Kelso, Sylvia. "'Across Never': Postmodern Theory and Narrative Praxis in Samuel R. Delany's Nevèrÿon Cycle." *Science Fiction Studies*, vol. 24, no. 2, July 1997, pp. 289–301.

Kohut, Heinz. *The Analysis of the Self: A Systematic Approach to the Psychoanalytic Treatment of Narcissistic Personality Disorders*. International Universities P, 1971.

Krašovec, Primož, and Marko Bauer. "Scarlett Johansson Leaps to Your Lips.

An Interview with R. Scott Bakker." *Šum*, 18 June 2018, sumrevija.si/en/sum 9-scarlett-johansson-leaps-to-your-lips-an-interview-with-r-scott-bakker. Accessed 9 July 2020.

Kristeva, Julia. "From One Identity to Another." *Desire in Language: A Semiotic Approach to Literature and Art*, edited by Leon S. Roudiez, translated by Tomas Gora, Alice Jardine, and Leon S. Roudiez, Columbia UP, 1980, pp. 124–147.

———. "The Novel as Polylogue." *Desire in Language: A Semiotic Approach to Literature and Art*, edited by Leon S. Roudiez, translated by Thomas Gora, Alice Jardine, and Leon S. Roudiez, Columbia UP, 1980, pp. 159–209.

Kuang, R. F. "How to Talk to Ghosts." *Uncanny: A Magazine of Science Fiction and Fantasy*, March/April 2018, uncannymagazine.com/article/how-to-talk-to-ghosts. Accessed 18 June 2020.

———. *The Poppy War*. Harper, 2018.

Lanser, Susan Sniader. *The Narrative Act: Point of View in Prose Fiction*. Princeton UP, 1981.

Łaszkiewicz, Weronika. *Fantasy Literature and Christianity: A Study of the Mistborn, Coldfire, Fionavar Tapestry and Chronicles of Thomas Covenant Series*. McFarland, 2018.

Le Guin, Ursula K. "From Elfland to Poughkeepsie." 1973. *The Language of the Night: Essays on Fantasy and Science Fiction*. Revised ed., edited by Ursula K. Le Guin, HarperCollins, 1989, pp. 78–91.

———. *Tehanu*. 1990. Bantam, 1991.

———. *The Tombs of Atuan*. 1970. Aladdin, 2001.

Lehrer, Jonah. "Spoilers Don't Spoil Anything." *Wired*, 10 Aug. 2011, wired.com/2011/08/spoilers-dont-spoil-anything. Accessed 7 Aug. 2020.

Leiber, Fritz. "Afterword." *The Best of Fritz Leiber*. Nelson Doubleday, 1974, pp. 298–301.

———. "The Bazaar of the Bizarre." 1963. *Swords Against Death*. Ace, 1970, pp. 222–251.

———. "Ill Met in Lankhmar." 1970. *Swords and Deviltry*. Grafton, 1979, pp. 122–191.

———. "The Jewels in the Forest." 1939. *Swords Against Death*. Ace, 1970, pp. 20–62.

Levine, Caroline. *Forms: Whole, Rhythm, Hierarchy, Network*. Princeton UP, 2015.

Lukács, Georg. *The Theory of the Novel*. 1920. Translated by Anna Bostock, MIT Press, 1971.

Lynch, Scott. *The Lies of Locke Lamora*. Bantam, 2006.

Mandala, Susan. *Language in Science Fiction and Fantasy: The Question of Style*. Continuum, 2010.

Manlove, Colin N. *The Impulse of Fantasy Literature*. Kent State UP, 1983.

Martin, George R. R. *A Storm of Swords*. Bantam, 2000.

Martínez, M. Angeles. "Storyworld Possible Selves and the Phenomenon of Narrative Immersion: Testing a New Theoretical Construct." *Narrative*, vol. 22, no. 1, 2014, pp. 110–131.

McKillip, Patricia. *The Riddle-Master of Hed*. Del Rey, 1976.

Mendlesohn, Farah. *Rhetorics of Fantasy*. Wesleyan UP, 2008.

Miéville, China. "Marxism and Fantasy: Editorial Introduction." *Historical Materialism*, vol. 10, no. 4, 2002, pp. 39–49.

———. "On World Building." Del Rey Internet Newsletter, Number 98, March 2001. Accessed 17 August 2010.

Miller, Christopher R. *Surprise: The Poetics of the Unexpected from Milton to Austen*. Cornell UP, 2015.

Miller, D. A. *The Novel and the Police*. U of California P, 1988.

Miller, J. Hillis. "*Wuthering Heights* and the Ellipses of Interpretation." *Notre Dame English Journal*, vol. 12, no. 2, 1980, pp. 85–100.

"Min's Viewings." *Encyclopaedia WoT*, encyclopaedia-wot.org/prophecies/viewings.html. Accessed 24 Aug. 2020.

Mobley, Jane. "Toward a Definition of Fantasy Fiction." *Extrapolation*, vol. 15, 1973, pp. 117–128.

Moorcock, *Elric of Melniboné*. 1972. *The Sleeping Sorceress—Chronicles of the Last Emperor of Melniboné: Volume 3*. Ballantine, 2008.

———. "Foreword." *Wizardry and Wild Romance: A Study of Epic Fantasy*. Austin, TX: Monkeybrain, 2004.

———. "Putting a Tag on It." 1961. *Elric: The Stealer of Souls—Chronicles of the Last Emperor of Melniboné: Volume 1*. Ballantine, 2008.

———. *Stormbringer*. 1965. *Elric: The Stealer of Souls—Chronicles of the Last Emperor of Melniboné: Volume 1*. Ballantine, 2008.

Naas, Michael. *Miracle and Machine: Jacques Derrida and the Two Sources of Religion, Science, and the Media*. Fordham UP, 2012.

Numb. "Re: Back Cover Flaps." *17th Shard: The Official Brandon Sanderson Fan Site*, 25 April 2014, 17thshard.com/forum/topic/7777-back-cover-flaps. Accessed 24 Aug. 2020.

Nünning, Ansgar. "Reconceptualizing the Theory, History and Generic Scope of Unreliable Narration: Towards a Synthesis of Cognitive and Rhetorical Approaches." *Narrative Unreliability in the Twentieth-Century First-Person Novel*, edited by Elke D'hoker and Gunther Martens, Walter de Gruyter, 2008, pp. 29–76.

O'Connell, Mark. "The Empathic Paradox: Third-Person Narration in John Banville's First-Person Narratives." *Orbis Litterarum*, vol. 66, no. 6, 2011, pp. 427–447.

Olson, Barbara K. *Authorial Divinity in the Twentieth Century: Omniscient Narration in Woolf, Hemingway, and Others*. Bucknell UP, 1997.

Oziewicz, Marek. *One Earth, One People: The Mythopoeic Fantasy Series of Ursula K. Le Guin, Lloyd Alexander, Madeleine L'Engle and Orson Scott Card*. McFarland, 2008.

Palmer-Patel, C. *The Shape of Fantasy: Investigating the Structure of American Heroic Epic Fantasy*. Routledge, 2020.

Parsons, Deke. *J. R. R. Tolkien, Robert E. Howard and the Birth of Modern Fantasy*. McFarland, 2015.

Pascal, Roy. *The Dual Voice: Free Indirect Speech and Its Functioning in the Nineteenth-Century European Novel*. Manchester UP, 1977.

Pittock, Murray. "Rider Haggard and *Heart of Darkness*." *Conradiana*, vol. 19, no. 3, 1987, pp. 206–208.

Priest, Christopher. "David Gemmell." *The Guardian*, 1 Aug. 2006, the guardian.com/news/2006/aug/02/guardianobituaries.booksobituaries. Accessed 14 Aug. 2020.

Pringle, David. *Modern Fantasy: The Hundred Best Novels—An English-Language*

Selection, 1946–1987. Peter Bedrick Books, 1988.

Purdie, Susan. *Comedy: The Mastery of Discourse.* Harvester, 1993.

Puschmann-Nalenz, Barbara. "Reconceptualisation of Frame Story and Nested Narrative in 21st-Century Novels: *The Fall of Troy* and *Ragnarok.*" *AAA: Arbeiten aus Anglistik und Amerikanistik,* vol. 41, no. 2, 2016, pp. 49–72.

"R. F. Kuang on Writing Through Difficult Scenes." *88 Cups of Tea,* 88cupsoftea.com/rf-kuang.

Rancière, Jacques. "Interview with the Machete Group (2009): Farewell to Artistic and Political Impotence." *The Politics of Aesthetics: The Distribution of the Sensible,* edited by Gabriel Rockhill, Bloomsbury Academic, 2013, pp. 77–81.

———. *Mute Speech: Literature, Critical Theory, and Politics.* 1998. Translated by James Swenson, Columbia UP, 2011.

———. *The Politics of Aesthetics: The Distribution of the Sensible.* 2000. Translated by Gabriel Rockhill, Bloomsbury Academic, 2013.

Rand, Nicholas. "Translator's Introduction: Toward a Cryptonymy of Literature." *The Wolf Man's Magic Word: A Cryptonymy,* by Nicolas Abraham and Maria Torok, 1976, U of Minnesota P, 1986, pp. li–lxix.

Ransom, John Crowe. "The Woman as Poet." *The World's Body,* Louisiana State UP, 1938, pp. 76–110.

Raskin, Victor. *Semantic Mechanisms of Humor.* D. Reidel, 1985.

Rawls, Melanie. "Witches, Wives and Dragons: The Evolution of the Women in Ursula K. Le Guin's Earthsea—An Overview." *Mythlore,* vol. 26, no. 3, 2008, pp. 129–149.

Ray745. "[No Spoilers] Questions on Sales Figures for Brandons Books." *Reddit,* 4 May 2018, reddit.com/r/Stormlight_Archive/comments/8h25ie/no_spoilers_question_on_sales_figures_for. Accessed 26 Aug. 2020.

Reid-Pharr, Robert F. "Disseminating Heterotopia.'" *African American Review,* vol. 28, no. 3, 1994, pp. 923–933.

Rossen, Jake. "The Reason Movie Trailers Give So Much Away." *Mental Floss,* 23 April 2021, mentalfloss.com/article/643997/why-do-movie-trailers-give-so-much-away. Accessed 26 April 2021.

Rowe, John Carlos. "Gender, Sexuality, and Work in *In the Cage.*" *Tales of Henry James,* edited by Christof Wegelin and Henry B. Wonham, Norton, 2003, pp. 483–502.

Royle, Nicholas. *The Uncanny.* Manchester UP, 2003.

Ryan, Vanessa L. "The Physiological Sublime: Burke's Critique of Reason." *Journal of the History of Ideas,* vol. 62, 2001, pp. 265–279.

Said, Edward. "Identity, Authority, and Freedom: The Potentate and the Traveler." *Reflections on Exile and Other Essays.* Harvard UP, 2000, pp. 386–404.

Sanderson, Brandon. *The Alloy of Law: A Mistborn Novel.* Tor, 2012.

———. *Arcanum Unbounded: The Cosmere Collection.* Tor, 2016.

———. *Elantris.* Tor, 2005.

———. *The Hero of Ages.* Tor, 2008.

———. *Mistborn: The Final Empire.* Tor, 2006.

———. *The Way of Kings.* Tor, 2010.

———. *The Well of Ascension.* Tor, 2007.

Sarvan, C. P. "Under African Eyes." *Conradiana,* vol. 8, 1976, pp. 233–239.

Schuyler, William M., Jr. "Deconstructing Deconstruction: Chimeras of Form and Content in Samuel R. Delany." *Journal of the Fantastic in the Arts,* vol. 1, no. 4, 1988, pp. 67–76.

Scroggins, Mark. *Michael Moorcock: Fiction, Fantasy and the World's Pain.* McFarland, 2016.

Senior, W. A. *Stephen R. Donaldson's Chronicles of Thomas Covenant: Variations on the Fantasy Tradition.* Kent State UP, 1995.

Sondheimer, S. W. "R. F. Kuang on *The Poppy War,* Peace, and Confronting History." *Book Riot,* 8 Aug. 2018, bookriot.com/2018/08/08/r-f-kuang-on-the-poppy-war. Accessed 18 June 2020.

Spencer, Kathleen L. "Deconstructing *Tales of Nevèrÿon:* Delany, Derrida, and the 'Modular Calculus, Parts I–IV.'" *Essays in Arts and Sciences,* vol. 14, May 1985, pp. 59–89.

"Spiritweb." *Stormlight Archive Wiki,* stormlightarchive.fandom.com/wiki/Spiritweb. Accessed 24 Aug. 2020.

Spivack, Charlotte. *Merlin's Daughters: Contemporary Women Writers of Fantasy.* Greenwood Press, 1987.

Spivak, Gayatri Chakravorty. *Other Asias.* Blackwell, 2008.

Stark, Ryan J. *Rhetoric, Science, and Magic in Seventeenth-Century England.* Catholic U of America P, 2009.

Stevenson, Frank. "Enclosing the Whole: Woolf's 'Kew Gardens' as Autopoietic Narrative." *Journal of the Short Story in English,* vol. 50, Spring 2008, pp. 137–152.

Stockwell, Peter. "Miltonic Texture and the Feeling of Reading." *Cognitive Stylistics: Language and Cognition in Text Analysis,* edited by Elena Semino and Jonathan Culpeper, John Benjamins, 2002, pp. 73–94.

Strunk, William, Jr., and E. B. White. *The Elements of Style.* 4th ed., Longman, 1999.

Stubby the Rocket. "How Many Times Does Braid-Tugging and Skirt-Smoothing Happen in the Wheel of Time?" *Tor.com,* 24 March 2017, tor.com/2017/03/24/how-many-times-does-braid-tugging-and-skirt-smoothing-happen-in-the-wheel-of-time. Accessed 24 Aug. 2020.

Sugarbullet. "Re: The Real Meaning of the Poem." *Theoryland,* 7 Feb. 2005, www.theoryland.com/theories.php?func=5&rec=77&theo=2014. Accessed 24 Aug. 2020.

Suvin, Darko. "Considering the Sense of 'Fantasy' or 'Fantastic Fiction': An Effusion." *Extrapolation,* vol. 41, 2000, pp. 209–247.

———. *Metamorphoses of Science Fiction: On the Poetics and History of a Literary Genre.* Yale UP, 1979.

Swinfen, Ann. *In Defence of Fantasy: A Study of the Genre in English and American Literature since 1945.* Routledge, 1984.

Tillyard, E. M. W. *The Epic Strain in the English Novel.* Essential Books, 1958.

Todorov, Tzvetan. *The Fantastic: A Structural Approach to a Literary Genre.* Translated by Richard Howard, P of Case Western Reserve U, 1973.

Tolkien, J. R. R. "On Fairy-Stories." *The Tolkien Reader,* Ballantine, 1966, pp. 33–99.

Vance, Jack. *Lyonesse.* Ace, 1987.

VanderMeer, Jeff. *City of Saints and Madmen.* Prime, 2002.

Walkowitz, Rebecca L. *Cosmopolitan Style: Modernism Beyond the Nation.* Columbia UP, 2006.

Walsh, Richard. *The Rhetoric of Fictionality: Narrative Theory and the Idea of Fiction.* Ohio State UP, 2007.

Watt, Ian. *Conrad in the Nineteenth Century.* U of California P, 1979.

Wells, Martha. *The Death of the Necromancer.* Eos, 1998.

Wickham, Kim. "Identity, Memory, Slavery: Second-Person Narration in N. K. Jemisin's The Broken Earth Trilogy." *Journal of the Fantastic in the Arts,* vol. 30, no. 3, 2019, pp. 392–411.

Williams, Joseph M. *Style: Ten Lessons in Clarity and Grace.* 7th ed., Longman, 2003.

Williamson, Jamie. *The Evolution of Modern Fantasy: From Antiquarianism to the Ballantine Adult Fantasy Series.* Palgrave Macmillan, 2015.

Wise, Dennis Wilson. "A Brief History of EPVIDS: Subjectivity and Evil Possessed Vampire Demon Swords." *Journal of the Fantastic in the Arts,* vol. 31, no. 1, 2020, pp. 83–103.

———. "History and Precarity: Glen Cook and the Rise of Picaresque Epic Fantasy." *Journal of the Fantastic in the Arts,* vol. 30, no. 3, 2019, pp. 331–351.

Wolfe, Gary K. *Critical Terms for Science Fiction and Fantasy: A Glossary and Guide to Scholarship.* Greenwood Press, 1986.

Wolfe, Gene. *The Knight.* Tor, 2004.

Zerweck, Bruno. "Historicizing Unreliable Narration: Unreliability and Cultural Discourse in Narrative Fiction," *Style,* vol. 35, no. 1, 2001, pp. 151–178.

Žižek, Slavoj. *The Sublime Object of Ideology.* Verso, 1989.

Zunshine, Lisa. *Why We Read Fiction: Theory of Mind and the Novel.* Ohio State UP, 2006.

Index